Women's Suffrage

Women's Suffrage

THE COMPLETE GUIDE TO THE NINETEENTH AMENDMENT

Tiffany K. Wayne, Editor

BLOOMSBURY ACADEMIC
NEW YORK • LONDON • OXFORD • NEW DELHI • SYDNEY

BLOOMSBURY ACADEMIC
Bloomsbury Publishing Inc
1385 Broadway, New York, NY 10018, USA
50 Bedford Square, London, WC1B 3DP, UK
29 Earlsfort Terrace, Dublin 2, Ireland

BLOOMSBURY, BLOOMSBURY ACADEMIC and the Diana logo
are trademarks of Bloomsbury Publishing Plc

First published in the United States of America by ABC-CLIO 2020
Paperback edition published by Bloomsbury Academic 2024

Copyright © Bloomsbury Publishing Inc, 2024

Cover photo: *End of the Climb*. Political cartoon celebrating women's suffrage, by *New York World* cartoonist Kirby Rollin, 1920. (Everett Collection Historical/Alamy Stock Photo)

All rights reserved. No part of this publication may be reproduced or
transmitted in any form or by any means, electronic or mechanical,
including photocopying, recording, or any information storage or retrieval
system, without prior permission in writing from the publishers.

Bloomsbury Publishing Inc does not have any control over, or responsibility for,
any third-party websites referred to or in this book. All internet addresses given
in this book were correct at the time of going to press. The author and publisher
regret any inconvenience caused if addresses have changed or sites have
ceased to exist, but can accept no responsibility for any such changes.

Library of Congress Cataloging-in-Publication Data
Names: Wayne, Tiffany K., 1968-editor.
Title: Women's suffrage : the complete guide to the nineteenth amendment /
Tiffany K. Wayne, editor.
Description: Santa Barbara, California : ABC-CLIO, 2020. |
Includes bibliographical references and index.
Identifiers: LCCN 2019057146 (print) | LCCN 2019057147 (ebook) |
ISBN 9781440871986 (hardcover) | ISBN 9781440871993 (ebook)
Subjects: LCSH: Women—Suffrage—United States—History—Encyclopedias.
Classification: LCC JK1896 .W67 2020 (print) |
LCC JK1896 (ebook) | DDC 324.6/23097303—dc23
LC record available at https://lccn.loc.gov/2019057146
LC ebook record available at https://lccn.loc.gov/2019057147

ISBN: HB: 978-1-4408-7198-6
PB: 979-8-7651-2689-9
ePDF: 978-1-4408-7199-3
eBook: 979-8-2161-6768-6

To find out more about our authors and books visit www.bloomsbury.com
and sign up for our newsletters.

Contents

List of Entries, vii

Guide to Related Topics, ix

List of Primary Documents, xi

Introduction, xiii

Chronology of Women's Suffrage in the United States, xxi

A–Z Entries, 1

Primary Source Documents, 193

About the Editor and Contributors, 307

Index, 311

List of Entries

Addams, Jane (1860–1935)
African American Women and Suffrage
Alpha Suffrage Club
American Association of University Women (AAUW)
American Equal Rights Association
American Woman Suffrage Association (AWSA)
Anthony, Susan B. (1820–1906)
Antisuffrage Movement
Beard, Mary Ritter (1876–1958)
Belmont, Alva Vanderbilt (1853–1933)
Bethune, Mary McLeod (1875–1955)
Blackwell, Alice Stone (1857–1950)
Blake, Lillie Devereux (1833–1914)
Blatch, Harriot Stanton (1856–1940)
Bloomer, Amelia Jenks (1818–1894)
Brown, Olympia (1835–1926)
Burns, Lucy (1879–1966)
Cary, Mary Ann Shadd (1823–1893)
Catt, Carrie Chapman (1859–1947)
College Equal Suffrage League
Congressional Union
Davis, Paulina Kellogg Wright (1813–1876)
Dorr, Rheta Childe (1866–1948)
Eastman, Crystal Catherine (1881–1928)
Equal Rights Amendment (ERA)
Equal Rights Party
Field, Sara Bard (1882–1974)
Fifteenth Amendment (1870)
Fourteenth Amendment (1868)
Gage, Matilda Joslyn (1826–1898)
Gordon, Kate (1861–1932)
Harper, Frances Ellen Watkins (1825–1911)
Harper, Ida Husted (1851–1931)
History of Woman Suffrage
Hooker, Isabella (1822–1907)
International Woman Suffrage Alliance (IWSA)
International Women's Movement
Jewish Women and Suffrage
La Follette, Belle Case (1859–1931)
League of Women Voters
Lee, Mabel Ping-Hua (1896–1966)
Lockwood, Belva (1830–1917)
Milholland, Inez (1886–1916)
Minor v. Happersett (1875)
Mott, Lucretia Coffin (1793–1880)

National American Woman Suffrage Association (NAWSA)
National Association of Colored Women (NACW)
National Association Opposed to Woman Suffrage
National Woman Suffrage Association (NWSA)
National Woman's Party (NWP)
New Departure
New England Woman Suffrage Association
Nineteenth Amendment (1920)
Park, Maud Wood (1871–1955)
Paul, Alice (1885–1977)
Pollitzer, Anita Lily (1894–1975)
Presidential Politics and Suffrage
Rankin, Jeannette (1880–1973)
Revolution, The
Rose, Ernestine (1810–1892)
Ruffin, Josephine St. Pierre (1842–1924)
Schneiderman, Rose (1882–1972)
Seneca Falls Convention (1848)
Shafroth-Palmer Amendment
Shaw, Anna Howard (1847–1919)
Silent Sentinels
Stanton, Elizabeth Cady (1815–1902)
Stevens, Doris (1892–1963)
Stone, Lucy (1818–1893)
Suffrage Procession of 1913
Suffragist, The
Talbert, Mary Burnett (1866–1923)
Temperance Movement
Terrell, Mary Church (1863–1954)
Truth, Sojourner (ca. 1797–1883)
United States v. Susan B. Anthony (1873)
Vernon, Mabel (1883–1975)
Washington, Margaret Murray (1865–1925)
Weil, Gertrude (1879–1971)
Wells-Barnett, Ida Bell (1862–1931)
Western States and Suffrage
Willard, Frances (1839–1898)
Winning Plan
Woman Citizen, The
Woman's Christian Temperance Union (WCTU)
Woman's Era, The
Woman's Journal
Women's Political Union
Women's Trade Union League (WTUL)
Woodhull, Victoria (1838–1927)

Guide to Related Topics

People
Addams, Jane (1860–1935)
Anthony, Susan B. (1820–1906)
Beard, Mary Ritter (1876–1958)
Belmont, Alva Vanderbilt
 (1853–1933)
Bethune, Mary McLeod (1875–1955)
Blackwell, Alice Stone (1857–1950)
Blake, Lillie Devereux (1833–1914)
Blatch, Harriot Stanton (1856–1940)
Bloomer, Amelia Jenks (1818–1894)
Brown, Olympia (1835–1926)
Burns, Lucy (1879–1966)
Cary, Mary Ann Shadd (1823–1893)
Catt, Carrie Chapman (1859–1947)
Davis, Paulina Kellogg Wright
 (1813–1876)
Dorr, Rheta Childe (1866–1948)
Eastman, Crystal Catherine
 (1881–1928)
Field, Sara Bard (1882–1974)
Gage, Matilda Joslyn (1826–1898)
Gordon, Kate (1861–1932)
Harper, Frances Ellen Watkins
 (1825–1911)
Harper, Ida Husted (1851–1931)
Hooker, Isabella (1822–1907)
La Follette, Belle Case (1859–1931)
Lee, Mabel Ping-Hua (1896–1966)
Lockwood, Belva (1830–1917)
Milholland, Inez (1886–1916)
Mott, Lucretia Coffin (1793–1880)
Park, Maud Wood (1871–1955)
Paul, Alice (1885–1977)
Pollitzer, Anita Lily (1894–1975)
Rankin, Jeannette (1880–1973)
Rose, Ernestine (1810–1892)
Ruffin, Josephine St. Pierre
 (1842–1924)
Schneiderman, Rose (1882–1972)
Shaw, Anna Howard (1847–1919)
Stanton, Elizabeth Cady (1815–1902)
Stevens, Doris (1892–1963)
Stone, Lucy (1818–1893)
Talbert, Mary Burnett (1866–1923)
Terrell, Mary Church (1863–1954)
Truth, Sojourner (ca. 1797–1883)
Vernon, Mabel (1883–1975)
Washington, Margaret Murray
 (1865–1925)
Weil, Gertrude (1879–1971)
Wells-Barnett, Ida Bell (1862–1931)
Willard, Frances (1839–1898)
Woodhull, Victoria (1838–1927)

Organizations
Alpha Suffrage Club
American Association of University Women (AAUW)
American Equal Rights Association
American Woman Suffrage Association (AWSA)
College Equal Suffrage League
Congressional Union
Equal Rights Party
International Woman Suffrage Alliance (IWSA)
League of Women Voters
National American Woman Suffrage Association (NAWSA)
National Association of Colored Women (NACW)
National Association Opposed to Woman's Suffrage
National Woman Suffrage Association (NWSA)
National Woman's Party (NWP)
New England Woman Suffrage Association
Silent Sentinels
Woman's Christian Temperance Union (WCTU)
Women's Political Union
Women's Trade Union League (WTUL)

Publications
History of Woman Suffrage
Revolution, The
Suffragist, The
Woman Citizen, The
Woman's Era, The
Woman's Journal

Events
Equal Rights Amendment (ERA)
Fifteenth Amendment (1870)
Fourteenth Amendment (1868)
Minor v. Happersett (1875)
New Departure
Nineteenth Amendment (1920)
Seneca Falls Convention (1848)
Shafroth-Palmer Amendment
Suffrage Procession of 1913
United States v. Susan B. Anthony (1873)
Winning Plan

Movements
African American Women and Suffrage
Antisuffrage Movement
International Women's Movement
Jewish Women and Suffrage
Presidential Politics and Suffrage
Temperance Movement
Western States and Suffrage

List of Primary Documents

Elizabeth Cady Stanton, Declaration of Sentiments (1848)
Lucretia Coffin Mott, Discourse on Woman (1849)
Ernestine Rose, *On Woman's Rights* (1851)
"The Nonsense of It" (1866)
Sojourner Truth, Address to the American Equal Rights Association (1867)
Fourteenth Amendment (1868)
An Act to Grant to the Women of Wyoming Territory the Right of Suffrage (1869)
Fifteenth Amendment (1870)
Victoria Woodhull, Address before the House of Representatives (1871)
United States v. Susan B. Anthony, U.S. District Court, Canandaigua, New York (1873)
George W. Julian, "The Slavery Yet to Be Abolished" (1874)
Alexander Graham Bell, Letters on Woman Suffrage (1875)
Minor v. Happersett (1875)
The Declaration of Rights of the Women of the United States (1876)
Isabella Beecher Hooker, *The Constitutional Rights of the Women of the United States* (1888)
Frances E. W. Harper, "Woman's Political Future" (1893)
Alice Stone Blackwell, *Why Women Should Vote* (1896)
Harriot Stanton Blatch, "Woman as an Economic Factor" (1898)
Florence Kelley, "Child Labor and Women's Suffrage" (1905)
Women Opponents of Suffrage, "Why the Home Makers Do Not Want to Vote" (1909)
Theodore Roosevelt, "Women's Rights; and the Duties of Both Men and Women" (1912)

Helen Keller, "Why Men Need Woman Suffrage" (1913)
Jane Addams, "If Men Were Seeking the Franchise" (1913)
Emmeline Pankhurst, "Freedom or Death" (1913)
Margaret Hinchey, Address on Working Women (1913)
Mary Ritter Beard, "The State Rights Shibboleth" (1914)
Anna Howard Shaw, Recollections of NAWSA Conventions (1915)
Massachusetts Anti-Suffrage Committee (1915)
NAACP Testimonials on Women's Suffrage (1915)
Mary Church Terrell, "Woman Suffrage and the 15th Amendment" (1915)
Alice Paul, Letter on Imprisonment (1917)
Imprisoned Suffragists' Letter to the Prisoner Commissioners (1917)
A. Philip Randolph, "Woman Suffrage and the Negro" (1917)
Carrie Chapman Catt, Address to Congress on Women's Suffrage (1917)
Nineteenth Amendment (1920)
Crystal Eastman, "Now We Can Begin" (1920)
Documents from the League of Women Voters (1921)
National Woman's Party Platform (1922)

Introduction

At the time of this encyclopedia's publication, four years will have passed since Hillary Clinton's historic run as the Democratic Party candidate in the presidential election of 2016. Her critics accused her of playing the "gender card" during her campaign as she embraced the historic potential of her candidacy as well as a feminist vision in her platform. Clinton supporters declared "I'm with Her" on T-shirts and bumper stickers, emphasizing the gender of their chosen candidate. In 2007, the first time Hillary Clinton sought the Democratic nomination, 88 percent of Americans said they would vote for a female candidate for president, up from just 33 percent who said they would do so in 1937, the first time the Gallup Poll asked that question (Malone 2016).

Beginning with Victoria Woodhull in 1872, many women have run in the presidential primaries, seeking the nomination not only from the two major parties but also as representatives of third parties ("Run like a Girl"). Both the Democratic and Republican Party tickets have each included one female vice-presidential candidate, although both tickets lost in the general elections (Geraldine Ferraro in 1984 as the running mate of Walter Mondale, and Sarah Palin in 2008 as John McCain's running mate).

Indeed, while the 2019–2020 primary election cycle again reached historic milestones, with five women appearing on the Democratic presidential debate stage (including one woman of color), women still hold significantly fewer positions in state and national public office. It was not until 1974, more than 50 years after American women achieved national suffrage, that Ella Grasso of Connecticut was elected as the nation's first female governor in her own right, not as a proxy or replacement for a husband. Currently, in 2019, only 9 out of 50 states have a female governor. And, to date, there has *never* been a black female governor.

According to the U.S. House of Representatives and U.S. Senate websites, there are record numbers of women in Congress in 2019, but, overall, women still hold just one-quarter of the seats in both the House of Representatives and the Senate, where women fill 25 out of 100 seats. While this is the highest percentage of women ever in Congress, these are recent increases; of the *total* number of women who have ever been elected to the House or the Senate, one-third and one half of those, respectively, are serving right now.

Turning to the judicial branch, in its 230-year history, there have only been four female justices on the U.S. Supreme Court, three of whom are *currently* serving and two of those were appointed only recently, in 2009 and 2010. In a 2015 interview, Justice Ruth Bader Ginsburg (confirmed in 1993 as the second woman on the Court) said in an interview, "People ask me sometimes, when—when do you think it will it be enough? When will there be enough women on the court? And my answer is when there are nine" (PBS NewsHour 2015).

Clearly the struggle for women's inclusion in the political life of the nation did not end with ratification of the Nineteenth Amendment nor did it begin there. The specific events and momentum leading to that historic moment in August 1920, when the final state ratified the women's suffrage amendment, began, in the most immediate sense, when the suffragists protested at the White House on the day of Woodrow Wilson's inauguration in March 1913.

Or, perhaps it more accurately began when the national women's movement organized around a single issue with the creation of the National American Woman Suffrage Association (NAWSA) in 1890.

Or, perhaps the road to a national amendment began with the state-by-state achievements, with Wyoming as the first territory (1869) and then the first state (1890) to grant women suffrage.

Or, perhaps the credit is due to an earlier generation of women's rights activists who dared to list "her inalienable right to the elective franchise" as one of the most radical demands in the Declaration of Sentiments drafted at the Seneca Falls convention of 1848.

Or, perhaps the struggle to fulfill the promise of democracy was set in motion when the Constitution was ratified in 1789 with no provision for voting rights, and enshrining chattel slavery for another two generations.

Or, to the even earlier founding document upon which the Declaration of Sentiments was explicitly modeled, the Declaration of Independence, which dared to assert upon the world stage in 1776 the enlightened idea that "all men are created equal."

Or, perhaps the American women's movement for political rights began in that same year, when the very idea of the nation of the United States was not yet fully formed, with the missed opportunity behind Abigail Adams's plea to her revolutionary husband: "By the way in the new Code of Laws which I suppose it will be necessary for you to make I desire you would Remember the Ladies." In this letter of March 31, 1776, she went on to warn him, somewhat playfully, but ultimately presciently, that "if perticuliar care and attention is not paid to the Ladies we are determined to foment a Rebellion, and will not hold ourselves bound by any Laws in which we have no voice, or Representation" (Adams Family Papers). American women did, indeed, eventually foment a rebellion, one that has taken us into our fourth century, from 1776 to 1848 to 1920 to today.

Nothing in the original U.S. Constitution (or in the subsequent Bill of Rights) guaranteed any citizen either a right to vote or protection from discrimination. It would take several more constitutional amendments, and a fair amount of federal legislation, to institutionalize those features of our democracy. Indeed, the founders did not set out to create a direct democracy, but rather a republic, a representative democracy ruled by elite property-holding men making decisions for the good of all. Several decades into the experiment, by the 1850s, the nation had made great strides toward "democratization" with the oxymoronic concept of "universal white male suffrage," meaning that property ownership or wealth was slowly (state-by-state) discarded as a legal requirement for voting.

This expansion of white male political rights stood in stark contrast to the lack of rights for either African Americans or women of any race, but by the 1850s both the abolitionist and women's rights movements were in full force and organized to assert those rights. A major change occurred in the mid-nineteenth century with the end of slavery and the ratification of two additional constitutional amendments expanding voting rights: the Fourteenth Amendment (1868), guaranteeing equal protection under the law for all citizens, and the Fifteenth Amendment (1870), prohibiting states from denying voting rights based on race (but not sex).

Constitutional change still did not guarantee the free exercise of the franchise for black men, and the civil rights movement spent another 100 years (and beyond) countering the effects of and protesting state and local-level obstacles to black voting and office-holding, such as poll taxes, literacy tests, gerrymandering, lack of education, difficult voter registration processes, intimidation, and violence. It took another 50 years—between the ratification of the Fifteenth Amendment in 1870 and the Nineteenth Amendment in 1920—and many state-by-state victories before a federal amendment extended the right to vote to all American women.

The next major constitutional change to voting rights also involved the rights of African Americans, as the Twenty-Fourth Amendment, ratified in 1964, outlawed poll taxes. This amendment was achieved within the context of the new Civil Rights Acts of 1964 and 1965, prohibiting racial discrimination by governments and public agencies, and the even more expansive Voting Rights Act of 1965, which still, nearly 100 years after the Fifteenth Amendment was ratified and 45 years after the Nineteenth, was needed in order to protect black voters in the South.

The next major change in national voting rights came with the Twenty-Sixth Amendment, ratified in 1971, changing the voting age from 21 to 18. This amendment was passed in the context of a Vietnam War draft requiring young men to fight before they were old enough to vote and, in fact, some had proposed this age change for the exact same reason soon after the Civil War. Besides registering for a draft, young people have other civic roles and responsibilities, leading some to argue today that people as young as 16 should be allowed to vote, and that this would improve voter participation among young people. In our American system of federalism, states retain control or power over the voter registration process, as well as over the logistics of running elections. Debates continue over the voting rights of homeless individuals without a permanent address, of inmates or felons both during and after incarceration, and over methods of voter registration or voter ID requirements, all varying by state. These issues clearly have enormous implications not only for individual civil rights, but for election outcomes.

Another issue in voter registration efforts is low voter turnout, especially among specific groups, such as youth and minorities. Celebrities as well as interest groups get involved in voter registration drives each general election cycle and social media makes it easier than ever to reach potential voters, and yet voter apathy remains a real issue for democracy in the United States and globally. In the United States, overall turnout among all eligible voters has consistently been between 50 and 60 percent for most of the twentieth and into the twenty-first century. While voter turnout varies by age, educational level, income, race or ethnicity, or other factors, women have consistently turned out to vote in higher numbers than men in every presidential election since 1964 (Center for American Women and Politics 2019).

The movement to secure votes for women always worked alongside other social and civil rights movements. The suffrage movement had its own leaders, organizations, newspapers, strategies, and events, all documented in this volume. But, from the overlap between abolitionism and women's rights among antebellum reformers, to the connection between black civil rights and women's rights in the Reconstruction Era, to the efforts of Progressive Era women labor leaders to recruit working-class women to the suffrage cause, to the re-emergence of the women's movement out of the civil rights movements of the 1960s and 1970s, to LGBTQ rights and the global connections between human rights and women's rights, the story of the women's movement has always been the story of the broader, and continual, expansion of the democratic promise of the United States.

So, what does the history of women's suffrage teach us about the future of gender equality and democracy in the United States? In an interview toward the end of her life, suffragist Alice Paul said, "There is nothing complicated about ordinary equality" (Gallagher 1974). And yet, the story of American women's participation in our nation's political processes—from voting to office-holding to holding other positions of decision-making to incorporating (or even hearing) the voices of women of color at all levels—has been incredibly long and complicated. Alice Paul was central to that story and often takes center stage in the story of the dramatic years and months leading up to final passage of the Nineteenth Amendment. Yet, she herself complicated her own movement and legacy by favoring political expediency over lasting coalitions and a commitment to true equality, literally pushing aside the presence of black women in the movement.

That legacy remains with us today. The historical connection between abolitionism, black civil rights, and women's rights, means that black women were often at the center of these social movements, and yet, the racism of white women often limited the radical potential of these voices and these coalitions to strengthen the movement. Perhaps the fight for the vote—and the subsequent struggles for women's broader political participation—would have seen greater or swifter progress if the work of women of color had not been dismissed or made invisible by white women in the movement, or in subsequent histories of the movement.

While the increase in the number of female presidential candidates between 2016 and 2020 might seem exponential, the struggle for women, as well as all African Americans and other groups, to be included in the promise of democracy in this country has crept along at an embarrassing pace. Celebrating the anniversary of the ratification of the Nineteenth Amendment reminds us that it took 100 years to get to this point, and we still have a long way to go. According to Equality Can't Wait, a campaign launched by Melinda Gates to bring awareness to the issue, based on the historical rates of progress, it will take another 208 years to reach full gender equality in this country in the key areas of economics, politics, education, and health (Equality Can't Wait).

In the fight for "ordinary equality," it would be easy to focus on the vote as a single issue, but the suffragists were also birth control advocates, peace activists, temperance proponents, labor organizers, educators, anti–child labor activists, and anti-lynching activists, concerned about maternal mortality, child health, and immigrant rights, and pushing their way as women into the professions.

Their true legacy to us is understanding that the vote, and a political voice, was needed in order to do something about so many other issues. Let us build on this legacy as we move forward into the next 100 years.

Tiffany K. Wayne

Further Reading

Adams Family Papers. "Letter from Abigail Adams to John Adams, 31 March–5 April 1776." Massachusetts Historical Society. https://www.masshist.org/digitaladams/archive/doc?id=L17760331aa.

Center for American Women and Politics. "Gender Differences in Voter Turnout." Eagleton Institute of Politics, Rutgers University, September 16, 2019. http://www.cawp.rutgers.edu/sites/default/files/resources/genderdiff.pdf.

Equality Can't Wait. https://equalitycantwait.evoke.org/

Gallagher, Robert. "'I was arrested, of course . . .' An Interview with the Famed Suffragette, Alice Paul." *American Heritage* 25, no. 2 (February 1974). https://www.americanheritage.com/alice-paul-i-was-arrested-course.

Malone, Clare. "From 1937 to Hillary Clinton, How Americans Have Felt about a Woman President." *FiveThirtyEight*, June 9, 2016. https://fivethirtyeight.com/features/from-1937-to-hillary-clinton-how-americans-have-felt-about-a-female-president/.

PBS NewsHour. "When Will There Be Enough Women on the Supreme Court? Justice Ginsburg Answers That Question." PBS.org, February 5, 2015. https://www.pbs.org/newshour/show/justice-ginsburg-enough-women-supreme-court.

"Run like a Girl." NursingClio.org. https://nursingclio.org/topics/run-like-a-girl/.

United States House of Representatives. "House Service & Seniority: Total Members of the House & State Representation." *History, Art & Archives*, U.S. House of Representatives, January 3, 2019. https://history.house.gov/Institution/Total-Members/Total-Members/.

United States House of Representatives. "Women in Congress: Historical Data." *History, Art & Archives*, U.S. House of Representatives. https://history.house.gov/Exhibitions-and-Publications/WIC/Historical-Data/Historical-Data---Nav/.

United States Senate. "Women in the Senate." U.S. Senate. https://www.senate.gov/artandhistory/history/common/briefing/women_senators.htm.

Chronology of Women's Suffrage in the United States

1776
Abigail Adams writes to her husband, John Adams, to "remember the ladies" in forming a new government; the American Declaration of Independence asserts that "all men are created equal."

1789
The new U.S. Constitution is ratified; with no federal voting provisions, voting rights are left to the individual states.

1807
The New Jersey legislature revises earlier state constitution, which granted suffrage rights to any property-owning resident, including women or free blacks, and restricts the right to vote to property-owning white male citizens.

1833
Oberlin College opens as the first coeducational college in the United States, admitting both men and women as students; Oberlin also admitted both black and white students.

1836
Wesleyan College in Georgia is founded as the first college chartered specifically for women; several other women's colleges are subsequently founded in the mid-nineteenth century, including Mount Holyoke (1837), Vassar (1861), Wellesley (1875), and Smith (1875).

1838
Abolitionist Sarah Grimké publishes *Letters on the Equality of the Sexes* in response to a "Pastoral Letter" from the congregational churches of

Massachusetts denouncing the public reform work of the Grimké sisters. Kentucky passes the first state women's suffrage law allowing female heads of households to vote in school and local elections.

1840

Elizabeth Cady Stanton, Lucretia Mott, and other American abolitionists attend the World Anti-Slavery Convention in London where they are radicalized by the exclusion of female delegates and commit themselves to working for the rights of women.

1844

Female textile workers in Lowell, Massachusetts, organize the Female Labor Reform Association to advocate for the rights of working women, including a 10-hour workday.

1848

The first American women's rights meeting is held in Seneca Falls, New York. Organized by Elizabeth Cady Stanton and Lucretia Mott, the convention presents a "Declaration of Sentiments," signed by 100 attendees, calling for equal treatment for women and "the right to the elective franchise."

New York passes a comprehensive Married Women's Property Law which becomes the model for other states.

Amelia Bloomer founds *The Lily*, the first American journal published by and for women; the paper is initially focused on the temperance movement but expands to include arts, literature, and dress reform for women.

1850

The first statewide women's rights convention is held in Salem, Ohio.
The first National Women's Rights Convention, held in Worcester, Massachusetts, and presided over by Paulina Wright Kellogg Davis, is attended by more than 1,000 people.

1851

Sojourner Truth delivers her "Ar'n't I a Woman?" speech at a women's rights convention in Akron, Ohio.

The second National Women's Rights Convention is again held in Worcester, Massachusetts, with Paulina Wright Kellogg Davis as president.

1852

The third National Women's Rights Convention is held in Syracuse, New York, with Lucretia Mott as president; a special committee on the issue of women's suffrage is formed.

1853

The fourth National Women's Rights Convention is held in Cleveland, Ohio, with Frances Dana Parker Gage as president.

1854

The fifth National Women's Rights Convention is held in Philadelphia, Pennsylvania, with Ernestine Rose as president.

1855

The sixth National Women's Rights Convention is held in Cincinnati, Ohio, with Martha Coffin Wright as president.

1856

The seventh National Women's Rights Convention is held in New York City, with Lucretia Mott as president.

North Carolina is the last state to end property qualifications for voting, achieving universal white male suffrage in all states.

1857

In *Dred Scott v. Sandford*, the U.S. Supreme Court declares that African Americans are not considered "citizens" under the U.S. Constitution.

1858

The eighth National Women's Rights Convention is again held in New York City, this time with Susan B. Anthony as president; a committee is formed to discuss the need for women to hold elective office and to demand suffrage at the state level.

1859

The ninth National Women's Rights Convention is again held in New York City, with Lucretia Mott presiding.

1860

The tenth and final pre–Civil War National Women's Rights Convention is again held in New York City, with Martha Coffin Wright presiding.

1863

The Women's National Loyal League is formed in New York City by Susan B. Anthony, Lucretia Mott, Elizabeth Cady Stanton, and others committed to supporting the Union cause and ending slavery.

1865

The Thirteenth Amendment to the U.S. Constitution is ratified, abolishing slavery in the United States, freeing some 4 million enslaved African Americans.

Elizabeth Cady Stanton and Susan Anthony start a national "Petition for Universal Suffrage," calling for a constitutional amendment to "prohibit the several states from disenfranchising any of their citizens on the ground of sex."

1866

The eleventh National Women's Rights Convention is held in New York City, with Elizabeth Cady Stanton presiding; Frances Ellen Watkins Harper delivers an address challenging racial discrimination.

The American Equal Rights Association is organized, dedicated to the goal of universal suffrage—founded by Susan B. Anthony, Elizabeth Cady Stanton, Frederick Douglass, and others.

1868

The Fourteenth Amendment to the U.S. Constitution is ratified, establishing citizenship for the former slaves and guaranteeing "equal protection of the laws" for all citizens; the Constitution includes the word "male" for the first time, referring to "male inhabitants" as citizens with voting rights to be protected.

As part of the Reconstruction Era debates over black civil rights, Samuel C. Pomeroy, a Republican Senator from Kansas, introduces a constitutional amendment that would grant universal suffrage for all U.S. citizens, but the proposal is tabled.

Susan B. Anthony and Elizabeth Cady Stanton begin publishing the women's suffrage paper, *The Revolution*.

1869

Debates over ratification of the Fifteenth Amendment, extending voting rights to African American men, splits the women's movement between the National Woman Suffrage Association (NWSA), which opposes the Fifteenth Amendment because it does not guarantee universal suffrage, and the

American Woman Suffrage Association (AWSA), which supports the Fifteenth Amendment as a step forward in the fight for equality.

The final National Women's Rights Convention of the nineteenth century is held in Washington, D.C., attended by Susan B. Anthony, Lucretia Mott, Elizabeth Cady Stanton, and others.

A woman suffrage bill and hearing are introduced into the U.S. House of Representatives for the first time.

The Wyoming territory grants women the right to vote.

1870

The Fifteenth Amendment to the U.S. Constitution is ratified, extending voting privileges to African American men, but omitting "sex" as a protected category, by making it unconstitutional for states to deny the vote "on account of race, color, or previous condition of servitude."

Lucy Stone founds the women's rights newspaper, the *Woman's Journal*, as the paper for the American Woman Suffrage Association (AWSA).

Utah territory grants voting rights to women.

1871

Paulina Kellogg Wright Davis publishes *A History of the National Woman's Rights Movement* to document the first 20 years of the U.S. women's movement.

In response to the violence and intimidation of the Ku Klux Klan, the U.S. Congress passes a series of Enforcement Acts to protect African American voting rights, as well as secure the right to serve on juries and to hold office.

1872

Victoria Woodhull is the first woman to run for president of the United States, as the candidate for the Equal Rights Party, with Frederick Douglass named as her vice presidential running mate.

Susan B. Anthony and a group of other women are arrested in Rochester, New York, for attempting to vote in the presidential election.

Sojourner Truth attempts to vote in Battle Creek, Michigan, but is turned away.

1873

In *United States v. Susan B. Anthony*, a district federal court in New York finds against Anthony, tried for "unlawful voting," denying the claim that the Fourteenth Amendment protects women's rights to vote as citizens.

1874

The Woman's Christian Temperance Union (WCTU) is founded by Annie Wittenmyer. Under the leadership of Frances Willard, who becomes president of the WCTU in 1879, the organization is a key force in the fight for women's suffrage.

1875

In *Minor v. Happersett*, the U.S. Supreme Court rules that the Fourteenth Amendment to the Constitution does not guarantee the right to vote for women as citizens.

1878

Aaron Sargent, a Republican Senator from California, introduces a proposed constitutional amendment for women's suffrage in Congress for the first time; the next day, suffragists testify before the U.S. Senate on the issue of women's suffrage.

The U.S. Senate receives 30,000 signatures on petitions for women's suffrage, but decides to leave the matter to the states and the question is "indefinitely postponed" as a congressional issue.

1881

The first volume of the *History of Woman Suffrage* is published, edited by Elizabeth Cady Stanton, Susan B. Anthony, and Matilda Joslyn Gage.

1882

The U.S. Senate approves a resolution to establish a Select Committee on Woman Suffrage; five months after its founding, the committee recommends a federal women's suffrage amendment.

Volume 2 of the *History of Woman Suffrage* is published, edited by Elizabeth Cady Stanton, Susan B. Anthony, and Matilda Joslyn Gage.

1883

Washington territory grants voting rights to women.

1886

Volume 3 of the *History of Woman Suffrage* is published, edited by Elizabeth Cady Stanton, Susan B. Anthony, and Matilda Joslyn Gage.

1887

The U.S. Senate votes on a women's suffrage amendment (the Anthony Amendment) for the first time; with 50 Senators present and voting, the amendment is defeated with 16 votes for, 34 against.

Montana territory grants voting rights to women.

Kansas grants women the right to vote in municipal elections.

Women in the Utah territory (who had the vote since 1870) lose the right to vote under the Edmunds-Tucker Act, intended to restrict the economic and political power of Mormons and prevent the spread of polygamy.

1890

The National American Woman Suffrage Association (NAWSA) is formed, merging the two post–Civil War suffrage organizations, the NWSA and AWSA, into one, with Susan B. Anthony as first president of NAWSA.

Wyoming becomes a state and is the first state with full voting rights for women (women had been voting in the Wyoming territory since 1869).

1892

Ida B. Wells starts her nationwide anti-lynching campaign following the murders of three African American men in Memphis, Tennessee.

Olympia Brown forms Federal Suffrage Association to push for a constitutional amendment.

1893

Colorado grants women the right to vote in an amendment to the state constitution—the following year (1894) three Colorado women are elected to the state legislature.

New Zealand is the first independent nation to grant women the right to vote.

1895

Elizabeth Cady Stanton's controversial book, *The Woman's Bible*, is published, challenging women's subordination in traditional Judeo-Christian religions.

1896

The National Association of Colored Women is formed in Washington, D.C., with Mary Church Terrell as first president of the organization.

Idaho grants women suffrage.

Women in Utah regain the right to vote with statehood.

1897

The National American Woman Suffrage Association (NAWSA) begins publishing the *National Suffrage Bulletin*.

1900

The International Ladies' Garment Workers' Union (ILGWU) is founded in New York City.

Carrie Chapman Catt becomes president of NAWSA.

1902

Volume 4 of *The History of Woman Suffrage* is published, edited by Ida Husted Harper.

Women in Australia gain the right to vote.

1903

The National Women's Trade Union League (WTUL) is formed to improve working conditions for women.

1904

Anna Howard Shaw becomes president of NAWSA.

1906

Women in Finland gain the right to vote.

1907

Harriot Stanton Blatch organizes the Equality League of Self-Supporting Women, comprising more than 20,000 factory, laundry, and garment workers on New York City's lower East Side.

1909

The National Association for the Advancement of Colored People (NAACP) is founded to promote and protect black civil rights, including the right to vote.

1910

Major suffrage parades are organized in both New York City and Washington, D.C., and continue periodically until 1913.

The Women's Political Union (formerly known as the Equality League of Self-Supporting Women) organizes the first major suffrage parade in New York City.

Washington state grants women the right to vote through a state constitutional amendment; the territorial government had previously enacted women's suffrage, only to have it overturned by the courts.

1911

California grants women the right to vote through a state constitutional amendment.

1912

The Progressive Party becomes the first national political party to adopt a woman suffrage platform; candidate Theodore Roosevelt.

Women granted the right to vote in Arizona, Kansas, and Oregon.

1913

Alice Paul and Lucy Burns form the Congressional Union for Woman Suffrage, a subcommittee of and eventual replacement for the Congressional Committee of NAWSA.

Over 8,000 suffragists march in a parade in Washington, D.C., on the eve of Woodrow Wilson's presidential inauguration, the largest suffrage parade to date.

Suffragists submit over 75,000 pro-suffrage amendment signatures to the U.S. Senate.

Belle Case La Follette, Wisconsin suffragist and wife of Republican Senator Robert La Follette, speaks before the U.S. Senate in support of the federal women's suffrage amendment.

Kate Gordon helps found and serves as president of the Southern States Woman Suffrage Conference, promoting a state-by-state approach rather than a federal amendment.

The Seventeenth Amendment to the U.S. Constitution is ratified, allowing direct election of Senators by citizens of a state rather than by state legislatures.

Alaska territory grants voting rights to women.

The Illinois Suffrage Act grants women in Illinois the right to vote in municipal elections and in the presidential election.

Women granted the right to vote through state constitutional amendments in Arizona, Kansas, and Oregon.

Women in Norway gain the right to vote.

1914

The U.S. Senate votes on a women's suffrage amendment for the second time; with 69 Senators present and voting, the amendment is defeated with 35 votes for, 34 against.

The General Federation of Women's Clubs formally endorses women's suffrage.

Women granted the right to vote through state constitutional amendments in Montana and Nevada.

1915

The U.S. House of Representatives votes on a women's suffrage amendment for the first time; the amendment is defeated with 174 votes for, 204 against.

Carrie Chapman Catt resumes the presidency of NAWSA for a second term.

In *Guinn v. United States*, the U.S. Supreme Court strikes down literacy tests for voting as unconstitutional.

Women in Denmark and Iceland gain the right to vote.

1916

Jeannette Rankin of Montana becomes the first woman elected to the U.S. Congress as a member of the House of Representatives.

Margaret Sanger opens the first birth control clinic in Brooklyn, New York.

The National Woman's Party (NWP) is founded by Alice Paul.

Carrie Chapman Catt unveils her "Winning Plan" to reenergize the efforts of NAWSA by focusing on suffrage campaigns in winnable states and passage of a federal amendment.

1917

The "Silent Sentinels" begin picketing in front of the White House in protest against President Wilson's lack of support for women's suffrage; over the next two years, more than 2,000 women participate in the protest and several suffragists, including leaders Alice Paul and Lucy Burns, are arrested and jailed for obstructing traffic.

In April, the U.S. Congress approves a resolution declaring war against Germany and enters World War I; Representative Jeannette Rankin, the only female member of Congress, dissents and votes against war.

New York anti-suffragist Alice Hay Wadsworth, wife of Republican Senator James Wadsworth Jr. and president of the National Association Opposed to

Woman Suffrage, testifies before the U.S. Senate in opposition to the federal suffrage amendment.

In November, jailed suffragists at the Occoquan Workhouse in Virginia are abused and beaten in what became known as the "Night of Terror."

Women granted the right to vote in New York through state constitutional amendment, the first eastern state to grant full suffrage.

Women in Nebraska, North Dakota, and Rhode Island granted the right to vote in presidential elections.

Arkansas women granted the right to vote in primary elections.

Women in Russia gain the right to vote.

1918

World War I ends with an armistice agreement on November 11th.

The U.S. House of Representatives votes on a women's suffrage amendment for the second time; the amendment is approved with 274 votes for, 136 against, but the amendment is subsequently narrowly defeated in the U.S. Senate, with 53 votes for, 31 against.

President Woodrow Wilson addresses the U.S. Senate and announces his support for passage of the women's suffrage amendment.

Women granted the right to vote through state constitutional amendments in Michigan, Oklahoma, and South Dakota.

Women in Texas granted the right to vote in presidential elections.

Women in Austria, Canada, Estonia, Georgia, Germany, Hungary, Kyrgyzstan, Latvia, Lithuania, Poland, Russia, and the United Kingdom gain the right to vote.

1919

In the months before ratification of the Nineteenth Amendment, women in Indiana, Iowa, Ohio, Maine, Minnesota, Missouri, Tennessee, and Wisconsin are granted the right to vote in presidential elections.

In February, the U.S. Senate votes on a women's suffrage amendment for the fourth time, defeating the amendment with 55 for and 29 against.

In May, the U.S. House of Representatives votes for the third time on the women's suffrage amendment, approving the amendment again with 304 for, 90 against.

On June 4th, the U.S. Senate votes on a women's suffrage amendment for the fifth time, approving the amendment with 66 for, 30 against.

Having now passed both houses of Congress, the Nineteenth Amendment is sent to the states for ratification; by the end of 1919, 22 states have ratified the suffrage amendment.

Women in Belarus, Luxembourg, the Netherlands, and Ukraine gain the right to vote.

1920

On August 18, 1920, Tennessee becomes the 36th state—the final state needed—to ratify the Nineteenth Amendment to the U.S. Constitution.

Connecticut is the 37th state to ratify the Nineteenth Amendment on September 14, 1920.

August 26, 1920, the Nineteenth Amendment is formally adopted as part of the U.S. Constitution, by proclamation of Secretary of State Bainbridge Colby.

The League of Women Voters is founded by Carrie Chapman Catt to replace NAWSA and promote women's political involvement after the Nineteenth Amendment is ratified.

Women in Kentucky granted the right to vote in presidential elections.

Women in Albania, Czechoslovakia, and Slovakia gain the right to vote.

1921

Margaret Sanger founds the American Birth Control League, eventually renamed Planned Parenthood Federation of America.

Vermont ratifies the Nineteenth Amendment.

Women in Armenia, Azerbaijan, and Sweden gain the right to vote.

1922

Volumes 5 and 6 of the *History of Woman Suffrage* are published by NAWSA, edited by Ida Husted Harper.

In two cases, *Fairchild v. Hughes* and *Leser v. Garnett*, the U.S. Supreme Court upholds the constitutional validity of the ratification process of the Nineteenth Amendment against anti-suffrage challenges.

Women in Ireland gain the right to vote.

1923

The Equal Rights Amendment, authored by Alice Paul for the National Woman's Party, is first introduced in the U.S. Congress; the ERA would be reintroduced in each subsequent session of Congress between 1923 and 1972.

Delaware ratifies the Nineteenth Amendment, having originally rejected it in 1920, the last state to do so until the 1940s.

1924

Native Americans gain full U.S. citizenship through the Indian Citizenship Act (or Snyder Act), but many are still prevented from voting under state laws.

Women in Kazakhstan, Mongolia, Saint Lucia, and Tajikistan gain the right to vote.

1927

Women in Turkmenistan gain the right to vote.

1929

Women in Ecuador gain the right to vote.

1930

Women in Turkey gain the right to vote.

1931

Women in Sri Lanka and Spain gain the right to vote.

1932

Hattie Wyatt Caraway of Arkansas is the first woman elected to the U.S. Senate.

Women in Brazil, Maldives, Uruguay, and Thailand gain the right to vote.

1934

Women in Cuba gain the right to vote.

1935

Mary McLeod Bethune organizes the National Council of Negro Women.

Women in Myanmar (Burma) and Puerto Rico gain the right to vote.

1937

Women in the Philippines gain the right to vote.

1938
Women in Uzbekistan gain the right to vote.

1939
Women in El Salvador gain the right to vote.

1941
President Franklin Roosevelt signs an Executive Order prohibiting racial or ethnic discrimination in defense industries, the first federal action against employment discrimination.

Maryland ratifies the Nineteenth Amendment, having originally rejected it in 1920.

1942
Women in the Dominican Republic gain the right to vote.

1943
The Magnuson Act repeals the Chinese Exclusion Act of 1882, allowing some Chinese immigrants to become naturalized citizens and to vote.

1944
In *Smith v. Allwright*, the U.S. Supreme Court struck down racial discrimination in state voting laws by ruling that all-white primary elections were unconstitutional.

Women in Bulgaria, France, and Jamaica gain the right to vote.

1945
Women in Croatia, Indonesia, Italy, Japan, Senegal, Slovenia, and Togo gain the right to vote.

1946
The newly organized United Nations establishes the Commission on the Status of Women, an international committee to promote gender equality and women's empowerment.

Women in Cameroon, Djibouti, Guatemala, Liberia, Macedonia, North Korea, Panama, Romania, Trinidad and Tobago, Venezuela, Vietnam, and Yugoslavia gain the right to vote.

1947

Women in Argentina, Malta, Mexico, Pakistan, Singapore, and Taiwan gain the right to vote.

1948

The Universal Declaration of Human Rights, created in part by Eleanor Roosevelt, is accepted by the United Nations.

Women in Belgium, Israel, Niger, Seychelles, South Korea, and Suriname gain the right to vote.

1949

Women in Bosnia and Herzegovina, Chile, China, Costa Rica, Indonesia, and Syria gain the right to vote.

1950

Women in Barbados, Haiti, and India, as well as aboriginal women in Canada, gain the right to vote.

1951

Women in Antigua and Barbuda, Dominica, Grenada, Nepal, Saint Kitts and Nevis, and Saint Vincent and the Grenadines gain the right to vote.

1952

The McCarran-Walter Act (also known as the Immigration and Nationality Act of 1952) repeals race restrictions in the immigration and citizenship process, allowing Asian immigrants, including Japanese Americans and Korean Americans, to become U.S. citizens with voting rights for the first time.

Virginia ratifies the Nineteenth Amendment, having originally rejected it in 1920.

Women in Bolivia, Côte d'Ivoire, Greece, and Lebanon gain the right to vote.

1953

Alabama ratifies the Nineteenth Amendment, having originally rejected it in 1919.

Women in Bhutan and Guyana gain the right to vote.

1954
Women in Colombia gain the right to vote.

1955
Women in Belize, Cambodia, Eritrea, Ethiopia, Ghana, Honduras, Nicaragua, and Peru gain the right to vote.

1956
Women in Benin, Comoros, Egypt, Gabon, Mali, Mauritius, and Somalia gain the right to vote.

1957
Women in Malaysia and Zimbabwe gain the right to vote.

1958
Women in Burkina Faso, Chad, Guinea, and Laos gain the right to vote.

1959
Women in Madagascar, Morocco, San Marino, Tanzania, and Tunisia gain the right to vote.

1960
The federal Food and Drug Administration (FDA) approves oral contraceptives.

Women in Cyprus, Gambia, and Tonga gain the right to vote.

1961
President John F. Kennedy establishes the President's Commission on the Status of Women and appoints former First Lady Eleanor Roosevelt as head.

The Twenty-Third Amendment to the U.S. Constitution is ratified, allowing residents of Washington, D.C., to vote in presidential elections and choose electors.

Women in Burundi, Malawi, Mauritania, Paraguay, Rwanda, and Sierra Leone gain the right to vote.

1962
Women in Algeria, the Bahamas, Monaco, Uganda, and Zambia, and aboriginal women in Australia, gain the right to vote.

1963

President John F. Kennedy signs into law the Equal Pay Act, outlawing wage discrimination based on sex.

Betty Friedan's book, *The Feminine Mystique*, is published, inciting a new wave of feminism focused on women's roles in both public and private life.

Women in the Congo Republic, Equatorial Guinea, Fiji, Iran, Kenya, Libya, and Morocco gain the right to vote.

1964

President Lyndon B. Johnson signs into law the Civil Rights Act, outlawing race and sex discrimination in education, employment, and public accommodations.

The Twenty-Fourth Amendment is ratified, abolishing poll taxes in voting, in particular affecting African Americans in the South, where many such practices persisted.

Civil rights activist Fannie Lou Hamer challenges the all-white Democratic Party national convention by running for Congress as a member of the Mississippi Freedom Democratic Party.

Margaret Chase Smith announces her candidacy for the Republican Party nomination for president, the first woman to seek a major party's nomination; her name was ultimately on the ballot in six state primaries.

Women in Afghanistan, Papua New Guinea, Sudan, Tanzania, and Zambia gain the right to vote.

1965

President Lyndon B. Johnson signs into law the Voting Rights Act, enforcing the Fifteenth Amendment by prohibiting racial discrimination in voting practices.

In *Griswold v. Connecticut*, the U.S. Supreme Court rules that married couples may obtain birth control information based on a right to privacy.

Women in Botswana and Lesotho gain the right to vote.

1966

The National Organization for Women (NOW) is founded by Betty Friedan and others, eventually becoming the largest women's rights association in the nation.

In *Harper v. Virginia Board of Elections*, the U.S. Supreme Court rules that poll taxes are an unconstitutional restriction of voting rights.

1967

President Lyndon Johnson issues Executive Order 11375, banning gender discrimination in federal employment.

The United Nations passes a Declaration on the Elimination of Discrimination against Women to address women's global human rights.

Women in the Democratic Republic of the Congo, Kiribati, and People's Republic of Yemen gain the right to vote.

1968

Charlene Mitchell is the Communist Party candidate for president in the general election, the first African American woman to run for president; her name appears on the ballot in two states.

Women in Nauru and Swaziland gain the right to vote.

The Equal Employment Opportunity Commission (founded in 1965) rules that separating job advertisements by gender is illegal.

Shirley Chisholm is the first black woman elected to the U.S. Congress as a Representative from New York.

A group of women's liberationists, the New York Radical Women, organize a protest of the Miss America Pageant in Atlantic City, New Jersey, as degrading to women.

1969

Florida ratifies the Nineteenth Amendment, having never held a vote on it during the original ratification process in 1920.

South Carolina ratifies the Nineteenth Amendment, having originally rejected it in 1920.

1970

Representative Martha Griffiths of Michigan files a discharge petition demanding that the Equal Rights Amendment receive a full hearing in the U.S. House of Representatives.

Georgia ratifies the Nineteenth Amendment, having originally rejected it in 1919.

Louisiana ratifies the Nineteenth Amendment, having originally rejected it in 1920.

Women in Andorra and the Arab Republic of Yemen gain the right to vote.

1971

The ERA is approved by the House of Representatives in a vote of 354 for, 24 against, and sent to the U.S. Senate for a full vote.

The National Women's Political Caucus is founded by Gloria Steinem, Bella Abzug, and Shirley Chisholm to encourage women to seek public office.

North Carolina ratifies the Nineteenth Amendment, having never held a vote on it during the original ratification process in 1920.

The Twenty-Sixth Amendment to the U.S. Constitution is ratified, lowering the national voting age from 21 to 18.

Women in Switzerland gain the right to vote.

1972

The U.S. Senate approves the ERA with a vote of 84 for, 8 against; having now passed both houses of Congress, the amendment is sent to the states with a seven-year deadline for ratification.

The League of Women Voters, founded in 1920, endorses the Equal Rights Amendment.

Conservative activist Phyllis Schlafly organizes a national STOP ERA campaign.

Congresswoman Shirley Chisholm announces her candidacy for president of the United States, the first woman to seek the Democratic Party nomination.

Title IX of the Education Amendments prohibits discrimination in schools based on gender, which increases women's participation in athletic programs.

Women in Bangladesh gain the right to vote.

1973

President Richard Nixon proclaims August 20th as Women's Equality Day in commemoration of the date women gained the right to vote in 1920 with adoption of the Nineteenth Amendment to the U.S. Constitution.

The U.S. Supreme Court decision in *Roe v. Wade* establishes a woman's legal right to abortion based on the trimester framework.

The AFL-CIO, the largest national federation of trade unions, endorses the ERA.

1974

Ella Grasso of Connecticut is the first woman elected as governor of a U.S. state in her own right, not filling the position as a replacement for a spouse.

Women in Jordan gain the right to vote.

1975

The United Nations declares 1975 the Year of the Woman, and March 8th is celebrated as International Women's Day.

Women in Angola, Cape Verde, Mozambique, and Vanuatu gain the right to vote.

1976

President Jimmy Carter creates the National Advisory Committee on Women, with New York Congresswoman Bella Abzug as chair.

Women in Nigeria gain the right to vote.

1977

Following up on 1975 as the international Year of the Woman, a National Women's Conference is held in Houston, Texas, chaired by Congresswoman Bella Abzug.

Indiana is the 35th state to ratify the ERA, the last state before the original deadline expires; it would be 40 years before another state ratified the amendment.

Alice Paul, leading suffragist and author of the ERA, dies in New Jersey at age 92.

Women in Guinea-Bissau gain the right to vote.

1978

Representative Elizabeth Holtzman of New York introduces a bill to extend the deadline for ERA ratification from 1978 to 1982; both houses of Congress approve the extension.

NOW organizes a women's March for Equality and 100,000 people gather in Washington, D.C., in support of the Equal Rights Amendment.

The Pregnancy Discrimination Act bans hiring and firing discrimination based on pregnancy.

Women in Moldova and the Solomon Islands gain the right to vote.

1979
Women in the Marshall Islands, Micronesia, and Palau gain the right to vote.

1980
The media and NOW report a national "gender gap" in voting for the first time in the presidential election, with more women voting for pro-ERA Democratic candidate Jimmy Carter over Republican Ronald Reagan.

Women in Iraq gain the right to vote.

1981
Sandra Day O'Connor (nominated by President Ronald Reagan) is confirmed as the first female justice on the U.S. Supreme Court.

1982
The Equal Rights Amendment fails to achieve ratification by the extended deadline; 35 out of 38 needed states had ratified by this date.

1984
Geraldine Ferraro is chosen as the running mate for Democratic presidential hopeful Walter Mondale, the first female vice presidential candidate for one of the two major parties.

Mississippi ratifies the Nineteenth Amendment, having originally rejected the amendment in 1920.

Women in Liechtenstein gain the right to vote, the last European country to extend voting rights to women.

1986
President Ronald Reagan signs the Uniformed and Overseas Citizens Absentee Voting Act, protecting voting rights for American citizens serving abroad during elections.

Women in the Central African Republic gain the right to vote.

1987
The U.S. Congress designates March as Women's History Month.

1989
Women in Namibia gain the right to vote.

1990
Women in Western Samoa gain the right to vote.

1993
Ruth Bader Ginsburg (nominated by President Bill Clinton) becomes the second woman appointed to the U.S. Supreme Court.

President Bill Clinton signs the National Voter Registration Act to facilitate easier voter registration processes.

1994
President Bill Clinton signs into law the Violence against Women Act to investigate and prosecute more crimes against women.

Women in post-apartheid South Africa gain the right to vote.

1995
The United Nations Fourth World Conference on Women is held in Beijing; First Lady Hillary Rodham Clinton delivers the keynote address, outlining an international agenda for women's human rights.

1997
Madeline Albright is sworn into office as the first female U.S. Secretary of State.

1999
In *Davis v. Monroe County Board of Education*, the U.S. Supreme Court rules that, under Title IX of the Education Amendments of 1972, a school can be held liable for damages due to sexual harassment of a student.

Women in Qatar gain the right to vote.

2002
President George W. Bush signs into law the Help America Vote Act, to improve voting systems and election processes.

Women in Bahrain gain the right to vote.

2003
Women in Oman gain the right to vote.

2005

Women in Kuwait gain the right to vote.

2006

Women in the United Arab Emirates gain the right to vote.

2007

Democrat Nancy Pelosi of California becomes the first woman to serve as Speaker of the U.S. House of Representatives.

2008

Alaska governor Sarah Palin is selected as the vice presidential running mate for Republican presidential hopeful John McCain.

Former Congresswoman Cynthia McKinney is the Green Party candidate for president in the general election.

2009

President Obama signs into law the Lily Ledbetter Fair Pay Restoration Act, amending the statute of limitation for filing complaints against employers for gender-based pay discrimination.

2012

Activist Jill Stein is the Green Party candidate for president in the general election.

2013

In *Shelby v. Holder*, the U.S. Supreme Court strikes down certain provisions of the Voting Rights Act of 1965 as unconstitutional based on jurisdiction; the ruling is largely seen as a civil rights setback.

2015

In *Obergefell v. Hodges*, the U.S. Supreme Court rules that same-sex marriage is legal in all 50 states.

Women in Saudi Arabia gain the right to vote in municipal elections.

2016
Hillary Clinton wins the nomination as the presidential candidate for the Democratic Party, the first female nominee of one of the major parties; Clinton wins the popular vote by almost 3 million votes in the general election but does not secure enough electoral college votes to win the presidency.

Activist Jill Stein garners more than 1.4 million votes in the general election as the Green Party candidate for president.

2017
Nevada ratifies the Equal Rights Amendment, the first state to do so in 40 years, reviving interest in challenging the 1982 ratification deadline set by Congress.

2018
Illinois is the 37th state to ratify the Equal Rights Amendment.

2020
Virginia becomes the 38th state (the final state needed) to ratify the Equal Rights Amendment, first introduced in 1923; the question of whether the amendment met the ratification deadline and can be added to the U.S. Constitution will likely be decided by the courts.

Sources

Adams, Jad. *Women and the Vote: A World History.* New York: Oxford University Press, 2014.

Dodd, Lynda G. "Parades, Pickets, and Prison: Alice Paul and the Virtues of Unruly Constitutional Citizenship." *Journal of Law and Politics* 24 (2008): 339–443. http://lyndagdodd.com/2_Research/Research_4_Dodd_FINAL_Alice%20Paul%20Paper.pdf

National Organization for Women (NOW). "Chronology of the Equal Rights Amendment, 1923–1996." https://now.org/resource/chronology-of-the-equal-rights-amendment-1923-1996/

U.S. Senate. "Timeline: The Senate and the 19th Amendment." *Woman Suffrage Centennial.* https://www.senate.gov/artandhistory/history/People/Women/Nineteenth_Amendment_Vertical_Timeline.htm

Wayne, Tiffany K., ed. *Women's Rights in the United States: A Comprehensive Encyclopedia of Issues, Events, and People.* Santa Barbara, CA: ABC-CLIO, 2014.

Women Suffrage and Beyond. https://womensuffrage.org/?page_id=69

Addams, Jane (1860–1935)

Social reformer, pacifist, and suffragist Jane Addams was a leader in the American settlement house movement, cofounding Hull House in Chicago in 1889 with Ellen Gates Starr. Hull House provided services to Chicago's poor and immigrant communities and provided a forum for increased civic activism by Addams and the other middle-class women reformers who were involved, convincing them of the need for the vote in order to carry out a broader agenda of social and municipal reform.

Addams was born in Cedarville, Illinois. Her widowed father was a wealthy banker who sent Addams to the Rockford Female Seminary and then to the Woman's Medical College in Philadelphia, where she completed one year of training. After Addams's father died in 1881, she dropped out of medical school and went to Europe, where she observed the Toynbee Hall project that combined charity efforts to offer legal aid, inexpensive meals, and literacy classes to the poor in London slums. Upon her return to the United States in 1889, Addams rented a deserted Chicago mansion, renovated it, and called it Hull House. With the help of young middle-class volunteers, and charitable donations from wealthy benefactors, the center sought to ease the suffering of immigrant women and families in Chicago slums. Eventually the center grew into a complex of 13 buildings that provided many services, including day care, free medicines, playground areas, and a gymnasium. It offered a variety of classes including English literacy, sewing, bookbinding, art, music, and cooking. It promoted cultural enrichment with concerts and exhibitions and offered advice about working hours, working safety, and child labor practices, emphasizing the importance of keeping children in school rather than sending them to work in factories.

Addams, Jane

Jane Addams, an American sociologist, pacifist, and feminist who cofounded Hull House, the nation's first settlement house. (National Archives)

Besides helping people directly with their everyday needs, Addams also initiated a massive social research project to investigate the causes of poverty and crime. She hired college-educated women to undertake interviews and observations. Hull House workers compiled statistical data about the living and working conditions of Chicago's poorest neighborhoods. The results and recommendations were published in 1895 in *Hull House Maps and Papers*. Addams used the report findings to push for state and federal progressive reforms such as inspections of factories and housing, child labor laws, and union recognition. In 1903, Addams helped found the Women's Trade Union League to address women's rights in the workplace, and in 1908 she participated in and founded the Immigrants' Protective League to help recent immigrants. Addams wrote about her experiences in *Twenty Years at Hull-House* (1910) and *The Second Twenty Years at Hull-House* (1930). She also wrote social studies and commentaries mostly based on her lectures, including *Democracy and Social Ethics* (1902), *Newer Ideals of Peace* (1907), and *The Spirit of Youth and the City Streets* (1909).

When World War I began in Europe in 1914, Addams led a peace parade in New York and, in 1915, she met with other American pacifists in

Washington, D.C., to organize peace efforts. The meeting resulted in the founding of the Woman's Peace Party. At the international level, Addams served as president of the Women's International League of Peace and Freedom (WILPF). Although her opposition to war was a humanitarian effort, when the United States entered the war in 1917, Addams's pacifism appeared unpatriotic to many people. In addition, her support of immigrants at Hull House, particularly Germans, led to widespread criticism and charitable contributions almost entirely disappeared. Nevertheless, Addams continued to publicly oppose the war. After the war, Herbert Hoover, director of the U.S. Department of Food Administration, commissioned Addams to lead a humanitarian aid project in Europe supplying survivors with food and clothes. Upon her return to the United States in 1920, she helped found the American Civil Liberties Union to protect the rights of the underrepresented poor.

Addams had supported women's rights since her college days, but she became more directly involved in the women's suffrage movement because she felt that her agenda of municipal and national reforms would be more easily attained if women could vote. She spoke regularly at suffrage conventions and served as vice president of the National American Woman Suffrage Association (NAWSA) between 1911 and 1914. Addams addressed the International Woman Suffrage Alliance in London in 1908 and again in Budapest in 1913. In 1911, she campaigned in support of the Illinois suffrage bill, traveling around the state by train to collect petition signatures. She wrote a speech on "The Woman and the State," part of which was published in 1913 as "If Men Were Seeking the Franchise." In 1912, she worked with NAWSA to push the Republican Party to include women's suffrage on its platform, but when the Republicans failed to do so, Addams publicly supported Progressive Party candidate Theodore Roosevelt, a controversial move within NAWSA, which declared itself nonpartisan. She resigned from NAWSA in 1914 over the states' rights compromise made with the proposed Shafroth-Palmer Amendment.

After the ratification of the Nineteenth Amendment in 1920, Addams focused primarily on peace activism. In 1931, Addams was awarded the Nobel Peace Prize. She died of cancer four years later at the age of 75. Her funeral service was held at Hull House.

Rolando Avila and Tiffany K. Wayne

Further Reading

Diliberto, Gioia. *A Useful Woman: The Early Life of Jane Addams.* New York: Scribner, 1999.

African American Women and Suffrage

Black women were active as suffragists throughout the history of the women's rights movement. Their appeals for the vote were part of the larger civil rights agenda, from abolitionism in the first half of the nineteenth century, to the racial uplift and women's club movements at the turn of the twentieth century. As African American suffragists rarely focused solely on the vote for women as a separate or even primary reform issue, black women's participation in the struggle for the vote has been a story of exclusion or marginalization within national suffrage organizations and, subsequently, from many contemporary and later histories of the movement. For black women, the struggle for the political and economic enfranchisement of African Americans in the 50-year period between the ratification of the Fifteenth Amendment in 1870, which extended voting rights to black men, and the ratification of the Nineteenth Amendment in 1920, which granted the right to vote to all American women, required also addressing the problems of segregation, lynching and violence, poll taxes and literacy tests to prevent black men from voting, and the lack of black officeholders as policy makers.

Before the Civil War, the abolitionist and women's rights causes shared members, ideas, and strategies. The emergence of a separate women's rights movement, traditionally marked by the 1848 meeting at Seneca Falls, New York, was already a culmination of more than a decade of collaboration between black and white activists in the antislavery cause. Finding a moral and personal imperative to end slavery, black and white women alike had few opportunities and many critics for speaking and writing in public forums.

In 1832, writer and educator Maria Stewart was the first American woman known to speak before an audience of both men and women, black and white. Stewart called upon black women, in particular, as having a special role and position to speak against slavery and injustice. Probably the most well-known black female speaker of the mid-nineteenth century was Sojourner Truth, a former slave and abolitionist who highlighted the gendered aspects of racism against black women at her 1850 speech at the National Women's Rights Convention in Akron, Ohio. Both Stewart and Truth had white women allies, including many Quakers who believed in spiritual equality and a commitment to nonviolence. However, black women speakers could speak from personal experience about the connection between racial and gendered discrimination.

Despite the fact that the organized women's movement arose directly from women's public activism in the antislavery cause, those alliances were broken in the post–Civil War split over the question of civil and political rights for former slaves. The ratification of the Fifteenth Amendment to the U.S. Constitution in 1870 effectively granted black men the right to vote by including "race," but explicitly excluding "sex," as a protected category against which states could not discriminate in determining voting rights. In 1869, two women's suffrage organizations formed: the National Woman Suffrage Association (NWSA), which opposed the Fifteenth Amendment because it excluded women, and the American Woman Suffrage Association (AWSA), which supported the Fifteenth Amendment as a necessary step toward full equality. The two organizations institutionalized a deep racial division and emphasized the inability of some white women to see the necessity of black women's perspectives and commitments.

The national suffrage organizations reunited in 1890 as the National American Woman Suffrage Association (NAWSA), incorporating new strategies and reaching out to younger women and working-class women. Although NAWSA was dominated by white leadership, many black women were affiliated with the national movement. By the end of the nineteenth century, however, black clubwomen and reformers were also organizing in larger numbers on a range of issues affecting African Americans, from education to economic independence, to anti-lynching and voting rights. Women's suffrage was just one aspect of the larger voting rights issue for African Americans; even with the constitutional right to vote, black men were politically disenfranchised through southern strategies such as poll taxes, literacy tests, and violence and intimidation to keep them from exercising that right. Additionally, black political participation included the need for more black officeholders and women's groups, such as Ida B. Wells's Alpha Suffrage Club in Chicago, to work toward getting black men elected to office before women could vote and hold office themselves.

Prominent African American suffragists of the early twentieth century, such as Ida B. Wells, Mary McLeod Bethune, Mary Church Terrell, and Josephine St. Pierre Ruffin, included suffrage in their broader goals as clubwomen, educators, and anti-lynching activists, but largely worked outside of, or were explicitly excluded from, the national suffrage organizations. NAWSA leadership, in particular, pursued a strategy of distancing themselves from the question of votes for African American women in exchange for support from white southern lawmakers who did not want to enfranchise more black voters. In 1913, Ida B. Wells refused to accept NAWSA's request for a segregated women's suffrage parade at Woodrow Wilson's inauguration in Washington, D.C., with Wells joining the other white delegates from

Illinois mid-parade. This action seemed to exemplify the division and racism within the national suffrage movement, but the parade was only the most public display of a longer and broader history of black women's marginalization and overt racism in the movement.

While fighting alongside white women to achieve their own full legal and political equality, including the right to vote, black women were also challenging the racism, segregation, violence, and discrimination that prevented all African Americans from fully participating in the political system. This dual, or multiple, agenda sometimes put black women at odds with white suffrage organizations and leadership, although many individual alliances were made along the way. Black women created their own organizations and directed their own suffrage strategies, while also challenging white suffragists by demanding that *all* women's voices be included.

This intersectional vision of reform positioned black women to continue to be outspoken public activists on a range of civil rights issues after and beyond women gaining the vote with ratification of the Nineteenth Amendment in 1920, as African American political rights continued to be threatened throughout the twentieth century and beyond.

Tiffany K. Wayne

Further Reading

Knupfer, Anne Meis. *Toward a Tenderer Humanity and a Nobler Womanhood: African American Women's Clubs in Turn-of-the-Century Chicago.* New York: NYU Press, 1996.

Schechter, Patricia A. *Ida B. Wells-Barnett and American Reform, 1880–1930.* Chapel Hill: University of North Carolina Press, 2001.

Terborg-Penn, Rosalyn. *African American Women in the Struggle for the Vote, 1850–1920.* Bloomington: Indiana University Press, 1998.

Alpha Suffrage Club

The Alpha Suffrage Club was founded in Chicago in 1913 by suffragist and anti-lynching activist Ida B. Wells. The Alpha Suffrage Club was an organization to promote voting rights for African American women, who were excluded from many mainstream suffrage groups and activities, but the group also focused on the suppression of black male voting rights and on the need to elect more black men to office. The Alpha Suffrage Club strove for nonpartisanship, and their main goal was to register and educate black women voters, as well as to affect local politics by mobilizing black voters to vote for black officeholders in Chicago. Wells founded the club with support from her white colleagues in the Illinois suffrage movement, Belle Squire and Virginia Brooks.

Ida B. Wells was an active suffragist and national reformer but had come into conflict with white leaders of the National American Woman Suffrage Association (NAWSA) who pursued a strategy of distancing themselves from African American women's groups for fear of alienating white southern suffrage advocates and politicians. The issue famously and publicly drew attention when leaders of the 1913 Washington, D.C., suffrage parade organized by Alice Paul of the Congressional Union of NAWSA asked Wells to march in a separate black women's section, rather than marching with the Illinois contingent. Wells refused and joined mid-parade alongside the other white women from Illinois, including her friends Squire and Brooks.

That same year, Wells returned to Illinois to lobby the state legislature for passage of the Illinois Equal Suffrage Act (IESA) of 1913, which granted Illinois women the right to vote for president in national elections and to vote for certain local offices, though Illinois women still could not vote for state-level representatives or senators. The IESA passed, and Wells wanted to build on this new role for African American women by educating and encouraging them to have an impact on local and city politics, influencing the outcome of elections for aldermen in their neighborhoods.

Alpha Suffrage Club members went door-to-door in Chicago to register black women voters, held meetings to encourage women's political participation and civic duties, and posted information on voting locations on election days. Indeed, due to the efforts of Wells and the Alpha Suffrage Club, black women voter turnout was high and, in 1915, resulted in the election of Republican Oscar De Priest as the first black alderman in Chicago. It was reported that one-third of the votes for De Priest came from black women. City politics had an even larger impact on African American representation in national politics, as De Priest's position in Chicago eventually launched him to the U.S. Congress, where he served in the House of Representatives between 1929 and 1935.

The Alpha Suffrage Club published a newsletter, the *Alpha Suffrage Record*, and went on to support other black candidates for aldermen and mayor. In the process, it empowered and organized black women as activists and as voters at a time when their voices and their interests were ignored by national suffrage organizations. With the passage of the Nineteenth

Amendment in 1920, Ida B. Wells shifted her political activism away from supporting black male candidates to promoting women, including herself, as officeholders.

Tiffany K. Wayne

Further Reading

Knupfer, Anne Meis. *Toward a Tenderer Humanity and a Nobler Womanhood: African American Women's Clubs in Turn-of-the-Century Chicago.* New York: NYU Press, 1996.

Schechter, Patricia A. *Ida B. Wells-Barnett and American Reform, 1880–1930.* Chapel Hill: University of North Carolina Press, 2001.

Terborg-Penn, Rosalyn. *African American Women in the Struggle for the Vote, 1850–1920.* Bloomington: Indiana University Press, 1998.

American Association of University Women (AAUW)

The American Association of University Women (AAUW) (originally named the Association of Collegiate Alumnae) was founded in 1881 by a group of college alumnae from several schools with the purpose of promoting research and information about higher education. The AAUW advocated for and supported women pursuing higher education and entrance into the professions. The association was cofounded by Ellen Swallow Richards and Marion Talbot. Richards was the first American woman to receive a degree in chemistry, which she received from Vassar College in 1870. She pursued advanced studies at the Massachusetts Institute of Technology (MIT) and had a lifelong commitment to women's scientific and technical education. Talbot, a student of Richards, later became a professor and Dean of Women at the University of Chicago.

The AAUW's first research report, *Health Statistics of Women College Graduates,* was published in 1885 and found that attaining a college education did not negatively impact women's health, especially their reproductive health, a widely held belief in the late nineteenth century as more women entered into higher education and the professions. In 1888, the AAUW awarded its first financial fellowship of $350 to support Ida Street, a researcher at the University of Michigan. In 1919, AAUW members held a special fundraising drive to raise money to support the radium experiments of Marie Curie.

Although not a political organization by definition, in 1915 the AAUW membership voted to formally support women's suffrage. For over a century, the work of the AAUW has supported women's entrance into public life through its research and reports about the obstacles and discrimination that women face in pursuit of higher education and jobs, including issues in primary and secondary education for girls, women's access to universities, academic appointments and promotion, political participation and voting rights, equal pay, and sexual harassment.

Headquartered in Washington, D.C., in the twenty-first century the AAUW has over 1,000 chapters nationwide and partners with 800 colleges and universities to continue its work.

Tiffany K. Wayne

Further Reading

Gould, Suzanne. "AAUW's Long Road to Women's Suffrage." *American Association of University Women*, August 23, 2013. https://www.aauw.org/2013/08/23/road-to-womens-suffrage/.

Levine, Susan. *Degrees of Equality: The American Association of University Women and the Challenge of Twentieth-Century Feminism*. Philadelphia, PA: Temple University Press, 1995.

"Our History: The Story of AAUW's Place in Women's History." *American Association of University Women*. https://history.aauw.org.

American Equal Rights Association

The first national organization to campaign for both black and female suffrage, the American Equal Rights Association (AERA) organized in 1866 with Lucretia Mott as president. Supporters included abolitionists from the American Anti-Slavery Society as well as men and women who supported the women's rights movement before the American Civil War. The AERA lasted only three years, dissolving in 1869 over the debate on black male suffrage with the Fifteenth Amendment to the U.S. Constitution, and was replaced by two new organizations to focus on women's suffrage: the American Woman Suffrage Association and the National Woman Suffrage Association.

The women's rights movement developed in the antebellum period as part of a broader era of social and moral reform that included the abolition of slavery, educational reform, penal reform, temperance, and other issues focused on securing changes to the legal, political, civil, and social structure of American society. In the 1830s, some reformers began to question women's limited public role in reform movements such as abolitionism. In 1865, with the abolition of slavery and the end of the Civil War, abolitionist Wendell Phillips assumed leadership of the American Anti-Slavery Society (AASS). In January 1866, Susan B. Anthony proposed a merger between the AASS and the women's rights movement to fight for universal suffrage. Phillips blocked the proposal, claiming that reformers must first secure black male suffrage. In response to the AASS's rejection, Anthony along with Lucy Stone organized the Eleventh Annual National Women's Rights Convention, the first such gathering since the Civil War. At that convention, supporters voted to establish the American Equal Rights Association and announced plans to launch lobbying and petition campaigns in several states.

In 1867, the AERA launched two major state-level political campaigns. In Kansas, two referenda were placed before voters. The first called for black male suffrage, and the second called for female suffrage. Elizabeth Cady Stanton and Anthony campaigned vigorously for both proposals. Stone supported only the measure for extending the franchise to black men. Both referenda were defeated. In New York, a state convention had been called to consider two revisions to the U.S. Constitution, including the enfranchisement of women. Newspaper editor and abolitionist Horace Greeley chaired the New York suffrage committee, but stunned Stanton and others when he abandoned women's suffrage, citing a lack of public support.

After the failed campaigns of 1867, the AERA became increasingly divided. Both sides advocated universal suffrage yet differed in their approach. Stone was willing to defer female suffrage until black political rights had been secured, while Stanton and Anthony insisted that both women and black men should be enfranchised at the same time. The ratification of the Fourteenth Amendment in 1868 affirmed black men's status and rights as American citizens but remained silent on the question of full citizenship rights for women. After the AERA met for the last time in 1869, Anthony and Stanton formed the National Woman Suffrage Association (NWSA), adopting an independent political stance and working on a broad range of women's issues. Stone and her allies formed the American Woman Suffrage Association (AWSA), which attempted to work with the Republican Party to advance both black civil rights and women's rights.

In 1870 the Fifteenth Amendment was ratified, prohibiting states from denying to citizens the right to vote on the basis of race, color, or previous condition of servitude. However, the amendment omitted any reference to gender, essentially securing the vote for black men but rendering women's political exclusion complete. Supporters of the NWSA and the AWSA reunited in 1890, forming the National American Woman Suffrage Association (NAWSA). The NAWSA became the primary promoter of female suffrage, playing a key role in securing the ratification of the Nineteenth Amendment in 1920, which guaranteed women the right to vote.

Julie Holcomb

Further Reading

Cott, Nancy. *No Small Courage: A History of Women in the United States*. New York: Oxford University Press, 2000.

Dudden, Faye E. *Fighting Chance: The Struggle over Woman Suffrage and Black Suffrage in Reconstruction America*. New York: Oxford University Press, 2011.

Faulkner, Carol. *Lucretia Mott's Heresy: Abolition and Women's Rights in Nineteenth-Century America*. Philadelphia: University of Pennsylvania Press, 2011.

Wellman, Judith. *The Road to Seneca Falls: Elizabeth Cady Stanton and the First Woman's Rights Convention*. Urbana: University of Illinois Press, 2004.

American Woman Suffrage Association (AWSA)

The American Woman Suffrage Association (AWSA) was an organization that worked to achieve women's right to vote from 1869 until 1890. The AWSA formed when the American Equal Rights Association (AERA), which was founded in 1866 to fight for "universal suffrage" for black Americans and for women after the Civil War, disbanded in 1869 over disagreements related to the ratification of the Fourteenth and Fifteenth Amendments to the U.S. Constitution. The National Woman Suffrage Association (NWSA) formed at the same time, and each group worked toward the shared goal of women's suffrage using different strategies and tactics. In 1890, the AWSA and the NWSA merged to form the National American Woman Suffrage Association (NAWSA).

Led by Lucy Stone, Julia Ward Howe, and Henry Blackwell, among others, the AWSA was primarily comprised of former AERA members who

American Woman Suffrage Association (AWSA)

A delegation of officers of the National American Woman Suffrage Association. Front row, left to right: Mrs. Maud Wood Park, Dr. Anna Howard Shaw, Mrs. Carrie Chapman Catt, and Mrs. Helen H. Gardener. Second row: Miss Rose Young, Mrs. George Bass, and Miss Ruth White. (National Archives)

supported the ratification of the Fourteenth and Fifteenth Amendments to the Constitution. The Fourteenth Amendment broadened the definition of citizenship to include former slaves and guaranteed equal protection and due process to all citizens. However, it also introduced the first gendered language into the Constitution, declaring that any state that limits the enfranchisement of *male* citizens would be subject to decreased apportionment. Further, the Fifteenth Amendment protected citizens' right to vote without discrimination based on race and condition of former servitude but said nothing of sex. Because both amendments focused on granting citizenship rights to African American men but did not guarantee women the right to vote, some members felt that the AERA should not support their ratification. Others saw them as a step in the right direction, even if women's suffrage was left out. The AERA disbanded over the issue of black male suffrage, and its members split into either the AWSA or the NWSA. While the NWSA was initially considered more radical and embraced a broader range of issues related to gender equality and women's rights, the AWSA focused primarily on the vote and sought to make women's suffrage an issue that would appeal to mainstream American values. The AWSA was also the larger of the two organizations and allowed men to join (whereas the NWSA did not). Beginning in 1870, AWSA published a newspaper, the *Woman's Journal*, under the editorship of founder Lucy Stone.

In the 1880s, AWSA allied itself with the Woman's Christian Temperance Union (WCTU), an organization dedicated to the prohibition of alcohol, as well as other moral and social reform issues. The WCTU and the AWSA took advantage of a widespread belief at the time that women were morally superior to men to argue that women's presence in politics could be a "purifying" force. The alliance proved to be mutually beneficial. Because temperance was largely a women's movement, the WCTU realized that women's suffrage would give their cause much more political influence, and the conservative and religious WCTU was able to market women's suffrage to more conservative women who might otherwise be against it.

The alliance between the AWSA and the WCTU had some limited success. It did, for example, lead to a surge in more traditional women and men converting to the suffrage cause, and some western states and territories passed suffrage legislation by the end of the nineteenth century. Bolstered by this state-by-state success, and led by a new generation of suffragists with different strategies and reform commitments, in 1890 the AWSA and the NWSA merged to form the National American Woman Suffrage Association. NAWSA worked toward women's suffrage until the passage of the Nineteenth Amendment in 1920, which granted women the right to vote.

Tessa Ditonto

Further Reading

Dudden, Faye E. *Fighting Chance: The Struggle over Woman Suffrage and Black Suffrage in Reconstruction America*. New York: Oxford University Press, 2011.

Ford, Lynne E. *Women and Politics: The Pursuit of Equality*. Boston, MA: Cengage, 2011.

Freeman, Jo. *A Room at a Time: How Women Entered Party Politics*. Lanham, MD: Rowman & Littlefield, 2000.

McMillen, Sally G. *Lucy Stone: An Unapologetic Life*. New York: Oxford University Press, 2015.

Anthony, Susan B. (1820–1906)

Susan Brownell Anthony was one of the major leaders of the nineteenth-century American women's rights movement, a suffragist who was known for her public speeches, publications, and organizational leadership. Although trained as a teacher, Anthony spent much of her life as an activist. Alongside her friend and long-time collaborator Elizabeth Cady Stanton, Anthony supported the abolition of slavery and the recognition of rights for all persons, but when the women's movement split in the 1860s over a continued focus on civil rights after black men gained the vote with the Fifteenth Amendment, Anthony and Stanton founded the National Woman Suffrage Association (NWSA), which focused exclusively on securing a federal amendment for women's suffrage.

Susan B. Anthony (left) and Elizabeth Cady Stanton were pioneers in the fight for women's rights and suffrage. (Library of Congress)

Anthony was born the second of six children, in Adams, Massachusetts, on February 15, 1820, to Quakers Daniel Anthony and Lucy Read. Unlike many of her female counterparts, Anthony's family ensured that both she and her sisters received a strong education, which ultimately led her to attend Deborah Moulson's Select Seminary for Females in Philadelphia and subsequently become a schoolteacher. Despite the benefits of such a positive upbringing, the financial panic of 1837 undermined the security of the Anthony family, leaving Susan to support her family until 1849 when she began to manage her family's estate. Anthony remained opposed to marriage throughout her life, believing that the institution and subsequent domestic life were a means to entrap women.

As early as 1837, while still teaching, Anthony became politically involved by attending antislavery conventions and was an active member in the American Anti-Slavery Society. In 1848, Anthony joined the Daughters of Temperance and began making public speeches about women's rights. In 1851, Anthony met Stanton, with whom she would work throughout her life. Around this time Anthony also met other women reformers, such as Lucy Stone, Antoinette Brown (Blackwell), Amelia Bloomer, and Lucretia Mott. In 1852, Anthony also helped form the New York Temperance Society and spoke at the World Temperance Convention, arguing that women had the right to divorce drunk and violent husbands. Soon afterward, Anthony began petitioning to reform property rights and divorce legislation to recognize the legal and economic rights of women.

During the Civil War, Anthony and Stanton founded and organized the Woman's National Loyal League, which petitioned against slavery. After aiding the Union Army, supporting the Republican Party, and organizing women in support of abolition, Anthony was astonished when the Fourteenth and Fifteenth Amendments were introduced utilizing masculine language and focusing specifically on the rights of black men. Controversy over the exclusion of women from the Fifteenth Amendment created a divide within the abolitionist and women's movements. In 1869, Anthony and Stanton formed the National Woman Suffrage Association (NWSA), while Stone and her husband, Henry Blackwell, led the American Woman Suffrage Association (AWSA).

As president of NWSA, Anthony published the women's rights journal *The Revolution* from 1868 to 1870, which ultimately became financially insolvent, leaving Anthony in debt. Anthony sought to challenge women's citizenship rights under the U.S. Constitution in the courts and was arrested for attempting to vote on November 5, 1872. Despite refusing to pay her fine, the district court in New York declined to pursue the matter, denying Anthony the means of an appeal to the U.S. Supreme Court.

Between 1881 and 1886, Anthony, Stanton, and Matilda Joslyn Gage published the first three volumes of the *History of Woman Suffrage*. In 1897, she worked with Ida Husted Harper to draft a two-volume autobiography, *The Life and Work of Susan B. Anthony* (1898). In 1890, Anthony had helped reunify the competing women's rights organizations into the National American Woman Suffrage Association (NAWSA) and, from 1892 until 1900, served as president of this organization. Anthony traveled widely and remained active as a speaker for the women's suffrage cause well into her later years. In 1906, Anthony attended and even briefly participated in the annual NAWSA convention, but soon afterward her health declined. On March 13, 1906, she passed away at her home in Rochester, New York, without seeing women gain the right to vote nationwide.

In 1878, Anthony had first introduced a constitutional amendment in Congress that would have prevented sex discrimination in voting rights. Publicly known as the Anthony Amendment, a federal amendment granting American women the right to vote did not pass Congress until 1919, and the Nineteenth Amendment was ratified by the states in 1920.

Sean Morton and Tiffany K. Wayne

Further Reading

Baker, Jean H. *Sisters: The Lives of America's Suffragists*. New York: Hill and Wang, 2005.

Barry, Kathleen. *Susan B. Anthony: A Biography of a Singular Feminist*. New York: New York University Press, 1988.

Burns, Ken, and Geoffrey C. Ward. *Not for Ourselves Alone: The Story of Elizabeth Cady Stanton and Susan B. Anthony*. New York: Alfred A. Knopf, 1999.

Sherr, Lynn. *Failure Is Impossible: Susan B. Anthony in Her Own Words*. New York: Times Books, 1995.

Antisuffrage Movement

The antisuffrage movement was a late nineteenth-century response to the international women's rights movement. The antisuffrage movement had both male and female members. Opponents of suffrage had various reasons for their position. Some believed that women had no innate interest in politics, would be less knowledgeable voters, and that involvement in the public sphere in any way interfered with or distracted from women's duties within the home as wives and mothers. Others were not against women having a more public role but feared that the right to vote would actually diminish women's political influence by compromising the influence they had built through social reform and civic housekeeping, public activities justified not in the name of equality, but often as self-sacrificing and as an extension of women's roles in the home.

Headquarters of the National Association Opposed to Woman Suffrage in the United States in 1911. (Library of Congress)

In addition, the ballot would potentially open up career opportunities and political power, and some antisuffragists contended that these changes in the name of equality would actually negatively impact women by removing special privileges and protections for women, such as protective labor laws. These same arguments were used to oppose ratification of an Equal Rights Amendment in the 1920s and again in the 1970s. Political power, it was further pointed out, had corrupted women rulers such as Catherine II of Russia and Mary, Queen of Scots.

Organized voices against women gaining the vote escalated after the Civil War, as the suffrage movement itself organized and became more focused on this single issue. A petition to the U.S. Congress against woman suffrage was published by *Godey's Lady's Book* in 1871 and antisuffragists protested at state suffrage conventions throughout the late 1800s. By the 1890s, the first state-level antisuffrage organizations were formed in Massachusetts, New York, Iowa, and several western states and territories, where women first won the vote, and the National Association Opposed to Woman Suffrage (NAOWS) was founded in 1911 by Josephine Dodge, an advocate of day care for working mothers. Opponents of woman suffrage soon had their own newspapers, such as the *Anti-Suffrage Review*, *The Anti-Suffragist*, and *The Women's Protest*. The movement became global with the creation of the Women's National Anti-Suffrage League in London in 1908.

While the antisuffrage movement was generally a conservative effort, other forces and fears played an important part in the movement. In the early twentieth century, feminism was often linked to socialism and other radical ideas, but socialist Emma Goldman and other radical thinkers contended that the inequalities between the sexes required revolution, not participation in the existing political process. Because the temperance movement had so much female support, brewers and saloon-based organizations also opposed women's suffrage, reasoning that if women had the vote they would vote to ban alcohol sales. White southerners were divided on enfranchising more white women to shore up white supremacy but also feared extending the vote to black women. Likewise, antisuffrage activists pointed to Utah Territory, which had given women the vote not as a nod to female political equality but instead to increase the number of Mormon voters. Other critics worried that women's suffrage simply functioned to double married men's votes because their wives would vote as they were told. The focus of these antisuffrage arguments was less about women's rights or equality and more about political concerns over the influence of different types of voters if all women gained the vote.

American women gained the right to vote with the passage of the Nineteenth Amendment in 1920 and some antisuffrage activists continued to oppose women's participation in politics, or remained active in national politics themselves as conservative opponents of social welfare, pacifist, and equality platforms.

Amy H. Forss and Tiffany K. Wayne

Further Reading

Benjamin, Anne. *A History of the Anti-Suffrage Movement in the United States from 1895 to 1920*. Lewiston, NY: Edwin Mellen, 1991.

Goodier, Susan. *No Votes for Women: The New York State Anti-Suffrage Movement*. Chicago: University of Illinois Press, 2013.

Howard, Angela, and Sasha Renae Adams Tarrant, eds. *Opposition to the Women's Movement in the United States, 1848–1929*. New York: Garland, 1997.

Thurner, Manuela "'Better Citizens without the Ballot': American AntiSuffrage Women and Their Rationale during the Progressive Era." *Journal of Women's History* 5, no. 1 (Spring 1993): 33–60.

B

Beard, Mary Ritter (1876–1958)

Activist, historian, and archivist Mary Ritter Beard was a suffragist and member of the National Woman's Party (NWP), but she also made remarkable contributions to the field of women's history through her books, and through her preservation of primary documents chronicling women's contribution to American history.

Born on August 5, 1876, Mary Ritter was the fourth of seven children born to Eli, an activist and lawyer, and his wife, Narcissa, in Indianapolis, Indiana. After graduating as valedictorian of her high school, she attended DePauw University, where she was Kappa Alpha Theta and class president. She was greatly influenced by her German professor, who taught her to see her studies in a broader context by using literature, culture, and philosophy in lectures, and by her sorority sisters, who refused to be limited by conventional courses and activities for women. DePauw University was also where she met her husband, Charles Austin Beard, who also became a noted historian.

Upon graduation in 1897, Mary Beard became a schoolteacher in Greencastle, Indiana, while Charles went to England to further his studies. He returned a year later, and they married in 1900. The couple returned to England, where Beard befriended socialists and radicals such as the British suffragettes, Christabel and Emmeline Pankhurst. When the Beards' daughter was born in 1902, the couple returned to the United States. Mary then became involved with the Women's Trade Union League (WTUL) and the National Woman's Party (NWP). While part of the NWP, she was a member of the board and editor of *The Suffragist*, and she organized, lectured, and participated in demonstrations.

After the Nineteenth Amendment was passed in 1920, Mary focused on women's place in history. She collaborated with her husband on several history textbooks that were used in American high schools, including *American Citizenship* (1914) and *Rise of American Civilization* (1927). Although her husband gained fame for these works, historians and the public largely ignored Mary's part in these publications. Traditionally, historians and archivists had not thought that material on women's history was significant. Mary Beard disagreed and argued that women had made significant contributions to human history throughout all time periods and were equally responsible as men for defining social values.

Mary began collecting both published and unpublished materials related to women's activities throughout world history to create an archive and educational center for future researchers. In 1935, she received a large donation of materials from Hungarian feminist and peace activist Rosika Schwimmer and established the World Center for Women's Archives (WCWA) in New York. The WCWA gathered funds and endorsements from the likes of Eleanor Roosevelt, Frances Perkins, and others. The WCWA initially garnered the financial support it needed for its large goal. However, it soon had disagreements over racial issues and organizational approaches. After five years of a lack of solidarity and financial woes, Mary resigned from the WCWA. In that short time, she had identified historical records of women in private households, historical societies, and various archives. She promoted an exhibit of women including a collection at the Library of Congress and also compiled secondary sources important to women's studies. After the WCWA folded, Mary returned some materials to the original owners and donated parts of the collection to various colleges, forming the foundation for important women's history archives at the Schlesinger Library at Radcliffe College and the Sophia Smith Collection at Smith College. Ironically, Beard destroyed many of her own personal papers and, when she died in 1958, her letters to her husband showing their collaborative efforts were destroyed. Mary and Charles Beard were interred together in Ferncliff Cemetery in Westchester, New York. Today she is considered one of the most significant founders of the movement to add women to historical studies.

Sarah Nation

Further Reading

Cott, Nancy. F., ed. *A Woman Making History: Mary Ritter Beard through Her Letters*. New Haven, CT: Yale University Press, 1991.

Trigg, Mary K. *Feminism as Life's Work: Four Modern American Women through Two World Wars*. New Brunswick, NJ: Rutgers University Press, 2014.

Turoff, Barbara K. *Mary Beard as Force in History*. Dayton, OH: Wright State University Press, 1979.

Voss-Hubbard, Anke. "No Document—No History: Mary Ritter Beard and the Early History of Women's Archives." *American Archivist* 58 (1995): 16–30.

Belmont, Alva Vanderbilt (1853–1933)

Alva Belmont was a wealthy socialite and activist who used her money and influence to support the women's suffrage movement. She became president of the National Woman's Party (NWP) in 1921, after ratification of the Nineteenth Amendment granting American women the right to vote.

A wealthy New York socialite due to her first marriage to an heir to the Cornelius Vanderbilt railroad fortune, Alva Belmont turned her attention in her fifties to the women's rights cause after the death of her second husband. Inspired by a lecture by suffrage activist Ida Husted Harper, she threw herself into the cause, sponsoring meetings and lectures at her mansions, organizing fundraising efforts among her wealthy friends, using her name and political connections to gain support for women's suffrage, and donating her own time and money primarily to work with the Congressional Union of the National American Woman Suffrage Association (NAWSA) and then to the National Woman's Party.

Belmont first became politically active in support of working women's rights in New York in the early 1900s. The year 1909 proved to be a turning point for Belmont's public activism. She made headlines in New York City when she paid the bail for shirtwaist factory strikers who had been arrested on the picket line, and hosted a rally attended by thousands in support of equal pay and the vote for working women. Although criticized by some union leaders and labor activists because she was a member of the Gilded Age wealthy elite, against whom workers were fighting, Belmont joined the board of the Women's Trade Union League (WTUL) and fought for working women's right to vote.

In 1909, she also founded the Political Equality League in New York to campaign for votes for New York state politicians who supported women's suffrage. As leader of the Political Equality League, Belmont gathered together a who's who of Progressive Era reform speakers at her meetings, including Rose Schneiderman of the WTUL, Julia Lathrop of the U.S. Children's Bureau, and Florence Kelley of the National Consumers League. Belmont soon joined NAWSA and, at the invitation of NAWSA president and friend, Anna Howard Shaw, she traveled to London as a delegate to the International Women's Suffrage Association (IWSA), later the International Alliance of Women (IAW), where she was influenced by the strategies and tactics of English activists such as Emmeline Pankhurst. Upon her return, Belmont paid for a building in New York City to house NAWSA offices and helped organize a 1912 New York City suffrage parade. Belmont again attended the IWSA conference in Budapest in 1913.

Belmont's Political Equality League was eventually merged with the Congressional Union, a NAWSA committee headed by Lucy Burns and Alice Paul with the purpose of pressuring the sitting Democratic Congress and president in support of a suffrage amendment. Belmont, along with her daughter, Consuelo Vanderbilt, hosted women's rights meetings in the 1910s, and in 1917, Belmont helped organize the picketing of the White House which brought the Congressional Union into conflict with NAWSA leadership. She helped fund a western tour in support of women's suffrage, and worked with Alice Paul to create the National Woman's Party, serving on the executive board and then as president of the NWP from 1921 until her death in 1933. In 1929, she purchased a building as the Washington, D.C., headquarters for the NWP, a site that remains as the Belmont-Paul Women's Equality National Monument, dedicated in 2016.

In her post-suffrage work with the NWP throughout the 1920s and early 1930s, Belmont remained active in support of women's equality and political participation. She lived in France during her later years and served on the International Advisory Council of the NWP, monitoring women's international legal and political status from abroad. Although she had an important role as a primary benefactor for the women's suffrage movement in its final critical years of the 1910s and beyond (she left another $100,000 to the National Woman's Party upon her death in 1933), Alva Belmont offered more than financial support and was an activist and leader in her own right.

Tiffany K. Wayne

Further Reading
Hoffert, Sylvia D. *Alva Vanderbilt Belmont: Unlikely Champion of Women's Rights*. Bloomington: Indiana University Press, 2012.

Neuman, Johanna. *Gilded Suffragists: The New York Socialites Who Fought for Women's Right to Vote.* New York: NYU Press, 2017.

Stuart, Amanda Mackenzie. *Consuelo and Alva Vanderbilt: The Story of a Daughter and a Mother in the Gilded Age.* New York: HarperCollins, 2005.

Bethune, Mary McLeod (1875–1955)

Mary Jane McLeod was born on July 10, 1875, in Mayesville, South Carolina. She was the 15th of 17 children born to Samuel and Patsy McLeod, both of whom, like her older siblings born before the American Civil War, were slaves. In her youth Mary picked cotton but also attended a Methodist mission school, and her early efforts earned her a scholarship in 1888 to attend Scotia Seminary in North Carolina. Graduating in 1893, she enrolled in what is now Moody Bible Institute in Chicago, intending to become a missionary in Africa. However, upon learning that African Americans were not chosen for such assignments, she altered her plans, became a teacher, and worked in Presbyterian schools in Georgia and South Carolina.

In 1898 Mary McLeod married Albertus Bethune, and in 1899 they had a son. The young family moved to Florida, and in 1904 Mary Bethune founded the Daytona Normal and Industrial Institute. While the school originally focused on industrial and religious training, Bethune ultimately moved it in a more academic direction. The Board of Trustees boasted some of the biggest names in American business,

Mary McLeod Bethune, an early twentieth-century African American reformer and educator. (Library of Congress)

including major supporter and longtime board chair James Gamble of Proctor and Gamble as well as John D. Rockefeller Jr.

Albertus left the family after eight years of marriage, but the couple remained formally married until his death in 1918. In 1911 the Daytona Normal and Industrial Institute expanded its offerings, adding nursing classes to the curriculum and eventually the opening of a hospital, which operated until 1931. In 1923 the school merged with Cookman Institute for Men in Jacksonville, becoming Bethune-Cookman College. Bethune served as the school's president, the centerpiece of her professional career, from 1904 until 1942 and then again briefly from 1946 to 1947.

A longtime civil rights activist, during World War I Bethune pressured the Red Cross to integrate, and she was also active in the anti-lynching campaign. Bethune focused especially on the education and economic independence of girls and women and in 1912 she joined the Equal Suffrage League of the National Association of Colored Women (NACW). Beyond the legal right to vote, Bethune was also concerned about the legal and social obstacles for African Americans attempting to exercise that right, and spoke out against poll taxes and literacy tests, as well as organized voter registration efforts. She was elected president of the NACW in 1924 and in 1935 she brought together black women from different organizations and founded the National Council of Negro Women (NCNW), serving as president from 1935 to 1949. She also served as vice president of the National Association for the Advancement of Colored People from 1940 to 1955.

Bethune's experience and expertise led to her being recruited for governmental service, where she served on presidential commissions under Presidents Calvin Coolidge and Herbert Hoover. She became a close personal friend of Eleanor Roosevelt, and that relationship helped to make Bethune a prominent adviser, both officially and unofficially, within the New Deal. In addition, Bethune helped bring together a group of black advisers for President Franklin Roosevelt, a body that came to be known as the "black cabinet." Along with A. Philip Randolph, Bethune played a key role in convincing Roosevelt to establish the Federal Committee on Fair Employment Practices in 1941. During World War II Bethune served as an aide to the secretary of war, holding the position of assistant director of the Women's Army Corps. In that role, she oversaw the creation of the first officer candidate schools for women and was an unyielding advocate on behalf of African American women who sought the opportunity to serve in the armed forces.

Mary McLeod Bethune died in 1955 and is buried on the grounds of Bethune-Cookman College, the institution that serves as a testament to her never-ending efforts to foster equality and opportunity for all through education.

William H. Pruden III

Further Reading

McCluskey, Audrey Thomas, and Elaine M. Smith. *Mary McLeod Bethune: Building a Better World; Essays and Selected Documents.* Bloomington: Indiana University Press, 1999.

"Our Founder—Dr. Bethune." Bethune-Cookman University. https://www.cookman.edu/about_BCU/history/our_founder.html.

Blackwell, Alice Stone (1857–1950)

Alice Stone Blackwell was born in East Orange, New Jersey, on September 14, 1857, the only child of Henry Browne Blackwell and Lucy Stone, both leaders in the women's suffrage movement. Alice's mother, Lucy, attended Oberlin College and was the first woman from Massachusetts to obtain a college degree. Alice's aunt, Elizabeth Blackwell, was the first woman in the United States to graduate from medical school.

While Alice Blackwell was still young, the family moved to the Boston area, where she attended the Chauncy Hall School and graduated as class president and Phi Beta Kappa from Boston University in 1881. After her graduation, she began working for the *Woman's Journal*, a publication created in 1870 by her parents to further the cause of women's suffrage. When her mother died in 1893, Blackwell became editor in chief of the *Woman's Journal*, a position she held for 35 years. Her father was involved in the publication until his death in 1909.

Blackwell, along with her parents, was a member of the American Woman Suffrage Association (AWSA). During her time as editor of the *Woman's Journal*, she worked with members of AWSA and the National Woman Suffrage Association (NWSA) to reconcile these rival factions of the women's suffrage movement into one unified group. The first convention of this new society, the National American Woman Suffrage Association (NAWSA), was held in February 1890. Blackwell served as the recording secretary for NAWSA for nearly 20 years. She also served as honorary president of the

Massachusetts League of Women Voters and president of the New England Woman Suffrage Association and the Massachusetts Woman Suffrage Association.

Around the time she became editor of the *Woman's Journal*, Blackwell branched out into other reform endeavors. She met Ohannes Chatschumian in Leipzig, Germany, and together they founded a group called the Friends of Armenia, a society dedicated to fighting for the human rights of the Armenian people. She served in this society with other prominent American women, including Julia Ward Howe, and with Chatschumian she began a project to translate Armenian poetry into English. Blackwell published *Armenian Poems* in 1896 and also published translations of works from Russian, Yiddish, Spanish, Hungarian, and French.

Blackwell, a self-identified socialist, became involved in many different social reform groups, including the Friends of Russian Freedom, the Woman's Christian Temperance Union, and the National Association for the Advancement of Colored People. Her letters in support of various causes were so militant that one of Boston's newspapers would not print her work.

After Blackwell left editorship of the *Woman's Journal*, she began writing a biography of her mother, *Lucy Stone: Pioneer of Woman's Rights*, which was published in 1930. Boston University awarded Blackwell an honorary doctorate in humanities in 1945. Alice Stone Blackwell went blind near the end of her life and died on March 15, 1950, in Cambridge, Massachusetts.

Elizabeth Bass

Further Reading

"Alice Stone Blackwell, 1857–1950." Dorchester Antheneum, n.d. http://www.dorchesteratheneum.org/page.php?id=38.

Hays, Elinor Rice. *Those Extraordinary Blackwells: The Story of a Journey to a Better World.* New York: Harcourt and Brace, 1967.

Merrill, Marlene Deahl, ed. *Growing Up in Boston's Gilded Age: The Journal of Alice Stone Blackwell, 1872–1874.* New Haven, CT: Yale University Press, 1990.

Blake, Lillie Devereux (1833–1914)

Lillie Devereux Blake was a fiction writer for the first 25 years of her career. Then, in 1882, she began to publish essays on women's rights, eventually lecturing and arranging suffrage conventions across the United States in an effort to win the right to vote.

Blake was born into a wealthy and distinguished family in 1833, in Raleigh, North Carolina. She attended Apthorp's School for Girls in New Haven, Connecticut, before taking the Yale College course from tutors at home. She made her social debut at age 17 and soon was renowned for her beauty and active social life.

She married in 1855 and made her home in St. Louis, Missouri, but in 1859 her husband died of alleged suicide, leaving Blake a penniless, single mother. She turned to writing, having already published some of her work in magazines to moderate success, to support herself and her two daughters. She published her first novel, *Southwold*, the same year of the death of her husband. The book told the story of a woman who, rejected by the man she loves, becomes "bold and even unfeminine" in her opinions, especially with her claims that Christianity harms women's status, only to commit suicide by the end of the novel. Blake then went on to serve as a correspondent in Washington, D.C., during the Civil War, contracted by the *New York Evening Post*, *New York World*, *Philadelphia Press*, and *Forney's War Press*.

Blake led a number of successful campaigns for woman suffrage legislation at the state level while serving as president of both the New York State Woman Suffrage Association (1879 to 1890) and the New York City Woman Suffrage League (1886 to 1900). Her efforts not only secured the vote for women in school elections but also led to legislation requiring that women physicians be available in mental institutions, that matrons be on hand in police stations, that chairs be provided for saleswomen, that women be employed as census takers, that mothers and fathers be recognized as joint guardians of their children, that Civil War nurses be eligible for pensions, and that women be eligible to sit in the state constitutional convention.

Blake became an active member of the National Woman Suffrage Association (and, after 1890, the National American Woman Suffrage Association [NAWSA]). She organized NAWSA's Committee on Legislative Advice, and served as chair from 1895 to 1899, during which time she published a leaflet of legal advice for her fellow suffragists. Ultimately, her interest in reforms other than suffrage led to conflict with fellow activist Susan B. Anthony, who maintained that the focus should remain solely on suffrage. Blake was also active in the movement that resulted in the founding of Barnard College in 1889.

Blake's last novel, *Fettered for Life; or, Lord and Master* (1874) highlighted issues such as domestic abuse, unjust marriage laws, and lack of educational opportunities for women. The protagonist, similar to Blake, was a successful reporter, but unlike Blake, she adopted male attire so that she could move about freely and look for work.

Ill health forced Blake into retirement in 1905. She died in 1913 at the age of 80.

Amy Bizzarri

Further Reading

Blake, Katherine Devereux, and Wallace, Margaret Louise. *Champion of Women: The Life of Lillie Devereux Blake.* New York: Fleming H. Revell Company, 1943.

Farrell, Grace. *Lillie Devereux Blake: Retracing a Life Erased.* Amherst: University of Massachusetts Press, 2002.

Blatch, Harriot Stanton (1856–1940)

Women's rights activist Harriot Eaton Stanton Blatch played a significant part in revitalizing the women's suffrage movement in the early 1900s.

Blatch was born on January 20, 1856, in Seneca Falls, New York. She was the sixth child of antislavery reformer Henry Brewster Stanton and suffragist and women's rights advocate Elizabeth Cady Stanton. In 1862 Henry moved the family to New York City to take an appointment with the New York Customs House. The family left New York City in 1868. Harriot graduated from all-female Vassar College in Poughkeepsie, New York, in 1878. After her graduation, she and her mother worked with Susan B. Anthony to produce the multivolume *History of Woman Suffrage*.

In 1880, Harriot Stanton left for Europe with her brother Theodore but was called to return home to care for her mother, who had fallen ill. She met her

Suffragist Harriot Stanton Blatch, taken ca. 1915–1920. (Library of Congress)

future husband, Englishman William Blatch, on board the ship that returned her to the United States. Upon her return to her parents' home in Tenafly, New Jersey, she and her mother worked with Anthony to produce the second volume of the *History of Woman Suffrage*. After the volume was completed, mother and daughter traveled to Europe to allow Stanton to recuperate. William and Harriot were married in England in 1882 and Blatch lost her U.S. citizenship, a deprivation made more unjust by the fact that her brother had married a foreign national but was able to keep his citizenship. During her time in England, Blatch became active in reform societies, including the Women's Local Government Society, the Women's Franchise League, and the Fabian Society. While in England she gave birth to two daughters, Nora and Helen. Helen died at age of four. Blatch obtained a master's degree from Vassar for a study of English rural working women and lived in England until 1902.

When the Blatches returned to the United States, Harriot Blatch became involved in several reform societies, including the Women's Trade Union League and the National American Woman Suffrage Association. She founded the Equality League of Self-Supporting Women in 1907 to recruit working-class women to the fight for women's suffrage. In doing so, she helped revitalize the movement, which had floundered in the late 1800s. Recognizing the importance of the vote for promoting issues such as workers' rights, fair wages, and job safety, she helped organize open-air marches and meetings. The Equality League later became the Women's Political Union and then the National Woman's Party.

Unlike many women's rights organizers who were pacifists, Blatch supported U.S. involvement in World War I and was the director of the Food Administration's Speakers Bureau and the Woman's Land Army, which organized female volunteers to do farm labor. In 1918, Blatch wrote a book, *Mobilizing Woman-Power*, describing the contributions of women to the war effort during World War I as an argument for extending the franchise to women in Great Britain and the United States. She describes women as working side by side with men to win the war. In his introduction to the work, former U.S. president Theodore Roosevelt acknowledged women's wartime contributions.

After the war, Blatch embraced pacifism and joined the Socialist Party. She ran for public office in New York as a Socialist but did not win. After William's death in 1915, Blatch regained her U.S. citizenship. She and her brother Theodore edited a collection of their mother's papers titled *Elizabeth*

Cady Stanton: As Revealed in Her Letters, Diary, and Reminiscences, published in 1922.

Blatch co-wrote her memoir, *Challenging Years: The Memoirs of Harriot Stanton Blatch*, with National Woman's Party activist and author Alma Lutz. The work was published in 1940. Harriot Stanton Blatch died on November 20, 1940.

Elizabeth Bass

Further Reading
DuBois, Ellen Carol. *Harriot Stanton Blatch and the Winning of Woman Suffrage.* New Haven, CT: Yale University Press, 1997.

Bloomer, Amelia Jenks (1818–1894)

Amelia Jenks Bloomer was a temperance leader, suffragist, and publisher of one of the first female-produced newspapers, *The Lily.*

Born in Homer, New York, in 1818, Amelia Jenks followed the path of Emma Willard, Catherine Beecher, and other educated women of the early nineteenth century by becoming a teacher, one of the few professions open to women at the time. In 1840, she married newspaperman Dexter Bloomer and moved to Seneca Falls, New York. Her husband was involved in politics, and she worked with him on William Henry Harrison's presidential campaign.

Bloomer wrote for several newspapers under pseudonyms—most frequently "Gloriana." She joined the temperance movement in Seneca Falls and helped start the Ladies Temperance Society in 1848. At the initial organizing meeting, a committee formed to publish an organizational newspaper, *The Lily: A Ladies' Journal, Devoted to Temperance and Literature.* Before the first edition went to print, however, the committee dissolved, and Bloomer was left as *The Lily*'s writer, editor, and publisher.

Bloomer attended the first Seneca Falls Convention on women's rights in 1848 but did not sign the convention's Declaration of Sentiments. Women's rights topics were soon included in *The Lily*, with articles written by Elizabeth Cady Stanton and Susan B. Anthony. Bloomer introduced the two prominent activists to each other in 1851. Bloomer's primary contribution to the women's rights movement was through dress reform. The limiting clothing worn by nineteenth-century women (corsets, multiple petticoats, bustles, and heavy long skirts) represented to many the social and physical restrictions placed on women. In *The Lily*, Bloomer championed practical women's clothing. Bloomer was introduced to the "new costume" of a knee-length dress worn over loose trousers, worn by many nineteenth-century reformers, when Elizabeth Cady Stanton's cousin, Elizabeth Smith Miller, began wearing the outfit. The "Turkish costume," as it was also called, had a less-confining fit and reduced weight, which were practical and comfortable. Bloomer and other reformers, including Stanton and Anthony, embraced the outfit, and Bloomer published sewing patterns in *The Lily*. Bloomer never took credit for the outfit, but it became known as the "Bloomer costume," and a woman wearing baggy pants under a shortened dress was called a "Bloomer." Gradually, the billowy pants themselves became known as "bloomers."

Controversy swirled around the radical clothing, with critics claiming that the pants were unfeminine. Bloomer and other dress reformers countered that there was nothing feminine about dirty, wet hems draped around women's ankles. The freedom to move naturally enhanced female health, while the shorter skirt's reduced yardage was economical. When Horace Greeley, a renowned newspaper reporter, wrote about Bloomer and the pantaloons, dress reform became international news. *The Lily*'s circulation catapulted from 500 subscriptions to 4,000. Dress reform indirectly made women's rights issues a public topic.

Bloomer and her husband went on to own a newspaper in Ohio, where they took a stand on equal employment for women. When they hired a woman to help run the printing presses, the male staff threatened to quit. The Bloomers responded by replacing the workers who threatened to quit with progressive-minded men and hiring three additional women. In 1854, Bloomer sold *The Lily* before moving to the frontier town of Council Bluffs, Iowa.

Amelia Bloomer was one of the first women to speak publicly about suffrage in Iowa and was elected president of the Iowa Women's Suffrage Association in 1871. She championed an 1873 revision to the Iowa legal code that removed all distinctions between male and female property owners. Once women in Iowa owned property equally, individuals such as Bloomer petitioned the U.S. Congress that taxation on their property resulted in taxation without the right to vote for representation—an important shift in tactics to obtain women's suffrage.

Bloomer died on December 30, 1894, a quarter of a century still before American women gained the right to vote with the Nineteenth Amendment.

Keri Dearborn

Further Reading

Fischer, Gayle V. *Pantaloons and Power: Nineteenth Century Dress Reform in the United States.* Kent, OH: Kent State University Press, 2001.

Brown, Olympia (1835–1926)

Olympia Brown was a Universalist minister, the first woman ordained by full denominational authority. (Antoinette Brown Blackwell was the first American woman minister ordained by an independent congregation.) Olympia Brown was one of the few earlier generation suffragists to live long enough to vote after the ratification of the Nineteenth Amendment in 1920.

Olympia Brown was born on January 5, 1835, in Prairie Ronde, Michigan. Denied admission to the University of Michigan because of her gender, she attended Mount Holyoke and Antioch College, graduating from the latter in 1860. After helping with the arrangements to have Antoinette Blackwell preach at Antioch—the first woman Brown had seen preach—Brown decided to become a minister herself. She entered the St. Lawrence University theological school and was ordained in 1863.

Brown married John Henry Willis in 1873 but continued to use her maiden name. In 1866, Susan B. Anthony invited Brown to attend a suffrage meeting; Brown became a champion of women's rights and a charter member of the American Equal Rights Association. In 1868, she organized a convention in Boston that led to the formation of the New England Woman Suffrage Association. Brown continued her suffrage activity after the family moved to Wisconsin so that Brown could accept pastorship of a church in Racine. From 1884 to 1912, she served as president of the Wisconsin Woman Suffrage Association. In 1887, she unsuccessfully sued election officials in the city of Racine for having denied her the vote. That year, she resigned her pastorate to work full-time for the suffrage cause.

In addition to her activities in Wisconsin, Brown maintained her commitment to suffrage on a national level, becoming vice president of the National Woman Suffrage Association (NWSA) in 1884. However, her commitment was to a suffrage amendment to the U.S. Constitution, rather than to the state-by-state strategy for which NWSA worked. To promote a constitutional amendment, she helped form the Federal Suffrage Association in Chicago in 1892. She served as its vice president until 1902, when the group was reorganized and renamed the Federal Equality Association (FEA). A year later,

Brown was named president of the association, serving in that capacity until 1920. She was also a member of the Congressional Union for Woman Suffrage. In 1917, while in her eighties, she picketed the White House with the National Woman's Party (NWP), passing out literature holding President Woodrow Wilson responsible for the failure to pass a federal suffrage amendment. She continued marching in women's suffrage demonstrations until 1920 and was also involved with the Women's International League for Peace and Freedom (WILPF).

From 1893 to 1900, Brown managed *The Racine Times*, a newspaper owned by her husband. She authored *Acquaintances, Old and New, among Reformers* (1911). A lifelong feminist, Brown was involved in reform activities until her death in Baltimore, Maryland, on October 23, 1926.

Elizabeth Frost-Knappman

Further Reading

Bidlack, Beth. "Olympia Brown: Reading the Bible as a Universalist Minister and a Pragmatic Suffragist." In *Breaking Boundaries: Female Biblical Interpreters Who Challenged the Status Quo*, edited by Nancy Calvert-Koyzis and Heather Weir, 125–143. New York: T & T Clark, 2010.

Coté, Charlotte. *Olympia Brown: The Battle for Equality.* Racine, WI: Mother Courage Press, 1988.

McBridge, Genevieve G. *On Wisconsin Women: Working for Their Rights from Settlement to Suffrage.* Madison: University of Wisconsin Press, 1993.

Burns, Lucy (1879–1966)

Suffragist and women's rights advocate Lucy Burns cofounded the National Woman's Party (NWP). Burns's collaboration and activism with NWP cofounder Alice Paul was pivotal to the passage and ratification of the Nineteenth Amendment in 1920.

Burns was born in Brooklyn, New York, on July 28, 1879, to an Irish Catholic family. A brilliant student of language and linguistics, she graduated from Packer Institute in 1899, Vassar College in 1902, and Yale University in 1903. While studying at the University of Bonn in 1909, she traveled to England and became interested in the work of British suffragettes Emmeline and Christabel Pankhurst. Burns became an activist with the Pankhursts, learning the art of street rallies, and worked as an organizer in Scotland until 1912. Burns and Alice Paul met in a London police station after they were arrested for demonstrating outside Parliament. The two women returned to the United States and formed an alliance and a lifelong friendship, not unlike that of Elizabeth Cady Stanton and Susan B. Anthony a generation earlier.

In 1913, Paul was the chair and Burns the cochair of the Congressional Committee for the National American Woman Suffrage Association (NAWSA). Tasked with lobbying Capitol Hill for national suffrage, the NAWSA leadership and Paul disagreed on strategy. When Burns was arrested for chalking meeting notices on a sidewalk, NAWSA leadership worked to remove them both from the organization. Paul and Burns left NAWSA in 1914 to form the National Woman's Party (NWP) and pursued more militant strategies, such as protesting in front of the White House for eight hours a day, six days a week. President Wilson had given lip service to the cause of suffrage but, when the United States entered World War I, the president thwarted progress on the suffrage cause in Congress and painted the suffragists as unpatriotic.

When a Russian envoy visited the White House, Burns prominently displayed a banner declaring that Russian women had more freedom than American women because they could vote. Burns and other so-called Silent Sentinels demonstrated outside the White House from January 1917 until the Nineteenth Amendment passed both houses of Congress in mid-1919. President Wilson actively worked to break the protestors. Police and onlookers incited violence against the women and several suffragists were arrested and sent to Occoquan Workhouse in Virginia. Burns and Paul leaked reports of the conditions. Stories of upper-class women locked in the same quarters as women with criminal records and black women made the Washington elite squeamish, and Wilson was forced to pardon them. Burns kept the campaigns going, building sympathy and support with every arrest.

In November 1917, Lucy Burns was among those arrested and sent to Occoquan. November 15 became known as the "Night of Terror," when Burns and her fellow protestors were beaten and terrorized. Burns was handcuffed with her hands above her head and, after declaring a hunger strike, was placed in solitary confinement and force-fed. They could not pry Burns's mouth open, so a glass tube was shoved up her nostril, causing significant bleeding and pain. Sympathizers named the women "Iron-Jawed Angels."

After legal maneuvering and a public outcry, the White House ordered that the prisoners be released without condition on November 27 and 28. Burns was arrested and jailed seven times, more than any American suffragist. Burns and other suffragists who had been jailed toured the country on "The

Prison Special" train. Dressed in prison garb, the suffragists packed houses nationwide, encouraging condemnation of the Wilson administration's shameful treatment of women. Burns increased the pressure through more protests and watch fires. With national and international opinion shifting, Wilson called for a special session of Congress and in May 1919, the amendment was approved and sent to the states for ratification.

After the Nineteenth Amendment was ratified in 1920, Lucy Burns retired from political life, returning to Brooklyn to live with her family. In 1923, her youngest sister died in childbirth, and Burns reared her newborn niece as her own. Burns became committed to Catholicism and worked with the Catholic Church until her death in 1966.

Jennifer Oliver O'Connell

Further Reading

Clift, Eleanor. *Founding Sisters and the Nineteenth Amendment.* Hoboken, NJ: Wiley, 2003.

Haesly, Richard, ed. *Women's Suffrage.* Farmington Hills, MI: Greenhaven, 2003.

Zahniser, J. D., and Amelia Fry. *Alice Paul: Claiming Power.* New York: Oxford University Press, 2014.

C

Cary, Mary Ann Shadd (1823–1893)

Mary Ann Shadd Cary was a journalist, lawyer, educator, suffragist, and civil rights activist. She achieved prominence largely because of her antebellum work on black immigration to Ontario, Canada, and through her journalistic endeavors as one of the first black woman newspaper publishers.

Mary Ann Shadd was born on October 9, 1823, the eldest of 13 children to free, property-owning blacks in Wilmington, Delaware. Her father, Abraham Shadd, was a well-known abolitionist and was involved in the Underground Railroad, helping fugitive slaves. Mary Ann was privately educated and taught in black schools. In 1849, her first printed letter appeared in abolitionist Frederick Douglass's *The North Star* newspaper, and she also published a pamphlet titled "Hints to the Colored People of the North." In 1851, she attended a convention with pro-emigration abolitionists Martin R. Delany, John Scoble, and Henry Walton Bibb in Toronto, Canada. She was so moved by the messages of these leaders that she subsequently moved to Windsor in Ontario, Canada, to what was then called "Canada West." Black emigrationists advocated for blacks to relocate to other countries, such as Canada, Mexico, and Haiti, and some pro-emigration leaders wanted a black return to West Africa. Shadd argued that Canada was best for black migration because of its close proximity to the United States, similar climate, language, and religion, and economic opportunities. She worked to improve life for black émigrés in Ontario, Canada, and in 1851, she opened a racially integrated school for black and white students. She taught there under the auspices of the American Missionary Association, serving as the sole black missionary.

In 1852, Mary Ann Shadd published *A Plea for Emigration; or Notes of Canada West, in Its Moral, Social and Political Aspect, with Suggestions Respecting Mexico, West Indies and Vancouver's Island, for the Information of Colored Emigrants* urging blacks to leave the United States. Because of her activism and outspokenness, she was fired from her job, and her school was forcibly closed in 1853. She moved to journalism and, in 1854, Shadd published the first edition of the *Provincial Freeman*, an abolitionist newspaper. She named Samuel Ward as the editor and Rev. Alex McArthur as coeditor in name only because newspaper publishing was viewed as men's work. The *Provincial Freeman* became extremely popular throughout Canada and the United States, although Shadd endured heavy criticism because of her gender and her political work. In 1856, she married Thomas F. Cary, a barber, and became a stepmother to his three children. They had two more children, but Thomas Cary died in 1860, the same year the last issue of the *Provincial Freeman* was published. Mary Ann Shadd Cary remained active throughout the Civil War and served as a Union Army recruiter. She returned to live in the United States, teaching in Detroit and Washington, D.C. In 1869, she enrolled in Howard University Law School, but, upon graduation, was denied access to the bar because of her sex.

Shadd Cary had published articles on women's education and the need for economic independence, and reported on women's rights lectures, in the *Provincial Freeman* as early as the 1850s. She had specifically mentioned the vote in an earlier editorial entitled "Can You Tell Where We Stand on Women's Rights?" By the 1870s, she had become active in the women's suffrage movement and was affiliated with the National Woman Suffrage Association (NWSA), the splinter group formed by Susan B. Anthony and Elizabeth Cady Stanton in protest over black men gaining the vote with the Fifteenth Amendment. Shadd Cary was among a group of both black and white women (including Anthony) who adopted a strategy of attempting to register to vote and showing up at the polls as an act of civil disobedience in order to challenge women's citizenship status under the Fourteenth Amendment.

Shadd Cary addressed the House Judiciary Committee on women's suffrage in 1872, arguing women's rights as taxpayers and calling to remove the word "male" from the U.S. Constitution. She attended the 1878 NWSA convention, where the group adopted a strategy of supporting whichever party promoted women's suffrage—whether Democratic or Republican—a controversial position among black activists, most of whom held allegiance to the post-Reconstruction Republican Party.

Mary Ann Shadd Cary ultimately fought for women's suffrage in both the United States and Canada. She died of stomach cancer on June 5, 1893, in Washington, D.C.

Deirdre Benia Cooper Owens and Tiffany K. Wayne

Further Reading

Rhodes, Jane. *Mary Ann Shadd Cary: The Black Press and Protest in the Nineteenth Century.* Bloomington: Indiana University Press, 1998.

Sangster, Joan. *One Hundred Years of Struggle: The History of Women and the Vote in Canada.* Vancouver: University of British Columbia Press, 2018.

Terborg-Penn, Rosalyn. *African American Women in the Struggle for the Vote, 1850–1920.* Bloomington: Indiana University Press, 1998.

Catt, Carrie Chapman (1859–1947)

Advocate for women's suffrage and international peace, both in the United States and abroad, Carrie Chapman Catt served as president of the revitalized National American Woman Suffrage Association (NAWSA) from 1900 to 1904, and again from 1915 to 1920. In 1920, after the Nineteenth Amendment was passed, she founded the League of Women Voters. She was also a prominent proponent of world peace and cofounded the Woman's Peace Party.

Carrie Clinton Lane, the daughter of Lucius and Maria Clinton Lane, was born in Ripon, Wisconsin, on January 9, 1859. In 1866, her family moved to a farm near Charles City, Iowa. After she graduated from high school, she entered the Iowa Agricultural College (now Iowa State University) in Ames, Iowa. She graduated as valedictorian in 1880 with a degree in general science, the only woman in her class. She worked as a law clerk and then as a schoolteacher and principal in Iowa and was appointed superintendent of schools in 1883, one of the first women in the United States to hold that post.

In 1885 Carrie Lane married Leo Chapman, the publisher and editor of the *Mason City Republican.* The following year, he went to San Francisco in search of a new job. She was traveling to join him when he died a few days before her arrival. She worked for a newspaper in San Francisco before returning to Charles City, where she joined the Iowa Woman Suffrage Association and began to write and speak in support of women's suffrage.

In 1890, she married George Catt, a wealthy engineer and fellow alumnus of Iowa Agricultural College who supported her work, both personally and financially. Carrie Chapman Catt began to work for the NAWSA, speaking at its national convention in 1890, and in 1892 she advocated passage of a suffrage amendment in a speech before the U.S. Congress. In 1900 she succeeded Susan B. Anthony as president of NAWSA and began speaking, planning campaigns, and organizing women nationwide.

In 1902, Catt helped to organize the International Woman Suffrage Alliance (IWSA), which eventually had groups in 32 countries. In 1904, she resigned as president of NAWSA to care for her sick husband. He died in 1905, closely followed by the death of her friend Susan B. Anthony in 1906 and both her younger brother and mother in 1907. Grief-stricken and emotionally exhausted, Catt's doctors suggested that she travel abroad to rest, but instead she spent the next eight years touring the world to promote the cause of women's suffrage and pacifism worldwide.

In 1915, Catt returned to the United States and resumed the presidency of NAWSA. That same year, spurred on by the outbreak of World War I, she and Jane Addams founded the Woman's Peace Party. At NAWSA's annual convention in 1916, Catt revealed what she called her "Winning Plan," which involved pursuing suffrage at both the state and national levels and working hard to procure at least partial voting rights in states that were resistant. In 1917, New York state passed a suffrage referendum, the first eastern state to do so. That same year the United States entered World War I, and in a seeming contradiction, Catt supported the decision as a strategy to highlight the loyalty of the suffragists.

After the Nineteenth Amendment was ratified in 1920, Catt resigned from the presidency of the NAWSA and founded the League of Women Voters to provide education for the nation's new female voters. In 1920, she ran for vice president of the United States on the ticket of the Georgist Commonwealth Land Party, a party founded on the single-tax principles of Henry George. In 1923, Catt and Nettie Rogers Shuler published *Woman Suffrage and Politics: The Inner Story of the Suffrage Movement*.

Catt again advocated for antiwar and disarmament groups during the 1920s and 1930s, and was a staunch supporter of the League of Nations and, later, the United Nations. In 1933, in response to Adolf Hitler's use of Jews as the scapegoat for Germany's problems, she founded the Protest Committee of Non-Jewish Women against the Persecution of Jews in Germany. For her work she received the American Hebrew Medal. In 1940, she organized her final event, the Woman's Centennial Conference in New York City, celebrating the feminist movement in the United States. Carrie Chapman Catt died in New Rochelle on March 9, 1947. Iowa State University established the Carrie Chapman Catt Center for Women and Politics in 1992.

Nancy Snell Griffith

Further Reading

Du Bois, Ellen Carol. *Woman Suffrage and Women's Rights*. New York: New York University Press, 1998.

Fowler, Robert Booth. *Carrie Chapman Catt: Feminist Politician*. Boston, MA: Northeastern University Press, 1986.

Rupp, Leila J. *Worlds of Women: The Making of an International Women's Movement*. Princeton, NJ: Princeton University Press, 1997.

Van Voris, Jacqueline. *Carrie Chapman Catt: A Public Life*. New York: Feminist Press at the City University of New York, 1987.

College Equal Suffrage League

The College Equal Suffrage League (CESL) was founded in 1900 by Maud Wood Park and Inez Haynes (Gillmore) Irwin to promote women's suffrage movement participation by younger women. Both Park and Irwin attended Radcliffe College and, soon after graduating, Park attended the 1900 convention of the National American Woman Suffrage Association (NAWSA) in Washington, D.C. She found that very few young women were involved in the movement. Park then committed to educating college women about the history and contributions of the leaders of the women's suffrage movement and to inspiring their more active participation in the national movement to secure a federal amendment for women's voting rights. Together, their efforts also inspired NAWSA leadership to more actively recruit college students and alumnae.

Park and Irwin formed the first CESL in Boston, Massachusetts, and worked to establish branches of the CESL at college campuses throughout the nation. The CESL sponsored speakers, organized suffrage meetings on campuses, published suffrage articles in campus newspapers, and participated in public marches. In 1908, enough branches had been formed that they joined together to form the National College Equal Suffrage League (NCESL), recognized as a sub-committee by NAWSA. Bryn Mawr College

President M. Carey Thomas was the first president of the NCESL and Maud Wood Park served as vice president. The NCESL disbanded in 1917, after which many of its members continued to work for NAWSA and the campaign for the federal amendment.

Not only did the College Equal Suffrage League contribute to the national women's suffrage movement by mobilizing new members, but it stood as an early model for student activism that would characterize other social and civil rights movements of the twentieth century.

Tiffany K. Wayne

Further Reading

"Bryn Mawrters as Suffragists: The National College Equal Suffrage League." Bryn Mawr College Library Special Collections. http://www.brynmawr.edu/library/exhibits/suffrage/ncesl.html.

Knupfer, Anne Meis, and Christine Wovshner, eds. *The Educational Work of Women's Organizations, 1890–1960*. New York: Palgrave Macmillan, 2008.

Mead, Rebecca J. *How the Vote Was Won: Woman Suffrage in the Western United States, 1868–1914*. New York: NYU Press, 2004.

Congressional Union

Formed in 1913 and led by suffragists Alice Paul and Lucy Burns, the Congressional Union for Woman Suffrage was a controversial though effective organization that focused on passage of a constitutional amendment guaranteeing American women the right to vote in federal elections. The Congressional Union was originally formed to support the work of the Congressional Committee of the National American Woman Suffrage Association (NAWSA), but NAWSA, led by Carrie Chapman Catt, eventually cut ties with the Congressional Union. The Congressional Union became the organizational and membership foundation of Alice Paul's National Woman's Party, formed in 1916.

Along with suffrage activists such as Lucy Burns, Mabel Vernon, and Olympia Brown, Alice Paul was inspired by the more militant suffragist activities of the Women's Social and Political Union in Britain. Paul felt stifled by the American women's suffrage organizations (specifically NAWSA's) unwillingness to openly confront both the public and politicians in their efforts to secure the vote. Under Paul's direction, the Congressional

Union introduced new strategies to the national movement, such as picketing the White House, holding massive demonstrations and parades, and, eventually, subjecting themselves to arrest for loitering and obstructing traffic. Lucy Burns was arrested in both England and the United States and, at one point, Alice Paul received a seven-month prison sentence and went on a hunger strike, during which she was force-fed with a metal tube.

Within a year of its founding, the Congressional Union boasted a membership of 4,500. It became so successful that it raised more than $50,000 and ran its own all-female periodical, *The Suffragist*. The leaders of NAWSA broke ties and funding from the Congressional Union in late 1913 over the CU's strategy of holding the party in power responsible for women's suffrage and refusing to support Democratic members of Congress or the president, unless or until they supported women's suffrage. After World War I broke out in 1914, this opposition to the presidential administration of Woodrow Wilson was seen as particularly unpatriotic.

In 1916, the Congressional Union became the National Woman's Party with Alice Paul as its head. In 1918, President Woodrow Wilson proposed that suffrage be granted as a "war measure." Passed in the House, the federal women's suffrage amendment stalled and was defeated in the Senate that year, as well as the next. The National Woman's Party again forced the issue into Congress in 1920, where it finally passed the House and the Senate. The measure became the Nineteenth Amendment to the U.S. Constitution after Tennessee became the required 36th state to ratify it into law.

Jason Newman and Tiffany K. Wayne

Further Reading

Ware, Susan. *Modern American Women*. New York: McGraw Hill, 2002.

Woloch, Nancy. *Women and the American Experience*. New York: McGraw Hill, 1994.

Davis, Paulina Kellogg Wright (1813–1876)

Paulina Kellogg Wright Davis was an abolitionist, social reformer, and editor, as well as the founder of the New England Woman Suffrage Association.

She was born in Bloomfield, New York, on August 7, 1813, to Ebenezer Kellogg and Polly Saxton. When Davis was seven years old, her parents both died, and she moved to Le Roy, New York, to live with her aunt, an orthodox Presbyterian. In 1853, Paulina Kellogg married a like-minded reformer, Francis Wright, a wealthy businessman from Utica, New York. The couple did not like the proslavery attitude of many churches, both southern and northern. They joined the New York Anti-Slavery Society, working as members of the executive committee. Like many antebellum women in the North, Paulina Wright's involvement in the antislavery movement led to an interest in other social justice movements, including female health reform, the legal rights of married women, and women's education. Many antebellum Americans believed that teaching girls physiology and mathematics was a waste of time and was even deleterious to female health. She began to give public lectures on anatomy, physiology, and women's health to single-sex audiences. With the help of a mannequin imported from Paris, she explained the details of female anatomy, and her lecture series was criticized as distasteful and shocking in the extreme. Nonetheless, she continued lecturing and began encouraging women to become doctors, reasoning that women might overcome their embarrassment about physical ailments if they had a female doctor.

Francis Wright died in 1845, and Paulina then married Thomas Davis, a jewelry manufacturer, women's rights supporter, and future member of the

Rhode Island State Senate and the U.S. Congress. The New York legislature passed the Married Women's Property Act in 1848, granting women rights over property of their own. In July 1848, Lucretia Mott and Elizabeth Cady Stanton called the Seneca Falls Convention to discuss women's civil rights, but Paulina Davis could not attend. Two years later she helped Mott, Stanton, Lucy Stone, and Abby Kelly Foster organize the first National Women's Rights Convention in Worcester, Massachusetts. Nearly 1,000 people, largely men, from 11 different states passed resolutions demanding equal rights for women in the areas of education and marriage. Davis presided over the meeting and gave the opening address.

At the 1852 convention, Davis decided to launch the monthly women's magazine, *The Una*, named after a character in Edmund Spenser's *Faerie Queene*. Davis was both the editor and sole financier of the magazine, which addressed issues of labor, marriage, suffrage, and education as they affected women. *The Una* was devoted to the "elevation of woman" and to discussing the rights of women and projecting their aspirations. Davis's editorials called for equality between husband and wife, equal pay for the genders, respect for women, and more opportunities in various professions. She wrote that women were not to be "crushed into idiocy to make them lovely and beloved." The magazine was discontinued after two years and nine months due to financial constraints as well as differences of opinion between Davis and her new co-editor Caroline Dall regarding whether their paper should focus on activism or literature.

In 1868 Davis helped found the New England Woman Suffrage Association, and the following year she served as president of the Rhode Island Suffrage Association. After the Civil War, she split with the New England suffrage groups and with many of her former abolitionist colleagues over the question of black men gaining the vote with the Fifteenth Amendment. Davis allied herself with Susan B. Anthony and Elizabeth Cady Stanton's organization, the National Woman Suffrage Association (NWSA), which focused exclusively on the vote for women, and wrote articles for the NWSA journal, *The Revolution*. The year 1870 marked the 20th anniversary of the first National Women's Rights Convention. Davis served as president of the 1870 convention in recognition of her immense contribution to the first generation of the American women's rights struggle. In 1871, she published *A History of the National Woman's Rights Movement*. Davis died at her home in Providence, Rhode Island, on August 24, 1876.

Patit Paban Mishra

Further Reading

Clymer, John F. *This High and Holy Moment: The First National Woman's Rights Convention, Worcester, 1850*. Fort Worth, TX: Harcourt Brace, 1999.

Dudden, Faye E. *Fighting Chance: The Struggle over Woman Suffrage and Black Suffrage in Reconstruction America*. New York: Oxford University Press, 2011.

Tonn, Mari Boor. "The Una, 1853–1855: The Premiere of the Woman's Rights Press." In *A Voice of Their Own: The Woman Suffrage Press, 1840–1910*, edited by Martha Solomon. Tuscaloosa: University of Alabama Press, 1991.

Wayne, Tiffany K. *Woman Thinking: Feminism and Transcendentalism in Nineteenth-Century America*. Lanham, MD: Rowman & Littlefield, 2005.

Dorr, Rheta Childe (1866–1948)

Rheta Childe Dorr was a suffragist and muckraking journalist of the Progressive Era who was the first editor of *The Suffragist*, the official paper of the Congressional Union for Woman Suffrage, precursor to the National Woman's Party. She used her platform as a journalist to promote not only women's suffrage but also the rights of children and working women. Throughout her career, Dorr promoted the work of the women's club movement, believing in the power of organized womanhood as the key to social and political change, and the need for the vote in order to effect that change.

Born in Omaha, Nebraska, Rheta Childe briefly attended the University of Nebraska before moving to New York City to work as a journalist. She was politicized to women's issues at around age 12 after sneaking out with her sister to hear a lecture by Susan B. Anthony and Elizabeth Cady Stanton in Lincoln, Nebraska. She was reprimanded by her parents after a list of those who paid money to join the National Woman Suffrage Association that night was published in the local newspaper. She recounted this story, and her early awakening to what she termed "class war between the male and the female of the species," in her 1924 autobiography, *A Woman of Fifty*.

Rheta Childe married John Pixley Dorr in 1892 and briefly moved to Seattle, Washington. The couple had one child, Julian, in 1896, but separated by 1898. In her autobiography, Dorr herself pinpointed the tension that led to the demise of the marriage as an argument over "the labor question," in which her husband showed anti-union sentiments. Indeed, after separating from her husband, Dorr returned to New York with her child, found work as a journalist, and in 1902 became the women's page editor at the New York *Evening Post*, for which she wrote articles supporting labor unions, improved working conditions, socialism, and women's suffrage.

Dorr joined both the Women's Trade Union League and the General Federation of Women's Clubs, where she served as chair of the GFWC's Committee on Industrial Conditions of Women and Children. She advocated for the eight-hour day, a minimum wage, and the vote for working women, as well as industrial education for girls and education for the children of working mothers. She even went undercover to report on factory working conditions. In 1910, Dorr published *What Eight Million Women Want*, a compilation based on her previous reporting on working women's issues. The title referred to the estimated 8 million American women earning a wage outside their homes according to the most recent census data at that date. Like other suffragists who focused on working-class women's issues—such as Harriot Stanton Blatch—Dorr saw the need for working women to have a voice in politics if they were to improve their own situation, and the need for middle-class reformers to help them.

In 1906, Dorr attended and reported on the International Woman Suffrage Association meeting in Copenhagen. In the 1910s, Dorr became even more active in the women's suffrage movement, writing about the national versus state strategies of the suffragists, about women winning the vote in the West, and meeting British suffragists such as Emmeline and Christabel Pankhurst. In 1913 Alice Paul sought out Dorr to serve as editor of *The Suffragist* newspaper. After just a few months Dorr resigned over editorial disagreements with Paul, though she remained supportive of Paul's work and of the Congressional Union's strategy of pushing for a constitutional amendment for women's suffrage.

During World War I, Dorr was a European correspondent to the New York *Evening Mail*, reporting on the war and the Bolshevik Revolution in Russia, about which she also published a book, *Inside the Russian Revolution* (1917). After the war, Dorr wrote her own autobiography and began work on a biography of the woman who had sparked her own feminist consciousness as a young girl, *Susan B. Anthony: The Woman Who Changed the Mind of a Nation*, published in 1928. The Anthony biography was a post-suffrage attempt to revive Anthony's role in the history of the movement and introduce her to a new generation of young women. It was also a defense of Anthony and Elizabeth Cady Stanton's particular strategies and positions in that history in that it recounted earlier splits among the suffragists, but sidestepped the overt racism of Anthony and Stanton in their opposition to black male suffrage under the Fifteenth Amendment, ratified in 1870.

Rheta Childe Dorr died in Pennsylvania in 1948, at the age of 81.

Tiffany K. Wayne

Further Reading

Adams, Katherine H., and Michael L. Keene. *Alice Paul and the American Suffrage Campaign.* Chicago: University of Illinois Press, 2010.

Bradley, Patricia. *Women and the Press: The Struggle for Equality.* Evanston, IL: Northwestern University Press, 2005.

Burt, Elizabeth V. "Rheta Childe Dorr." In *Encyclopedia of American Journalism*, edited by Stephen L. Vaughn, 143–144. New York: Routledge, 2007.

DuBois, Ellen Carol. *Harriot Stanton Blatch and the Winning of Woman Suffrage.* New Haven, CT: Yale University Press, 2007.

Gottlieb, Agnes Hooper. *Women Journalists and the Municipal Housekeeping Movement, 1868–1914.* Lewiston, NY: Edwin Mellen Press, 2001.

Schilpp, Madelon Golden, and Sharon M. Murphy. *Great Women of the Press.* Carbondale: Southern Illinois University Press, 1983.

Eastman, Crystal Catherine (1881–1928)

Lawyer, women's rights activist, socialist, and pacifist Crystal Eastman contributed to the suffragist movement, advocated on behalf of civil rights, and helped to found the National Civil Liberties Bureau, now known as the American Civil Liberties Union (ACLU).

Born in 1881 in Massachusetts and later raised in New York, Eastman was the third of four children born to Samuel Elijah Eastman and Annis Bertha Ford. Both of Eastman's parents were ministers of the Congregationalist Church in Elmira, a town that had historically supported the abolition of slavery, the Underground Railroad, and early socialist ideology. Eastman's mother was one of the first women to be ordained as a minister. Exposed to the progressive attitudes developed in Elmira, both Crystal Eastman and her brother Max became activists.

Eastman graduated from Vassar in 1903 and went on to earn a master's degree in sociology from Columbia University and a law degree from the New York University Law School in 1907. She contributed criticism of laws on behalf of her main causes: women's rights, especially the right for financial independence, and workers' rights, including safety and health.

Eastman worked as a journalist with the *Pittsburgh Survey* investigating factory conditions for workers. As a result of her investigations she wrote and published one of her major works, *Work Accidents and the Law* (1910). This work was utilized in one of the first major legal cases for workers' compensation reform.

In addition to her contributions to workers' rights, Eastman was an advocate of women's suffrage. Although both women's rights and socialism were important to Eastman, she carefully differentiated them in her writings. For her both were fundamental to American equality, and the fulfillment of one would not necessarily eradicate the injustices of the other. She worked with Lucy Burns and Alice Paul in the Congressional Union and then the National Woman's Party. When the Nineteenth Amendment was ratified in 1920, Eastman co-authored the Equal Rights Amendment with Paul, recognizing that gaining the vote was just one step in women's larger struggle for equality.

Active in antiwar efforts, Eastman joined the American Union Against Militarism (AUAM) in 1915. This pacifist organization conducted demonstrations and lectures and wrote literature against U.S. involvement in World War I. Eastman was elected as the executive director, lending her law expertise to the AUAM's cause. As the AUAM continued expanding its efforts to advocate on behalf of protestors who were being silenced by the government, the organization inspired the National Civil Liberties Bureau (CLB), an organization dedicated to free speech. In her pacifism, Eastman joined other women's rights advocates such as Jeannette Rankin, the first woman in Congress, who voted against America's entry into both World War I and World War II, and Jane Addams, founder of the Women's International League for Peace and Freedom (WILPF) and winner of the Nobel Peace Prize. Eastman conceived of the CLB as more than a lobbyist group for antimilitarism; the group advocated on behalf of all issues related to civil liberties. Others such as Lillian

Crystal Eastman, an American feminist who fought for a wide variety of causes during the early twentieth century, including women's suffrage, socialism, and new relationships between men and women outside of marriage. (Library of Congress)

Wald, chair of the AUAM, found Eastman's mission too radical. In its early years, the CLB was active in providing support to war dissenters through litigation, lobbying, and education. In 1920, the CLB underwent reform and changed its name to the American Civil Liberties Union (ACLU). It was the first civil rights organization in the United States dedicated to preserving the rights and liberties of all Americans.

In 1916, in the midst of her antiwar work, Eastman married English activist Walter Fuller. It was her second marriage. Earlier she briefly married and then divorced Wallace Benedict. In 1918, Eastman retired from the CLB due to health issues. With Fuller, Eastman had two children, Jeffrey and Annis. Fuller returned to England at the end of World War I. Eastman followed him to London after she was blacklisted for being a leftist in 1920 and could not find work. In London, Eastman wrote for *Time and Tides* and *Equal Rights*, both women's rights journals.

Eastman died in 1928 after battling nephritis. Walter Fuller had died the previous year, leaving their two young children to be raised by friends. For her work in civil rights, Crystal Eastman was inducted into the ACLU National Women's Hall of Fame in 2002.

Cynthia M. Zavala

Further Reading

Aronson, Amy. *Crystal Eastman: A Revolutionary Life*. New York: Oxford University Press, 2020.

Cook, Blanche Wiesen, ed. *Crystal Eastman on Women and Revolution*. New York: Oxford University Press, 1978.

Walker, Samuel. *In Defense of American Liberties: A History of the ACLU*. Carbondale: Southern Illinois University Press, 1990.

Equal Rights Amendment (ERA)

The Equal Rights Amendment (ERA) is a proposed constitutional amendment that would guarantee women equal rights before the law. Drafted by Alice Paul and the National Woman's Party, the ERA was first introduced in the U.S. Congress in December 1923 by Representative Daniel R. Anthony Jr. (the nephew of Susan B. Anthony) and Senator Charles Curtis, both of Kansas. The ERA was introduced into each subsequent session of Congress until it was finally passed by the required two-thirds vote of both the House

Equal Rights Amendment (ERA) | 51

Equal Rights envoys of the National Woman's Party in Rapid City, South Dakota, where the delegation, consisting principally of western women, saw President Coolidge and asked that he garner support for the Equal Rights Amendment in 1927. (Library of Congress)

and the Senate in 1972. At the time of its passage it had a seven-year deadline by which it had to be ratified by the states. By 1977, the ERA had been ratified by 35 of the needed 38 states but, even with another three-year extension, no new states ratified between 1979 and the extended deadline of 1982. It has been reintroduced in subsequent sessions of Congress but has not attained the necessary support of the House and Senate.

Originally known as the Mott Amendment in honor of Lucretia Mott, a prominent nineteenth-century abolitionist, feminist, and social reformer, the amendment sought to guarantee men and women equality before the law. First introduced in 1923, 75 years after the Seneca Falls Convention and in the aftermath of the implementation of the Nineteenth Amendment granting women the vote, women's rights advocates saw it as a logical next step. The original amendment, as drafted by feminist leader Alice Paul, stated simply that "Men and women shall have equal rights throughout the United States and every place subject to its jurisdiction" in addition to the standard enforcement provision that "Congress shall have the power to enforce this article by appropriate legislation." However, over the course of the ensuing 50 years as the amendment was continuously reintroduced into session after session of Congress and the language was altered slightly so that when it finally passed in 1972, the core provision of the proposed amendment states simply that "Equality of rights under the law shall not be denied or abridged by the United States or by any state on account of sex."

Riding the wave of the women's rights movement of the 1960s and powered by the well-organized efforts of the National Organization for Women (NOW), the Women's Equity Action League (WEAL), and newly organized National Women's Political Caucus (NWPC), 22 states ratified the ERA by the end of the first year. But while another eight states affirmed their support in 1973, only three more joined in 1974, and only one each was added in 1975 and 1977.

Indeed, after the quick start, a well-organized and well-funded opposition developed, and each remaining state became a battleground not only over the political or legal rights of women but also over gender roles. Phyllis Schlafly, a one-time congressional candidate and longtime conservative activist, formed an organization called STOP ERA and offered an alternative vision of what the United States would look like in the aftermath of ratification. With a campaign that encouraged fears about an end to protective legislation, coed bathrooms, and women in combat and subject to the draft, as well as the end of child support for divorced mothers (none of which was true), strong resistance to the amendment developed among those claiming to be advocates of a traditional American way of life that they had known before the civil rights and feminist movements of the 1960s had changed the nation. To conservative Americans, equal rights for women foretold frightening societal upheaval.

Meanwhile, some advocates of the principle of equal rights have argued that a constitutional amendment is unnecessary and that the Fourteenth Amendment's guarantee of equal protection as enforced by the Supreme Court was an adequate defense of women's rights. At the same time, others argue that many states subsequently passed equality amendments to their own constitutions, making a federal amendment redundant. Still, many feminist activists saw the need for the ERA as a symbolic constitutional commitment and continued to lobby Congress for renewed support and state legislatures for ratification. Three additional states—Nevada, Illinois, and Virginia—ratified the original ERA in 2017, 2018, and 2020, respectively, bringing the number of state ratifications to the 38 needed and renewing debates about the ratification deadline.

William H. Pruden III and Tiffany K. Wayne

Further Reading

Epps, Garrett. *Democracy Reborn: The Fourteenth Amendment and the Fight for Equal Rights in Post–Civil War America*. New York: Holt Paperbacks, 2007.

Mansbridge, Jane J. *Why We Lost the ERA*. Chicago: University of Chicago Press, 1986; new ed. 2015.

Mathews, Donald G., and Jane Sherron DeHart, eds. *Sex, Gender, and the Politics of ERA: A State and a Nation*. New York: Oxford University Press, 1990.

Neuwirth, Jessica. *Equal Means Equal: Why the Time for an Equal Rights Amendment Is Now*. New York: The New Press, 2015.

Equal Rights Party

In the nineteenth century, two women (both suffragists) ran for president of the United States as candidates of the Equal Rights Party: Victoria Clafin Woodhull and Belva Ann Bennett Lockwood. Woodhull announced that she would be a candidate for president in a letter to the *New York Herald* on April 2, 1870. That same year, she began publishing her own newsletter, the *Woodhull & Claflin's Weekly*, with her sister. Through her newsletter, Woodhull invited reformers from a variety of causes to attend a convention at the Apollo Hall in New York City in May 1872. After adopting a platform for the newly formed Equal Rights Party, Woodhull accepted the party's nomination, although at 33 she did not meet the constitutionally required age of 35 to serve as president. African American social reformer, abolitionist, orator, and writer Frederick Douglass was nominated as the party's candidate for vice president. However, Douglass never acknowledged the nomination, and historical accounts are inconclusive as to whether he was even aware of it.

During the campaign, Woodhull advocated for many political and social reforms, including an eight-hour workday, changes to the income tax system, new divorce laws, the enfranchisement of women, improved civil rights, and the abolition of capital punishment. Her positions on these issues garnered some support from trade unionists, socialists, and women suffragists. However, some women's suffrage leaders, including Susan B. Anthony and Elizabeth Cady Stanton, were shocked by some of Woodhull's more extreme ideas and supported Democratic Party presidential candidate Horace Greeley, who was running against incumbent president Ulysses Grant, the Republican Party candidate, in the election. On Election Day in 1872, Woodhull was in jail after being charged under the Comstock Act with sending obscene materials through the U.S. mail. She received no electoral votes, and there are no records of how many popular votes were cast in her favor. Grant won reelection.

In 1884, Belva Lockwood of New York became the second woman to run for president as a candidate of the Equal Rights Party. Lockwood practiced law and was the first woman admitted to practice before the U.S. Supreme Court in 1879. Lockwood also taught school, managed property, lobbied for women's suffrage, campaigned for candidates, and reported for newspapers. When her efforts to include a women's suffrage plank in the 1884 Republican Party's platform failed at its national convention, Lockwood proposed that women should run for office, even though they could not vote, as no law prevented them from serving if elected. She was subsequently nominated by the Equal Rights Party to be its presidential candidate in 1884 and chose Marietta Stow, editor of the *Woman's Herald of Industry*, to be her running mate.

One of many reform candidates running in 1884, Lockwood campaigned for women's suffrage, equal legal rights regardless of gender or race, and diplomatic policies focused on peace. Despite her commitment to equal rights for women, Lockwood's candidacy was opposed by some suffrage leaders who believed it brought ridicule to their cause. Lockwood was the first woman whose name appeared on a national ballot and received over 4,000 votes, but was easily defeated by Democratic Party candidate Grover Cleveland.

Lockwood ran for president as the Equal Rights Party candidate again in 1888 with Charles S. Wells as her running mate, but Cleveland was reelected president in 1888.

Dianne G. Bystrom

Further Reading

Falk, Erika. *Women for President: Media Bias in Eight Campaigns*. Chicago: University of Illinois Press, 2009.

Freeman, Jo. *We Will Be Heard: Women's Struggles for Political Power in the United States*. Lanham, MD: Rowman & Littlefield, 2008.

Norgren, Jill. *Belva Lockwood: The Woman Who Would Be President*. New York: NYU Press, 2007.

F

Field, Sara Bard (1882–1974)

Sara Bard Field worked in the national suffrage movement by campaigning for women's right to vote in the western states of California, Oregon, and Nevada. In 1915, she was chosen by Alice Paul to make a 5,000-mile cross-country trip by car to deliver a suffrage petition to President Woodrow Wilson. She was a member of the National American Woman Suffrage Association (NAWSA) and became a prominent leader in the National Woman's Party (NWP).

Sara Bard Field was born in Cincinnati, Ohio, on September 1, 1882, and moved to Detroit, Michigan, as a young child. At age 18, she married a much-older minister named Albert Erghott and accompanied him to India and Burma for his missionary work. Upon returning to the United States, the couple and their two young children lived in Cleveland, Ohio, and then moved to Portland, Oregon. Field joined the Oregon Equal Suffrage League and campaigned for women's suffrage throughout Oregon and Nevada. In 1914, the couple divorced and her husband was awarded custody of the children. Field followed them to California to be near her children.

In 1915, the Congressional Union (CU) of NAWSA participated in the Panama-Pacific International Exposition in San Francisco. Over the course of several months at the expo, the group gathered over 500,000 signatures in support of national women's suffrage. As a publicity stunt, CU leader Alice Paul chose Field to drive the petition across country and hand-deliver it to President Wilson. On September 16, 1915, Field and two other women who owned and drove the car began the cross-country automobile tour, arriving in Washington, D.C., three months later. Paul maximized the publicity for the cause by arranging for Field to give speeches in towns along the way, meet with city officials, enter into parades, and give interviews to local papers. Field sent regular updates on the journey to be published in *The Suffragist*, the newspaper of the CU. The trip culminated in December 1915 with a dramatic arrival at the Capitol building and a White House reception, but the women received an uncommitted response from President Wilson and were turned away from presenting their petition in person on the floor of the House of Representatives.

Field remained a popular speaker and reporter on women's suffrage and addressed the 1916 Chicago convention of the National Woman's Party. In 1917, she spent time in Rhode Island to assist New York suffragist and movement benefactor Alva Belmont write her memoirs. In February 1921, Field gave an address in the capitol rotunda to present to the U.S. Congress a marble statue of women's rights pioneers Susan B. Anthony, Lucretia Mott, and Elizabeth Cady Stanton.

In 1938, Field married writer Charles Erskine (C. E.) Wood, for whom she had previously worked as an assistant, and in the 1920s and 1930s she wrote and published her own books of poetry: *The Pale Woman* (1927), the award-winning *Barabbas* (1932), and *Darkling Plain* (1936). The couple moved in elite literary and reform circles in San Francisco's Bay Area. Sara Bard Field Wood died in California in 1974.

Tiffany K. Wayne

Further Reading

Adams, Katherine H. and Michael L. Keene. *Alice Paul and the American Suffrage Campaign.* Urbana and Chicago: University of Illinois Press, 2008.

Fry, Amelia R. "Sara Bard Field: Poet and Suffragist." *Suffragists Oral History Project.* Berkeley: Regents of the University of California, 1979. https://oac.cdlib.org/view?docId=kt1p3001n1&query=&brand=oac4.

Fifteenth Amendment (1870)

The Fifteenth Amendment to the U.S. Constitution was approved by both houses of Congress in February 1869 and ratified by the required number of states in 1870. The text of the Fifteenth Amendment reads: "The right of citizens of the United States to vote shall not be denied or abridged by the United States or by any State on account of race, color, or previous condition of servitude." By specifically excluding "sex" as a protected category, the Fifteenth Amendment effectively granted the vote to black men, leading to debates and a split within the women's rights movement over support for the Fifteenth Amendment and its implications for the women's suffrage cause.

The Fifteenth Amendment was the third and final of the Reconstruction Era amendments meant to address the civil and political rights of African Americans after the Civil War. The Thirteenth Amendment abolished slavery and was ratified in 1865, and the Fourteenth Amendment, defining citizenship for former slaves and establishing the principle of equality under the law, was ratified in 1868. These three amendments were passed by a predominantly Republican-controlled Congress, as Southern Democrats had been disenfranchised by the Civil War. The Fifteenth Amendment was, in part, a partisan effort to secure black support for the Republican Party. As soon as the amendment was drafted and proposed in Congress, women's rights advocates petitioned Congress to take advantage of expanding suffrage rights to include women, but male members of Congress explicitly excluded "sex" as a category of protected rights.

Wendell Phillips famously said it was "the negro's hour" in referring to the opportunity of the Reconstruction Era to constitutionally redress the wrongs of slavery. The American Equal Rights Association (AERA) had been founded in 1866 by prominent former abolitionists and women's rights advocates (including Elizabeth Cady Stanton, Susan B. Anthony, Frederick Douglass, and Lucy Stone) in order to promote civil rights, including the vote, for African Americans and for women after the Civil War. Anthony and Stanton's opposition to the Fifteenth Amendment was originally one of principle, arguing for no compromise on full equal rights, universal suffrage, for all adult citizens. However, opposition to the limits of the amendment slid into racist criticism of the idea that former slaves, as well as Irish and Chinese immigrant men, could cast votes while educated white women could not. Defining the debate as one between "blacks" versus "women" also ignored the civil and political rights of black women.

The AERA was disbanded in 1869 after the Fifteenth Amendment passed both houses of Congress and suffrage advocates subsequently split into two separate groups: Anthony and Stanton founded the National Woman Suffrage Association (NWSA) to focus on the vote for women and Lucy Stone led supporters of the Fifteenth Amendment in a broader civil rights alliance with creation of the American Woman Suffrage Association (AWSA). This split in the women's movement, over suffrage strategies and over racial alliances, persisted until 1890 when the two factions merged into a new national organization of the next generation with the National American Woman Suffrage Association (NAWSA).

Although the Fifteenth Amendment was intended to constitutionally secure voting rights for black men, localities throughout the post–Reconstruction Era South instituted literacy tests, poll taxes, or allowed violence and intimidation to prevent black men and, after the Nineteenth Amendment, black women from exercising their right to vote. It would take the Voting Rights Act nearly one hundred years later, as well as other Supreme Court decisions and civil rights legislation, to continually reaffirm and protect the enfranchisement of American citizens.

Tiffany K. Wayne

Further Reading

Dudden, Faye E. *Fighting Chance: The Struggle over Woman Suffrage and Black Suffrage in Reconstruction America*. New York: Oxford University Press, 2011.

Free, Laura E. *Suffrage Reconstructed: Gender, Race, and Voting Rights in the Civil War Era*. Ithaca, NY: Cornell University Press, 2015.

Gordon, Ann D. "Stanton and the Right to Vote: On Account of Race or Sex." In *Elizabeth Cady Stanton: Feminist as Thinker*, edited by Ellen Carol DuBois and Richard Candida Smith, 111–127. New York: New York University Press, 2007.

Fourteenth Amendment (1868)

The Fourteenth Amendment to the U.S. Constitution was passed on June 13, 1866, and ratified on July 9, 1868, declaring "all persons born or naturalized in the United States" to be full citizens of both the United States and the individual states, thus incorporating former African American slaves as full citizens of the United States. While the Thirteenth Amendment (ratified in 1865) abolished slavery throughout the United States, the Fourteenth Amendment protected the rights of the former slaves by establishing due process and equal protection under the law as constitutional principles applying to all citizens. It also established the counting of all persons residing in a state for purposes of representation, nullifying the compromise in Article I of the original 1787 Constitution, which allowed for only three-fifths of slaves to be counted for purposes of representation and taxation of the states. The Equal Protection Clause of the Fourteenth Amendment has had broad civil rights implications beyond the nineteenth century, in regard to both racial and gender equality, and was quickly taken up by women's rights activists arguing in support of women's suffrage.

While the Fourteenth Amendment was intended to recognize the rights of former slaves, the text of the amendment marks the first time that the term "male" appeared in the Constitution, in the section linking political representation of the states to the protection of male suffrage. Therefore, despite the initial support of suffragists for both racial equality and for the Fourteenth Amendment to guarantee citizenship to former slaves, the inclusion of such language frustrated advocates who had linked the two causes on the basis of natural rights and wished to apply the previously gender neutral language of citizenship to expand women's rights.

Despite this, some women's rights advocates, including Julia Ward Howe and Lucy Stone, supported the passage of the Fourteenth Amendment, while others, such as Susan B. Anthony and Elizabeth Cady Stanton, sought its revision to include all citizens regardless of class, race, or sex. Other members of the women's movement maintained that despite the limitation of voting rights to men, the equal protection clause in the Fourteenth Amendment nonetheless could be used as a basis to support full suffrage for women. After black male voting rights were further secured with the ratification of the Fifteenth Amendment in 1870, the debate regarding this issue divided the women's rights movement into two groups: the American Woman Suffrage Association and the National Woman Suffrage Association, with both striving for a constitutional amendment specifically guaranteeing women the right to vote.

The extensive controversy over the intentions and applicability of the Fourteenth Amendment not only divided the women's suffrage movement between 1869 and its reunification in 1890, but led to a number of legal challenges to the law throughout the late nineteenth century. In 1869, Myra Bradwell, who graduated from law school and passed the bar, challenged the decision prohibiting her from practicing law. In *Bradwell v. Illinois* (1873), Bradwell argued that the state of Illinois violated the Fourteenth Amendment's equal protection provision and the privileges and immunities clause, which prevented a state from treating citizens in a discriminatory manner. However, the U.S. Supreme Court ruled against Bradwell, declaring that the right to pursue a legal career was not a privilege accorded all citizens under the Fourteenth Amendment.

Similarly, in the 1870s a number of challenges to both state and federal law were made under the argument that women's suffrage was guaranteed by the Fourteenth Amendment. However, these too were rebuffed by the courts, which decided that suffrage was also not a privilege accorded under the law. The late nineteenth- and early twentieth-century women's movement continued to focus on securing suffrage at the state level until there was enough support for constitutional change with the 1920 ratification of the Nineteenth Amendment, granting women full voting rights. It was not until the 1971 Supreme Court decision in *Reed v. Reed* that discrimination and unequal treatment on the basis of sex was determined to be a violation of the Fourteenth Amendment's equal protection clause. The Fourteenth Amendment was also the basis of majority opinions in U.S. Supreme Court cases declaring racial segregation unconstitutional in *Brown v. Board of Education* (1954), applying due process and privacy rights in *Roe v. Wade* (1973), and securing same-sex marriage equality in *Obergefell v. Hodges* (2015).

Sean Morton and Tiffany K. Wayne

Further Reading

Dudden, Faye E. *Fighting Chance: The Struggle over Woman Suffrage and Black Suffrage in Reconstruction America.* New York: Oxford University Press, 2011.

Flexner, Eleanor, and Ellen Fitzpatrick. *Century of Struggle: The Woman's Rights Movement in the United States.* Cambridge, MA: Harvard University Press, 1996.

G

Gage, Matilda Joslyn (1826–1898)

Matilda Joslyn Gage fought for women's suffrage, abolitionism, and Native American rights and was, along with Susan B. Anthony and Elizabeth Cady Stanton, one of the primary coauthors of the multivolume *History of Woman Suffrage.*

Matilda was born on March 24, 1826, in Cicero, New York, to Hezekiah and Helen Leslie Joslyn. Like many women of her day, Gage's abolitionist work led her to take a greater role in the other causes, including women's rights. At the age of 18, she married fellow abolitionist Henry Hill Gage, and the home they shared with their five children became a stop on the Underground Railroad that operated through the end of the American Civil War. In 1850, Matilda Gage signed a public petition refusing to comply with the newly created Fugitive Slave Act, which made it illegal to assist runaway slaves.

Gage was the youngest speaker at the National Women's Rights Convention in Syracuse, New York, in 1852. She continued to speak on both subjects through the Civil War while also preparing hospital supplies, hosting fundraising events in support of the Union Army, and caring for her own children. In 1869, she joined the National Woman Suffrage Association (NWSA), founded by Elizabeth Cady Stanton, and wrote for its newspaper, *The Revolution.* Gage served as secretary of the New York State Women's Suffrage Association and, in 1871, Gage along with a group of 10 other women attempted to cast votes in Vincland, New Jersey, but failed. This was a late-nineteenth-century strategy of women suffragists and the following year, Susan B. Anthony, her coworker in NWSA, was arrested and fined after attempting to vote in Rochester, New York.

Gage served as vice president of NWSA as well as chairperson of the Executive Committee, and was elected president from 1875 to 1876. On July 4, 1876, during the centennial celebration, Gage along with four other suffragists presented the Declaration of the Rights of the Women of the United States, a document she cowrote. The next year she petitioned the U.S. Congress to grant women voting rights. Gage contended that criminals could gain the right to vote, but law-abiding female citizens were denied that right. Although her petition was not heard, it did create publicity on behalf of the NWSA.

In addition to women's suffrage, Gage also advocated for easier divorce procedures for married women and equal pay in employment. In her speeches and articles, she addressed issues such as sexual and domestic abuse, trafficking in women, the rights of females over their bodies, and medical care for prostitutes. She also highlighted women's achievements in many areas where they had been dismissed, such as science and the military.

Gage was also committed to the freedom of all people irrespective of race. In the 1870s, she wrote frequently about the unfair treatment of Native Americans and highlighted what she felt was a superior form of government found in the six-nation Iroquois Confederacy, which balanced power between genders. For her efforts, the Mohawk nation adopted her as a ceremonial member of the people.

Although Gage cowrote the first three volumes of *History of Woman Suffrage* (1881–1887), her *Woman, Church, and State* (1893) was her most widely known work. It contained her controversial belief that the church served as an instrument of the subordination of women by blaming them for original sin. In 1895, she and Elizabeth Cady Stanton coauthored *The Woman's Bible*, a rewriting of the Christian Bible that removed the subordination of women and replaced it with statements of male and female equality.

In 1890, NWSA ceased to exist, merging with the other main women's rights organization to form the new National American Woman Suffrage Association (NAWSA), and Gage founded a new group, the Woman's National Liberal Union, which focused on a variety of social justice issues. She served as president of the new organization and editor of its publication, the *Liberal Thinker*, until her death in 1898.

Patit Paban Mishra

Further Reading

Brammer, Leila R. *Excluded from Suffrage History: Matilda Joslyn Gage, Nineteenth-Century American Feminist.* Westport, CT: Praeger, 2000.

Rivette, Barbara S. *Fayetteville's First Woman Voter: Matilda Joslyn Gage.* Fayetteville, NY: Matilda Joslyn Gage Foundation, 2006.

Wagner, Sally Roesch. *Sisters in Spirit: Haudenosaunee (Iroquois) Influence on Early American Feminists.* Summertown, TN: Native Voices, 2001.

Gordon, Kate (1861–1932)

Kate Gordon stands as one of the most influential women of Progressive Era Louisiana. A vocal advocate of women's rights in every realm, from healthcare to judicial reform, she is best remembered for her role as the director of the 1918 campaign for woman suffrage in the state of Louisiana, the first such statewide push for women's voting rights in the American South.

Born on July 14, 1861, in New Orleans, Kate's mother, Margaret, was herself an early advocate of women's suffrage: after attending an 1853 meeting focused on women's rights in New York, Margaret returned to Louisiana with the pledge to encourage her children to join the movement toward equality. Her father, too, was a proponent for equal rights, publicly opposing the taxation of women without representation.

An 1896 lecture by Colorado suffragist Mary C. C. Bradford at a local Unitarian meeting convinced Gordon to work for change. Bradford urged the women attending the meeting to "stand for women." Gordon's first step was to join the groundbreaking Portia Club, a New Orleans based women's rights organization. Then, in 1892, Gordon and her sister, Jean, established the ERA Club (Equal Rights Association), one of the largest women's clubs with a social reform agenda in the southern United States.

Gordon tirelessly advocated for public health reforms, fighting for better flood control and clean water. In 1899, she organized women entitled to vote (by virtue of being property taxpayers) in a special bond election to finance improvements in New Orleans' sewage and drainage systems. Her organizational efforts highlighted the potential impact of women voters. In 1906, she organized the Louisiana Anti-Tuberculosis League, eventually establishing the first hospital in the state of Louisiana for the treatment of victims of the deadly bacterial disease. She also fought to allow women to be admitted to the Tulane University School of Medicine.

The Portia Club and ERA Club eventually merged to form the Louisiana State Suffrage Association, which Gordon headed from 1904 until 1913. The association advocated not only for women's suffrage but also for children's rights, including child labor reform and the establishment of a juvenile justice system. She went on to become the vice president and corresponding secretary of the National American Woman Suffrage Association.

Gordon firmly sustained, however, that the right to vote should not be mandated by a national amendment but rather on a state by state basis. Gordon opposed ratification of the Nineteenth Amendment after it passed Congress in 1919. She founded the Southern States' Woman Suffrage Conference in 1913 and actively campaigned against the Nineteenth Amendment, fearing that by allowing the federal government to oversee voting rights, the social order in the South would fall into ruin. For this reason, she drew criticism from many of her peers who accused her of racist views.

Gordon died August 24, 1932, at the age of 71 and is buried in the historic Metairie Cemetery in New Orleans.

Amy Bizzarri

Further Reading

Gilly, B. H. "Kate Gordon and Louisiana Woman Suffrage." *Louisiana History* 24, no. 3 (Summer 1983): 289–306.

Green, Elna C. *Southern Strategies: Southern Women and the Woman Suffrage Question.* Chapel Hill: University of North Carolina Press, 1997.

Wheeler, Marjorie Spruill, ed. *Votes for Women!: The Woman Suffrage Movement in Tennessee, the South, and the Nation.* Knoxville: University of Tennessee Press, 1995.

Harper, Frances Ellen Watkins (1825–1911)

One of the founding members and vice president of the National Association of Colored Women (NACW), Frances Ellen Watkins Harper was also a published poet, novelist, teacher, and suffragist.

Frances Watkins was born to free parents (whose names are not known) in Baltimore, Maryland, on September 24, 1825. Her uncle, an influential educator and abolitionist, William Watkins, raised her after her parents died and she studied at her uncle's Academy for Negro Youth until she was 13 years old. Exposed to activism at a young age, she first gave voice to her thoughts in poetry, publishing *Forest Leaves* in 1845. In 1850, she moved to Ohio temporarily to become the first female vocational teacher at Union Seminary, where the infamous abolitionist John Brown was principal. In 1853, Maryland passed a law that ultimately prevented free blacks from returning to the state. As a result, Frances moved to Philadelphia, where she became acquainted with William Still, a free black abolitionist who worked for the Underground Railroad. With Still, she assisted runaway slaves in reaching freedom in Canada.

Frances Watkins published *Poems on Miscellaneous Subjects* in 1854. The year also marked the beginning of her public speaking career on the abolitionist lecture circuit. She shifted her writing toward that cause and was eventually appointed to a permanent position as a lecturer with the Anti-Slavery Society of Maine. In 1859, Watkins published the first short story by an African American, titled "Two Offers," which was serialized in the *Anglo-African Magazine*. Because of her commitment, she remained an influential and well-known figure in several reform movements until 1860, when she married

Frances Ellen Watkins Harper, an African American abolitionist, suffragist, and poet. (Library of Congress)

widower Fenton Harper, moved to Ohio, and took on a reduced public role to care for his three children. Together the couple would have one daughter, Mary, who followed her mother into the educational field.

After her husband's death, Harper returned to lecturing and became involved in the women's suffrage movement. By addressing primarily black women and advocating the growing role they would play in racial politics, she also became more involved with the developing women's club movements of her time. She eventually served as vice president of the Philadelphia Woman's Christian Temperance Union (WCTU).

Harper continued to publish, often with the *Christian Recorder*, which serialized three novellas: *Minnie's Sacrifice* (1869), *Sowing and Reaping: A Temperance Story* (1876–1877), and *Trial and Triumph* (1888–1889). Her arguably most renowned work, however, was *Iola Leroy, or Shadows Uplifted*, an 1892 novel chronicling the journey of a mixed-race woman and her brother, a soldier in a colored unit of the Union Army, as he fights to rescue her from the throes of slavery. The novel provides a startling portrait of the American Civil War and the antebellum South, interweaving social commentary and a feminist stance to demand equality for blacks, depicting black women as strong and independent.

Eventually Harper returned to Philadelphia, where she continued to support women's suffrage and participate in a number of organizations including the WCTU, the National Association of Colored Educators, and the NACW, which she helped found in 1894 as a precursor to the National Association for the Advancement of Colored People. In 1897, Harper was elected vice president of the NACW. Frances Ellen Watkins Harper died in Philadelphia on February 20, 1911, leaving behind a literary legacy and contributions to social and political change essential in the long-lasting fight for equal women's and African American rights.

Christopher Allen Varlack

Further Reading

Boyd, Melba Joyce. *Discarded Legacy: Politics and Poetics in the Life of Frances E. W. Harper, 1825–1911.* Detroit, MI: Wayne State University Press, 1994.

Field, Corinne T. "Frances E. W. Harper and the Politics of Intellectual Maturity." In *Toward an Intellectual History of Black Women*, edited by Mia Bay et al., 110–126. Chapel Hill: University of North Carolina Press, 2015.

Foster, Frances Smith, ed. *A Brighter Coming Day: A Frances Ellen Watkins Harper Reader.* New York: Feminist Press at CUNY, 1990.

Parker, Alison M. *Articulating Rights: Nineteenth-Century American Women on Race, Reform, and the State.* DeKalb: Northern Illinois University Press, 2010.

Harper, Ida Husted (1851–1931)

Ida Husted Harper was a reporter and writer who campaigned vigorously through her writing and leadership for American women's right to vote. She collaborated with Susan B. Anthony on the multi-volume *History of Woman Suffrage* and later became Anthony's official biographer.

Harper began her career in Indiana as a columnist in 1878 for the *Terre Haute Saturday Evening Mail*, and then she was recruited by labor organizer Eugene V. Debs to write for the *Fireman's Magazine*, a publication for railroad workers. Her earlier work in the *Saturday Evening Mail* reflected her commitment to the temperance movement and a focus on the traditional sphere of women as homemakers. As her writing career progressed, she put her voice into the service of the rights of women by decrying inequality—a position that earned letters of complaint from male readers of the newspaper. Her columns began to question the conventional wisdom about a woman's satisfaction with her role of wife and the standards of pay inequality for women who chose to work outside the home or who had to support themselves. Harper's writing, in both the newspaper and the magazine, revealed

Harper, Ida Husted

Ida Husted Harper, an author and activist who played a major role in the final campaign that won women the vote. Harper also documented the last years of the suffragist movement and the life of one of its most important leaders: Susan B. Anthony. (Library of Congress)

her growing realization that women's inequality could never be addressed without access to the ballot box.

Harper first became acquainted with Susan B. Anthony in the late 1870s when Debs invited the famous proponent of women's equality to a meeting in Indiana. In 1887, Harper acted as state secretary of the Indiana chapter of Anthony's National Woman Suffrage Association (NWSA), where she coordinated several conventions. In the late 1890s, after divorcing her husband and attending Stanford University in California, Harper focused her life on the suffrage movement. She became the press secretary for the National American Woman Suffrage Association (NAWSA) in 1896 and dedicated her time to achieving state suffrage in California. Shortly thereafter, Susan B. Anthony asked Harper to be her official biographer. Harper lived with Anthony in order to research and write *The Life and Work of Susan B.*

Anthony, published in two volumes in 1898. The two women also collaborated on the fourth volume of the *History of Woman Suffrage* (1902). Harper wrote two more volumes of the *History of Woman Suffrage* in 1922, which brought the work up-to-date.

Throughout this period Harper continued her journalism career, writing syndicated columns for major newspapers across the country and editing a woman's page for *Harper's Bazaar* from 1909 to 1913, a magazine that addressed political concerns as well as domestic ones. In 1916, Harper headed the Leslie Bureau of Suffrage Education, which was part of the NAWSA. As an accomplished writer and thinker, Harper issued articles, press releases, and letters that contributed to the passage of the Nineteenth Amendment in 1919.

Harper ultimately saw the passage of the amendment that granted American women the right to vote, outliving many of the movement's pioneers. She died in Washington, D.C., in March 1931 at the age of 80.

Leslie Birdwell Shortlidge

Further Reading

D'Angelo, Dolores A. "Ida A. Husted Harper." *Cyclopedia of World Authors*, edited by Frank N. Magill and Tracy Irons-Georges, 4th rev. ed. Amenia, NY: Salem Press, 2003.

Graham, Sara Hunter. "The Suffrage Renaissance: A New Image for a New Century, 1896–1910." In *One Woman, One Vote: Rediscovering the Woman Suffrage Movement*, edited by Marjorie Spruill Wheeler. Troutdale, OR: NewSage Press, 1995.

Jones, Nancy Baker. "A Forgotten Feminist: The Early Writings of Ida Husted Harper, 1878–1894." *Indiana Magazine of History* 73, no. 2 (1977): 79–101.

History of Woman Suffrage

The *History of Woman Suffrage* is a six-volume work documenting the nineteenth- and early-twentieth-century women's suffrage movement, published between 1881 and 1922. The project began under the direction of Elizabeth Cady Stanton and Susan B. Anthony, and the primary coeditors were Matilda Joslyn Gage and Ida Husted Harper. The compilers of the early volumes of *History of Woman Suffrage* saw the need to record the history of the movement they had begun and secure their own place and leadership in that history. The first volume, however, was "Affectionately Inscribed to the Memory of" key figures in the broader historical and international women's rights movement—names such as Mary Wollstonecraft, Harriet Martineau, Margaret Fuller, and Lucretia Mott, among many others—acknowledging the inspiration and traditions of feminist thought that brought the authors and editors to their place in the late nineteenth and early twentieth centuries.

As early as 1876, Anthony had planned for a single-volume history of the women's movement based on documents and letters she had preserved. After the death of founding women's rights activist Lucretia Mott in 1880, Stanton and Anthony saw the need to record the history of the already nearly 30-year movement in the United States, but they soon realized the project would encompass more than one volume; the first volume ultimately covered only the pre–Civil War era. Because of their role in that early history, the early volumes generally focus on the commitments and activities of Stanton and Anthony through the post-Civil War era, during a time when the women's movement was split over the issue of black male voting rights. The volumes edited by Anthony and Stanton emphasize the history of their own organization, the National Woman Suffrage Association (NWSA), founded in 1869, rather than their rival organization, the American Woman Suffrage Association (AWSA), which was led by Lucy Stone. The two organizations would merge in 1890 as the National American Woman Suffrage Association (NAWSA), and Stanton's daughter, Harriot Stanton Blatch, later contributed an essay on the contributions of AWSA, but Stone herself was not involved in the volumes.

The first three volumes published in 1881, 1882, and 1886, were primarily written and edited by Stanton, Anthony, and Gage. Some of the material included as chapters in those early volumes was also published in the suffrage newspaper, *The National Citizen and Ballot Box*, edited by Gage. The volumes were expensive to print and purchase, but Anthony donated copies to libraries and to members of Congress. The fourth through sixth volumes were edited by journalist and Anthony biographer Ida Husted Harper, with Volume 4 published in 1902 and Volumes 5 and 6 not appearing until 1922, after ratification of the Nineteenth Amendment and long after the passing of both Anthony and Stanton. The later volumes included detailed information about state-level organizations and national suffrage conventions, as well as information about the international women's movement.

The six volumes ultimately provide scholars with over 5,000 pages of history, reflections, documents, and details on the U.S. women's suffrage movement at the local, state, and national levels. In the introduction to the first volume, published in 1881, the editors defined the women's suffrage movement as "the most momentous reform that has yet been launched on the world." Despite the limitations and politics of writing about a history in which they had direct involvement, their efforts to record the history of feminism at all was a significant step in creating the field of women's history. As Anthony noted in the text, "Men have been faithful in noting every heroic act of their half of the race, and now it should be the duty, as well as the pleasure, of women to make for future generations a record of the heroic deeds of the other half."

Tiffany K. Wayne

Further Reading

Barry, Kathleen. *Susan B. Anthony: A Biography of a Singular Feminist*. New York: Ballantine Books, 1988.

Griffith, Elizabeth. *In Her Own Right: The Life of Elizabeth Cady Stanton*. New York: Oxford University Press, 1984.

Tetrault, Lisa. *The Myth of Seneca Falls: Memory and the Women's Suffrage Movement, 1848–1898*. Chapel Hill: University of North Carolina Press, 2014.

Hooker, Isabella (1822–1907)

Isabella Beecher Hooker, a notable suffragist and reformer, was born in February 1822 at Litchfield, Connecticut, to Reverend Lyman Beecher and Harriet Porter. Her older half sisters included Harriet Beecher Stowe, the author of *Uncle Tom's Cabin* (1852), and education reformer Catharine Beecher. Isabella attended the Western Female Institute and the Hartford Female Seminary, founded by her sister Catharine. In 1839, Isabella Beecher met fellow progressive John Hooker, a clerk at a law office. After a two-year engagement, John opened his own office, and they married in August 1841.

While abolitionism was the couple's first cause, Isabella Hooker also became interested in the rights of women. She associated herself with prominent women's rights advocates and in 1868 organized the New England Woman Suffrage Association. After the schism in the American Equal Rights Association, Hooker joined the radical wing, the National Woman Suffrage Association (NWSA), in May 1869. In the same year, she organized the Connecticut Woman Suffrage Association (CWSA) and served as president of the organization from 1869 to 1905. Hooker focused the group's efforts on lobbying in state legislatures and later in Congress for women's suffrage and other rights.

In 1871, Hooker organized at her own expense a suffragist convention in Washington, D.C., where a constitutional amendment was prepared by the suffragists demanding voting rights as citizens of the United States under the Constitution. Although this petition failed, Hooker and her husband co-authored a petition in the Connecticut General Assembly that provided property rights to married women and presented it every year for seven years until it passed in 1877.

What became known as the Beecher-Tilton Scandal Case caused a rift among the family, specifically among the Beecher sisters. In 1872, free love advocate Victoria Woodhull printed an article accusing Hooker's brother, famed clergyman and abolitionist Henry Ward Beecher, of conducting an adulterous affair even as he hypocritically preached against free love from the pulpit. The article resulted in Woodhull's imprisonment for breaking the Comstock Law by sending obscene material through the mail. Hooker supported her friend, Woodhull, while her sister Harriet Beecher Stowe supported their brother. Woodhull was eventually released on a technicality, and Henry Ward faced a church inquiry in which he was exonerated from all charges.

Distanced from her family, Hooker along with her husband began to tour cities such as Washington, Boston, and New York, lecturing on women's issues. In 1888, Hooker planned the first International Convention of Women. In 1890, she attended the deliberations when the NWSA and the American Woman Suffrage Association merged into the National American Woman Suffrage Association to combine their efforts in the fight for voting rights. The next year she published *Women in Politics and Jurisprudence*, which argued that both politics and law required a combination of male and female perspectives to function ideally.

In 1892, Hooker joined Elizabeth Cady Stanton, Susan B. Anthony, and Lucy Stone to present the case of suffragists before the U.S. Senate Committee on Women's Suffrage. Hooker dealt with the theme of the unfair treatment of Americans under the law. She alienated herself from her relatives, such as her grandniece Charlotte Perkins Gilman, because of her strong opinion against divorce and against career taking precedence over motherhood. Toward the latter part of her life she became interested in Spiritualism, a religious movement that held that the spirits of the dead could and did communicate with the living. Some of Hooker's friends disapproved of her interest in Spiritualism, but the movement did have many adherents among reformers of the era.

After the death of her husband in 1901, Isabella Beecher Hooker continued her efforts for the cause of suffrage but ceased appearing in public on the matter, preferring to write papers and letters to congressional representatives. She died after a stroke on January 25, 1907, and was buried at Cedar Hill Cemetery in Hartford.

Patit Paban Mishra

Further Reading

Boydston, Jeanne, et al., eds. *The Limits of Sisterhood: The Beecher Sisters on Women's Rights and Woman's Sphere.* Chapel Hill: University of North Carolina Press, 1988.

Campbell, Susan. *Tempest-Tossed: The Spirit of Isabella Beecher Hooker.* Middletown, CT: Wesleyan University Press, 2014.

Foster, John T., Jr., and Sarah Whitmer Foster. *Beechers, Stowes, and Yankee Strangers: The Transformation of Florida.* Gainesville: University Press of Florida, 1999.

White, Barbara A. *The Beecher Sisters.* New Haven, CT: Yale University Press, 2003.

International Woman Suffrage Alliance (IWSA)

The International Woman Suffrage Alliance (IWSA) was founded in 1904 in Berlin, Germany, by an international group of women's rights activists and suffragists, including Americans Susan B. Anthony and Elizabeth Cady Stanton. Initially formed as a suffrage organization in 1926, after women had won the vote in many Western European countries and in the United States, the organization changed its name to the International Women's Alliance (IWA).

The idea for an international suffrage organization was formulated at a meeting of the International Council of Women (ICW) in Washington, D.C., in 1902. The ICW was a global gathering of women's rights organizations pursuing a broader reform agenda in human rights, peace, and worker's rights. Although the ICW was founded by and included among its membership several American suffragists, including Anthony and Stanton, the ICW was not focused solely on the vote. The idea for an International Woman Suffrage Alliance was formulated out of that ICW meeting. The IWSA was formally organized at the next biannual convention in Berlin in 1904. The IWSA was headquartered in London, and the first president of the IWSA was an American, Carrie Chapman Catt, who served simultaneously as the president of the National American Woman Suffrage Association (NAWSA). The organization published its own monthly newspaper, *Jus Suffragi* (Latin for "The Right of Suffrage"), between 1906 and 1924. The journal later became the *International Women's News*.

Except for breaks during World War I and World War II, when some of the representative nations were at war with one another, the IWSA and IAW met every two or three years in locations throughout Europe. During and between the world wars, however, individual members used their organizational and political skills gained through the international suffrage movement to work for various other causes, such as peace among nations, or to combat gender inequality and human rights violations against women and children, thus cementing a connection between the global women's rights and peace movements. After World War I, the IWSA was affiliated with the League of Nations (a precursor to the United Nations), and in 1915 some IWSA members formed another international women's organization, the Women's International League for Peace and Freedom (WILPF).

In the twenty-first century, the IAW continues to represent women's and human rights organizations from around the world, and consults to the UN Committee on the Status of Women, in particular supporting nations in the ratification and implementation of the UN's Convention on the Elimination of All Forms of Discrimination Against Women (CEDAW). The United States has not ratified CEDAW.

Tiffany K. Wayne

Further Reading

Alonso, Harriet Hyman. *Peace as a Women's Issue: A History of the U.S. Movement for World Peace and Women's Rights.* Syracuse, NY: Syracuse University Press, 1993.

International Alliance of Women. https://womenalliance.org/.

Rupp, Leila J. *Worlds of Women: The Making of an International Women's Movement.* Princeton, NJ: Princeton University Press, 1997.

International Women's Movement

Women gained the right to vote in countries across Europe and North America in the period between the 1880s and 1920s. This era was marked by the rapid spread of globalization, imperialism, nationalism, and World War I (1914–1918). Another wave in the extension of women's rights around the globe occurred after World War II, with women gaining the right to vote in many countries in Latin America, Africa, or Asia in the 1940s and 1950s. The expansion of women's political rights often emerged from movements for the rights of other groups, such as workers, immigrants, or people of color. The timing of women's suffrage has also historically coincided with the larger needs of the nation as a whole, whether political, economic, or military. The international history of women gaining the right to vote has therefore been uneven across time and geography.

In the United States, women's right to vote was secured with the passage of the Nineteenth Amendment in 1920. Although the timing was specific to U.S. women's involvement in Progressive Era politics and in World War I, this milestone was achieved during a period notable for the rise of international suffrage movements. Women in Canada, Russia, Germany, and the United Kingdom also gained the right to vote in the years immediately after the end of World War I, as women held more public roles as workers and as reformers, demanding participation in the political process. In most cases, including the United States, women's suffrage was not granted with a single legislative or constitutional change, but rather was a more complicated process with voting rights granted with distinctions of class or property-holding, race, region, marital status, literacy, military service, and, of course, age.

While the international women's suffrage movement gained momentum in the early twentieth century, women in many Western countries had been organizing for and demanding political rights for many generations. This was true in France and in the new United States, where authoritative relationships were openly questioned with the overthrow of monarchies and calls for "natural rights" of the Revolutionary era. These debates did not immediately lead to the vote for women, but they did lead to changes in women's access to education, their rights to their own property and wages, and, throughout the nineteenth century, their entrance into the professions and greater participation in public life, and eventually organized suffrage movements.

By the late 1800s, women had voting rights in various colonies, localities, or states around the globe, and the International Woman Suffrage Alliance (IWSA; later renamed the International Alliance of Women) first met in 1902 and included representatives from North America and Northern Europe. The first independent nations to grant full female suffrage were in Northern Europe in the early 1900s: Finland, Iceland, and Sweden. It is not coincidental that Finland, the first European nation to grant women the right to vote in 1906, also had the first group of female MPs (members of Parliament) elected to office in 1907.

Throughout the late nineteenth and early twentieth century, women gained not only suffrage rights in various nations but also other legal and economic rights, such as access to education and the professions, property rights, protections as workers, and birth control. The "woman question" was taken up across the political, ideological, and economic spectrum, not solely in Western democracies. For example, women's rights were part of the call for social equality in the Bolshevik Revolution and Russian women gained the right to vote under communist leadership in 1917, three years before women in the United States.

Although feminist movements also began in France, Italy, and Japan in the 1800s, it was not until the late 1940s that women in these countries gained the right to vote, as women's suffrage was seen as a valuable part of post–World War II nation rebuilding. During the 1930s and 1940s, Latin American countries such as Argentina, Brazil, El Salvador, Venezuela, and others also extended women's suffrage rights.

In South Africa, the right to vote was, not surprisingly, divided along racial lines. White women gained the vote in 1930, and a complicated system of regional and local voting rights existed through the mid-twentieth century. It was not until the post-apartheid era of racial desegregation in the government that voting rights were fully extended to nonwhite citizens in 1994. In just a few decades, South Africa has subsequently achieved a notable level of female representation in national elected office.

Different political contexts affected women's suffrage in South Asia in the twentieth century. In India, the suffrage movement arose under British imperialism and then as part of Indian nationalism beginning in the early 1900s. As in other countries, Indian feminists argued that women's participation in politics would strengthen national politics and pave the road to modernization. Under British colonial rule the right to vote varied by province and economic status. After independence in 1947, the new Indian constitution addressed not only voting rights, but equal pay and anti-gender discrimination legislation. Women throughout India were granted full voting rights in the constitution (alongside many men previously barred from voting) in 1950 and India elected a female prime minister, Indira Gandhi, in 1966.

In many regions of the Middle East, the focus has not been on women's voting rights directly but on threats to free elections and civil and human rights violations in conflict zones. In Afghanistan, women gained the right to vote in a new constitution in 1964, but that was reversed under Taliban rule between 1996 and 2001. Women's political rights were reinstated and Afghanistan's first democratic elections were held in 2004. In more politically and economically stable Middle Eastern countries, for example, Saudi Arabia and United Arab Emirates, the right to vote was extended to women in the early 2000s and in 2015 the first women were elected to public office. This is in a context, however, in which other gender-based segregation and restrictions still limit women's full participation in public life.

The story of how women won the right to vote worldwide is not a single narrative of a struggle fought for and progress achieved. Through the twentieth and into the twenty-first century, there have been many different roads to suffrage based on different political, cultural, and national contexts at different historical moments. In some countries, full or universal suffrage passed, while in others there were regional, religious, or racial restrictions. In some national contexts, women achieved suffrage through broad constitutional changes, while in others the right to vote was won slowly, state-by-state or province-by-province. And in non-democratic systems without free and open elections, the political participation of all citizens, both men and women, remains limited.

Tiffany K. Wayne

Further Reading

Adams, Jad. *Women and the Vote: A World History.* New York: Oxford University Press, 2014.

Daley, Caroline, and Melanie Nolan, eds. *Suffrage and Beyond: International Feminist Perspectives.* Auckland, New Zealand: Auckland University Press, 1994.

Rupp, Leila J. *Worlds of Women: The Making of an International Women's Movement*, Princeton, NJ: Princeton University Press, 1997.

J

Jewish Women and Suffrage

The role of Jewish women in the American women's suffrage movement is directly tied to the history of immigration and the labor movement of the late nineteenth and early twentieth centuries. Jewish women worked through labor organizations and trade unions to advocate for the rights and protections of working and immigrant women, and the vote became a means to an end in bringing about these reforms. Middle-class Jewish women were also politically activated through involvement in the women's club movement and as temperance reformers. Although Jewish women were sometimes excluded on religious grounds from mainstream Christian and church-based reform organizations; they pursued a broader reform agenda through their own organizations; for example, the National Council of Jewish Women (NCJW) introduced them to politics through emphasizing the special civic responsibility of Jewish women.

The Jewish League for Woman Suffrage (JLWS) was founded in England in 1912, the only specifically Jewish organization dedicated to women's suffrage. The JLWS linked the rights of women to the broader political enfranchisement of European Jews in an era of rising anti-Semitism, as well as linked the secular and religious in advocating for women's political rights. The activism of Jewish women in the United Kingdom was more directly connected to their religious identity than in the United States, and no separate Jewish suffrage organization was founded in the United States. Instead, American Jewish women worked within other reform organizations to expand the political, educational, and workplace rights of women.

Some of the most prominent suffrage battles and leaders arose in New York in the 1910s. New York state was central to women's suffrage organizing and legislative battles, and hosted a large percentage of the nation's new immigrant and working-class population. Rose Schneiderman, an immigrant from Poland, founded the Women's Trade Union League (WTUL) in 1903. She and other Jewish labor leaders and socialists (such as Clara Lemlich) organized wage-earning women to strike and brought many working women into the suffrage movement. Schneiderman spoke out publicly after the 1911 Triangle Shirtwaist Factory fire killed 146 workers, most of them young immigrant women. Jewish anarchist Emma Goldman supported women's rights but did not believe that the vote would bring full equality as long as the current government system was in place.

Maud Nathan was probably the most well-known Jewish woman activist of the early twentieth century. She was president of the New York Consumers' League for 30 years and advocated for the vote as necessary for modern Jewish American women to contribute to civil society. In 1912, she published an article in the *American Hebrew* newspaper on "Jewesses in the Suffrage Movement." Nathan represented the United States at the first meeting of the International Woman Suffrage Association (IWSA) in Berlin in 1904. Other Jewish feminists, such as Aletta Jacobs of the Netherlands and Rosika Schwimmer of Hungary, were active within the international women's movement, as representatives not of Jewish women's organizations, but of their individual nations.

Some Jewish men also supported suffrage: the Men's League for Suffrage was led by Rabbi Steven Wise, and Maud Nathan's husband, Frederick Nathan, publicly supported women's suffrage, writing a 1915 article on "Women and Democracy." As in the broader society, there were also some prominent Jewish voices among the antisuffragists as well, including Maud Nathan's own sister, Annie Nathan Meyer, founder of Barnard College, the women's college of Columbia University in New York. Although a strong advocate for women's higher education, Meyer argued against the need for the vote as a tool for women's influence in society.

Jewish women suffragists were sometimes subjected to anti-Semitism and anti-immigrant attitudes by other suffragists. Elizabeth Cady Stanton's multi-volume *The Woman's Bible* of the 1890s blamed the Judeo-Christian tradition for women's subordinate status. Many suffragists distanced themselves from Stanton's radical work, but, according to Stanton herself, a group of Jewish women approached her to argue that women were honored in their religion.

In the final years leading up to ratification of the Nineteenth Amendment, Jewish women emerged as leaders in the national suffrage organizations, including the National American Woman Suffrage Association (NAWSA) and the National Woman's Party (NWP). Gertrude Weil worked for NAWSA on pro-ratification efforts in North Carolina, and Caroline Katzenstein became executive secretary of the Pennsylvania delegation of the NWP and worked closely with Alice Paul on a national suffrage tour in 1916.

Tiffany K. Wayne

Further Reading

Klapper, Melissa R. *Ballots, Babies, and Banners of Peace: American Jewish Women's Activism, 1890–1940.* New York: New York University Press, 2013.

Kuzmack, Linda Gordon. *Woman's Cause: The Jewish Woman's Movement in England and the United States, 1881–1933.* Columbus: Ohio State University Press, 1990.

L

La Follette, Belle Case (1859–1931)

Lawyer and journalist Belle Case La Follette of Wisconsin dedicated much of her public life to securing women's suffrage both in her home state and at the national level. She was the wife of Progressive politician Robert La Follette and in 1913 Belle La Follette gave a speech before the U.S. Senate Committee on Women's Suffrage. She was also among the suffragists who met directly with President Woodrow Wilson to pressure him to support a women's suffrage amendment.

Isabelle Case was born on April 21, 1859, to a Wisconsin farm family. She attended the University of Wisconsin–Madison where she heard several suffrage leaders speak and where she met her future husband, Robert La Follette. Upon their graduation from college, Belle taught school and Bob attended law school. The two married in 1881 and Bob became a country district attorney before being elected to the U.S. House of Representatives in 1884. Belle decided to study law as well and, in 1885, was the first woman to graduate from the University of Wisconsin Law School.

Bob La Follette went on to serve three terms as a Representative, returned to Wisconsin to serve as governor, and was later elected to the U.S. Senate, where he served for over 20 years under several presidents. Throughout this time, both Bob and Belle La Follette were active in Progressive reform causes. Together they founded and published *La Follette's Weekly Magazine*, founded in 1909 and renamed *The Progressive* in 1929. Belle wrote weekly articles for the paper and used it as a forum for women's suffrage activism.

In 1910, Belle joined the National American Woman Suffrage Association (NAWSA) and served on the national board. She gave a speech on women's equal citizenship rights before the U.S. Senate on Women's Suffrage in 1913, when Bob La Follette was a sitting Senator from Wisconsin. Belle worked with NAWSA to secure a national suffrage amendment, but in 1912 she devoted her efforts to the campaign for a suffrage referendum back in her home state of Wisconsin, touring the state and giving public lectures. The referendum was defeated and women in Wisconsin had to wait until passage of the Nineteenth Amendment for full voting rights. Belle La Follette was present in the Senate chamber in June 1919 when the Senate voted to approve the Nineteenth Amendment and send it to the states for ratification. One week after the Senate vote, Wisconsin was among the first states to ratify the new amendment.

Belle La Follette fought for other progressive causes as well, including anti-segregation and pacifism. She was one of the founders of the Woman's Peace Party in 1915, a precursor to the Women's International League for Peace and Freedom. She continued to advocate for peace and international arms reductions throughout the 1920s. Bob La Follette died in 1925, and both of their sons remained active in Wisconsin Progressive politics, as a long-term governor (Philip) and U.S. Senator (Robert, Jr.). Belle died on August 18, 1931, in Washington, D.C. *The Progressive* magazine, the successor to their original *La Follette's Weekly Magazine*, continues publication today.

Tiffany K. Wayne

Further Reading

Unger, Nancy C. *Belle La Follette: Progressive Era Reformer.* New York: Routledge/Taylor & Francis, 2016.

Unger, Nancy C. "Belle La Follette's Fight for Women's Suffrage: Losing the Battle for Wisconsin, Winning the War for the Nation." *Wisconsin Magazine of History* 102, no. 4 (Summer 2019): 28–41. https://scholarcommons.scu.edu/history/105/.

League of Women Voters

The League of Women Voters (LWV) was founded on February 14, 1920, just six months before the Nineteenth Amendment to the U.S. Constitution giving women the right to vote was ratified. Since its founding, the LWV has been a nonpartisan, activist, grassroots organization whose leaders believe that citizens should play a critical role in public policy and advocacy.

Members pose outside of the headquarters of the National League of Women Voters with miles of signatures for the World Court Proposal. (Library of Congress)

U.S. suffrage leader Carrie Chapman Catt proposed the creation of a new organization for women voters to "finish the fight" for women's political participation in her presidential address at the 50th convention of the National American Woman Suffrage Association (NAWSA) in St. Louis, Missouri, in 1919. The LWV was initially formed within the NAWSA and comprised of organizations in the states where women's suffrage had already been attained. The national LWV was officially organized in Chicago, Illinois, the following year. Maud Wood Park served as the first president of the LWV. She had helped steer the Nineteenth Amendment through Congress in the last two years before ratification; however, it was clear that the legislative goals of the LWV would not be exclusively focused on women's issues. The LWV is structured so that members at the local, state, and national levels study and recommend public policy issues of interest and then agree to take action through lobbying and advocacy. For example, in the post-suffrage era of the 1930s, LWV members worked successfully for the enactment of the Social Security and Food and Drug Acts and launched a nationwide civil service reform campaign in support of a merit system of selecting government personnel.

The LWV helped lead the effort to establish the United Nations and ensure participation by the United States, and the LWV was one of the first organizations officially recognized by the United Nations as a nongovernmental organization. The LWV also supported the creation of the World Bank, the International Monetary Fund, and NATO. In 1951, the LWV began publishing *The National Voter* magazine. And, in 1957, the LWV established its League of Women Voters Education Fund.

In the 1960s, the LWV focused its energy on equality of opportunity and supported equal access to education, employment, and housing. In the 1970s, the LWV worked for the passage of the Equal Rights Amendment, and also sponsored the 1976 nationally televised presidential debates. The LWV also sponsored the nationally televised presidential debates in 1980 and 1984 but withdrew as sponsor of the general election debates in 1988. In 2011, the LWV launched its Power the Vote campaign to oppose measures to restrict access to voting that particularly affect minorities, students, the elderly, and rural voters and help bring those cases to court. In October 2017, the LWV filed an amicus brief in *Gill v. Whitford*, a case that could have changed how redistricting is done across the country, arguing that partisan gerrymandering violates the First Amendment and the Equal Protection Clause of the U.S. Constitution. In the twenty-first century, the League of Women Voters continues its original work on voter education, increasing voter participation, and protecting civil liberties and voters' rights.

Dianne G. Bystrom

Further Reading

"History." *League of Women Voters.* https://www.lwv.org/about-us/history.

Sharer, Wendy B. *Vote and Voice: Women's Organizations and Political Literacy, 1915–1930.* Carbondale: Southern Illinois University Press, 2004.

Stevens, Jennifer A. "Feminizing Portland, Oregon: A History of the League of Women Voters in the Postwar Era, 1950–1975." In *Breaking the Wave: Women, Their Organizations, and Feminism, 1945–1985*, edited by Kathleen A. Laughlin and Jacqueline L. Castledine, 55–172. New York: Routledge, 2010.

Stuhler, Barbara. *For the Public Record: A Documentary History of the League of Women Voters.* Westport, CT: Praeger, 2003.

Young, Louise M. *In the Public Interest: The League of Women Voters, 1920–1970.* New York: Praeger, 1989.

Lee, Mabel Ping-Hua (1896–1966)

Mabel Ping-Hua Lee was a passionate suffragist who mobilized the Chinese American community to support women's right to vote, even though she would never benefit from a women's suffrage amendment. Even after the passage of the Nineteenth Amendment in 1920, she was banned from voting due to the 1882 Chinese Exclusion Act.

Born in Guangzhou, China, in 1896, Lee studied English at a missionary school. She was the first woman to be awarded a Boxer Indemnity Scholarship, which granted her a study visa to the United States. She joined her father, who was already working as a missionary in New York City, in 1905. She lived with her family in a tenement building at 53 Bayard Street in Chinatown.

Lee became an active part of New York City's suffrage movement when she was a teenager. When the New York City suffragists held a parade in 1912 to advocate for women's voting rights, 16-year-old Lee, then a student at Erasmus Hall High School in Brooklyn, led the parade, on horseback, an act so bold it earned her a mention in the *New York Times*. Over 10,000 people attended the parade.

She went on to study at Barnard College, founded as an all-women's school when Columbia University refused to admit women. She joined the Chinese Students' Association and wrote feminist essays for *The Chinese Students' Monthly* and soon became a sought-after speaker. In her 1915 speech to the Women's Political Union, a speech that came to be titled "The Submerged Half," Lee pleaded to Chinese people both in the United States and abroad, for "a wider sphere of usefulness for the long-submerged women of China. I ask for our girls the open door to the treasury of knowledge, the same opportunities for physical development as boys and the same rights of participation in all human activities of which they are individually capable."

In 1921 Lee graduated from Columbia University, the first Asian-American woman to do so, with a PhD in economics and a dissertation on "The Economic History of China: With Special Reference to Agriculture." Although she often dreamed of moving back to China, she instead chose to fight for change in her own community, taking over her father's role at the First Chinese Baptist Church of New York City. As director, a role she served from 1926 to 1966, Lee introduced English classes and work-skills training in everything from typing to carpentry. Under her leadership, the church began offering health assistance, established a kindergarten, and soon became the first "self-supporting Chinese church in America." The church also hosted social activities that helped parishioners, many of whom were newly arrived immigrants, to form friendships and find a home amidst the hustle and bustle of New York City.

Although the Nineteenth Amendment gave women across the country the right to vote in 1920, Chinese American women, like Lee, could not vote until 1943 due to the Chinese Exclusion Act, a federal law in place from 1882 to 1943 that limited Chinese immigration and prevented Chinese immigrants from becoming citizens.

Mabel Lee never married. She dedicated her life to serving her church and her fellow Chinese Americans. She died in 1966.

Amy Bizzarri

Further Reading

Lee, Mabel. "China's Submerged Half." Unpublished Speech. ca. 1915. Files in First Chinese Baptist Church (FCBC). https://timtsengdotnet.files.wordpress.com/2013/12/mabel-lee-speech-china_s-submerged.pdf.

May, Grace. "Leading Development at Home: Dr. Mabel Ping Hua Lee (1896–1966)." *William Carey International Development Journal*, November 1, 2016. https://wciujournal.wciu.edu/women-in-international-development/2018/10/14/leading-development-at-home-dr-mabel-ping-hua-lee-18961966.

Lockwood, Belva (1830–1917)

Belva Ann Lockwood was an early women's rights activist, lawyer, political party leader, and U.S. presidential candidate during the late nineteenth century. She was a passionate advocate for women's rights throughout her career, becoming the first woman to present a case in front of the U.S. Supreme Court in 1879. Lockwood served as the presidential candidate for the Equal Rights Party in the 1884 and 1888 presidential elections. Her political efforts had a far-reaching impact on women's suffrage, women's legal and political rights, civil rights, and antiwar activism.

Belva Ann Bennett was born in Royalton, New York, on October 24, 1830, into a family of farmers. She attended local schools until she was 14, becoming a schoolteacher for her rural community. After marrying at 18 and being widowed at 22, she earned a degree at Genesee College and moved to Lockport, New York, to teach in 1857. Shortly after moving, Lockwood met and befriended prominent women's rights activist Susan B. Anthony and became

Lockwood, Belva

Lawyer Belva Lockwood brought about significant change in the laws restricting the rights of women during the late nineteenth century. She organized the first suffrage group in Washington, D.C., in 1867 and was the presidential candidate of the Equal Rghts Party in 1884. (Library of Congress)

involved in social reform activities, such as temperance, educational reform, women's suffrage, and the abolition of slavery. The young teacher established a girls' school in Washington, D.C., in 1866. By 1867, she met and married Ezekiel Lockwood.

In 1867, Lockwood cofounded the Universal Franchise Association (UFA) with a group of black and white suffragists. She served as the UFA president for several years. Lockwood also joined the National Woman Suffrage Association (NWSA), led by Anthony and Elizabeth Cady Stanton. In addition to promoting voting rights, Lockwood lobbied extensively for a bill to ensure federally employed women would receive equal pay and to fight gender-based employment discrimination. She lent her political support to numerous bills and causes, including marital and estate law reform, state voting rights for women, and increasing women's access to educational and civil service professions.

During the mid-nineteenth century, women who wanted to practice law were denied admission to law school, state and district bar associations, and the courts. Lockwood had studied the law privately while working as a teacher and, after Columbian College in Washington, D.C., rejected her in 1869, Lockwood enrolled at the new National University Law School. The university refused to grant her diploma or admission to the District of Columbia bar, but she lobbied to gain admission to the bar by 1873.

Lockwood started her own practice working in divorce and criminal cases. When she attempted to present a patent case for the court of claims, the judge refused her as an attorney based on the legal principle of coverture, in which a married woman's legal status was taken over by her husband's status. She then drafted a congressional bill that would allow women to practice law in federal courts, working with Senator Aaron Sargent to get the bill signed into law in 1879. Lockwood also requested admission to the Supreme Court bar and was accepted as its first female member. In 1880, she became the first woman to present a case before the Supreme Court and sponsored the admission of Samuel Lowery, the first African American lawyer to argue a case in the U.S. Supreme Court.

In the 1880s, Lockwood became involved with the Equal Rights Party, a national party that promoted legal and social equality for women and was headed by women's rights activist Victoria Woodhull, who was the first female presidential candidate in 1872. In 1884, Lockwood's platform highlighted issues ignored by both Democrats and Republicans, including suffrage, federal appointments of women, equal legal rights regardless of gender or race, and diplomatic policies focused on peace. Lockwood gained enough support to get her name on the presidential ballot and she ran a second presidential campaign in 1888. After her two unsuccessful campaigns, she moved away from pursuing office to focus on her legal career, writing for newspapers, supporting various women's rights organizations, and touring internationally for the antiwar Universal Peace Union. Lockwood continued touring and working until her death at 86 years old in 1917.

Katherine Warming

Further Reading

Klebanow, Diana, and Franklin L. Jonas. *People's Lawyers: Crusaders for Justice in American History.* Armonk, NY: M. E. Sharpe, 2003.

Morello, Karen Berger. *The Invisible Bar: The Woman Lawyer in America, 1638 to the Present.* New York: Random House, 1986.

Norgren, Jill. *Belva Lockwood: The Woman Who Would Be President.* New York: New York University Press, 2007.

Norgren, Jill. *Rebels at the Bar: The Fascinating, Forgotten Stories of America's First Women Lawyers.* New York: New York University Press, 2013.

M

Milholland, Inez (1886–1916)

Inez Milholland Boissevain was a lawyer and suffragist during the late nineteenth and early twentieth centuries. She came to national prominence leading the 1913 woman suffrage parade in Washington, D.C., organized by the National American Woman Suffrage Association (NAWSA) and was an advocate for women's right to vote throughout her life through NAWSA and the National Woman's Party.

Milholland was born on August 6, 1886, in Brooklyn, New York, to a family of wealthy social reformers and journalists. The Milhollands exposed their daughter to gender and racial politics as a young woman, protesting against racist Jim Crow laws and meeting with activists such as Mary Church Terrell and Mary White Ovington, cofounders of the National Association for the Advancement of Colored People (NAACP). Milholland attended prestigious schools in New York, London, and Berlin before enrolling at Vassar College, then open only to women, in 1905. Milholland invited speakers like writer Charlotte Perkins Gilman and suffragist Harriot Stanton Blatch to a student protest rally in 1908, pressuring the administration to allow suffrage debates.

After graduating from Vassar in 1909, Milholland participated in militant suffrage rallies in England and the United States, was arrested picketing for striking factory workers with the Socialist Party and Women's Trade Union League, and wrote antiwar news correspondence in Italy during World War I. She also publicly promoted a radical "free love" philosophy and access to birth control, fought the use of capital punishment, and joined the NAACP. In the midst of her political activism, Milholland also attended law school from 1909 to 1912 at New York University.

Around 1911, Milholland became actively involved in the National American Woman Suffrage Association (NAWSA). Working within NAWSA, she made public appearances at political events and demonstrated for women's voting rights in London and the United States. During these events, newspapers and magazines often portrayed Milholland as a symbol of the twentieth-century suffrage movement due to her education, physical beauty, and independent personality. NAWSA leaders saw her glamorous image as an asset to the organization; in 1913, Alice Paul, chair of NAWSA's Congressional Committee, chose Milholland to lead the organization's public demonstrations. Paul organized the 1913 women's suffrage parade, which was held in Washington, D.C., one day prior to Woodrow Wilson's presidential inauguration. Milholland headed the parade on a white horse in medieval costume, leading 8,000 marchers, bands, and floats in front of an unruly crowd of more than 500,000 people.

Inez Milholland, a labor lawyer and suffrage leader, ca. 1911. (Library of Congress)

After breaking away from NAWSA's more moderate political stance, Paul and Lucy Burns formed the radical National Woman's Party (NWP) in 1916. Milholland joined the new party and in the fall of 1916, she took a month-long train tour of the western United States, encouraging voters to vote against President Woodrow Wilson's Democratic Party and support the cause of women's suffrage. Milholland developed a severe illness, pernicious anemia, and was quickly weakened by her public speaking duties. In October 1916, during a speech in California, she collapsed onstage while speaking and died in the hospital shortly afterward, on November 25, at the age of 30.

Her reported last words on stage—"President Wilson, how long must women wait for liberty?"—became a slogan for the NWP.

In the wake of her death, the NWP held a memorial service for Milholland at the U.S. Capitol and began a silent protest carrying banners in front of the White House gates bearing her words and other phrases critical of the Wilson administration. The "Silent Sentinel" campaign raised enormous public awareness of the suffrage movement, pressuring President Wilson to open discussions on the suffrage issue by 1918.

Katherine Warming

Further Reading

Dodd, Lynda G. "Parades, Pickets, and Prison: Alice Paul and the Virtues of Unruly Constitutional Citizenship." *Journal of Law and Politics* 24, no. 4 (2008): 339–433.

Iron Jawed Angels. Directed by Katja von Garnier. New York: HBO Films, 2004.

Lumsden, Linda J. *Inez: The Life and Times of Inez Milholland*. Bloomington: Indiana University Press, 2004.

Nicolosi, Ann Marie. "'The Most Beautiful Suffragette': Inez Milholland and the Political Currency of Beauty." *Journal of the Gilded Age and Progressive Era* 6, no. 3 (2007): 286–309.

Stovall, James Glen. *Seeing Suffrage: The Washington Suffrage Parade of 1913, Its Pictures, and Its Effect on the American Political Landscape*. Knoxville: University of Tennessee Press, 2013.

Minor v. Happersett (1875)

The U.S. Supreme Court decision *Minor v. Happersett* (1875) ruled that the Fourteenth Amendment to the U.S. Constitution (ratified in 1868) did not guarantee women a right to vote. Rather, the Court ruled that while women were considered citizens under the U.S. Constitution, the determination of voting eligibility resided not with the federal government but instead with the states, a historic tradition that the recently adopted Fourteenth Amendment did nothing to alter.

The case began in the aftermath of the 1872 election when Virginia Minor's attempt to register to vote was rebuffed by St. Louis registrar Reese Happersett. Minor was a founder of the Woman Suffrage Association of Missouri in 1867, and she and her husband Francis were also members of the National

Woman Suffrage Association (NWSA), headed by women's rights activists Elizabeth Cady Stanton and Susan B. Anthony.

The NWSA sought to use the 1872 election to force the issue of women's suffrage, hoping to gain support and publicity for their cause. As part of that effort, Minor sought to register to vote on October 15, 1872, but she was refused on the grounds that she was a woman. Many women attempted to register and vote in the elections that year, including Susan B. Anthony in New York, and were arrested, but Minor responded to her rejection by bringing suit against the government. Ironically, the suit had to be filed by her husband because married woman could not file suit in Missouri courts. The suit argued that women were citizens under the Fourteenth Amendment, and so states could not abridge their right to vote. The Minors lost in local court and appealed. In May 1873, the Missouri Supreme Court rejected the appeal, ruling that the Fourteenth Amendment was aimed at protecting the rights of the newly freed slaves and was not intended to prevent the states from limiting the franchise to men.

The Minors appealed to the U.S. Supreme Court and the Court's unanimous decision, authored by Chief Justice Morrison Waite and handed down in March 1875, addressed two fundamental issues. The first was whether the Fourteenth Amendment defined women as citizens. The Court also considered whether a citizen's right to vote could be denied by the states. In his decision, the chief justice asserted that the Fourteenth Amendment reaffirmed women's citizenship but that they had been citizens before the amendment's passage. Using history and legal research, he made the definitive assertion that women were citizens of the United States.

Waite next turned his attention to the question of women's right to vote, undertaking a historical review of the nation's treatment of that right and process and its relationship to citizenship. At the outset, Waite noted that the Constitution did not explicitly guarantee the right to vote to citizens. Waite noted that the states can and have extended the right of suffrage but have also withdrawn it, and that voting restrictions—and rights—were decisions left to each individual state. On behalf of the unanimous Court, the chief justice concluded that there was no universal right to vote attached to citizenship, and thus a state could, as Missouri had done in the case of Virginia Minor, legitimately deny female citizens the right to vote.

The Supreme Court's decision represented a setback for the advocates of women's suffrage. Denied a judicial solution, the movement shifted its focus to a state-by-state campaign to gain the vote or the pursuit of a constitutional amendment that would guarantee women's right to vote. Over the course of the next 50 years, suffrage advocates used both approaches. While a number of states, especially in the developing West, opened the franchise to women, it was not until ratification of the Nineteenth Amendment in 1920 that women were guaranteed the right to vote throughout the United States.

William H. Pruden III

Further Reading

Basch, Norma. "Reconstructing Female Citizenship: Minor v. Happersett." In *The Constitution, Law, and American Life: Critical Aspects of the Nineteenth-Century Experience*, edited by Donald G. Nieman, 52–66. Athens: University of Georgia Press, 1992.

DuBois, Ellen Carol. *Woman Suffrage and Women's Rights.* New York: New York University Press, 1998.

Elliott, Ward E. Y. "Minor v. Happersett." In *The Oxford Guide to United States Supreme Court Decisions*, 2nd ed., edited by Kermit L. Hall and James W. Ely Jr., 214–216. New York: Oxford University Press, 2009.

Ray, Angela G., and Cindy Koenig Richards. "Inventing Citizens, Imagining Gender Justice: The Suffrage Rhetoric of Virginia and Francis Minor." *Quarterly Journal of Speech* 93, no. 4 (2007): 375–402.

Mott, Lucretia Coffin (1793–1880)

Abolitionist, women's rights activist, and social reformer Lucretia Coffin Mott was born on January 3, 1793, in Nantucket, Massachusetts, to sea captain Thomas Coffin and Anna Folger Coffin. Staunch Quakers, they sent Lucretia to the Nine Partners Quaker Boarding School, managed by the Society of Friends, where she worked as an assistant teacher after graduation. She met fellow teacher James Mott at a Philadelphia antislavery meeting, and they married in April 1811. The couple became involved in various causes and raised their five children to be activists along with them. Lucretia Mott focused on abolitionism, female empowerment, and pacifism. In accordance with the religious teachings of her childhood, she visualized all three as essential parameters for a just society without discrimination on grounds of race, color, or gender.

After a split in the ranks of Quakers in 1817, Lucretia and James joined the liberal branch led by Elias Hicks. The Hicksites were not that particular about rigid rules, unlike the orthodox faction, and emphasized inward reflection and peace. Mott formally received recognition as a Quaker minister in 1821 and became involved in disseminating her ideas of faith as well as equality. A die-hard opponent of slavery, she began to preach in African American churches from 1829. Mott and her husband supported a boycott on free produce, meaning goods produced by slave labor. Although she and her husband were among the organizers of the American Anti-Slavery Society (AASS) and she spoke at its first meeting, she was debarred from further participation when the other male organizers voted to exclude women from its membership.

Mott's experience with male dominance in abolitionist groups made her determined to fight for women's equality as well. In December 1833, she organized the Philadelphia Female Anti-Slavery Society, open to black and white women from its inception. She continued to lecture throughout the state of Pennsylvania against slavery and became friends with many prominent free blacks such as Frederick and Sarah Douglass. The Mott home became a known stop on the Underground Railroad. After the AASS dropped its agenda of female exclusion, Mott became an executive board member of its Pennsylvania branch. In 1837, she became one of the organizers of the Anti-Slavery Convention of American Women.

The Motts traveled to London in 1840 as delegates to the World Anti-Slavery Convention, but Lucretia Mott and the other female delegates were refused admittance because of their gender. Their experiences of exclusion in the antislavery movement led Mott and one of the other female delegates, Elizabeth Cady Stanton, to later organize the first women's rights conference, the Seneca Falls Convention in New York in July 1848. Both women contributed to the writing of the Declaration of Sentiments, which put forth the concerns of the conference in a style and language modeled on the Declaration of Independence. Mott also authored the book *Discourse on Woman* (1850), addressing the status of education and low pay for women. She was one of the organizers along with Stanton, Lucy Stone, Paulina Wright Davis, and Abby Kelley Foster of the first National Women's Rights Convention in Worcester, Massachusetts, in October 1850. Mott was elected president of the third national meeting in 1852, held in Syracuse, New York, and continued to attend meetings until the outbreak of the Civil War.

In 1864, Mott, her husband, and other Hicksites founded Swarthmore College as a safe-haven for Quakers seeking coeducation in the natural sciences. She and her husband were also instrumental in founding the first medical school for women in the United States, the Female Medical College of

Pennsylvania, as well as what became the Moore College of Art, also originally for women to study design.

In May 1866, Mott, Stanton, and Stone established the American Equal Rights Association, and Mott served as its first president. The association worked for women's suffrage and civil rights for African Americans but in 1869 it split into two factions over the question of granting voting rights to African American males. The American Woman Suffrage Association (AWSA) chose to support the Fifteenth Amendment despite the fact that it ignored women's suffrage. At first Mott tried to bring a rapprochement between the two but was unsuccessful, so she joined the National Woman Suffrage Association (NWSA), which focused solely on passage of a federal amendment for the enfranchisement of women.

At the same time Mott also served as vice president of the Universal Peace Union and became the president of the Pennsylvania Peace Society in 1870. She presided over an important NWSA convention in Philadelphia on July 4, 1876. Her last speech was in July 1878 at Rochester, New York, to commemorate the 30th anniversary of Seneca Falls Convention. A life dedicated to the cause of equality for women and African Americans came to an end when she contracted pneumonia and died on November 11, 1880, at her home in Pennsylvania. Reflecting on her life philosophy was "I have no idea of submitting tamely to injustice. . . . I will oppose it with all the moral powers with which I am endowed. I am no advocate of passivity."

Patit Paban Mishra

Further Reading

DeAngelis, Gina. *Lucretia Mott: Woman Suffragist*. Philadelphia, PA: Chelsea House Publishers, 2001.

Faulkner, Carol. *Lucretia Mott's Heresy: Abolition and Women's Rights in Nineteenth-Century America*. Philadelphia: University of Pennsylvania Press, 2011.

Marsico, Katie. *Lucretia Mott: Abolitionist & Women's Rights Leader*. Edina, MN: ABDO Publishing, 2008.

McMillen, Sally. *Lucy Stone: An Unapologetic Life*. New York: Oxford University Press, 2015.

Palmer, Beverly Wilson, ed. *Selected Letters of Lucretia Coffin Mott*. Urbana and Chicago: University of Illinois Press, 2002.

National American Woman Suffrage Association (NAWSA)

The National American Woman Suffrage Association (NAWSA) was an organization devoted to securing the right to vote for American women. NAWSA formed in 1890 when two rival suffrage organizations—the American Woman Suffrage Association (AWSA) and the National Woman Suffrage Association (NWSA)—merged. Led by a series of prominent suffragists as president, including Elizabeth Cady Stanton, Susan B. Anthony, Anna Howard Shaw, and Carrie Chapman Catt, NAWSA played a pivotal role in achieving women's suffrage by, first, working to change state-level policies and, later, lobbying for a federal constitutional amendment. Eventually growing to a membership of almost 2 million, NAWSA's efforts led directly to the passage of the Nineteenth Amendment in 1920, which gave women the right to vote. After the passage of the Nineteenth Amendment, NAWSA disbanded, and many of its members formed the League of Women Voters (LWV) to continue to work for women's rights and participation in politics.

In the post–Civil War era, the American women's movement split over the issue of black male suffrage. From 1869 until 1890, the AWSA and the NWSA worked separately for women's suffrage, relying on different strategies and different underlying philosophies. In a convention held on February 18, 1890, the two groups merged to form NAWSA. Elizabeth Cady Stanton, who was one of the organizers of the original Seneca Falls convention for women's rights and one of the founders of NWSA, was elected as the new organization's first president.

During the late nineteenth century, NAWSA worked primarily at the state level, with the goal of passing enough state suffrage amendments that a federal amendment would become inevitable. Between 1893 and 1896, four western states (Wyoming, Colorado, Idaho, and Utah) passed suffrage amendments. From 1895 to 1910, NAWSA campaigned to put women's suffrage on state ballots or referenda approximately 500 times, but no other state granted women's suffrage until Washington in 1910.

In 1895, NAWSA adopted a "southern strategy" that aimed to increase support for women's suffrage in the South by arguing that allowing women the right to vote would ensure white supremacy in the region. This strategy meant that black suffragists were largely excluded from the organization's activities. In 1900, Susan B. Anthony stepped down from the NAWSA presidency, and Carrie Chapman Catt took her place. Catt aimed to recruit wealthy and middle-class women who were active in the "women's club" movement, a "society plan" strategy that significantly increased the membership and resources available to NAWSA, though the desire of NAWSA's leadership to make the suffrage cause seem less radical to "society" women meant the continued marginalization of black and working women within the organization. Catt stepped down from the presidency in 1904, and Dr. Anna Howard Shaw was elected to take her place. By 1910 NAWSA was also working to appeal to other groups of women, including specifically those who worked outside the home, thanks to new ties and shared concerns with a broader range of Progressive reformers.

After 1910, a new generation of suffragists entered the ranks of NAWSA's leadership. Harriet Stanton Blatch, Alice Paul, and Lucy Burns had spent time in England campaigning for women's suffrage rights alongside British suffragists who often used much more radical direct protest techniques. They lobbied NAWSA to begin a new push for a federal constitutional amendment, and Paul and Burns were given permission and a small stipend to form a congressional committee in 1912. NAWSA's Congressional Committee held a large parade in support of women's suffrage in 1913 in Washington, D.C. Taking place the day before President Woodrow Wilson's inauguration, approximately 8,000 women marched (including on floats, chariots, and on horseback) to gain visibility for the suffrage movement. Although it started out peacefully, it ended in a near riot in which angry spectators assaulted and harassed parade participants while nearby police did nothing.

Fallout from the parade led NAWSA's leadership to denounce the Congressional Committee's tactics and pull both its funding and support. This led Paul and Burns to split from NAWSA altogether, forming the Congressional Union (CU) for Woman Suffrage, which would later become the National

Woman's Party (NWP) in 1916. The NWP continued to use radical protest tactics, including picketing the White House beginning in 1917, which ultimately led to the arrest and imprisonment of many of its members.

Carrie Chapman Catt resumed the presidency of NAWSA in 1915 and implemented a "Winning Plan" that focused most of the organization's resources on campaigning in states that were most likely to pass suffrage legislation. Catt was also willing to accept some compromise in states that considered granting suffrage to certain groups of women or in certain elections only. Between 1910 and 1920, several more states passed suffrage legislation, which put more pressure on Congress to act at the federal level, thanks in large part to NAWSA's efforts. The Nineteenth Amendment, which granted women the right to vote, was passed by Congress in 1919 and ratified by the states in 1920. At NAWSA's last convention in 1920, the League of Women Voters was formed.

Tessa Ditonto

Further Reading

Ford, Lynne E. *Women and Politics: The Pursuit of Equality*. Boston, MA: Cengage, 2011.

Freeman, Jo. *A Room at a Time: How Women Entered Party Politics*. Lanham, MD: Rowman & Littlefield, 2000.

Iron Jawed Angels. Directed by Katja von Garnier. New York: HBO Films, 2004.

Stevens, Doris. *Jailed for Freedom: American Women Win the Vote*. Edited by Carol O'Hare. Troutdale, OR: NewSage Press, 1995.

National Association of Colored Women (NACW)

The National Association of Colored Women (NACW) was the preeminent association of African American clubwomen from its founding in 1896 through the first decades of the twentieth century. The NACW grew rapidly and, within 20 years of its founding, had 50,000 members in more than 1,000 clubs around the country. African American women organized themselves around the need to uplift the race, improve educational and economic opportunities in their communities, and promote civil rights.

In the summer of 1892, elite black clubwomen came together in Washington, D.C., to form the Colored Woman's League of Washington, D.C. Led in part by Mary Church Terrell, a wealthy school principal, in 1894, the league began to affiliate with other women's leagues to become a national organization. The next year, Josephine St. Pierre Ruffin, a clubwoman from Boston and editor of the *Woman's Era* monthly journal, founded the National Federation of Afro-American Women. In 1896, to avoid competition and factionalism, the two organizations merged into the National Association of Colored Women, with Terrell as the first president. This new organization, whose motto was "Lifting as We Climb," listed as its goals promoting education for African American women, raising home standards, aid to women and children, especially working women and children, political rights for African Americans, and interracial understanding. The NACW first convened in 1897 in Nashville, where, in addition to emphasizing women, children, and the home, they discussed the convict lease system, Jim Crow conditions, especially in railroad travel, and lynching. In addition to social welfare, the NACW also promoted black history, and, in 1916, the NACW made a significant contribution to public history in raising funds to preserve and purchase the former home of civil rights leader Frederick Douglass.

Women's suffrage was but one issue that the NACW embraced as part of a broader platform of black political enfranchisement and participation. Founding members Josephine St. Pierre Ruffin and Mary Church Terrell were both active suffragists and in 1912 the NACW passed a resolution in support of national women's suffrage. In 1916 the NACW convention resolved to raise money for the National American Woman Suffrage Association (NAWSA) efforts in lobbying for the "Susan B. Anthony Amendment" to be added to the U.S. Constitution. Despite this support, members of the NACW also spoke out against NAWSA's racist strategy of promoting white southern unity in the suffrage cause by excluding black women suffragists in public events. Just as the NACW was originally founded due to black women's marginalization in the broader national women's club movement, some black women suffragists founded their own organizations to promote voting rights for African Americans.

By 1920, the NACW had over 300,000 members. After the passage of the Nineteenth Amendment in 1920, the group increasingly focused on internationalism and interracial cooperation. Prominent NACW women became involved in the Pan-African movement and joined global women's organizations. The most well-known clubwomen formed the International Council of Women of the Darker Races, an organization that studied conditions of women of color around the world and established correspondence with women's groups in Liberia, South Africa, Haiti, and Brazil. Clubwomen also became active in the Women's Division of the Commission on Interracial Cooperation (CIC), a regional group begun after Atlanta clubwoman Lugenia Burns Hope invited two white women to the 1920 meeting of the NACW. The CIC focused on issues such as improved working conditions for domestic servants and anti-lynching laws.

The NACW began to lose influence in the 1920s as the explicitly masculine Universal Negro Improvement Association (UNIA), led by Marcus Garvey, and the Harlem Renaissance moved the spotlight back on men as leaders. Furthermore, the changing sexual mores of the 1920s departed from the NACW's strict emphasis on chastity and moral improvement. In 1928, the NACW started a Better Homes drive to improve dress, manners, and hygiene for African American children; and two years later the NACW eliminated all other departments in order to focus exclusively on the mother, the home, and the child, as well as women in industry. African American women more interested in the political fight for civil rights increasingly turned to the National Council of Negro Women, established by former NACW president Mary McLeod Bethune.

Now known as the National Association of Colored Women's Clubs, the NACWC continues to provide fellowship for black women and social welfare benefits to African Americans around the country.

Joan Marie Johnson and Tiffany K. Wayne

Further Reading

Giddings, Paula. *When and Where I Enter: The Impact of Black Women on Race and Sex in America.* New York: William Morrow, 1984.

Leslie, LaVonne. *The History of the National Association of Colored Women's Clubs, Inc.: A Legacy of Service.* Washington, D.C.: Xlibris, 2012.

"Our History." National Association of Colored Women's Clubs. http://nacwc.org/history.

Salem, Dorothy. *To Better Our World: Black Women in Organized Reform.* Brooklyn, NY: Carlson, 1990.

White, Deborah Gray. *Too Heavy a Load: Black Women in Defense of Themselves, 1894–1994.* New York: W. W. Norton, 1999.

National Association Opposed to Woman Suffrage

From the start of the women's rights movement, there were people, politicians, and even some prominent women reformers who opposed the vote for women. Opposition to women's suffrage in the United States was expressed in newspaper editorials, political cartoons, and organizations dedicated to public education and to preventing suffrage legislation, including a federal amendment. Although opposition to women's suffrage existed since the mid-1800s, in the 1910s, many state-level antisuffrage groups were organized under the National Association Opposed to Woman Suffrage (NAOWS).

It is not surprising that the first organized group against women's suffrage was founded in the Northeastern states, where many social and moral reform efforts first emerged. In the 1890s, the Massachusetts Association Opposed to the Further Extension of Suffrage to Women published news on the antisuffrage movement in their paper, the *Remonstrance*, a "remonstrance" being the name for an antisuffrage protest petition against suffrage legislation proposed in the state. The paper also published lists and news about antisuffrage organization members in other states, as well as sent copies of the paper to members of Congress so the U.S. government could see that the antisuffrage movement was widespread.

It was not until the 1910s that, corresponding to the greater presence and more militant strategies of the National American Woman Suffrage Association (NAWSA), the antisuffrage movement gained greater momentum. The first national group, the National Association Opposed to Woman Suffrage (NAOWS), was formed in 1911, led by Josephine Dodge as president. Josephine Jewell Dodge was an educator who had attended Vassar College and later opened one of the first day nurseries in New York City to provide childcare for working mothers. She promoted a greater emphasis on education in early childhood and also became president of the National Federation of Day Nurseries. Dodge was president of the state-level New York State Association Opposed to Woman Suffrage when she left to take over as president of NAOWS from 1911 to 1917.

In 1913, NAOWS established headquarters in Washington, D.C., but the leadership remained tied to New York. Dodge was succeeded as president of NAOWS in 1917 by Alice Hay Wadsworth, the wife of a U.S. Senator from New York. That same year, women won the right to vote in the state of New York. Several more states then developed chapters of the NAOW. These chapters worked to defeat state-level suffrage measures as well as exert national pressure against a federal amendment to the U.S. Constitution.

Female members of the NAOWS were not necessarily against women's involvement in politics and did not see themselves as anti-progressive. Most were active in other reform organizations and involved in the late nineteenth- and early twentieth-century women's club movement and were publicly against the militant tactics of some suffragists. Most antisuffrage activists did take a more conservative view on gender roles but argued that women held a greater influence in public affairs in the home and through their existing organizations, and had a greater influence on policy and social change without the vote. They also argued that most American women did not want the right to vote, but rather that the measure was being pushed by a minority of suffrage advocates. The National Association Opposed to Woman Suffrage disbanded in 1920 after all American women gained the right to vote with ratification of the Nineteenth Amendment.

Tiffany K. Wayne

Further Reading

Goodier, Susan. *No Votes for Women: The New York State Anti-Suffrage Movement.* Urbana and Chicago: University of Illinois Press, 2013.

Marshall, Susan E. *Splintered Sisterhood: Gender and Class in the Campaign against Woman Suffrage.* Madison: University of Wisconsin Press, 1997.

National Woman Suffrage Association (NWSA)

The National Woman Suffrage Association (NWSA) was an organization that fought for full voting rights for American women. The NWSA formed in 1869, after the dissolution of the American Equal Rights Association (AERA), and eventually merged with the American Woman Suffrage Association (AWSA) in 1890 to form the National American Woman Suffrage Association (NAWSA). Unlike the AWSA, the National Woman Suffrage Association was formed out of debates over the protection of voting rights for black men with the post–Civil War passage of the Fourteenth Amendment (1868) and Fifteenth Amendment (1870) to the U.S. Constitution. The NWSA wanted to focus exclusively on the vote for women, whereas the AWSA continued to merge the women's rights and black civil rights agendas.

The AERA was formed immediately after the Civil War as a "universal suffrage" organization that worked toward ensuring suffrage rights both for former slaves and for women. Members of the AERA disagreed, however, about whether black suffrage or women's suffrage ought to take priority. These disagreements came to a head with the passage of the Fourteenth and Fifteenth Amendments to the Constitution. Because both amendments represented important advances for African Americans (and especially African American men) but did not address the rights of women, some members of the AERA supported the amendments, while others thought women's rights were being overlooked. Upon the AERA's dissolution, two rival organizations formed comprised of its former members. Whereas the AWSA proposed passing the Fifteenth Amendment and then working toward a separate amendment that would give women the right to vote, the NWSA called for amending the existing Fifteenth Amendment to include suffrage rights for women.

Headed by Elizabeth Cady Stanton and Susan B. Anthony, the NWSA focused instead on the constitutional rights of women. Drawing on the Fourteenth Amendment, members of NWSA argued that because women were citizens but did not have the right to vote, they were governed without consent and taxed without representation. The NWSA was also considered to be the more radical of the two organizations. For example, at first, they refused to admit men into the group, believing that the many men in leadership positions within the AERA were directly responsible for women's suffrage being left out of the Fourteenth and Fifteenth Amendments. The NWSA also called into question many of the existing institutions of the time, including marriage and the church, blaming them for society's strict gender roles and women's oppression. The NWSA used protest politics and supported women as candidates for various political offices. Susan B. Anthony, Virginia Minor, and other NWSA members attempted to vote in different elections and were arrested for doing so. In Minor's case, *Minor v. Happersett* (1875), the U.S. Supreme Court ruled that, while the Fourteenth Amendment guaranteed citizenship, not all citizens necessarily had the right to vote.

The NWSA was headquartered in New York, but held its national conventions in Washington, D.C. The organization created its own official newspaper, *The Revolution*, published weekly between 1868 and 1872. In 1890, the NWSA and the AWSA joined forces yet again and merged to form the NAWSA. Elizabeth Cady Stanton and Susan B. Anthony served as the first two presidents of the new suffrage organization, and NAWSA went on to lead the movement into the twentieth century for a constitutional amendment granting women the right to vote.

Tessa Ditonto

Further Reading

Dudden, Faye E. *Fighting Chance: The Struggle over Woman Suffrage and Black Suffrage in Reconstruction America*. New York: Oxford University Press, 2011.

Ford, Lynne E. *Women and Politics: The Pursuit of Equality*. Boston, MA: Cengage, 2011.

Freeman, Jo. *A Room at a Time: How Women Entered Party Politics*. Lanham, MD: Rowman & Littlefield, 2000.

Weiss, Elaine. *The Woman's Hour: The Great Fight to Win the Vote*. New York: Penguin/Random House, 2018.

Wheeler, Marjorie Spruil, ed. *One Woman, One Vote: Rediscovering the Woman Suffrage Movement*. Troutdale, OR: NewSage Press, 1995.

National Woman's Party (NWP)

The National Woman's Party (NWP) was an American women's suffrage organization that existed from 1916 until ratification of the Nineteenth Amendment in 1920. The NWP was formed by leaders of the Congressional Union (CU) for Woman Suffrage, which split from the National American Woman Suffrage Association (NAWSA) in 1913. Led by Alice Paul and Lucy Burns, the NWP used radical protest tactics to bring visibility to the suffrage cause. Along with the efforts of the more moderate and traditional NAWSA, the NWP was instrumental in achieving the right to vote for American women.

In 1912, Paul and Burns were both part of a new generation of suffragists who were frustrated with the slow progress being made by NAWSA's state-level activism. They had spent time in England learning radical protest tactics from British suffragists and convinced the NAWSA to form a Congressional Committee that would focus efforts on lobbying for a federal suffrage amendment. Headed by Paul and Burns, the Congressional Committee worked to increase support for a federal suffrage amendment in Washington, D.C. In March 1913, the Congressional Committee held a suffrage parade on the eve of President Woodrow Wilson's inauguration in which

8,000 women marched on foot, on horseback, and on floats. The parade ended in a near riot in which hostile crowds broke through barriers to assault and harass parade members while police took no action. Fallout from the parade led NAWSA to defund the Congressional Committee and condemn its militant tactics.

Paul and Burns decided to split from NAWSA later that year and formed the CU, which continued to work toward a federal amendment. In 1917, the CU became the National Woman's Party. The NWP's sole purpose was to fight for a federal suffrage amendment to the U.S. Constitution. It did not ally itself with either of the major political parties, but rather vowed to withhold its support from whichever party was in power until a suffrage amendment was passed. Practically, this meant that most of their activism was focused on President Wilson and the Democratic-controlled Congress. The NWP continued to use radical, nonviolent protest tactics, including parades, picketing, and other public demonstrations to increase visibility for the suffrage cause.

Beginning in January 1917, the NWP began a campaign of stationing picketers at the White House daily from dawn until dusk. Known as the "Silent Sentinels," picketers endured the cold while holding large banners that called for President Wilson to act on women's suffrage. This was the first time that picketing the White House was used as a political tactic and was, at first, met with support and sympathy from the public. With U.S. entry into World War I in April of that year, however, the NWP was expected to cease its demonstrations in a show of national unity. When they decided to continue picketing, sympathy and tolerance quickly turned to hostility. Numerous protestors were arrested and jailed.

After the Nineteenth Amendment was ratified in 1920 granting women the right to vote, Alice Paul and the National Woman's Party focused on securing an Equal Rights Amendment and briefly published a magazine called *Equal Rights*, a successor to the earlier paper, *The Suffragist*, edited by leaders of the NWP. In addition to promoting the ERA, in the 1920s and 1930s the NWP authored numerous pieces of legislation to protect working women with equal pay and advocated for the removal of protective labor laws that prevented women from working in all fields. The NWP's role in this work culminated with the Equal Pay Act of 1963. During and after World War II, the NWP expanded to promote women's rights and suffrage internationally and Paul founded the World's Woman's Party and helped incorporate women's rights issues into the charter of the new United Nations. The National Woman's Party served a key role as a political lobbying organization through the 1990s and continues into the twenty-first century as an educational and historical foundation, sponsoring a historical monument dedicated in Washington, D.C., in 2016 to honor Alice Paul and the NWP's fight for women's equality.

Tessa Ditonto and Tiffany K. Wayne

Further Reading

Ford, Lynne E. *Women and Politics: The Pursuit of Equality*. Boston, MA: Cengage, 2011.

Freeman, Jo. *A Room at a Time: How Women Entered Party Politics*. Lanham, MD: Rowman & Littlefield, 2000.

Iron Jawed Angels. Directed by Katja von Garnier. New York: HBO Films, 2004.

Lunardini, Christine A. *Alice Paul: Equality for Women*. New York: Routledge, 2013.

National Woman's Party. https://www.nationalwomansparty.org/

Southard, Belinda A. Stillion. *Militant Citizenship: Rhetorical Strategies of the National Woman's Party, 1913–1920*. College Station: Texas A & M University Press, 2011.

New Departure

The "New Departure" was a strategy of American women suffragists in the 1870s that involved directly appealing to the newly ratified Fourteenth Amendment to the U.S. Constitution by claiming that women had the right to vote based on their status as citizens of the United States and of the individual states. The primary strategy was to attempt to register and, if successful, proceed to cast a ballot, prompting arrest in hopes of pursuing the issue through the courts. Although dozens of suffragists around the country attempted to register to vote, in most cases local election officials simply turned women away from the polls, but two high-profile cases (that of Susan B. Anthony and Virginia Minor) defined the New Departure strategy and garnered national attention.

The civil and political rights of African Americans were expanded under the three post–Civil War constitutional amendments of the 1860s and 1870s: the Thirteenth Amendment (ratified in 1865) abolished slavery in the United States; the Fourteenth Amendment (1868) defined citizenship for former slaves; and the Fifteenth Amendment (1870) prohibited the denial of the right to vote based on race (but not sex), effectively extending the right to vote to black men. In 1869, the women's rights movement split over the ratification of the Fifteenth Amendment, with the National Woman Suffrage Association (NWSA) wanting to focus exclusively on the vote for women, and the American Woman Suffrage Association (AWSA) maintaining the alliance between black and white reformers from the abolitionist era to continue to work on a broad civil rights agenda. The NWSA, founded by Susan B. Anthony and Elizabeth Cady Stanton, implemented the New Departure strategy as a direct political action, hoping to build on the momentum created by the Fourteenth and Fifteenth Amendments to establish that women were citizens and that all citizens must have "equal protection of the laws," including the right to vote.

A large contingent of women had tried unsuccessfully to register to vote in Washington, D.C., in 1871, and the 1872 presidential election was the perfect opportunity to highlight the issue of women's rights as citizens. Virginia Minor, a Missouri suffragist, and her husband, lawyer Francis Minor, had written about women's right to vote based on the Fourteenth Amendment and Virginia Minor attempted to register to vote in St. Louis, Missouri, on October 15, 1872. Minor's request was denied and the Minors subsequently filed a lawsuit against election official Reese Happersett. The Missouri state court ruled against Minor and the case was appealed to the U.S. Supreme Court, which ruled in *Minor v. Happersett* (1875) that the right to vote was not a constitutional right guaranteed to citizens, but rather an issue left to the states.

On November 1, 1872, just a few weeks after Virginia Minor attempted to register and mere days before the presidential election, NWSA leader Susan B. Anthony, her three sisters, and several more women registered to vote in their hometown of Rochester, New York. Anthony expected to be turned away at the polls, but instead she and at least fourteen other women, having proved they were registered, were allowed to cast their votes for president on November 5, 1872. Anthony was arrested, but not jailed, and her case was brought before the New York federal circuit court, which decided against Anthony in *United States v. Susan B. Anthony* (1873). She was fined $100 by the court, a fine she never paid, but because the case was tried in a criminal court, she could not appeal to the U.S. Supreme Court.

Although both Anthony and Minor lost their court cases, their actions and trials brought a significant amount of national media attention to the cause of women's suffrage. The New Departure strategy, however, was ultimately unsuccessful and even damaging to the women's suffrage cause, as the U.S. Supreme Court decision against Minor closed the possibility of arguing for voting as a constitutional right. Over the next 50 years, American suffragists pursued dual strategies of securing women's voting rights on a state-by-state basis, while also fighting for a constitutional amendment prohibiting sex as a category in denying voting rights. Anthony, Stanton, and Matilda Joslyn Gage recorded details about the New Departure strategy, the Anthony trial, and the role of Virginia and Francis Minor, in Volume 2 of the *History of Woman Suffrage*, published in 1882.

Tiffany K. Wayne

Further Reading

Davis, Sue. *The Political Thought of Elizabeth Cady Stanton: Women's Rights and the American Political Tradition.* New York: New York University Press, 2008.

DuBois, Ellen Carol. *Woman Suffrage and Women's Rights.* New York: New York University Press, 1998.

New England Woman Suffrage Association

Abolitionism and women's suffrage were very closely aligned, with major figures often working on behalf of both causes. Two prominent abolitionists were Julia Ward Howe and Lucy Stone. Howe is perhaps most famous for her poem, "The Battle Hymn of the Republic," which became the anthem sung by soldiers for the Union cause. Stone was a writer and publisher in addition to being an eminent speaker for abolition and women's rights before the war. Stone even gained the attention and admiration of showman P. T. Barnum. Both Howe and Stone were major figures in the founding of the New England Woman Suffrage Association (NEWSA) in 1868, with Howe serving as the first president and Stone following her tenure.

NEWSA was born from the already-active network of women's organizations in the northeastern states. Speakers and activists such as Sarah and Angelina Grimké, southern women who renounced slavery and took up the cause of abolition, found an eager audience in the Northeast. Interestingly, the sisters had to defend their right—as women—to speak publicly against slavery. By the 1830s, they had become women's rights activists as well as abolitionists.

Worcester, Massachusetts, was the location for the first National Women's Rights Convention in 1850, with delegates invited from all across the country. Organized by Lucy Stone and other women from New England, the convention's goal was to bring like minds together and attempt to create national unity and cohesion around suffrage. One of the speakers at this convention was Sojourner Truth, former slave and prominent abolitionist.

NEWSA was also in the middle of the controversy over the Fifteenth Amendment, which prohibited discrimination in voting on the basis of "race, color, or previous condition of servitude," but did not prohibit discrimination on the basis of sex. Elizabeth Cady Stanton and Susan B. Anthony were not willing to forgo the pursuit of the rights of women to vote in favor of the rights of African American men to vote, while Julia Ward Howe declared that she would not vote as long as Frederick Douglass was denied the same right. Lucy Stone agreed with Stanton and Anthony, but she supported the position of Howe.

Suffragists hang posters in New England, ca. 1914. (Library of Congress)

New England suffragists also favored a state-by-state strategy to gain the vote, another point of disagreement with Stanton and Stone. In general, New Englanders believed in aligning themselves closely with the traditional spheres of influence for women, and concentrated on getting women on school boards in the region with voting rights in those bodies.

NEWSA members went on to form the American Woman Suffrage Association (AWSA), which was founded in opposition to the National Woman

Suffrage Association (NWSA) over the issues of votes for freedmen as well a local focus to gaining the vote.

Leslie Birdwell Shortlidge

Further Reading

DuBois, Ellen Carol. *Feminism & Suffrage: The Emergence of an Independent Women's Movement in America, 1849–1869.* Ithaca, NY: Cornell University Press, 1999.

Dudden, Faye E. *Fighting Chance: The Struggle over Woman Suffrage and Black Suffrage in Reconstruction America.* New York: Oxford University Press, 2011.

Michals, Debra. "Julia Ward Howe." National Women's History Museum. https://www.womenshistory.org/education-resources/biographies/julia-ward-howe.

Prescott, Heather Munroe. "Woman Suffrage in New England." National Park Service. https://www.nps.gov/articles/woman-suffrage-in-new-england.htm.

Nineteenth Amendment (1920)

The Nineteenth Amendment to the U.S. Constitution was ratified in 1920 and granted the vote to all American women by prohibiting states from restricting the right to vote based on sex. The call for women's right to vote was part of the broader antebellum women's movement, but it was not until the post–Civil War era that a national suffrage movement began, focused specifically on securing a constitutional amendment.

The movement for women's suffrage is usually dated to the Seneca Falls convention of 1848, where Elizabeth Cady Stanton drew up the Declaration of Sentiments that included a demand for the "inalienable right to the elective franchise." Women's suffrage was considered to be one of the more radical and controversial issues to emerge from the convention. After the Civil War, debates about the civil and political rights of formerly enslaved African Americans led women's rights activists to call for full suffrage for both women and African Americans, but the Fourteenth (1868) and Fifteenth (1870) Amendments to the Constitution secured citizenship and voting rights primarily to black men, making no specific provisions for women. In 1869, women's suffrage proponents split into two main groups, with the National Woman Suffrage Association opposed to adoption of the Fifteenth Amendment without voting rights for women, and the American Woman Suffrage

Association favoring black voting rights as a step toward full equality for women. The two groups finally merged into one national organization in 1890 as the National American Woman Suffrage Association (NAWSA).

Democratic Representative James Brooks of New York was the first to offer a women's suffrage amendment in Congress. He introduced his proposal in 1866 as an amendment to section 2 of the Fourteenth Amendment and again in 1869 as an addition to the Fifteenth Amendment. In *Minor v. Happersett* (1875), however, the U.S. Supreme Court rejected the argument that the Fourteenth Amendment automatically extended the right to vote to women as citizens. The Fifteenth Amendment subsequently became the model for the women's suffrage amendment (also called the Susan B. Anthony Amendment), which was introduced regularly in Congress from 1880 until it was proposed by the necessary majorities in 1919.

Opposition to a national suffrage amendment came from various corners. As the leadership of the Woman's Christian Temperance Union promoted women's suffrage, liquor business interests feared that women's suffrage would lead to adoption of a national prohibition on alcohol. In the South, fears were raised that an amendment granting women the right to vote might renew federal efforts to enforce the Fifteenth Amendment, prohibiting discrimination in voting on the basis of race. Southerners were a major source of support for the Shafroth-Palmer Amendment of 1914, which would have allowed each state to have a referendum (if so requested by 8 percent or more of the voters) on the women's suffrage issue rather than setting a single national standard. Some supporters of women's suffrage wanted the vote limited to white women.

Throughout the last half of the nineteenth century, several individual Western territories and states extended voting rights to women, increasing pressure over the need and timing of a federal amendment. In 1914, the Senate voted 35 to 34 for the federal amendment, with the House falling far shorter in 1915 with a vote of 174 to 204. That same year, under the leadership of Alice Paul, the Congressional Union (later the National Woman's Party) broke with NAWSA leadership and advocated more militant measures, including campaigns against all Democrats, who were generally less supportive of the amendment than Republicans. The Congressional Union also led a series of parades and controversial pickets outside the White House.

The 1919 ratification of the Eighteenth Amendment prohibiting the manufacture and sale of alcohol probably aided the Nineteenth Amendment, in that some of those who had opposed women's suffrage for fear that it would lead to Prohibition now had nothing more to lose. World War I also mobilized increasing numbers of women into the workforce and increased support for acknowledging their sacrifices. Initially a tepid supporter of voting rights for women, President Woodrow Wilson addressed the Senate in 1918 in support of the suffrage amendment, but it again fell short of the necessary votes, as it would in early 1919 as well. Wilson subsequently called a special session of Congress and the amendment finally succeeded, with the final Senate vote coming on May 28, 1919. Proposals to limit the vote to white women, to ratify the amendment by convention rather than by state legislatures, and to entrust states with primary enforcement powers were all rejected at this time.

The Nineteenth Amendment was sent to the states for approval by the required number and was ratified in just over a year. The 36th and final state vote needed for ratification came from Tennessee on August 18, 1920. The Tennessee state constitution contained a provision that the state legislature could not vote for a proposed amendment until after an intervening election, but both the U.S. solicitor general and Tennessee's attorney general declared this provision invalid. When the measure came up for a vote, a 24-year-old state representative named Harry Burn switched votes because of his mother's request to adopt the amendment, and another member did the same in order to call the vote up for reconsideration. The "Red Rose Brigade," consisting of opponents of the amendment (supporters wore yellow roses), subsequently left the state for Alabama to prevent a quorum on reconsideration, but after a series of complicated maneuvers, they proved unsuccessful. The U.S. Secretary of State apparently ignored a later House resolution of nonconcurrence.

The amendment was officially adopted as part of the U.S. Constitution on August 26, 1920. In *Leser v. Garnett* (1922), the U.S. Supreme Court rejected a challenge to this amendment, and in *Adkins v. Children's Hospital* (1923), the court cited the amendment in striking down a minimum-wage law for women in the District of Columbia. Partly on the basis of this precedent and on the basis of the long debates on this amendment, some recent authors have argued that the Nineteenth Amendment might be interpreted, particularly in conjunction with the Fourteenth Amendment, as a broader guarantee of women's rights.

John R. Vile and Tiffany K. Wayne

Further Reading

Baker, Jean H., ed. *Votes for Women: The Struggle for Suffrage Revisited.* New York: Oxford University Press, 2002.

Dudden, Faye E. *Fighting Chance: The Struggle over Woman Suffrage and Black Suffrage in Reconstruction America.* New York: Oxford University Press, 2011.

McMillen, Sally G. *Seneca Falls and the Origins of the Women's Rights Movement.* New York: Oxford University Press, 2008.

Wheeler, Marjorie S., ed. *One Woman, One Vote: Rediscovering the Woman Suffrage Movement.* Troutdale, OR: NewSage, 1995.

Wheeler, Marjorie S. *Votes for Women! The Woman Suffrage Movement in Tennessee, the South, and the Nation.* Knoxville: University of Tennessee Press, 1995.

P

Park, Maud Wood (1871–1955)

Maud Wood Park was both an American suffragist and a dedicated chronicler of the movement for women's right to vote. She cofounded the College Equal Suffrage League (CESL), an organization committed to bringing more young women into the national women's suffrage movement. In addition to her work with the CESL, and through the National American Woman Suffrage Association (NAWSA), in 1920, Park became the first president of the League of Women Voters (LWV).

Park became active as a suffragist in Boston, involved first with the Massachusetts Woman Suffrage Association. She then helped form the Boston Equal Suffrage Association for Good Government (BESAGG). The BESAGG sought to engage women's civic participation on a broad range of reform issues, for which the vote was necessary. It later became the foundation for the Boston League of Women Voters.

In 1900, Park founded the College Equal Suffrage League (CESL) with her Radcliffe College classmate, Inez Haynes Irwin, after finding that few college students were involved in the suffrage movement. Park and Irwin toured college campuses and ultimately created CESL chapters in over 30 states, which merged into the National College Equal Suffrage League (NCESL) in 1908 and was formally recognized by the National American Woman Suffrage Association (NAWSA). Park served as the first vice president of the NCESL under NCESL president, Carey M. Thomas, president of Bryn Mawr College. In 1909, Park had undertaken a global tour to assess the status of women worldwide. She returned with valuable perspective and was a sought-after lecturer on women's rights. Park relocated to Washington, D.C., to work with NAWSA, and worked tirelessly to lobby Congress for a federal amendment on women's suffrage.

From 1920 to 1924, Park served as president of the League of Women Voters. After suffrage was won with the Nineteenth Amendment, Park, as head of the LWV, focused on a range of social reform issues and lobbying efforts on legislation affecting women and children. She was instrumental in the passage of the Sheppard-Towner Maternity and Infancy Protection Act of 1921, providing federal funding for maternity and infant care, and the Cable Act of 1922, protecting the citizenship status of American women who married foreign men. Park's activities were representative of the maternal-focused Progressive Era efforts of politically active women in the years immediately following the granting of women's suffrage. She also supported the post–World War I creation of a League of Nations, precursor to the United Nations.

Maud Wood Park led the effort to involve young women in the suffrage movement and became the first president of the League of Women Voters. (Library of Congress)

From her days in founding the CSEL, Maud Wood Park was actively interested in and concerned about preserving the history of the women's suffrage movement. She wrote a play, *Lucy Stone*, performed in Boston in 1939. She also wrote a detailed account of NAWSA's suffrage battle in Congress called *Front Door Lobbying*, published in 1960, several years after her death in May 1955.

In 1943, Park donated her own personal papers, books, and materials related to her many years as a reformer and activist to Radcliffe College, a collection that became the foundation of the Schlesinger Library on the

History of Women in America, one of the most important archives devoted to women's history in the United States.

Tiffany K. Wayne

Further Reading

Knupfer, Anne Meis, and Christine Wovshner, eds. *The Educational Work of Women's Organizations, 1890–1960*. New York: Palgrave Macmillan, 2008.

Weatherford, Doris. *Women in American Politics: History and Milestones*. Los Angeles, CA: SAGE, 2012.

Wilson, Jan Doolittle. *The Women's Joint Congressional Committee and the Politics of Maternalism, 1920–1930*. Urbana: University of Illinois Press, 2007.

Paul, Alice (1885–1977)

Alice Paul was a leading suffragist in the final decades leading to the passage of the Nineteenth Amendment. Born into a prominent Quaker family and educated at universities in the United States and England, she became the chief strategist for the more militant wing of the U.S. women's suffrage movement. She founded the National Woman's Party and, after helping secure ratification of the Nineteenth Amendment to the U.S. Constitution granting women the right to vote in 1920, in 1923 she authored the Equal Rights Amendment (ERA), which has yet to be adopted.

Alice Stokes Paul was born on January 11, 1885, in Mount Laurel, New Jersey, to Tacie Parry and William Paul, a wealthy Quaker businessman. Her parents believed in gender equality and education for women. Paul earned a bachelor's degree in biology from Swarthmore College in 1905 and a master's degree in sociology in 1907 from the New York School of Philanthropy (now Columbia University). She then studied social work at a training school for Quakers in Woodbridge, England. Paul lived in England from 1907 to 1910 and, upon returning to the United States, earned a PhD in sociology from the University of Pennsylvania.

While studying in England and working as a caseworker for a London settlement house, Paul met militant English suffragettes Emmeline Pankhurst and her daughters, Christabel, Sylvia, and Adela. Paul joined their movement and learned their militant tactics, including heckling, picketing, rock throwing, and window smashing to raise public awareness for women's suffrage.

Upon her return to the United States in 1910, Paul called on members of the U.S. movement to embrace their tactics. In 1912, she joined the National American Woman Suffrage Association (NAWSA) and was appointed head of its Congressional Committee to work on a federal constitutional amendment granting women the right to vote. Paul organized a group of young women, many of whom had also worked with the Pankhursts in England, who were willing to depart from NAWSA's more conservative tactics.

Both Paul and Carrie Chapman Catt—the NAWSA president—shared the goal of universal suffrage. At the time, NAWSA concentrated its efforts on both state campaigns and a federal amendment. Instead, Paul wanted to focus all of NAWSA's funding and energy on an amendment to the U.S. Constitution. While the NAWSA leadership was willing to work with President Woodrow Wilson and members of the Democratic Party, Paul wanted to hold Wilson and his administration directly accountable for disenfranchising women. In 1914, NAWSA ended its relationship with the semi-autonomous Congressional Union. In 1916, Paul and her followers formed the National Woman's Party (NWP).

Most famously, the NWP organized more than 1,000 "silent sentinels" to picket the White House for 18 months beginning in January 1917. The sentinels stood at the White House gates, holding banners with attacks directed at Wilson. As the United States entered World War I in 1917, public sentiment turned against the suffragists for picketing a wartime president, but the NWP continued its protests and referred to the president as "Kaiser Wilson." Angry mobs attacked the sentinels and the police began to arrest the protesters, including Paul, for "obstructing traffic." When the women refused to pay the imposed fine, they were sent to Occoquan Workhouse in Virginia. While in prison, Paul and her fellow protestors demanded to be treated as political prisoners. However, they were instead met with brutal conditions. When Paul and several other imprisoned suffragists staged hunger strikes, they were forcibly fed. Eventually, newspaper accounts about the hunger strikes and prison conditions were met with public sympathy, demands for the women's release, and support for women's suffrage.

After ratification of the Nineteenth Amendment, Paul continued her education, earning a law degree from the Washington College of Law in 1922 and master's and doctoral degrees from American University in 1927 and 1928, respectively. She also continued working on behalf of equal rights for women. In 1923, Paul proposed an Equal Rights Amendment (ERA) to the U.S. Constitution, believing it would guarantee women complete equality with men. In 1944, Paul worked actively out of the NWP's headquarters in Washington, D.C., until relocating to the Connecticut countryside in 1972 due to failing health. She died in 1977 and in 1979, Paul was inducted into the National Women's Hall of Fame.

Barbara Burrell

Further Reading

Adams, Katherine H., and Michael L. Keene. *Alice Paul and the American Suffrage Campaign*. Urbana and Chicago: University of Illinois Press, 2008.

Alice Paul Institute. "Who was Alice Paul?" http://www.alicepaul.org/who-was-alice-paul/.

Kops, Deborah. *Alice Paul and the Fight for Women's Rights: From the Vote to the Equal Rights Amendment*. Honesdale, PA: Calkins Creek, 2017.

Walton, Mary. *A Woman's Crusade: Alice Paul and the Battle for the Ballot*. New York: St. Martin's Press, 2015.

Pollitzer, Anita Lily (1894–1975)

Anita Pollitzer was a philanthropist from a prominent family in Charleston, South Carolina, an arts promoter, and a women's rights activist. Pollitzer was born in Charleston on October 31, 1894. Her mother was the college-educated daughter of Jewish immigrants from Prague and her father was the owner of a cotton export company. She was raised in a progressive, civic-minded atmosphere and both of her sisters also became suffragists and reformers.

Anita Pollitzer attended Teachers College at Columbia University where she studied art and where she met and promoted the work of Georgia O'Keefe. It was Pollitzer who introduced O'Keefe's work to acclaimed New York photographer and art dealer Alfred Stieglitz, who would mentor and eventually marry O'Keefe. Pollitzer later studied law and earned a master's degree in international law, staying active not only in the suffrage cause but in issues related to global women's rights, equal pay for women, and immigrant citizenship status.

After graduating from college in 1916, Pollitzer worked closely with Alice Paul and the National Woman's Party (NWP). She marched in suffrage parades in Washington, D.C., and was among the "Silent Sentinels" who were arrested for picketing outside the White House, protesting the Woodrow Wilson administration in the months leading up to congressional approval of the suffrage amendment. She proved particularly useful to the NWP due to her southern background and connections, and she was dispatched by Paul to meet with Tennessee Republicans, including state legislator Harry T. Burn, to convince them to cast the final votes for ratification of the Nineteenth Amendment.

Pollitzer remained active with the NWP for decades after the ratification of the Nineteenth Amendment in 1920. She served as NWP national secretary, 1921–1926, and held various other positions, including as chairwoman, after Alice Paul stepped down in the late 1940s. She remained close to Paul and became active in the International Woman Suffrage Alliance (IWSA), supporting women's rights worldwide, and in Paul's World Woman's Party. In 1933, Pollitzer earned a degree in international law and her interest in global women's rights led to her serving as a delegate to the 1945 UN conference held in San Francisco. For several decades, Pollitzer was also an outspoken promoter of the post-suffrage Equal Rights Amendment, first proposed in 1923, as she gave speeches, wrote letters to legislators, and testified before congressional committees. Later in her life she published a memoir of her friendship with Georgia O'Keefe. Anita Pollitzer died in New York in 1975.

Tiffany K. Wayne

Further Reading

Klapper, Melissa R. *Ballots, Babies, and Banners of Peace: American Jewish Women's Activism, 1890–1940*. New York: New York University Press, 2013.

Weiss, Elaine. *The Woman's Hour: The Great Fight to Win the Vote*. New York: Penguin, 2018.

Presidential Politics and Suffrage

The Progressive Movement was part of a sweeping reform movement between 1890 and 1920 that sought to address problems related to rapid industrialization, urbanization, and immigration, including child labor, low wages and long hours, and terrible working conditions, as well as the corruption of city governments and squalid living conditions in America's major cities. Women's organizations, in particular, were active in securing protections for working women and sought the vote in order to advance change. Leaders such as Florence Kelley and Frances Perkins pressured local and state governments to limit the number of hours or times of day that women could work, as well as barring them from certain hazardous occupations. Sex-specific protective labor legislation by the states was upheld by the U.S. Supreme Court in *Mueller v. Oregon* (1908).

In this spirit of seeking government solutions to social and economic problems, the Progressive Era presidents had a much more expansive view of the president's role in the national reform dialogue. Theodore Roosevelt (president from 1901 to 1909) positioned himself as the champion of the working man and consumers against the interests of millionaires and big business. Railroads were a primary target for Roosevelt, and he pushed laws through Congress that eliminated railroad rebates and standardized railroad rates. He had his Justice Department bring suit against the railroad monopoly, Northern Securities, and the U.S. Supreme Court would break it up a couple of years later.

Although Theodore Roosevelt is not often regarded as a feminist, in 1880 he wrote his senior thesis at Harvard entitled "Practicability of Giving Men and Women Equal Rights," and argued for women not being required to take their husbands' names nor should the wedding vows include the word "obey" only for women. He also advocated for women's suffrage and, as a New York City commissioner, he pushed for women as members of the city's police department. Still, he felt that urban working women were restricting their reproductive lives too much and was much in favor of large families.

Roosevelt came down heavily in favor of women's suffrage only after he had been denied the Republican presidential nomination in 1912, which went to incumbent William Howard Taft. As late as 1911, Roosevelt was tepid in his support for women's suffrage, but in championing direct primaries he realized that to push for greater input from voters in the primary nomination process, but not for women to participate as voters, would be a political contradiction. In his platform, New Freedom, he unequivocally called for a national amendment for women's suffrage.

Woodrow Wilson, a Virginia Democrat and governor of New Jersey, ran against both Taft and Roosevelt in 1912 and sidestepped the issue of women's suffrage by claiming that it was an issue left to the states to decide. By 1912, only nine states had approved of women's suffrage in presidential elections, all of them out West. The National American Woman Suffrage Association (NAWSA) had been working on a state-by-state strategy, exactly what Wilson advocated as governor. Wilson won the election of 1912 and would continue with other Progressive reform issues, such as a national bank, an end to child labor, a reduction in the protective tariff, workmen's compensation, and a strengthening of existing antitrust laws.

Wilson's relationship to the suffrage issue and to the women's suffrage movement changed when the United States entered World War I in 1917. President Wilson had recently refused to endorse a national suffrage amendment at a meeting with suffragists early in 1917, but coupled with embarrassing protests outside the White House by Alice Paul, Lucy Burns, and the National Woman's Party, and hard-charging lobbying by NAWSA president Carrie Chapman Catt, Wilson found that he could no longer stem the tide of a national amendment by 1918.

By year's end, NAWSA's state-by-state campaign had increased the number of states where women could vote to twenty-two. Early in that year, the U.S. House of Representatives bowed to what seemed inevitable pressure by passing the Anthony Amendment, which would give women nationwide the ballot. President Wilson went before the U.S. Senate soon after to give his full support for the passage of the amendment "as a war measure." It was defeated by the slimmest of margins that year but was revived again in 1919. Suffragists pushed Wilson who then exercised his constitutional authority by calling Congress into session in the spring of that year, which then ratified the amendment, sending it to the states for authorization. On August 18, 1920, Tennessee became the thirty-sixth state to approve the amendment, thereby making it the law of the land.

Geoff Wickersham

Further Reading

Flehinger, Brett. *The 1912 Election and the Power of Progressivism: A Brief History with Documents*. Boston, MA: Bedford/St. Martin's, 2003.

Gable, John. "Theodore Roosevelt and Women's Suffrage." Public Broadcasting Service. www.pbs.org/wgbh/americanexperience/features/tr-gable/.

Milkis, Sidney M., and Michael Nelson. *The American Presidency: Origins and Development, 1776–2018*. 8th ed. Thousand Oaks, CA: CQ Press/SAGE, 2020.

Morris, Edmund. *The Rise of Theodore Roosevelt*. New York: Modern Library/Random House, 1979.

Morris, Edmund. *Theodore Rex*. New York: Modern Library/Random House, 2001.

"The Omaha Platform: Launching the Populist Party." *HISTORY MATTERS— The U.S. Survey Course on the Web*. historymatters.gmu.edu/d/5361/.

R

Rankin, Jeannette (1880–1973)

Jeannette Rankin was a politician, suffragist, and social activist. In 1916, four years before American women gained the right to vote, she became the first woman elected to the U.S. Congress, serving between 1917 and 1919. In 1918, she sat on the House Committee on Woman Suffrage and voted on an early House resolution on women's suffrage, proud to be, as she put it, "the only woman who ever voted to give women the right to vote." A lifelong pacifist, Rankin served in the House of Representatives again from 1941 to 1943 and thus had the unique opportunity to vote against U.S. entrance into both World War I and World War II.

Rankin was born on June 11, 1880, in the Montana Territory, the oldest of seven children born to John and Olive Rankin. The family was well-to-do by the standards of the time, and Rankin and her siblings were able to pursue higher education; her sister, Harriet Rankin, became Dean of Women at the University of Montana. Jeannette Rankin attended Montana State University (now the University of Montana), graduating in 1902 with a degree in biology. Later, she studied social work at the New York School of Philanthropy (now the Columbia University School of Social Work) and rhetoric, economics, and sociology at the University of Washington in Seattle.

From 1902 to 1916, Rankin learned more about social conditions in the United States. From the Telegraph Hill Neighborhood Association (a settlement house in San Francisco), to the slums of Boston and New York City, to a school for the deaf and an orphanage, Rankin saw firsthand the poverty, misery, and prejudice that many suffered. Like many Progressive Era women reformers, Rankin soon turned her enthusiasm, energy, and organizational skills to the cause of women's suffrage. She became president of the Montana Women's Suffrage Association and a field secretary for the National American Woman Suffrage Association (NAWSA). In 1914, Montana became the tenth state to grant women the right to vote; two years later Montana voters elected Rankin, a suffragist, to represent them in Congress.

In 1916, Rankin ran for Congress on the Republican ticket and, on November 6, became the first woman elected to the U.S. House of Representatives. Just five months later, on April 6, 1917, Rankin voted against entry of the United States into World War I. Although not the only member of Congress to vote against the war, she received harsh criticism and, in 1918, she was defeated in the Montana Republican primary when she ran for the U.S. Senate.

Between the world wars, Rankin continued to work toward ensuring lasting peace. In 1919, she attended the Second International Congress of Women for Permanent Peace along with Jane Addams, founder of Hull House; Lillian Wald, founder of the Henry Street Settlement; and Mary Church Terrell, president of the National Association of Colored Women. They spoke against the harsh penalties inflicted on the Triple-Entente and its allies and urged measures toward lasting reconciliation, but to no avail. Later, she became an active member of the Women's International League for Peace and Freedom (WILPF), founded the Georgia Peace Society, worked for the National Consumers' League and the National Council for the Prevention of War, and lobbied for the rights of prisoners of war and infants.

Rankin was elected to the U.S. House of Representatives again in 1940. The following year, the United States was attacked at Pearl Harbor. This time Rankin was the lone dissenting voice, the only member of Congress to vote against President Franklin D. Roosevelt's request for a declaration of war to enter World War II. Rankin had to have a police escort back to her office due to the anger at her vote. Rankin did not seek reelection in 1942 and returned to her farm in Georgia.

Rankin's legacy remains as both a suffragist and a pacifist. On January 15, 1968, 5,000 women calling themselves the Jeannette Rankin Brigade marched on Washington to protest the Vietnam War. Rankin herself marched along with Coretta Scott King at the front of the brigade. Rankin became the first member of the Susan B. Anthony Hall of Fame in 1972. She died on May 18, 1973, in Carmel, California. In 1985, a bronze statue of Rankin was placed in the U.S. Capitol. On its base are her words "I cannot vote for war."

Jenna L. Kubly

Further Reading

Lopach, James J., and Jean A. Luckowski. *Jeannette Rankin: A Political Woman.* Boulder: University Press of Colorado, 2005.

Smith, Norma. *Jeannette Rankin: America's Conscience.* Helena: Montana Historical Society Press, 2002.

The Revolution

The Revolution was published by Susan B. Anthony and Elizabeth Cady Stanton as the official newspaper of the National Woman Suffrage Association (NWSA) between 1868 and 1870. The paper was then sold to another publisher and continued in print until 1872.

The first issue of the weekly paper was published on January 8, 1868. The former alliance between the abolitionist and women's movements was split after the Civil War in debates over the ratification of the Fifteenth Amendment extending the right to vote to African American men, but not women. Publication of *The Revolution* allowed Stanton and Anthony to publicly express and organize around their views, and in 1869 they founded the NWSA to focus exclusively on women's suffrage; that same year, Lucy Stone and others created the American Woman Suffrage Association (AWSA), with its own rival paper, the *Woman's Journal*, in support of the Fifteenth Amendment as a step toward equality for all.

The Revolution was a controversial newspaper from the start not only due to the split in the women's movement but also because Anthony and Stanton accepted financial support for the paper from George Francis Train, a Democrat who had supported the women's suffrage campaign in Kansas at a time when the Republican press took an antisuffrage position. In associating herself with Train, Anthony was exploiting a political opportunity to expose the Republicans on the limits of their equality and civil rights agenda. The Democrats, however, were the party of slavery and of antiblack civil rights, and Train's racism and eccentric public presence, along with Anthony's opposition to the Fifteenth Amendment, embroiled *The Revolution*—and Anthony—in controversy.

Throughout the paper's four-year publication history, Anthony handled the business and financial affairs of the paper (she was listed on the masthead as "Proprietor"), and also wrote articles, but Stanton was the primary writer and editor. Their abolitionist friend, Parker Pillsbury, also served as co-editor during the first year, and prominent women's rights advocate Paulina Wright Davis took over as editor during the second year. The paper's motto was "Men, Their Rights and Nothing More. Women, Their Rights and Nothing Less."

Although Stanton had been arguing for the vote since the Seneca Falls convention of 1848, *The Revolution* helped coalesce Anthony and Stanton's post–Civil War position of adding protections based on sex into the text of the U.S. Constitution and providing a public forum for the emerging national suffrage movement. The paper helped directly connect the broader issues of the antebellum women's rights movement to the need for the vote, explaining in the very first issue that "we shall show that the ballot will secure for woman equal place and equal wages in the world of work; that it will open to her the schools, colleges, professions, and all the opportunities and advantages of life."

Although *The Revolution* gained more than 3,000 subscribers, by the spring of 1870, Anthony was $10,000 in debt and sold the paper to publisher Laura Curtis Bullard for $1.00. Bullard ran the paper until February 1872 as a broader, less radical, women's literary and social magazine, not focused solely on suffrage and political rights.

Tiffany K. Wayne

Further Reading

Dudden, Faye E. *Fighting Chance: The Struggle over Woman Suffrage and Black Suffrage in Reconstruction America.* New York: Oxford University Press, 2011.

Solomon, Martha M., ed. *A Voice of Their Own: The Woman Suffrage Press, 1840–1910.* Tuscaloosa: University of Alabama Press, 1991.

Streitmatter, Rodger. *Voices of Revolution: The Dissident Press in America.* New York: Oxford University Press, 2001.

Rose, Ernestine (1810–1892)

Ernestine Rose was a freethinking atheist women's rights activist who sought voting rights for all Americans regardless of race, gender, or immigration status. Her political and religious views distinguished her speeches from other advocates for abolitionism and women's rights of the time. She served as the presiding officer for numerous organizations and conventions and delivered powerful and provocative speeches advocating human rights in the United States.

Ernestine Louise Potowska (or Potowski) grew up in Piotrków, Poland, in a Jewish household. Her rabbi father taught her Hebrew and the Jewish Scriptures. At an early age, Ernestine began to question religious practices and resist her father's demand for unchallenged obedience. After her mother died, her father arranged a marriage for her, but she begged her betrothed to release her. When he refused, Ernestine successfully pleaded her case before a judge, arguing that she should not have to marry and should keep her dowry. Afterward, she opted to live in Berlin and England where she could pursue greater freedom.

In England, Ernestine Potowska was heavily influenced by the teachings and philosophy of Robert Owen. Owen's emphasis on religious freedom, women's rights, communal cooperation, and exchange of labor particularly resonated with her. In 1836, she and her new husband, William Rose, an Englishman, moved to New York, where they hoped to put their Owenite beliefs into practice. Ernestine Rose attended women's rights conventions and lectures in the 1840s. After years of organizing, speech writing, and appearing before the New York legislature, Ernestine and William's efforts to expand married women's property rights in New York succeeded in 1849.

Because William provided her support and financial assistance, Ernestine traveled through the Midwest delivering lectures on issues ranging from abolitionism to marriage reform. Her background as a freethinker contributed a rhetorical style distinct from her more religious contemporaries. Her speech at the second National Women's Rights Convention, held in Worcester, Massachusetts, in 1851, for example, received high praise from some but was criticized as too radical by others. Undeterred, Rose continued to argue that strict distinctions between men and women, particularly on a political level, were oppressive to both sexes and that universal suffrage was necessary to American democracy. She also expressed unpopular perspectives such as the view that oppression was caused by religious institutions and capitalism.

The rhetoric that Rose utilized for abolitionist speeches also significantly differed from her contemporaries by including black and white women. She also declined to argue that God was in favor of abolition or women's rights, a marked difference from most mid-nineteenth-century social activists, who grounded their work in Christian morality. In 1853, she delivered a speech at the British West Indian Emancipation anniversary hosted by the New York

Anti-Slavery Society in which she emphasized the necessity to free all citizens—especially women—rather than focusing solely on antislavery.

In 1854, Rose presided over the fifth National Women's Rights Convention, held in Philadelphia that year. She was criticized by some for her atheism, but Susan B. Anthony supported her right to speak.

During the American Civil War, Rose continued her public activism even as her health limited her activity. When Abraham Lincoln announced the Emancipation Proclamation in 1863, Rose criticized it as a half measure that did not mean real freedom for all slaves. After the Civil War, Rose spoke publicly in favor of equal rights for blacks and all women in both the United States and the United Kingdom. She remained an active political force until her death in England in 1892.

Cynthia M. Zavala

Further Reading

Anderson, Bonnie S. *The Rabbi's Atheist Daughter: Ernestine Rose, International Feminist Pioneer.* New York: Oxford University Press, 2017.

Kolmerten, Carol A. *The American Life of Ernestine L. Rose.* New York: Syracuse University Press, 1999.

Rose, Ernestine. *Mistress of Herself: Speeches and Letters of Ernestine L. Rose, Early Women's Rights Leader.* Edited by Paula Doress-Worters. New York: Feminist Press, 2008.

Ruffin, Josephine St. Pierre (1842–1924)

Suffragist, philanthropist, journalist, entrepreneur, and civil rights activist Josephine St. Pierre Ruffin was a champion of African American women's rights during the late nineteenth and early twentieth centuries and a key figure in the women's club movement. She served as editor of the *Woman's Era*, the first newspaper published by and for African American women. Josephine St. Pierre was born on August 31, 1842, in Boston, Massachusetts, the fifth daughter and youngest of six children to John and Eliza Matilda (Menhenick) St. Pierre. Ruffin's mother was a native of Cornwall, England. Her father had a mixed ancestry of African, French, and Native American. The St. Pierres were light-skinned but defined themselves as black Americans.

Although the St. Pierre family was well off, Josephine encountered racism early in her life. She was originally enrolled in a private school, but six months later her racial background was discovered, and she was expelled. Refusing to accept racial segregation, her parents enrolled her in integrated schools in neighboring Salem, Massachusetts. The state would sign legislation desegregating public schools in 1855, and Josephine enrolled in the Bowdoin Finishing School in Boston. In 1858, she married George Lewis Ruffin, the son of another prominent African American Boston family. The newlyweds left for Liverpool, England, but returned to the United States after the outbreak of the American Civil War. During the war years George attended Harvard Law School, and Josephine bore five children: Hubert, Florida, Stanley, George, and Robert (who died during infancy).

During the war, Ruffin recruited African American soldiers and worked with the U.S. Sanitary Commission, a predecessor of the American Red Cross. In 1869, her husband George became the first African American to graduate from Harvard Law School. His career advanced as he served in the state legislature and the Boston Common Council, and in 1883 he was appointed judge of the Charlestown municipal court, making him the first African American judge in the North. In 1870, Josephine Ruffin became a member of the Massachusetts Suffrage Association and served on the executive board of the Massachusetts Moral Education Association. In 1879, she founded the Kansas Relief Association, an organization that provided economic assistance to former slaves who moved west.

Ruffin developed a national reputation among social reformers for her work and called attention to the injustice of excluding black women from suffrage organizations. After her husband's sudden death in 1886, Ruffin dedicated herself full-time to the empowerment of African American women. In 1890, she began the *Woman's Era*, the first newspaper by and for black women. Ruffin financed, operated, and served as editor from 1890 to 1897.

In 1894, together with her daughter Florida, Ruffin organized the Woman's Era Club. The club promoted improvement for African Americans and provided scholarships for young African American women. In 1895, Ruffin organized the first national convention of African American women, in part to support Ida B. Wells in her anti-lynching campaign. During the meeting, the women created the National Federation of Afro-American Women. In 1896, this group merged with the Colored Women's League to create the National Association of Colored Women (NACW), with Mary Church Terrell as its first president and Josephine Ruffin serving as the first vice president. Ruffin continued to fight for equality as she attempted to desegregate the General Federation of Women's Clubs (GFWC) amidst resistance from southern white delegates, and in 1910 she helped form the National Association for the Advancement of Colored People (NAACP). During her later years Ruffin helped found the Boston branch of the NAACP, the League of Women for Community Service, the American Mount Coffee School Association in Liberia, and the Association for the Promotion of Child Training in Atlanta, Georgia. She died in 1924 in Boston. Josephine St. Pierre Ruffin's legacy is a commitment to forming alliances regardless of class, gender, or racial background to benefit all Americans.

Robert L. Thornton

Further Reading

Holden, Teresa Blue. "Josephine St. Pierre Ruffin and Mary Church Terrell: Women Who Influenced the DuBois vs. Washington Debate." In *Voices from within the Veil: African Americans and the Experience of Democracy*, edited by William H. Alexander et al., 300–312. Newcastle upon Tyne, UK: Cambridge Scholars Publishing, 2008.

Holden, Teresa Blue. "A Presence and a Voice: Josephine St. Pierre Ruffin and the Black Women's Club Movement." In *Bury My Heart in a Free Land: Black Women Intellectuals in Modern U.S. History*, edited by Hettie V. Williams, 53–80. Santa Barbara, CA: ABC-CLIO, 2018.

Porter, Susan L., ed. *Women of the Commonwealth: Work, Family, and Social Change in Nineteenth-Century Massachusetts*. Amherst: University of Massachusetts Press, 1996.

Streitmatter, Rodger. *Raising Her Voice: African-American Women Journalists Who Changed History*. Lexington: University of Kentucky Press, 1994.

Schneiderman, Rose (1882–1972)

Rose Schneiderman was a suffragist and women's labor organizer who held important positions in the federal government during the New Deal and later in New York's state labor department.

Rachel "Rose" Schneiderman was born on April 6, 1882, in what is now Poland and was then part of Russia. Her father, Adolph Samuel Schneiderman, a tailor, brought the family to the United States in 1890 when Schneiderman was six and settled the family of five in two rooms in the Lower East Side of New York City. Three years later, he died of brain fever, and Schneiderman had to leave school to care for the younger children while her mother worked in a sweatshop. Rose returned to school through sixth grade before leaving again to work as a store clerk and then stitching cap linings; her wages were $5 a week and the cap stitchers had to pay for their own sewing machines, thread, and electric power.

After three years, Schneiderman led a group of fellow workers to demand membership in the all-male United Cloth Hat and Cap Makers Union. She was elected secretary and organizer of the local women's chapter and, in 1904, she led a successful strike against the cap factories. Soon afterward, she joined the New York chapter of the Women's Trade Union League (WTUL), an alliance of female unionists and social workers that Jane Addams had helped found. In the winter of 1909 to 1910, Schneiderman led the WTUL in supporting a strike of some 25,000 mostly female workers in the New York City shirtwaist industry. She persuaded prominent society women to contribute funds and walk the picket line. The strike won concessions from employers in a widely hailed settlement and established the International Ladies' Garment Workers' Union (ILGWU) as an important union. Schneiderman joined the ILGWU as an organizer and traveled the country to promote unionization. Active in the women's suffrage movement as of 1910, Schneiderman worked with the National American Woman Suffrage Association (NAWSA) in New York and Ohio. She joined Harriot Stanton Blatch's Equality League of Self-Supporting Women and was chair of the industrial committee of New York's Woman's Suffrage Party. After the March 1911 Triangle Factory Fire in New York that killed 146 workers, many of them young immigrant women, Schneiderman was one of the most outspoken critics of industrial working conditions. Her work for women's suffrage was always in connection with her goals related to working women's rights and in 1919 she spoke at the first meeting of the International Congress of Working Women, in Washington, D.C. After the ratification of the Nineteenth Amendment in 1920, Schneiderman continued to pursue protective labor legislation for women, and for this reason did not support the Equal Rights Amendment of the National Woman's Party.

Schneiderman had become vice president of the national WTUL when she was appointed by President Woodrow Wilson to represent American women workers at the Paris Peace Conference in 1920. In 1923, she was a delegate to the International Federation of Trade Unions in Vienna. Under the National Recovery Act of President Franklin D. Roosevelt's New Deal, she was the only woman on the Labor Advisory Board, and she was a member of the president's "brain trust." In 1937, Governor Herbert Lehman appointed her secretary of the New York State Department of Labor, a post she held for seven years. Schneiderman resigned at age 60 but continued to serve her causes—typically, as a director of Bryn Mawr College's summer school for working women, to which she insisted that African American women be admitted. She was reelected annually as president of the national WTUL to the end of her life.

Rose Schneiderman spent her last years in the Jewish Home and Hospital in New York City, where she died on August 11, 1972, at the age of 88.

William McGuire, Leslie Wheeler, and Tiffany K. Wayne

Further Reading

Dubofsky, Melvyn, and Tine W. R. Van. *Labor Leaders in America*. Urbana: University of Illinois Press, 1987.

Eisenstein, Sarah. *Give Us Bread but Give Us Roses: Working Women's Consciousness in the United States, 1890 to the First World War.* New York: Routledge, 2013.

Orleck, Annelise. *Common Sense and a Little Fire: Women and Working-Class Politics in the United States, 1900–1965.* Chapel Hill: University of North Carolina Press, 1995.

Seneca Falls Convention (1848)

The Seneca Falls Convention, held on July 19–20, 1848, in Seneca Falls, New York, was the first American conference on women's rights. Participants were both female and male. The scope of the conference included not only the treatment of women but also how women's rights were connected to both abolitionism and the temperance movement. A document ratified at the conference was titled the "Declaration of Sentiments" and became a cornerstone of the women's rights movement. Its most controversial resolution was the demand that women have a "sacred right to the elective franchise."

Seneca Falls is a small town in western New York. Along with the nearby town of Waterloo, it was home to a large number of people who were members of the religious Society of Friends, otherwise known as Quakers. Many in the Seneca Falls area were Hicksite Quakers, named for the liberal Elias Hicks. This group espoused simplicity, temperance, opposition to war, abolition of slavery, and the rights of and equality between all women and men.

In 1840, the World Anti-Slavery Convention was held in London. In attendance from the United States were Quakers Lucretia Mott and Elizabeth Cady Stanton. Since women were excluded from the convention floor and forced to sit in a sectioned-off area, their conversation turned to the issue of women's rights and the possibility of there being a women's rights conference in the United States.

In the summer of 1848, with political revolutions swirling in Europe, Lucretia Mott was visiting her sister, Martha Coffin Wright, in upstate New York. One of the people invited to a social gathering with the sisters was Elizabeth Cady Stanton, from nearby Seneca Falls. Over tea, the group of women discussed a radical idea: mounting a convention to focus on the social, civil, and religious rights of women. They decided to schedule it while Mott, a powerful orator, was in town. This meant organizing the convention in just five days' time. They placed a small notice in the local newspaper, but most of the promotion was by word of mouth and they anticipated a small turnout. Stanton began itemizing grievances for a document to be based on the Declaration of Independence, which would be debated and ratified by the attendees.

At that time, American women were denied access to higher education, almost all professions, and many jobs. In the few careers they could enter they were paid less than men for doing the same job, and if they were married their wages legally belonged to their husbands. Under the legal principle of coverture, in which married women were "covered by" or had no independent legal identity from their husbands; if women brought property into a marriage they lost all claim to it, even if they divorced; if a husband divorced his wife, she could also lose custody of their children. Women were legally bound to endure abuse of all kinds by their husbands and to tolerate the basest behavior. The legal system, the government, and the elective process were all controlled by men.

The Declaration of Sentiments was drafted primarily by Elizabeth Cady Stanton and listed 18 grievances and 11 resolutions demanding the rights of women as equal members of the human race. Resolution 9 was the most radical, calling for the "elective franchise." Without the vote, reasoned Stanton, nothing would change. It was such a provocative notion that even Mott told Stanton, "Thee will make us ridiculous!"

Although it was a women's rights convention, it was considered improper for a lady to conduct a public meeting. James Mott, Lucretia's husband, chaired the conference. Women were, however, allowed to speak. Stanton stated that the purpose of the event was to address civil and political rights. She read the Declaration, invited comments, and amended the document based on suggestions. As predicted, the most contentious issue was the resolution calling for women's right to vote. It barely passed after former slave Frederick Douglass urged its passage. Stanton later wrote that she believed that those who opposed it did so out of fear that it would overshadow and compromise the other resolutions. But she decried the fact that women did not have the same right to vote as "drunkards, idiots, [and] horse racing rum-selling rowdies."

About 300 people attended the Seneca Falls Convention. Of that number, the final draft of the Declaration of Sentiments was signed by 100: 32 men and 68 women. The national press wrote scathingly about the conference. Some of the signers of the Declaration of Sentiments feared reprisals and asked that their names be removed from the document. But other women's rights conferences were held, and when Elizabeth Cady Stanton later published the first volume of her *History of Woman Suffrage* (published in 1881), she identified the Seneca Falls Convention as the beginning of the fight for women's suffrage in the United States.

Seventy-two years after the Seneca Falls Convention, the Nineteenth Amendment gave American women the right to vote in 1920. Among the original signers of the Declaration of Sentiments, Charlotte Woodward Pierce, who had attended the Seneca Falls convention as a teenager, was the only signer who lived to see all Americans gain the right to vote. At age 92 in 1920, she was in poor health and unable to go vote, but she lived long enough to see the culmination of what had begun in Seneca Falls.

Nancy Hendricks

Further Reading

McMillen, Sally. *Seneca Falls and the Origins of the Women's Rights Movement.* New York: Oxford University Press, 2009.

Tetrault, Lisa. *The Myth of Seneca Falls: Memory and the Women's Suffrage Movement, 1848–1898.* Chapel Hill: University of North Carolina Press, 2014.

Wellman, Judith. *The Road to Seneca Falls: Elizabeth Cady Stanton and the First Woman's Rights Convention.* Champaign: University of Illinois Press, 2004.

Shafroth-Palmer Amendment

The Shafroth-Palmer Amendment was a proposed constitutional amendment introduced into the U.S. Congress in 1914 to allow for individual state referendums on the question of woman suffrage if 8 percent of a state's voters petitioned to have it on the state ballot. Promoted by the Congressional Union of the National American Woman Suffrage Association (NAWSA), the amendment placed the issue of women's suffrage in the hands of state voters, thus departing from NAWSA's previous focus on national legislation or a federal amendment securing all voting rights, as with the Anthony Amendment.

Introduced in early 1914 in the U.S. Senate by Democratic Senator John F. Shafroth of Colorado, and in the House of Representatives by Democrat A. Mitchell Palmer of Pennsylvania, the state referendum proposal dominated discussion and debate among suffrage leaders in 1914 and 1915. The amendment had been the effort of the Congressional Union committee of NAWSA, whose role it was to lobby individual members of Congress in pursuit of garnering enough support from individual states to pass a federal suffrage amendment. Suffragists in support of the Shafroth-Palmer Amendment argued that they were not abandoning hope of establishing national voting rights by federal amendment, but rather were seeking political expediency by building on the momentum of suffrage rights won in individual states and assuaging concerns about state's rights by some (mostly Southern) members of Congress. Supporters envisioned that the amendment would lead to a lively national debate about women's suffrage arising from several states simultaneously.

Other members of NAWSA, however, criticized the Shafroth-Palmer Amendment (and the Congressional Union) for dividing the group's focus and for abandoning the many years of work toward the Anthony Amendment. Furthermore, some suffrage leaders pointed out that referring the issue to the states undermined efforts to put pressure on the president and Congress to have a national debate about women's suffrage. The leaders of NAWSA dropped support for the Shafroth-Palmer Amendment in 1915.

The detailed discussion about the Shafroth-Palmer Amendment within the suffrage ranks was documented in detail in Volume 5 of the *History of Woman Suffrage*, edited by Ida Husted Harper. It was published in 1922, after the Nineteenth Amendment was ratified, and covered the final years of the suffrage movement.

Tiffany K. Wayne

Further Reading

Vile, John R. *Encyclopedia of Constitutional Amendments, Proposed Amendments, and Amending Issues, 1789–2002*. 2nd ed. Santa Barbara: ABC-CLIO, 2003.

Shaw, Anna Howard (1847–1919)

Best known for her work in the women's suffrage movement, Anna Howard Shaw was also a medical doctor and one of the first women ordained as a minister in the Methodist church. Shaw played a key role in the creation of the new National American Woman Suffrage Association (NAWSA) in 1890 and served as president from 1904 to 1915, overseeing the organization's strategy to pursue a national constitutional amendment for women's suffrage.

Born on February 14, 1847, at Newcastle-on-Tyne in England, Anna was the third daughter and sixth child of Thomas and Nicolas Shaw. The family arrived in the United States in 1853 after surviving a harrowing ocean crossing. Settling in Massachusetts, Shaw received her earliest education in the local Lawrence schools before she and her family relocated to the Michigan wilderness when she was nine years old.

At the age of 15, to help with the family's tenuous finances, Anna began teaching, walking many miles to her school. Encouraged by ministers, she also began preaching, much to her family's disapproval. Determined to get a college education, she preached and lectured to raise the money,

Anna Howard Shaw, a minister, physician, women's suffrage leader, and well-known lecturer. A close colleague of Susan B. Anthony, Shaw was president of the National American Woman Suffrage Association from 1904 to 1915. (Library of Congress)

and despite family opposition, she attended Albion College from 1873 to 1875. However, before earning her degree she left her family and Michigan, enrolling in the Boston University School of Theology. The sole female in her class, she graduated in 1878. Despite her training and education, the New England Conference and the General Conference refused her ordination into the Methodist Episcopal Church. Switching denominations, in 1880 she became the first woman ordained by the Methodist Protestant Church. In 1878, Shaw became the pastor of a church in East Dennis, Massachusetts, and also began studying medicine at Boston University, receiving her MD degree in 1886.

In 1886, she resigned her parish posts and became a lecturer for the Massachusetts Women's Suffrage Association. While she was also involved in the Woman's Christian Temperance Union (WCTU) from 1886 to 1892, after coming under the influence of Susan B. Anthony, Shaw committed fully to the suffrage cause. Applying the oratorical skills that she had developed as a minister, she became the acknowledged voice of the movement. For the next decade, Shaw spoke all over the country. In 1900, with Anthony's support, Shaw won election as vice president of the NAWSA, a post she held until 1904 when, again at the insistence of Anthony, she succeeded Carrie Chapman Catt as president.

In over a decade in that post heading an organization rife with tension and infighting, Shaw oversaw the transformation of the NAWSA from a volunteer association to a professional organization based in New York City. Under Shaw the NAWSA first began to pay its staff as well as its president, a move that allowed her to devote herself full-time to the organization and the cause. Shaw declined reelection as president, and her tenure ended in 1915. As president, she oversaw a substantive growth in active membership and a more than tripled operating budget. Most important, during that time the number of states that adopted full woman suffrage increased from four to twelve.

In the aftermath of her retirement from the NAWSA presidency, in 1915 Shaw published *The Story of a Pioneer*, an autobiographical work that demonstrated how different her immigrant, independent, self-supporting, working woman experience had been from that of most of her contemporaries. She was recognized as one of the nation's foremost female leaders, and as World War I began, Secretary of War Newton Baker asked her to serve as chair of the Woman's Committee for the Council of National Defense. Her conscientious efforts to help maximize women's contributions to the war effort were recognized when she was awarded the Distinguished Service Medal by the federal government in May 1919. She was asked by representatives of the League to Enforce Peace to join former president William Howard Taft and Harvard University president Abbott Lawrence Lowell in a national speaking tour in support of ratification of the Treaty of Versailles. However, her involvement in the tour was cut short when she became ill in Illinois. Shaw was bedridden at her home in Moylan, Pennsylvania, until her death on July 2, 1919.

William H. Pruden III

Further Reading
Franzen, Trisha. *Anna Howard Shaw*. Urbana: University of Illinois Press, 2014.

Silent Sentinels

The Silent Sentinels was the term given to a group of suffragists organized by the National Woman's Party (NWP), who picketed at the gates of the White House six days a week from January 10, 1917, to June 4, 1919. The picketers' overall goal was to pressure President Woodrow Wilson to advocate for an amendment to the U.S. Constitution guaranteeing women the right to vote. Both the NWP and the National American Woman Suffrage Association (NAWSA) had sent numerous delegations to the president asking for his support, but he declined, saying that it was a matter to be left to his Democratic Party. Frustrated by the inaction of both Wilson and Congress, NWP members decided to begin picketing as a strategy.

Harriot Stanton Blatch, daughter of pioneering women's rights activist Elizabeth Cady Stanton, made a stirring speech calling on women to join the effort to "stand there as sentinels—sentinels of liberty, sentinels of self-government—silent sentinels," day after day until Wilson acted.

The press adopted the term "silent sentinels" from the speech and used it to refer to the picketers. Although the picketers had pledged their verbal silence, they held large banners with printed statements questioning whether the

Women's suffrage activists picket at the White House, 1917. (Library of Congress)

United States was truly a democratic and free nation. These statements were often controversial, particularly after the country entered World War I in April 1917. They held banners with statements such as "Democracy Should Begin at Home" and referred to the president as "Kaiser Wilson." The suffragists were criticized as "treasonable" and "seditious" and the picketers were increasingly subjected to violence and taunting from the crowds that would gather around them. Some had banners ripped from their hands, and others were knocked down and dragged. The White House responded with arrests of the picketers beginning on June 22, 1917. Most were charged with obstructing traffic and fined, but the women refused to pay the fines and some were jailed.

In September 1917, the U.S. House of Representatives held debates over the formation of a special committee to review the issue of women's suffrage. Congressmember Joseph Walsh, a Republican from Massachusetts, referred to the protesters as "iron-jawed angels" in a statement in opposition to the creation of the committee. Walsh's term for the picketers was picked up by the press when his statement was included in a September 25, 1917, *New York Times* article on the debate. During the debate, other congressmen also referred to the "nagging" of the picketers and expressed reluctance to vote in favor of the committee for fear that it would be seen as acquiescing to the protestors. Ultimately, the House voted 180 to 107 in favor of forming the committee.

By that time, jail times were lengthened for the protestors and the women were being sentenced to the Occoquan Workhouse in Virginia, where they endured unsanitary and brutal conditions. NWP leaders Lucy Burns and Mabel Vernon had been among the first arrested in June and on October 20, 1917, leader Alice Paul was arrested and sent to Occoquan as well. Paul was placed in solitary confinement and began a hunger strike, which inspired the other women to refuse food in solidarity. Several women were brutally force-fed by the prison doctors and on November 14, 1917, several suffragists were beaten and chained by prison guards in what became known as the "Night of Terror." The treatment of the women was reported in the newspapers and public sympathy, as well as political embarrassment for the Wilson administration, led to the release of the suffragists from prison in late November 1917.

The suffragists continued to picket the White House throughout 1918 and early 1919 while Congress debated the suffrage amendment. Over the two and a half years of protests, some 2,000 women picketed the White House.

The picketing finally ended on June 4, 1919, after Congress passed the Nineteenth Amendment and sent it to the states for ratification.

Nancy Beach and Tiffany K. Wayne

Further Reading

Adams, Katherine, and Michael L. Keene. *Alice Paul and the American Suffrage Campaign*. Urbana: University of Illinois, 2007.

DuBois, Ellen Carol. *Harriot Stanton Blatch and the Winning of Suffrage*. New Haven, CT: Yale University Press, 1997.

Stevens, Doris. *Jailed for Freedom*. New York: Liveright Press, 1920.

Stillion Southard, Belinda A. *Militant Citizenship: Rhetorical Strategies of the National Woman's Party, 1913–1920*. College Station: Texas A&M University Press, 2011.

Stanton, Elizabeth Cady (1815–1902)

Elizabeth Cady Stanton was one of the key figures of the nineteenth-century women's rights movement, an abolitionist, temperance advocate, dress reformer, and suffragist. A prominent lecturer and writer, Stanton was the author of several key documents within the early history of American feminism, including the Declaration of Sentiments resolutions of the Seneca Falls convention of 1848, *The Woman's Bible* (1895), and creator and collaborator on the early volumes of the *History of Woman Suffrage* (Volumes 1–3, published 1881–1886).

Born in Johnstown, New York, Elizabeth Cady's childhood was marked by her mother's severe bouts of depression caused by the death of 6 of her 11 children. Elizabeth received a sound formal education at the coeducational Johnstown Academy; following graduation her male classmates went to Union College, but Elizabeth had to content herself with the only option available to the female graduates—attending the Troy Female Seminary. She was familiar with legal issues from an early age, as her father was an attorney and later a congressman and judge. She would use this knowledge in her fight for, first, abolitionism, and then women's rights.

Her cousin Gerrit Smith was a prominent abolitionist and, in 1840, Elizabeth Cady married journalist Henry Brewster Stanton, an ardent abolitionist who studied law under Elizabeth's father and became an attorney. Deeply committed to abolitionism, the Stantons spent their honeymoon at the World

Anti-Slavery Convention in London. The female attendants were snubbed and forced to sit apart from the male delegates, opening Elizabeth Cady Stanton's eyes to women's subordinate role within public activism. In 1843, the family moved to Boston, in whose abolitionist circles they met Ralph Waldo Emerson, Louisa May Alcott, and Frederick Douglass, among others. They moved to Seneca Falls, New York, in 1847.

In 1848, along with Lucretia Mott, Stanton helped organize the first American women's rights convention, held in Seneca Falls, New York, July 19–20, 1848, where her Declaration of Sentiments included the first written demand for women's right to vote. In 1851, Stanton was introduced to Susan B. Anthony, with whom she would forge a most productive friendship that would last for over 50 years. Together they cofounded the short-lived Woman's State Temperance Society in 1852, wrote lectures and speeches, worked in the American Equal Rights Association, founded the National Woman Suffrage Association (NWSA), published a weekly periodical, *The Revolution* (1868–1870), and documented the early history of the women's suffrage movement, in which they played a major part. In 1890, the rival American Woman Suffrage Association (AWSA) and National Woman Suffrage Association (NWSA) merged into a new organization, the National American Woman Suffrage Association (NAWSA), with Stanton as its first president.

Believing that organized religion kept women in a position of inferiority, in the 1890s Stanton gathered together an international committee to create *The Woman's Bible*, a rewriting of the Bible aimed at developing a theology that allowed for women's freedom. The controversial work was published in two installments (1895 and 1898), and alienated Stanton from many in the suffrage movement in the final years of her life.

In 1898, Stanton published her autobiography, *Eighty Years and More: Reminiscences 1815–1897*. Stanton died of heart failure on October 26, 1902. Her daughter Harriot Stanton Blatch was a prominent member of the next generation of the women's suffrage movement.

M. Carmen Gómez-Galisteo and Tiffany K. Wayne

Further Reading

Baker, Jean H. *Sisters: The Lives of America's Suffragists*. New York: Hill and Wang, 2005.

Burns, Ken, and Geoffrey C. Ward. *Not for Ourselves Alone: The Story of Elizabeth Cady Stanton and Susan B. Anthony*. New York: Alfred A. Knopf, 1999.

DuBois, Ellen Carol, and Richard Candida Smith, eds. *Elizabeth Cady Stanton: Feminist as Thinker. A Reader in Documents and Essays.* New York: New York University Press, 2007.

Ginzberg, Lori D. *Elizabeth Cady Stanton: An American Life.* New York: Hill and Wang, 2009.

Griffith, Elisabeth. *In Her Own Right: The Life of Elizabeth Cady Stanton.* New York: Oxford University Press, 1985.

Tetrault, Lisa. *The Myth of Seneca Falls: Memory and the Women's Suffrage Movement, 1848–1898.* Chapel Hill: University of North Carolina Press, 2014.

Stevens, Doris (1892–1963)

When the Nineteenth Amendment was ratified in 1920, suffragist and author Doris Stevens published her own account of the suffrage movement, *Jailed for Freedom*. The book was Stevens's account of the struggles she and others endured on the path to ratification, including arrests, hunger strikes, and picketing of the White House. Stevens went on to become the first chair of the Inter-American Commission of Women, also known as the Comisión Interamericana de Mujeres, an organization established in 1928 that continues to this day.

Doris Stevens was born in Omaha, Nebraska, and educated at Oberlin College. Stevens provided organizing support for the Congressional Union, which was founded by Alice Paul and Lucy Burns, the organizers of the 1913 suffrage procession held the day before Woodrow Wilson's inauguration. Stevens was a Silent Sentinel, one of the women who picketed daily in front of the White House to protest for the passage of the Nineteenth Amendment. Stevens was also a leader of the National Woman's Party (NWP), a group that followed the lead of the British suffragettes by engaging in public protests. *Jailed for Freedom* recounts in detail the abuse faced by protestors who were beaten, jailed, and force-fed as they put themselves in harm's way in order to achieve the right to vote. Stevens herself was jailed, as were Paul and Burns. Many of the jailed protestors were kept in the Occoquan Workhouse, a now-closed facility located in Virginia, about 20 miles from the White House. There, the protestors were denied decent food or living conditions and kept in solitary confinement—a heavy price to pay for exercising their right to free speech.

Stevens supported the Equal Rights Amendment (ERA), first introduced in 1923, and also campaigned for international rights for women. In 1928, she was the head of a delegation of women who attended the Sixth International Conference of American States in Havana. While attending the conference, Stevens realized that rather than bringing enlightenment to Latin American women, she and the other U.S. delegates found a great deal of solidarity already in place. Stevens asked for the support of Latin American women in efforts to pass the ERA to help U.S. women fight gender discrimination. She also convinced the representatives from other countries to form the Inter-American Commission of Women, of which she was the leader.

Stevens continued to campaign for the international rights of women and was instrumental in ratifying a treaty to ensure that women would not lose the citizenship of their home country upon marrying internationally, and supported the establishment of feminist studies at colleges and universities. Doris Stevens died March 22, 1963, in New York City.

Leslie Birdwell Shortlidge

Further Reading

Marino, Katherine M. *Feminism for the Americas: The Making of an International Human Rights Movement.* Chapel Hill: University of North Carolina Press, 2019.

Threlkeld, Megan. *Pan-American Women: U.S. Internationalists and Revolutionary Mexico.* Philadelphia: University of Pennsylvania Press, 2014.

Walton, Mary. *A Woman's Crusade: Alice Paul and the Battle for the Ballot.* New York: Palgrave Macmillan 2010.

Stone, Lucy (1818–1893)

Lucy Stone was a prominent nineteenth-century U.S. women's rights advocate, suffragist, and abolitionist, who frequently gave public lectures, wrote articles, and edited publications to support such causes. She was a co-founder of the American Woman Suffrage Association (AWSA) and founder and editor of its paper, the *Woman's Journal*. Stone drew public attention as a feminist when she kept her own name and property after her marriage to prominent reformer Henry Browne Blackwell in 1855.

Born in West Brookfield, Massachusetts, on August 13, 1818, Lucy Stone was one of nine children born to farmers Francis Stone and Hannah

Matthews. Following her father's refusal to assist her or pay for her schooling, she was employed as a teacher and domestic worker. She attended Mount Holyoke Seminary in 1839 and later the Oberlin Collegiate Institute, a coeducational institution in Ohio, from 1843 to 1847. While at Oberlin, Stone was influenced by the advocacy of sisters Angelina and Sarah Grimké and became friends with Antoinette Brown, a supporter of women's rights.

In 1847, Stone graduated from Oberlin and soon began to give public speeches on the equality and rights of women, as well as advocating for the abolition of slavery as a member of the Massachusetts Anti-Slavery Society. Two years later, Stone was introduced to Susan B. Anthony and Elizabeth Cady Stanton, establishing a relationship that defined the women's movement for decades. During that same year, along with Abbey Kelley Foster and Paulina Wright Davis, she organized the the first National Woman's Rights Convention, held at Worcester, Massachusetts in 1850, an event which launched the national American women's rights movement.

In 1853, Stone began a two-year courtship with Henry Browne Blackwell. Their 1855 union, however, garnered national attention and criticism when it was publicly announced that Stone had kept her maiden name and maintained control of her property, arguing that to surrender either would lead her to lose independence and become subjugated. In 1857, Stone gave birth to her only child, Alice Stone Blackwell, who would later become involved in the women's suffrage movement and write a biography of her mother. After the Civil War, in 1866, Stone became a member of the American Equal Rights Association and in 1868 joined the New England Woman Suffrage Association. After black men won the right to vote with the passage of the Fifteenth Amendment in 1870, the alliance between the abolitionist and women's rights movement split between those who, like Stone, maintained that women's organizations must continue their support for the equality and civil rights of all persons, and those who resented the omission of women's voting rights from the Amendment and wanted to focus exclusively on (white) women's suffrage. Others, however, including Anthony and Stanton, withdrew their support for African American rights and formed the National Woman Suffrage Association (NWSA) in 1869. In response, Stone and Blackwell founded a competing organization known as the American Woman Suffrage Association (AWSA). Along with Blackwell and Mary Livermore, Stone founded and wrote for the women's rights publication, the *Woman's Journal*, and was the paper's editor from 1872 until 1882. In 1890, Stone aided in the merging of the AWSA with the NWSA and eventually joined the executive committee of the unified women's rights organization, the National American Woman Suffrage Association (NAWSA).

Along with Anthony and Stanton, Lucy Stone is considered one of the primary figures of the nineteenth-century women's rights movement. Her daughter, Alice Stone Blackwell, wrote a biography, *Lucy Stone: Pioneer of Woman's Rights*, which was published in 1930. Lucy Stone gave her last public women's rights address in May 1893 and passed away just a few months later, on October 18, 1893, in Dorchester, Massachusetts.

Sean Morton

Further Reading

Baker, Jean H. *Sisters: The Lives of America's Suffragists*. New York: Hill and Wang, 2005.

Kerr, Andrea Moore. *Lucy Stone: Speaking Out for Equality*. New Brunswick, NJ: Rutgers University Press, 1992.

McMillen, Sally Gregory. *Lucy Stone: An Unapologetic Life*. New York: Oxford University Press, 2015.

Suffrage Procession of 1913

In March 1913, young suffragists Alice Paul and Lucy Burns, working with the National American Woman Suffrage Association (NAWSA), used the inauguration of President Woodrow Wilson to stage the largest political march that the country had yet seen.

Alice Paul, leader of NAWSA's new Congressional Union, was greatly influenced by a British suffrage counterpart organization, the Women's Social and Political Union (WSPU). Members of the WSPU went on hunger strikes, bombed empty buildings, and heckled public figures in their campaign to secure the vote. When Paul lived in London to study, she participated in WSPU marches and rallies and was arrested and jailed on several occasions. She befriended fellow American Lucy Burns, and together they worked with the NAWSA's Congressional Committee to pursue a federal suffrage amendment. After disagreements with NAWSA leadership over their strategies and access to funding, in early 1913, Paul and Burns formed the Congressional Union and began organizing the parade to coincide with the presidential inauguration in March.

Suffrage Procession of 1913 | 147

The cover of the official program of the woman suffrage procession in Washington, D.C., on March 3, 1913. (Library of Congress)

On Monday, March 3, 1913, the day before the inauguration, between 5,000 and 10,000 supporters of suffrage marched down Pennsylvania Avenue. They were led by two women on horseback. On the black horse was Jane Burleson, a prominent suffragist from Texas. On the white horse was Inez Milholland, a writer and lawyer who devoted her life to many causes in addition to the suffrage movement. There were elaborate floats and vivid tableau of women in flowing white robes, variously representing America as the figure of Columbia, and personifications of virtues such as justice and liberty.

The parade was made up of women from all over the country as well as all over the world. American women marched in groups representing their home states or dressed in the clothing or costumes representing their professions. Writers wore dresses stained with ink, for example. Women who came from countries that had already gained suffrage, such as Sweden and Finland, marched near the head of the parade, and men who supported the effort marched at the rear.

Black women were instructed to march at the rear of the parade upon the insistence of southern delegates. However, reformer Ida B. Wells marched with the delegation from Illinois despite attempts by organizers, including Paul, to minimize the presence and participation of African American women. Wells's brave act was in defiance of the great majority of her Illinois peers, who assumed she had acquiesced to their instructions to relegate herself to an inferior position within the march. However, Wells stepped out of the crowd as the march advanced and joined with two of her white colleagues who supported her position. A photograph of these marchers later appeared in the *Chicago Daily Tribune*.

When President Wilson arrived in Washington on the same day, he was met by very few people at the train station. One of his staffers asked where all of the spectators were and was informed that they were gathered on Pennsylvania Avenue to watch the suffrage procession rather than the arrival of the new president.

The crowd of mostly male spectators on Pennsylvania, estimated at 500,000, taunted the suffragists in the procession, pressing so close that the women had to walk single file in places. Women were grabbed and shoved, tripped, cursed at, and insulted. The police, who were supposed to protect the marchers, joined in the verbal assaults in some cases, or simply watched and laughed as the marchers were tormented. The men who marched alongside the women were similarly abused, as some were called "henpecked," and asked where their skirts were. The Fifteenth Cavalry from Fort Myer, Virginia, were stationed just outside of the city upon the request of a friend of Paul's and had to be called in to supplement the inadequate police presence. During the parade, over 100 people went to the hospital, and the subsequent investigation of the police department's actions during the event resulted in the eventual departure of the police superintendent. Press coverage of the crowd's disruptive behavior contrasted with the orderly and peacefully marching women, and increased sympathy for the cause of suffrage.

The march, though it did not result in immediate suffrage for women, was part of the forward momentum of the movement and made clear to other women as well as men that the time was at hand. Still, in December 1913, NAWSA leadership cut ties with Alice Paul's Congressional Union due to disagreements over what NAWSA saw as the increasingly militant and unpatriotic strategies of marching and protesting a sitting president.

Leslie Birdwell Shortlidge

Further Reading

Dodd, Lynda G. "Parades, Pickets, and Prison: Alice Paul and the Virtues of Unruly Constitutional Citizenship." *Journal of Law and Politics* 24 (2008): 339–443.

Hendricks, Wanda A. "Ida B. Wells-Barnett and the Alpha Suffrage Club of Chicago." In *One Woman, One Vote: Rediscovering the Woman Suffrage Movement*, edited by Marjorie Spruill Wheeler. Troutdale, OR: NewSage Press, 1995.

Lunardini, Christine. *Alice Paul: Equality for Women*. New York: Routledge, 2012.

The Suffragist

The Suffragist was the weekly news journal of the Congressional Union (CU) of the National American Woman Suffrage Association (NAWSA). The paper was founded by CU leader, Alice Paul, and was published from 1913 until the passage of the Nineteenth Amendment in 1920. With the Congressional Union's strategy of emphasis on a federal amendment, Paul saw the need for a national paper to unify communication and promote a sense of national purpose among the many state and local organizations and chapters. Paul envisioned a weekly paper for reporting the most up-to-date progress, as well as a vehicle for near-constant publicity to keep suffrage news in the public eye.

At the time, NAWSA already had its own suffrage paper, the *Woman's Journal*, founded in 1870 by Lucy Stone and Henry Browne Blackwell for the American Woman Suffrage Association (AWSA). By 1913, the *Woman's Journal* had a circulation of 20,000 readers and would have had to approve Paul's request for a potentially competing paper. Paul proposed a smaller "weekly bulletin" that would not compete with, but rather supplement, the *Woman's Journal*, but ultimately *The Suffragist* was a thorough, full-length journal with its own agenda and readership. The *Woman's Journal* covered a broad range of issues, with an emphasis on educating readers about the women's movement, but Paul ran her paper as a single-issue, more political paper, focused on the passage of a federal suffrage amendment. Paul wanted to move away from trying to convince the public of the need for women's voting rights and instead targeted readers who already supported women's suffrage—they did not need to be convinced, rather they just needed to be informed and motivated.

Rheta Childe Dorr, suffragist and advocate for working women, served as the first editor of *The Suffragist* and the first issue was published on November 15, 1913. Within the first year, Dorr split with Paul over issues of editorial control, and Paul took on writing and editing the paper herself, with Lucy Burns as co-editor; other editors were handpicked by Paul to assist in the journal's later years.

The Suffragist was different from other reform and women's rights papers, not only in frequency and content, but in design and visual appeal. As part of Paul's strategy of marketing the suffrage cause as a modern and relevant issue, each issue of the paper included a full-page political cartoon. Beginning in June 1914, these cartoons were drawn by artist and suffragist Nina Evans Allender, who helped create a public image of the American suffragist as young, modern, and capable.

Throughout its publication in the years leading up to ratification of the Nineteenth Amendment, *The Suffragist* provided up-to-date news of Congressional Union activities, reprinted press coverage of the suffrage movement, and was intended to circulate not only among activists but also to put information into the hands of lawmakers, including members of Congress and the president. The overall tone of the paper was positive, highlighting the latest news and constant activity of the suffragists engaged in the forward movement toward a federal amendment.

Tiffany K. Wayne

Further Reading

Adams, Katherine H., and Michael L. Keene. *Alice Paul and the American Suffrage Campaign*. Urbana and Chicago: University of Illinois Press, 2008.

Endres, Kathleen L., and Therese L. Lueck, eds. *Women's Periodicals in the United States: Social and Political Issues*. Westport, CT: Greenwood Press, 1996.

Zahniser, J. D., and Amelia R. Fry. *Alice Paul: Claiming Power*. New York: Oxford University Press, 2014.

Talbert, Mary Burnett (1866–1923)

Suffragist Mary Burnett Talbert was among the most active African American reformers of the turn of the twentieth century. While she is best known for her work with the Niagara Movement (the foundation of the National Association of Colored People (NAACP)) and the National Association of Colored Women (NACW), she also had a prominent role in elevating the voices of women of color in the suffrage movement.

Mary Morris Burnett grew up in Oberlin, Ohio. She graduated from Oberlin College in 1886, at a time when few black women attained higher education. She taught at Bethel University and then served as assistant principal of Union High School in Little Rock, Arkansas, an extremely high-level position for an African American woman at that time. Mary Burnett married William Talbert in 1891 and moved with him to Buffalo, New York. She was a founding member of the Phyllis Wheatley Club, the first in Buffalo to affiliate with the National Association of Colored Women's Clubs (NACWC). She eventually served as president for both organizations. The Phyllis Wheatley Club established a settlement house and helped organize the first chapter of the NACWC in 1910.

Talbert's extensive lecturing and writing career, which took her to 11 nations around the world, focused on educating people on the specific and varied challenges and talents of black Americans. She spoke and wrote at length about the anti-lynching movement and enlisted the support of Jewish and white Christian women. She also worked to raise awareness of the specific skills and attributes of women of color within the suffrage movement as necessary to the overall development of the nation. She lobbied the support of white women's organizations and built alliances that became highly valuable to the fight for suffrage and for the future civil rights movement.

In 1915, she participated in "Votes for Women: A Symposium by Leading Thinkers of Colored Women" in Washington, D.C. In a 1915 article on "Women and Colored Women" in *The Crisis* (the official paper of the NAACP), she wrote, "I firmly believe that enlightened men are now numerous enough everywhere to encourage this just privilege of the ballot for women, ignoring prejudice of all kinds . . . by her peculiar position, the colored woman has gained clear powers of observation and judgement—exactly the sort of powers necessary to the building of an ideal country."

In addition to being one of the first women of color to serve as a nurse in World War I, Talbert worked to preserve places of historic importance to the black community, including Fredrick Douglass's house in Washington, D.C., and historic black churches. As a committed activist, educator, leader, and social reformer, Talbert said that "no Negro woman can afford to be an indifferent spectator of the social, moral, religious, economic, and uplift problems that are agitated around [her]" (quoted in Williams 1993). Mary Burnett Talbert died October 15, 1923, in Buffalo, New York. She was inducted into the National Women's Hall of Fame in 2005.

Larissa Brown Shapiro

Further Reading

Brooks-Bertram, Peggy, and Barbara Seals Nevergold, eds. *Uncrowned Queens, Volume 3: African American Women Community Builders of Western New York*. Albany: SUNY Press, 2005.

Terborg-Penn, Rosalyn. *African American Women in the Struggle for the Vote, 1850–1920*. Bloomington: Indiana University Press, 1998.

Williams, Lillian Serece. "Mary Morris Burnett Talbert." In *Black Women in America: An Historical Encyclopedia*, edited by Darlene Clark Hine, 1137–1139. Brooklyn, NY: Carlson Publications, 1993.

Williams, Lillian Serece. *Strangers in the Land of Paradise: The Creation of an African-American Community, Buffalo, New York, 1900–1940*. Bloomington: Indiana University Press, 1999.

Temperance Movement

The temperance movement aimed to limit or prohibit the consumption of alcohol in the United States. It had an enormous impact on American life in

Temperance Movement | 153

the nineteenth and early twentieth centuries, culminating with the prohibition of alcohol in the Eighteenth Amendment to the U.S. Constitution in 1919. The nationwide ban on the sale, production, and transportation of intoxicating beverages lasted from 1919 to 1933. Women were prime movers in the temperance movement, particularly within the Woman's Christian Temperance Union (WCTU).

The American Temperance Society was formed in 1826, emphasizing religion and morality. Because of the physical abuse and economic dependency that many women and children suffered at the hands of drunken men, the temperance movement and the women's rights movement were often merged through such advocates as Susan B. Anthony, Elizabeth Cady Stanton, and Frances Willard. Although dozens of dry organizations were formed, two of the most significant were the Anti-Saloon League (ASL), founded in 1893, and the WCTU, officially chartered

An 1874 Currier and Ives lithograph, "Women's Holy War: Grand Charge on the Enemy's Works," illustrates the aggressive mission and religious purpose of the crusaders against the sale and consumption of alcoholic beverages. The "Holy War" was the nineteenth-century crusade for temperance and prohibition, whose advocates were predominantly clergymen and women. Here a young woman in armor on a black horse leads a group of similarly garbed women on foot and on horseback. With large battle-axes they shatter barrels of beer, whiskey, gin, rum, and "Wine & Liquors." In the background are two banners: "In the Name of God and Humanity" and "Temperance League." The Woman's Christian Temperance Union, with Frances Willard at the helm, empowered women to act politically and forcefully within their communities to promote both abstinence and women's rights. (Library of Congress)

in 1894. While the slogan of the ASL was "The Church in action against the saloon," the WCTU widened its platform to include social reform and women's suffrage.

Although the WCTU was the first women's mass temperance organization, it also had many male supporters. Between 1901 and 1931, it essentially doubled its membership from more than 150,000 to its peak of almost 400,000. Annie Wittenmyer was the first president of the WCTU, and Frances Willard was elected WCTU president in 1879. As president for almost two decades, Willard expanded the organization's scope to include reform of prostitutes, prison reform, and women's suffrage, all of which she felt were connected to alcohol abuse and to women's need to protect themselves and have a voice in changing laws. This broad agenda was embodied in the WCTU motto during this time: "Do Everything."

Rather than moderation, the early twentieth-century temperance movement espoused the complete legal prohibition of alcohol. The movement attracted an unlikely coalition of conservatives, Progressive reformers, doctors, pastors, labor leaders, politicians, and the Ku Klux Klan (which was adamantly anti-immigrant). The issue of women's suffrage further complicated the temperance debate. Pro-alcohol and business groups vigorously opposed woman suffrage, fearing that women would vote en masse against alcohol, while temperance advocates supported woman suffrage for the same reason. As it turned out, Prohibition was achieved in the United States before women had the right to vote in 1920.

On January 16, 1919, the Eighteenth Amendment to the Constitution was ratified, banning the manufacture, sale, and transportation of "intoxicating liquors" in the United States. It did not outlaw the consumption of alcohol-related products. Congress then passed the Volstead Act to attempt to enforce the confusing, unpopular amendment. The Eighteenth Amendment was repealed in 1933 by ratification of the Twenty-First Amendment, the only instance in American history in which a constitutional amendment was repealed.

Nancy Hendricks and Tiffany K. Wayne

Further Reading

Bordin, Ruth. *Woman and Temperance: The Quest for Power and Liberty, 1873–1900*. Philadelphia, PA: Temple University Press, 1981.

Okrent, Daniel. *Last Call: The Rise and Fall of Prohibition*. New York: Scribner, 2011.

Tyrrell, Ian. *Reforming the World: The Creation of America's Moral Empire*. Princeton, NJ: Princeton University Press, 2010.

Tyrrell, Ian. *Woman's World/Woman's Empire: The Woman's Christian Temperance Union in International Perspective, 1880–1930*. Chapel Hill: University of North Carolina Press, 1991.

Worth, Richard. *Teetotalers and Saloon Smashers: The Temperance Movement and Prohibition*. Berkeley Heights, NJ: Enslow Publishers, 2009.

Terrell, Mary Church (1863–1954)

Educator, speaker, writer, and activist Mary Church Terrell worked to end racial and gender discrimination by promoting black women's rights and suffrage. She became the first black woman on the Washington, D.C., Board of Education and was the founder and first president of the National Association of Colored Women (NACW). Well into her eighties, she continued to push for integration of restaurants, theaters, and public lodgings in Washington, D.C.

Mary Eliza Church was born in 1863 in Memphis, Tennessee, to Robert Church and Louisa Ayers, both former slaves. Robert Church moved from Mississippi to Memphis, where he gained wealth as a real estate investor, allowing Mary and her brother to live a life of relative privilege. At the age of eight, she left home to attend primary school at Antioch College Model School in Yellow Springs, Ohio. The prejudice she experienced at the Model School marked a pivotal point in her awareness of racial prejudice. In 1875, at the age of 12, the family moved to Oberlin, Ohio. Mary graduated from high school in 1879 and enrolled in Oberlin College, where she developed an interest in writing. After completing Oberlin College, she was hired at Wilberforce University, where she taught reading, writing, French, and geology. After two years at Wilberforce, she accepted a position to teach Latin at the top-ranked M Street Colored High School in Washington, D.C. While working at the school, she met Robert Terrell, whom she eventually married.

In 1895, Mary Terrell became the first black woman appointed to the Washington, D.C., Board of Education, a post she held for 11 years. During her tenure as board member, she visited schools and worked to increase funding. She pushed for D.C. schools to celebrate Douglass Day in honor of Frederick Douglass, which may have inspired her friend Carter G. Woodson to create Negro History Week (later to become Black History Month).

Mary Church Terrell, an African American suffragist, was president of the National Association of Colored Women and a charter member of the National Association for the Advancement of Colored People. (Library of Congress)

Terrell traveled the world as an advocate for global peace through the end of racial prejudice. Terrell also embraced women's suffrage and became friends with Susan B. Anthony and participated in the National American Woman Suffrage Association (NAWSA), where she reminded the mostly white membership that women's suffrage should include all American women, not just white women. In 1904, Terrell accepted an invitation to speak at the International Congress of Women in Berlin, Germany. She was the only black woman present at the meeting. Terrell surprised the audience by delivering the address in German, French, and English and received a rousing ovation. During World War I, she picketed the White House with members of the Congressional Union, led by Alice Paul and Lucy Burns, to demand women's suffrage.

Terrell's passion for activism was further fueled by the deaths of her children and childhood friend. She had four children, but only her daughter survived past infancy. Terrell believed that if she had access to better medical facilities her children would have survived. Adding to her grief was the 1892 murder of her childhood friend Tom Moss and two of his acquaintances at the hands of a mob of white vigilantes. As a result, Terrell joined with Ida B. Wells in the anti-lynching movement. In 1892, she and other African American women founded the Colored Woman's League of Washington, D.C., which was organized to help African Americans by creating night classes, a nursery to help working women, two kindergarten classes, and cooking classes. In 1896, she became the first president of the newly organized National Association of Colored Women (NACW). In the years following 1898, Terrell became more vocal as she began a career as a lecturer, speaking to crowds as large as 4,000. In 1909, she became a charter member of the National Association for the Advancement of Colored People (NAACP) and established a branch in Washington, D.C.

At age 86, Terrell escalated her fight against segregation. She became chair of the Coordinating Committee for the Enforcement of the Washington, D.C., Anti-Discrimination Laws (CCEAD). The CCEAD was organized to fight discrimination and enforce the Anti-Discrimination Laws of 1872 and 1873. The laws were labeled as the "lost" laws because they were ignored and not enforced. In 1950, a judge ruled that even though the laws of the 1870s had not been repealed, they were invalid because of nonuse and therefore not recognized as law. The matter went before a U.S. court of appeals, where the 1950 decision was upheld. The decisions of both courts saddened Terrell and the CCEAD, but they continued to emphasize the legal validity of the Anti-Discrimination Laws.

On October 10, 1953, a celebration luncheon was held in honor of the 90-year-old Terrell. The event was held at a Washington, D.C., hotel that had recently begun the process of integration. Over 700 people attended, including family, friends, and political officials, including representatives of the Dwight Eisenhower administration. At the luncheon the Mary Church Terrell Fund was unveiled. The mission of the fund was to raise and use funds to fight discrimination and eradicate all Jim Crow era segregation statutes. The matter was finally heard before the U.S. Supreme Court, which ruled unanimously in the *Brown v. Board of Education* case that segregation was unconstitutional. The ruling was handed down in May 1954, just two months before Terrell's death. She had recorded her own experiences with a 1940 autobiography, *A Colored Woman in a White World*.

Roshunda L. Belton

Further Reading

Cooper, Brittney C. *Beyond Respectability: The Intellectual Thought of Race Women*. Urbana: University of Illinois Press, 2017.

Davis, Elizabeth Lindsay. *Lifting as They Climb*. New York: G. K. Hall, 1996.

Jones, Beverly Washington. *Quest for Equality: The Life and Writings of Mary Eliza Church Terrell, 1863–1954*. New York: Carlson Publishing, 1990.

Quigley, Joan. *Just Another Southern Town: Mary Church Terrell and the Struggle for Racial Justice in the Nation's Capital.* New York: Oxford University Press, 2016.

Truth, Sojourner (ca. 1797–1883)

Sojourner Truth was one of the most prominent African American abolitionists and women's rights activists of the nineteenth century. Her autobiography, *Narrative of Sojourner Truth: A Northern Slave* (published in 1850 by William Lloyd Garrison), provides historians with much of what is known about her early life. She was born into slavery and remained a slave for 30 years until she escaped. In 1827, her religious zeal propelled her to activism. Although illiterate, Truth was a powerful speaker who called not only for the end of slavery but also pointed out the hypocrisy of the racialized gender roles that proscribed different expectations for white and black women.

Born into slavery as Isabella Baumfree around 1797 in a Dutch-speaking area of New York, she was sold several times and renamed each time. Since she was brought up speaking Dutch, her second master beat her because she did not understand English. John Dumont, her master from 1810 to 1826, refused to free her as promised, Truth freed herself by fleeing from bondage with her infant daughter in late 1826, just a few months before slavery was abolished in New York on

Former slave Sojourner Truth, who advocated for abolition and women's rights. (Library of Congress)

July 4, 1827. She went by the name Isabella Van Wagenen, after the family that took her in. When Truth found out that Peter, one of her five children, had been sold to a slaveholder in Alabama, with the help of the Van Wagenens, she successfully sued for his release and return to her.

In 1827 Truth went through a social and spiritual rebirth, as did many women who participated in the Second Great Awakening. A deeply religious woman, she became absorbed in the revivals sweeping the nation. In the early 1830s she worked for Elijah Pierson, an evangelical reformer, and became involved with Robert Mathews and his Kingdom of Matthias. Although the kingdom's experiment with free love and relative equality failed and destroyed the lives of many of the people associated with it, Truth escaped the experience relatively unscathed.

In 1836, after one of her speeches, a local newspaper called Truth a "Black witch." Truth sued the newspaper for libel and won. Having been given many different names throughout her life, on June 1, 1843, Isabella Van Wagenen renamed herself Sojourner Truth because she believed that God had instructed her to travel and speak the truth. With an innate talent for oratory, she often left audiences spellbound. She preached against slavery and for women's rights. She often encountered negative reactions from listeners and sometimes violent crowds, who objected to her because she was both black and a woman. She was not deterred. Her religious zeal was the fuel behind her activities, and she spoke anywhere she had the opportunity to do so, from street corners to grand halls.

By the 1840s, Truth's activist reputation had spread. She met many social reformers and abolitionists including former slave and abolitionist Frederick Douglass, who published his life story in 1845, and radical abolitionist William Lloyd Garrison, who convinced Truth to dictate her life story so that he could publish it. The *Narrative of Sojourner Truth* (1850) increased Truth's fame and netted her a modest income. She delivered her most famous speech, "Ar'n't I a Woman," in 1851 at the Ohio Women's Rights Convention. Using black evangelical rhetorical style, the speech used repetition and questions to forcefully point out that women were as strong and capable as men and thus deserved full civil rights. The speech was transcribed and published in antislavery newspapers, and in 1863 a new version of Truth's speech was published by early women's rights activist, Frances Gage. Although historians have cautioned against the published speech as an accurate representation of Truth's tone and dialect (Gage changed some facts about Truth's life and gave New Yorker Truth a southern dialect, undoubtedly in an effort to have her speak as a "representative" slave), the speech, along with an 1863 article about Truth in the *Atlantic Monthly* by abolitionist author Harriet Beecher Stowe, transformed Truth into an American icon. Perhaps due to her fame and respect among abolitionists, President Abraham Lincoln agreed to meet with Truth during the American Civil War. With Lincoln's blessing, Truth helped recruit and nurse African American soldiers. After the war, she unsuccessfully petitioned President Ulysses S. Grant to give African Americans land in the West as reparations for slavery.

Truth spoke at other women's rights conventions of the 1850s and 1860s and in 1867 addressed the newly formed American Equal Rights Association, a post-abolitionist organization focused on winning the vote for African Americans and for all women. Soon after the Equal Rights Association was founded, the women's movement split over the question of black male suffrage with the ratification of the Fifteenth Amendment in 1870. In 1871, Truth spoke at a meeting of the American Woman Suffrage Association, the Boston-based suffrage organization founded by Lucy Stone in support of the Fifteenth Amendment.

Sojourner Truth retired from public activism in 1880 and died on November 26, 1883. Her sophisticated understanding of the intersection of racial and gender bias, born of her own experiences as a disenfranchised black woman, provided a clear articulation of the foundation of black feminist thought.

Rolando Avila and Tiffany K. Wayne

Further Reading

Grigsby, Darcy Grimaldo. *Enduring Truths: Sojourner's Shadows and Substance*. Chicago: University of Chicago Press, 2015.

Mabee, Carlton. *Sojourner Truth: Slave, Prophet, Legend*. New York: New York University Press, 1993.

Painter, Nell Irvin. *Sojourner Truth: A Life, a Symbol*. New York: Norton, 1996.

Stetson, Erlene, and Linda David. *Glorying in Tribulation: The Lifework of Sojourner Truth*. East Lansing: Michigan State University, 1994.

U

United States v. Susan B. Anthony (1873)

On November 5, 1872, Susan B. Anthony of Rochester, New York, cast her vote for the Republican presidential candidate Ulysses S. Grant, as well as for members of Congress. She was not the only suffragist to attempt to register and vote that election year as a planned protest, but her case led to a trial in federal court. Anthony was the leader of the National Woman Suffrage Association (NWSA), founded in 1869, and her actions were part of the New Departure strategy of the suffrage movement, a plan to test women's right to vote as citizens of the United States as defined by the Fourteenth and Fifteenth Amendments to the Constitution, recently ratified in 1868 and 1870. Her case was heard by a New York federal court in 1873, which ruled that the Constitution did not guarantee a right to vote for all citizens.

Anthony's protest began a few days before the general election when, on November 1, 1872, she planned to attempt to register to vote. Expecting to be turned away, thus initiating her test case, Anthony, along with her three sisters and a friend, somehow convinced the local election officials to allow them to register to vote. Anthony spread the news of their success and other women took advantage of the opportunity to register in Rochester. She and fourteen other women showed up at the polling place four days later. The election officials questioned their eligibility to vote, but as the women proved that they were newly registered voters, they were allowed to cast their ballots in the presidential election. She immediately penned a letter to her suffrage colleague, Elizabeth Cady Stanton, excitedly reporting on her actions and hoping that other women around the country were also trying to vote.

Although the women were not prevented from casting their ballots, a poll worker reported the women and nine days later a warrant was issued for the arrest of Anthony and the fourteen other women. On November 18, 1872, a federal marshal appeared at Anthony's home to arrest her. Two election officials were also arrested and questioned for allowing the women to register and vote. Anthony was charged with illegally voting, since she was "a person of the female sex." She enlisted Henry Selden as her lawyer and, at the hearing, Anthony was found guilty and bail was set for $500; Anthony refused to pay, but she was never held in jail. When the case reached the district court, Selden paid the increased $1,000 bail on her behalf. The case was referred to the circuit court in June 1873. At the end of the trial, Justice Ward Hunt asked if Anthony had anything to say and she delivered an impassioned speech about the violation of her rights as a citizen.

Judge Hunt ruled that voting was a right connected to state citizenship and, therefore, women had no constitutional or federal right to vote as U.S. citizens. While Anthony's case ended with a federal court decision, another case went to the U.S. Supreme Court, but with the same outcome. In October 1872, just a few weeks before Anthony registered in Rochester, suffragist Virginia Minor attempted to register to vote in St. Louis, Missouri. Minor's request was denied and she subsequently filed a lawsuit against election officials. After the Missouri state court ruled against Minor, the case was appealed to the U.S. Supreme Court, which ruled in *Minor v. Happersett* (1875) that the right to vote was not a constitutional right guaranteed to citizens but rather an issue left to the states. The need for a constitutional amendment explicitly granting women the right to vote became apparent, and the proposal that became the Nineteenth Amendment was known as the Anthony Amendment.

Tiffany K. Wayne

Further Reading

Dudden, Faye E. *Fighting Chance: The Struggle over Woman Suffrage and Black Suffrage in Reconstruction America.* New York: Oxford University Press, 2011.

Gordon, Ann D. "The Trial of Susan B. Anthony." *Federal Trials and Great Debates in United States History.* Federal Judicial Center, Federal Judicial History Office, 2005. https://www.fjc.gov/history/famous-federal-trials/us-v-susan-b-anthony-fight-womens-suffrage.

Hull, N. E. H. *The Woman Who Dared to Vote: The Trial of Susan B. Anthony.* Lawrence: University of Kansas Press, 2012.

V

Vernon, Mabel (1883–1975)

Mabel Vernon devoted her life's work to both the women's suffrage and pacifist movements. A key figure in the Congressional Union for Women's Suffrage, Vernon was a leader in a new generation of activists that called for civil disobedience. Indeed, she was one of the first American suffragists to spend time in jail for the cause.

Born into an influential Quaker family in Wilmington, Delaware, in 1883, Vernon attended Swarthmore College, where she befriended fellow suffragist Alice Paul. Upon graduation in 1906, she worked as a high school Latin and German teacher until Paul urged her to attend the 1912 National American Woman Suffrage Association (NAWSA) conference in Philadelphia. Inspired by the conference, Vernon quit teaching and began working as a local suffrage organizer, eventually moving on to the national level as a regional fund-raiser and recruiter for the Congressional Union, a militant suffrage group that campaigned for a constitutional amendment guaranteeing women's suffrage.

On July 4, 1916, Vernon, frustrated with the Democratic Party's recent adoption of a platform that advocated state's rights to choose suffrage yet continued to block national suffrage, interrupted President Woodrow Wilson's Independence Day address by directly asking, "Mr. President, if you sincerely desire to forward the interests of all the people, why do you oppose the national enfranchisement of women?" (quoted in Stevens 1995, 43). When Wilson won reelection in November 1916, Vernon again interrupted yet another presidential address, this time unfurling a suffrage banner that she had hidden inside her coat, an act that won national publicity for the cause.

Mabel Vernon, left, was National Executive Secretary of the National Woman's Party. Vernon is pictured with her friend, Mary Moss Wellborn. (Library of Congress)

Vernon was also responsible for organizing the Silent Sentinels campaign, an 18-month protest that began on January 10, 1917. She recruited volunteers to silently picket in front of the White House, drawing attention to Wilson's lack of support for suffrage. Vernon was charged with obstructing traffic while picketing and spent three days in jail rather than pay the $25 fine.

When the Congressional Union and the National Woman's Party (NWP) merged in March 1917, Vernon served as its secretary. When a NWP committee was able to secure an audience with President Wilson soon after he announced the U.S. entry into World War I, Mabel found her opportunity to speak strongly to the cause, and asked "If the right of those who submit to authority to have a voice in their own government is so sacred a cause to foreign people as to constitute the reason for our entering the international war in its defense, will you not, Mr. President, give immediate aid to the measure before Congress demanding self-government for the women of this country?" (quoted in Stevens 1995, 86). Wilson dismissed the question, and when Vernon repeated the question once again, she was swiftly escorted away by police.

Following the ratification of the Nineteenth Amendment in 1920, Vernon went on to pursue a master's degree in political science at Columbia University. Although she shifted her focus toward peaceful international relations, when she joined the Women's International League for Peace and Freedom (WILPF) and served as the director of the Peoples Mandate Committee for

Inter-American Peace and Cooperation, she continued to support women candidates for Congress and lobbied on behalf of the Equal Rights Amendment (ERA). Mabel Vernon died on September 2, 1975, at the age of 91.

Amy Bizzarri

Further Reading

Lunardini, Christine A. *From Equal Suffrage to Equal Rights: Alice Paul and the National Woman's Party, 1910–1928*. New York: New York University Press, 1986.

Stevens, Doris. *Jailed for Freedom: American Women Win the Vote*. Rev. ed. Troutdale, OR: NewSage Press, 1995.

Washington, Margaret Murray (1865–1925)

Margaret Murray Washington was a groundbreaking educator and activist in her own right, though she is largely remembered in history as the third wife of trailblazing intellectual and educator Booker T. Washington. Often referred to today as the "First Lady of Tuskegee" for her role as the first "Lady Principal" at the Tuskegee Institute, which later became Tuskegee University, Margaret Murray Washington was also the one-time acting president of the National Federation of Afro-American Women (NFAW), which she helped merge with the Colored Women's League (CWL) to form the National Association of Colored Women (NACW), an organization that supported temperance and women's suffrage rights.

Born March 9, 1865, in Macon, Mississippi, Margaret Murray's parents were sharecroppers; her father was an immigrant from Ireland and her African American mother was a washerwoman and possibly a former slave. Upon the death of her father, Margaret was raised by a Quaker couple who encouraged her to become a teacher, one of the few professional career paths available to women in her time. In 1889, she graduated from Fisk University with a degree in education.

A year later, Margaret Murray was named principal of the prestigious Tuskegee Institute, where she met Booker T. Washington, and reluctantly married him two years later.

Murray Washington, a member of Tuskegee's executive board, worked with her husband to expand the institute. She is responsible for writing many of Booker T. Washington's most memorable speeches. Upon her appointment as Dean of Women, she instituted "mother's meetings," a vital Tuskegee program that provided child care, education, and literacy training for women in central Alabama.

Murray Washington is credited with forming the National Association of Colored Women's Clubs (NACWC) in 1896, a group that went on to become the largest black women's organization of the early twentieth century. Armed with the self-help motto "Lifting as We Climb," the NACWC worked to unite black women in campaigns against lynching and Jim Crow laws and in favor of women's suffrage, while also working to improve education and care for both children and the elderly. By 1918, the NACWC boasted 300,000 members nationwide.

Margaret Murray Washington was an educator and advocate for the education of African Americans in the Jim Crow south during the late nineteenth and early twentieth centuries. (Library of Congress)

Different from white suffrage organizations, the NACWC also worked to raise awareness around lynching and segregation and saw the struggle for suffrage as an important goal that needed to be viewed through the lens of race. The organization worked to ensure that black men could cast ballots, too, raising awareness on the impossible literacy tests, poll taxes, and grandfather clauses that made it difficult for black men to exercise the right to vote that they had won in 1870.

Murray Washington was also responsible for editing and publishing the NACWC journal. She was often at odds with the activist Ida B. Wells-Barnett, who considered Murray Washington too conservative in her stance that change should be slow and incremental, with few public demands on whites. The NACWC was badly split between the two women's views, yet still elected Murray Washington president for four years, from 1912 to 1916, though the organization itself did adopt a more direct, confrontational style of protest in the years to follow.

In her later years, Margaret Murray Washington suffered from ill health, yet she refused to retire, working to found and serve as the first president of the short-lived International Council of Women of the Darker Races, an association dedicated to shining a spotlight on the conditions facing women and children of color around the world, in 1921. She continued to serve as the "Lady Principal" of the Tuskegee Institute until her death on June 4, 1925. In 1972, she was inducted in the Alabama Women's Hall of Fame.

Amy Bizzarri

Further Reading

Terborg-Penn, Rosalyn. *African American Women in the Struggle for the Vote, 1850–1920*. Bloomington: Indiana University Press, 1998.

Wheeler, Marjorie Spruill, ed. *Votes for Women!: The Woman Suffrage Movement in Tennessee, the South, and the Nation*. Knoxville: University of Tennessee Press, 1995.

Weil, Gertrude (1879–1971)

Gertrude Weil was a social activist in North Carolina. She was involved in a range of progressive causes and was a leading voice in women's suffrage in the southern states at the time of ratification of the Nineteenth Amendment.

Weil was born in Goldsboro, North Carolina, December 11, 1879, the daughter of Henry and Mina (née Rosenthal) Weil, German-Jewish immigrants. Her family was wealthy and employed domestic staff, both white and black, and helped to form Goldsboro's first synagogue in 1833. At age 16, Weil was sent to the Horace Mann School in New York City. There she met Margaret Stanton Lawrence, daughter of Elizabeth Cady Stanton. Lawrence was her physical education teacher and made a strong political impression on Weil, inspiring her to become a reformer.

Weil attended Smith College, where she lived in the home of Mary Louise Cable, sister to abolitionist novelist George Washington Cable. She met progressive reformers such as Jane Addams. In 1898, Weil's mother Mina established the Goldsboro Women's Club, dedicated to Charlotte Perkins Gilman, focused on community service and increasing women's role in social reform. In the presidential election of 1900, the Smith students created a mock election and this experience influenced Weil's later involvement in the suffrage movement. In 1901, Weil became the first alumna of Smith College from North Carolina.

After college, Weil returned to Goldsboro. She became involved in the Women's Club and the North Carolina Federation of Women's Clubs. In 1911, Weil then joined the National American Woman Suffrage Association (NAWSA). Weil found that the women's clubs and other Smith alumna were nonpolitical. To that end, in 1914, Weil cofounded the Goldsboro Equal Suffrage Association and became its first president, and also the vice president of the Federation. Soon after, she declined a nomination to be president of the Federation of Women's Clubs in order to focus on women's suffrage. When the Nineteenth Amendment was ratified in 1920, Weil was serving as the president of the North Carolina Equal Suffrage League. Despite the hard work of all the local suffragists, the state legislature of North Carolina refused to ratify. Weil went on to establish the North Carolina League of Women Voters to educate women on their voting rights.

Throughout her life, Weil continued to champion women's rights and progressive causes. In addition to women's equality, she worked on labor reform and civil rights, co-creating the Association of Southern Women for the Prevention of Lynching, and served on the North Carolina Commission on Interracial Cooperation and its successor for 25 years. Gertrude Weil died on May 3, 1971, at age 91, in Goldsboro, North Carolina; three days later, her home state of North Carolina finally ratified the Nineteenth Amendment.

Larissa Brown Shapiro

Further Reading

Johnson, Joan Marie. *Southern Women at the Seven Sister Colleges: Feminist Values and Social Activism, 1875–1915.* Athens: University of Georgia Press, 2008.

Klapper, Melissa R. *Ballots, Babies, and Banners of Peace: American Jewish Women's Activism, 1890–1940.* New York: New York University Press, 2013.

Rogoff, Leonard. *Gertrude Weil: Jewish Progressive in the New South.* Chapel Hill: University of North Carolina Press, 2017.

Wells-Barnett, Ida Bell (1862–1931)

Journalist and anti-lynching activist Ida B. Wells was born a slave to James and Elizabeth Wells in Holly Springs, Mississippi, in 1862, the eldest of eight children. Wells and her mother attended a school for freed slaves and learned to read and write. When both of her parents and one of her brothers died in an 1878 yellow fever epidemic, Wells, a teenager, took over the rearing of her siblings. To support the family, she taught school and took classes at Shaw University in Holly Springs to further her education. In 1879, she moved to Memphis, Tennessee.

In 1884, Wells paid for a first-class train ticket but was asked to move to the railroad car designated for blacks. When she refused, she was forcibly dragged off the train. Wells and her black lawyer filed suit against the Chesapeake & Ohio Railroad Company and were awarded $500. Although three years later the Tennessee Supreme Court overturned the ruling, the incident launched her career as a reformer and journalist. Wells began writing a weekly column for the *Living Way*. She also bought an interest in another black-owned newspaper, the *Memphis Free Speech and Headlight*, in 1889, and continued writing about racial issues under the pen name "Iola." After she wrote about the funding gap between white and black schools in the city, Wells was fired from her teaching job and turned to journalism full-time.

In 1892, Thomas Moss, a grocery store owner and Wells's friend, and two other men, Calvin McDowell and William Stewart, were lynched by a white mob; Wells published a stinging article denouncing the lynchings. She also began documenting other lynchings and concluded that their most common cause was that whites were infuriated by black success, thereby debunking the myth that black men were lynched because they raped white women. Her newspaper office was set afire, and a bounty was placed on her life. She left Tennessee for New York and began writing for the *New York Age*. Wells was the first activist to use empirical data to explain the lynching phenomenon. She penned three books on lynching, lectured about the crime overseas, supported a federal anti-lynching law, and worked with Jessie Daniel Ames, a white female anti-lynching activist who founded the Association of Southern Women for the Prevention of Lynching.

Wells also helped found clubs and organizations that supported women's rights and female suffrage. After her marriage in 1895 to Ferdinand L. Barnett, publisher of the *Chicago Conservator* newspaper, she continued her activism and continued to use Wells as her professional name. She promoted voting rights for women as part of a larger strategy of African American political participation, and she also fought for the enfranchisement of black men, who already had the vote, in the face of violence and intimidation. In 1910, Wells founded a women's Republican club in Chicago and in 1913 she founded the Alpha Suffrage Club to encourage black women's participation in local and city-level politics. The Alpha Suffrage Club promoted black male candidates and was largely responsible for the election of the city's first black alderman in 1915.

Wells was affiliated with the National American Woman Suffrage Association (NAWSA), but her commitments to exposing the connection between racial and gender inequality, and to highlighting racism within the women's movement, put her at odds with some white women suffrage leaders. At the 1913 march on Washington, D.C., NAWSA leaders requested that African American women walk in a separate delegation at the 1913 march on Washington, D.C., for fear of alienating white southern supporters of the suffrage cause; Wells refused and joined the other white Illinois state delegates mid-parade.

Wells knew and worked with some of the leading civil rights figures of her time, including Frederick Douglass, Booker T. Washington, W. E. B. Du Bois, and Marcus Garvey. She was also part of the Niagara Movement and helped to found the National Association for the Advancement of Colored People (NAACP). In 1930, she ran unsuccessfully for a seat in the Illinois state senate, but she died in 1931 of kidney disease.

Marilyn K. Howard and Tiffany K. Wayne

Further Reading

Davidson, James West. *"They Say": Ida B. Wells and the Reconstruction of Race.* New York: Oxford University Press, 2008.

DeCosta-Willis, Miriam. *The Memphis Diary of Ida B. Wells: An Intimate Portrait of the Activist as a Young Woman.* Boston, MA: Beacon Press, 1995.

Giddings, Paula J. *Ida: A Sword among Lions. Ida B. Wells and the Campaign against Lynching.* New York: Harper Collins, 2008.

Schecter, Patricia A. *Ida B. Wells-Barnett and American Reform, 1880–1930.* Chapel Hill: University of North Carolina Press, 2001.

Western States and Suffrage

The role of the western United States in procuring voting rights for women in individual states and territories was critical in generating momentum toward the passage of the Nineteenth Amendment. By the end of 1914, almost all of the western states and territories had equal suffrage. The earliest suffrage victories were in the frontier regions. Discussions of suffrage occurred often in the new territories because developing statehood involved basic constitutional questions, as well as a need for full political participation among smaller populations. Pioneer women took on suffrage as a cause, using the open political environment of small territories and motivation toward reform to put forward a broad women's rights agenda.

Until the passage of the Nineteenth Amendment, state elections were held to decide if women should have the right to vote. In 1869, the territory of Wyoming became the first to grant women the right to vote, followed by Utah territory in 1870, and Washington Territory in 1883. Colorado gained suffrage in 1893 and Idaho in 1896. Following a delay in progress when the People's (or Populist) Party lost popularity, other western states achieved suffrage and another wave of suffrage victories moved relatively swiftly with Washington in 1910, California in 1911, Alaska, Arizona, and Oregon in 1912, and Montana and Nevada in 1914.

The early wave of western suffragists began in the late 1860s. These women were radical and openly feminist, many coming from work in abolition, spiritualism, Unitarianism, and women's rights movements in the East. Many wrote, lectured, and published, including Clara Colby (Nebraska and Oregon), Laura DeForce Gordon (California), Caroline Nichols Churchill (Colorado), Emily Pitts-Stevens (California), and Emmeline B. Wells (Utah). These women were often divorced or widows and earning their own livelihoods. Printing and publishing were common vehicles for their political work, despite the biased and challenging environment. The first western women's rights journal was the *Pioneer*, published by Emily Pitts-Stevens in San Francisco from 1869 to 1873. Abigail Scott Duniway published the *New Northwest* from 1871 to 1887, Clara Colby issued the *Women's Tribune* from 1883 to 1909, and Mormon women, substantively Emmeline B. Wells, published *The Women's Exponent* for 42 years, from 1872 to 1914.

Early suffragists in the West viewed their frontier culture as more egalitarian, but this was very much the white women's experience only. Wealthier white women found educational and economic advantages to their frontier lives. Native, Asian, and Mexican-American women often had no interest in supporting the rights of the white women when they experienced disruption and dislocation at their hands. Further, many women did not find the West to be as egalitarian and liberating, instead finding it isolating, lonely, and a hard place to raise families.

By the end of the nineteenth century, the clash between radical and moderate women in the West grew as more mainstream temperance advocates and women's clubs joined the western suffrage movement, both making it less radical, and causing progress to slow. In the early 1900s, however, more and more working-class women were able to join the suffrage movement, giving it greater power and numbers. In the early twentieth century, eastern suffragists and activists, including ones who were also labor organizers or socialists, such as Charlotte Perkins Gilman and Alice Park, visited the West to work among miners in Nevada and other working-class men around the West. The western campaigns generated huge energy for the national movement through the 1910s, leading up to full national suffrage.

Not all western women, however, received the vote with ratification of the Nineteenth Amendment. Many Native American women were not considered U.S. citizens and thus were not able to vote, nor did state suffrage laws enfranchise indigenous women unless they had renounced their connection to their tribe. Suffragists only infrequently reached out to Native communities, however, some indigenous leaders believed that voting rights could be a powerful tool for protecting Native rights. In 1924, Zitkala-Sa, a Lakota writer and activist, lobbied Congress to secure suffrage for indigenous Americans. Partly as a result of her efforts, Congress passed the Indian Citizenship Act, which defined Native Americans as U.S. citizens. Even after passage of this law, however, many western states continued to disenfranchise indigenous people. Zitkala-Sa went on to co-found the National Council of American Indians, which focused on civil rights for Native people.

Despite struggles across race, class, and other differences, women of the West, supported by sister suffragists from the East, created a framework and a momentum that brought strength and longevity to the struggle for the Nineteenth Amendment.

Larissa Brown Shapiro

Further Reading

Duniway, Abigail Scott. *Path Breaking: An Autobiographical History of the Equal Suffrage Movement in Pacific Coast States*. 1914. Reprint, New York: Shocken Books, 1971.

Mead, Rebecca J. *How the Vote Was Won: Woman Suffrage in the Western United States, 1868–1914*. New York: New York University Press, 2004.

Ross-Nazzal, Jennifer M. *Winning the West for Women: The Life of Suffragist Emma Smith DeVoe*. Seattle: University of Washington Press, 2011.

Willard, Frances (1839–1898)

A founder and president of the national Woman's Christian Temperance Union (WCTU), Frances Willard was a dynamic and influential figure in late-nineteenth-century American reform. Frances Elizabeth Caroline Willard was born on September 28, 1839, in Churchville, New York. She grew up on a farm on the Wisconsin frontier. Educated largely at home by her mother, she studied for a year at the Milwaukee Female College, then transferred to Northwestern Female College in Evanston, Illinois, graduating in 1859. She became an educator, teaching at many schools in six different states, and after two years spent traveling in Europe with a wealthy friend, Willard accepted the presidency of the newly formed Evanston College for Ladies in 1870. When the college merged with Northwestern University in 1873, she became dean of women.

Willard had, meanwhile, helped organize the Association for the Advancement of Women. In 1874, not long after leaving Northwestern, she became president of the newly established Chicago Woman's Temperance Union and then secretary of the Illinois temperance association. She joined with other midwestern temperance leaders late in 1874 in forming the national WCTU.

In temperance, Willard found her life's work, but she was soon at odds with conservatives within the movement. Willard believed that a broad program of reform, including women's suffrage and the eight-hour day for workers, was necessary. In 1876, she was sharply criticized for trying to introduce a pro-suffrage resolution at the national WCTU convention. In 1877, Willard resigned as recording secretary, and she spent a year lecturing on suffrage throughout the country. Staying on as head of the WCTU's publications committee, she also promoted suffrage through the WCTU journal. In 1879, the more liberal element of the WCTU gained control of the organization and elected Willard president.

By 1889, the WCTU had 39 separate departments, including ones for suffrage; labor reform; female health and hygiene; and "society purity," focusing on the evils of rape and prostitution. There was also a mothers' department, a department of peace and arbitration, and departments concerned with the welfare of immigrants, African Americans, and prisoners. Each department served an educational purpose, while at the same time working for reform legislation. Willard further sought through her activities to link the WCTU with other women's rights and reform organizations. In

1887, she and four other women were elected by local church conferences as the first female delegates to the Methodist General Conference, but they were denied their seats. The following year, Willard played a leading role at the International Council of Women. She served as first president of the National Council of Women (1888–1890) and as vice president of the Universal Peace Union. In 1889, Willard helped found the General Federation of Women's Clubs.

Willard also worked to make the WCTU a force in national and international politics. With both major political parties refusing to endorse prohibition, she founded the Home Protection Party in 1880. Through this group, she was able to get the Prohibition Party to endorse women's suffrage and unite with it as the Home Protection Prohibition Party. In 1884, this party was probably responsible for the Republicans' losing the presidential election, but the alliance between the WCTU and the Prohibition Party fell apart soon afterward. Willard then sought unsuccessfully to get the Populist Party to endorse a prohibition plank in 1892 and again in 1895. After an 1883 visit to San Francisco's Chinatown, she vowed to fight opium addiction as well and circulated a petition calling on world leaders to act against alcohol and narcotic drugs. These efforts resulted in the founding of the World WCTU, which elected Willard as president in 1891.

Her health already on the decline, Willard died of influenza on February 17, 1898, at the age of 58. Thousands attended her funeral, and tens of thousands more took part in memorial processions throughout the country. Famous for her reform efforts, she was honored by the state of Illinois in 1905, when it placed a statue of her in the U.S. Capitol. By joining together home, family, religion, temperance, suffrage, and social reform under the banner of "home protection," Frances Willard succeeded in bringing an entire generation of conservative, middle-class women into new areas of public endeavor.

William McGuire and Leslie Wheeler

Further Reading

Baker, Jean H. *Sisters: The Lives of America's Suffragists.* New York: Hill and Wang, 2005.

Bordin, Ruth. *Frances Willard: A Biography.* Chapel Hill: University of North Carolina Press, 1986.

Bordin, Ruth. *Women and Temperance: The Quest for Power and Liberty, 1873–1900.* Philadelphia: Temple University Press, 1981.

Winning Plan

Carrie Chapman Catt, president of the National American Woman Suffrage Association (NAWSA), devised "The Winning Plan" as a strategy for women gaining the right to vote by beginning at the local level, building on state-level successes, and coalescing state achievements into a national movement toward a constitutional amendment. In doing so, she ended the movement's argument about whether women's suffrage was better pursued at the state level or by working for a federal amendment and instead combined the two strategies. Within four years "The Winning Plan" ushered in the passage of the Nineteenth Amendment to the U.S. Constitution, extending equal voting rights to women.

Following the winning of suffrage in several western states, and then the deaths of trailblazing suffrage leaders Elizabeth Cady Stanton in 1902 and Susan B. Anthony in 1906, leadership of the NAWSA was divided over goals and strategies for moving forward. Younger feminists such as Alice Paul and Lucy Burns had participated in militant demonstrations in England and joined with Harriot Stanton Blatch to establish the National Woman's Party (NWP). They aimed to pass a constitutional amendment and broke away from NAWSA to pursue more extreme tactics—parades, public protests, and hunger strikes. Catt, who had previously served as NAWSA's president, regained leadership in 1915 and, while recognizing that the status of the suffrage movement varied regionally, forced the issue of a united effort. She condemned acts of violence and protests and laid out a multi-branched plan similar to the strategy successfully used by Frances E. Willard and the Woman's Christian Temperance Union (WCTU) in their campaign to regulate alcoholic beverages.

"The Winning Plan" had a four-pronged strategy: (1) Women in states with full suffrage would press for passage of a constitutional amendment because they had the greatest potential influence over presidential and party politics; (2) States where women did not yet have full suffrage but where a state constitutional amendment was viable would press for a referendum at the state level; (3) Everyone in the movement would contribute what they could toward influencing national political policy toward full suffrage; and (4) Suffrage advocates in southern states would push for the vote on a local level.

Behind closed doors, the NAWSA leaders and state chapter presidents signed a pledge to adhere to Catt's plan. Miriam Folline Leslie, a self-made New York City magazine publisher born of French American descent in New

Orleans, willed her fortune to Catt to fund the plan. Over the next four years, Catt and the leaders of the NAWSA lobbied elected officials in Washington D.C., reestablishing House and Senate support. Catt also cultivated a personal friendship with President Woodrow Wilson and gained his endorsement for a constitutional amendment. By 1917, focused advocacy had secured limited voting rights in Arkansas, electing suffrage activist women to the state's 1918 Democratic State Convention. Concurrently, New York passed a state referendum on woman suffrage, creating momentum in the Northeast.

In February 1920, Catt led the NAWSA in establishing the League of Women Voters. The league aimed to inform women about democracy, candidates, and issues. The effort was effectively a fifth element of "The Winning Plan" that countered suffrage opponents' claim that women were ignorant of voting procedure and political choices. The strategy reached fruition when Tennessee became the 36th state to ratify the Nineteenth Amendment, and on August 26, 1920, women across the United States were officially guaranteed the right to vote.

Keri Dearborn

Further Reading

Baker, Jean, ed. *Votes for Women: The Struggle for Suffrage Revisited*. New York: Oxford University Press, 2002.

Frost-Knappman, Elizabeth, and Kathryn Cullen-Dupont. *Women's Suffrage in America*. New York: Facts on File, 2005.

Van Voris, Jacqueline. *Carrie Chapman Catt: A Public Life*. New York: Feminist Press at CUNY, 1996.

The Woman Citizen

During the final stages of the fight for women's suffrage, *The Woman Citizen* periodical had a critical role in reporting on the movement, reaching suffragists in all states as well as every member of the U.S. Congress. *The Woman Citizen* was founded in 1917, made possible with the financial backing of the Leslie Woman Suffrage Commission, which included a $1.8 million estate value bequest from Mrs. Frank Leslie, a New York magazine publisher, to Carrie Chapman Catt, president of the National American Woman Suffrage Association (NAWSA). Catt purchased the earlier women's rights paper, *Woman's Journal*, from Alice Stone Blackwell and moved it from Boston to

New York. She then merged the *Woman's Journal* with two other suffrage publications—the *Woman Voter* and the *National Suffrage News*—to form the *The Woman Citizen*.

The Woman Citizen reflected the strengths of each of the predecessor publications. The opening editorial explained that "for the first time in suffrage history, the strength of the suffrage propaganda can be concentrated in one journal under the aegis of the 'National.'" Catt entrusted editorial control of the paper to Rose Emmett Young, who worked with both Alice Stone Blackwell, a contributing editor, and Catt to produce a top-quality journal that became the official publication of NAWSA and all its state affiliates.

The Woman Citizen dealt with many political issues of interest to women, with feature stories covering everything from woman suffrage in Mexico, to an approval of the measure by the House of Commons in England; from the militarism and moral depravity of Germany, to women voting in Russia; from Maud Wood Park, chair of the NAWSA congressional committee, reporting on new developments in Congress, to accounts of how a U.S. suffragist was helping immigrants. However, the largest portion of the editorial content covered progress toward achieving the vote for American women within individual states and as a constitutional amendment. Copies of *The Woman Citizen* were also sent free of charge each week to members of Congress.

The paper editorially supported U.S. involvement in World War I, with an emphasis on the heroism and war work of women. Front covers of the paper depicted "Win the War Woman" in such occupations as physician, farmer, conductor, munitions worker, and knitter. However, the editor never missed an opportunity to link the war with the need for suffrage. As one front cover illustrated, a World War I soldier told Uncle Sam about his mother, "She Has Given Me to Democracy; Give Democracy to Her."

With the ratification of the Nineteenth Amendment in 1920, the publication continued on with a different editorial mission. The post-suffrage *Woman Citizen* would focus on political education and "help clarify issues, to help interpret economic and political interplay." The paper provided stories on the dismal economic realities faced by workingwomen and ways to reduce the high cost of living. Beginning in 1921, the League of Women Voters was given four pages in each issue, although *The Woman Citizen* no longer had formal ties with any organization and presented itself as "an independent, non-partisan organ." Rose Young remained editor until April 1921 (replaced by Virginia Roderick) and Carrie Chapman Catt contributed a feature known as "The Carrie Chapman Catt Citizen Course."

In the 1920s, with increasing production costs, *The Woman Citizen* began an aggressive subscription campaign in order to raise $25,000. The appeal was successful, and between 1921 and 1924, circulation increased from 8,000 to 20,000. In 1924, the paper cut back from a weekly issue to twice-monthly and then, in September 1925, to a monthly issue.

The Woman Citizen of the 1920s covered a range of controversial reform issues, including child labor, anti-lynching, and support for Prohibition. Perhaps due to the broader editorial content beyond women's political rights, as well as continued financial problems, in November 1927 the paper returned to the name, *The Woman's Journal*. By 1930, the publication was carrying stories about unemployment and public works programs and in 1931 the magazine ventured into radio, sponsoring 15-minute talks on "Current Events about Women" on NBC.

The May 1931 issue of *The Woman's Journal* had the largest amount of advertising ever, yet, with the Great Depression underway, the June 1931 issue was the paper's last issue.

Kathleen L. Endres

Further Reading

Huxman, Susan Schultz. "*The Woman's Journal*, 1870–1890: The Torchbearer for Suffrage." In *A Voice of Their Own: The Woman Suffrage Press, 1840–1910*, edited by Martha M. Solomon. Tuscaloosa: University of Alabama Press, 1991.

Lemons, J. Stanley. *The Woman Citizen: Social Feminism in the 1920s*. Urbana: University of Illinois Press, 1973.

Webb, Sheila M. "The Woman Citizen: A Study of How New Narratives Adapt to a Changing Social Environment." *American Journalism* 29, no. 2 (Spring 2012): 9–36.

Woman's Christian Temperance Union (WCTU)

The Woman's Christian Temperance Union (WCTU) was a women's social reform movement founded by Frances Willard and Annie Wittenmyer in 1874. Aimed at combating the destructive effects of alcohol abuse on the family and society, the WCTU grew out of the "Woman's Crusade," of 1873–74, when several founding members attended a talk in Cleveland, Ohio, by Dr. Dio Lewis on the "Duty of Christian Women" and were motivated to engage in a series of nonviolent protests. Within three months, alcohol had been removed from 250 communities. In the fall of 1874, a national convention was held in Cleveland, and the WCTU was officially formed with Annie Wittenmyer elected as the first president. The constitution of the WCTU called for the prohibition of the manufacture and sale of alcohol. By 1895, the WCTU had nearly 150,000 members and international chapters or "unions" in 10 countries. By 1883, the WCTU had embraced the cause of women's suffrage and was one of the most influential reform groups of the late nineteenth and early twentieth centuries.

Women were drawn to the temperance movement for several reasons. Personal tragedy, the loss of a family member, familial alcoholism, the cult of domesticity, and religion all played a part. Most temperance workers were members of Protestant denominations that stressed moral uplift, self-discipline, and personal reform. While the realities of spousal alcoholism, violence, and poverty brought some women to the temperance movement, the death of a spouse or child was more of a motivating factor for temperance work than having an alcoholic in the family. There was also a distinctive gender ideology of the temperance movement. For example, women were viewed as pillars of strength, morality, and loving-kindness, especially in the role of mother. Women needed to prevail against the disorder and corruption of men's public worlds. As mothers, women influenced the moral character of her children and as a citizen mother she would influence the moral character of society.

The leadership of the WCTU were experienced organizers and political activists. Annie Wittenmyer, the first president of the WCTU, was well known for her work with military hospitals during the Civil War. She organized a Methodist church, opened a free school for poor children, a retirement home for widows and nurses, and served as president of the Iowa State Sanitary Commission. During her time as president, Wittenmyer oversaw the creation of 1,000 affiliate WCTU chapters. She was also one of the leaders of the Woman's Temperance Crusade of 1873–74.

Frances Willard held the office of president of the WCTU from 1879 until her death in 1898 and was an educator and dean of the female college connected to Northwestern University. She was one of the most famous lecturers of her time. She had been an early supporter of women's suffrage because it was deemed necessary for "Home Protection." Under her leadership the WCTU shifted its focus from temperance exclusively to "Do Everything" reform. The WCTU expanded its reform focus to include health reform, child welfare reform, prison reform, and the reform of working conditions. Lillian Stevens served as president from 1898 to 1914 and was a tireless campaigner for delinquent women and children and served as a Maine delegate to the National Conference on Charities and Corrections.

Soon after the founding of the WCTU, members had to decide whether or not to endorse the franchise for women. Conservatives like Wittenmyer were against suffrage because they feared the churches might object, but when Frances Willard became WCTU president, they organized a committee on the franchise and the WCTU took a stance on women's suffrage. In 1883, the WCTU passed a resolution for equal and unlimited suffrage and they began to work diligently for the women's ballot. More militant suffragists felt betrayed that the WCTU was so willing to settle for limited franchise in state and municipal elections. Despite their common interest in securing the vote for women, the temperance and suffrage movements took separate paths. Suffragists sought state action and temperance reformers had been disappointed by the state's inability to pass anti-liquor laws. Some suffragists saw the temperance movement as a misguided religious movement to end drunkenness and not a political movement aimed at getting women the vote. Despite frequent animosity between the two groups, the WCTU formed the backbone of many suffrage movement campaigns. In many cases, the WCTU was the only organized reform group in small towns, and they became ardent supporters of the suffrage movement as the suffrage cause became more mainstream.

After the passage of the Nineteenth Amendment in 1920, membership in the WCTU declined. In 2015, their membership was approximately 5,000 and that year its quarterly journal, *The Union Signal*, published its last edition.

Kathleen R. Simonton

Further Reading

Bordin, Ruth. *Woman and Temperance: The Quest for Power and Liberty, 1873–1900*. New Brunswick, NJ: Rutgers University Press, 1990.

Giele, Janet Zollinger. *Two Paths to Women's Equality: Temperance, Suffrage, and the Origins of Modern Feminism*. New York: Twayne Publishers, 1995.

Tyrrell, Ian. *Woman's World/Woman's Empire: The Woman's Christian Temperance Union in International Perspective, 1880–1930*. Chapel Hill: University of North Carolina Press, 2010.

The Woman's Era

The Woman's Era was a Boston-based newspaper, the first national newspaper published by and specifically for African American women. Published monthly by suffragist and journalist Josephine St. Pierre Ruffin between 1894 and 1897, *The Woman's Era* both reported on and inspired the black women's club movement at the end of the nineteenth century by publishing on a variety of reform issues including suffrage, anti-lynching, temperance, and the educational and professional pursuits of African Americans. They also profiled prominent or historically important women, especially black women. As reformer Fannie Barrier Williams wrote in the June 1894 issue, "*The Woman's Era* is the face of our colored women turned upward to the star of hope."

Josephine Ruffin, along with her daughter, Florida Ruffin Ridley, was the founder of the Woman's Era Club in Boston in 1892, a black women's club with the motto "Help Make the World Better." Both Ruffin and her daughter were experienced writers and they founded *The Woman's Era* as the club's newspaper. On July 29, 1895, the First Congress of Colored Women met at Ruffin's urging, a call she organized and networked through the pages of *The Woman's Era*. The conference drew 104 delegates from 14 states and Washington, D.C.

When the National Federation of Afro-American Women (precursor to the National Association of Colored Women) was founded out of the Boston conference organized by Ruffin in 1895, *The Woman's Era* moved from serving a local Boston group to becoming the national voice of the expanding black women's club movement. The paper relied upon a network of state-level editors to report on local events and activities and women's club representatives from around the country corresponded with one another through its pages. In 1897, the paper was replaced by the *National Association News*, the official paper of the National Association of Colored Women, published by educator Margaret Murray Washington, wife of civil rights leader Booker T. Washington.

Excluded from both the white women's reform press and black periodicals dominated by male publishers, the publisher and editors of *The Woman's Era* helped connect black women's clubs in other cities and states—and ultimately build a national movement—by making visible the extent of black women's activism and participation in political and intellectual life at the turn of the century.

Tiffany K Wayne

Further Reading

Logan, Shirley Wilson. *We are Coming: The Persuasive Discourse of Nineteenth-Century Black Women*. Carbondale: Southern Illinois University Press, 1999.

McHenry, Elizabeth. *Forgotten Readers: Recovering the Lost History of African American Literary Societies*. Durham, NC: Duke University Press, 2002.

Streitmatter, Rodger. *Raising Her Voice: African-American Women Journalists Who Changed History*. Lexington: University of Kentucky Press, 2015.

Woman's Journal

The *Woman's Journal* was established in Boston in 1870 as the official newspaper of the New England based American Woman Suffrage Association (AWSA) and was one of the most important forums for the early women's rights movement. The *Woman's Journal* merged with another paper, *The Woman Citizen*, in 1917, and continued publication until 1931.

The periodical's founder, Lucy Stone, had already achieved a reputation as a reformer when she began her publishing venture. A longtime proponent of women's rights, she received frequent invitations to lecture on the subject. Although married to Henry Browne Blackwell at the time she formed the *Woman's Journal*, Stone did not change her name and continued to make appearances and to publish under her birth name.

Publication of the *Woman's Journal* seemed a logical extension of Stone's efforts to educate the general public about women's rights and advocate for women's suffrage. Through the crucial work of Stone and Blackwell, assisted by founding editor Mary A. Livermore, it appeared as a weekly newspaper, with the first issue made available on January 8, 1870. This date marked the second anniversary of a rival publication, *The Revolution*, the paper of the National Woman Suffrage Association (NWSA), led by Susan B. Anthony.

Although initially the paper was connected to the AWSA, it did not have a formal link to any single organization and sought to gain readers and represent women's issues across national constituencies. The publication gave the growing women's rights movement a voice with which to contest social injustices and readers encountered writings by an impressive array of the nation's thinkers and reformers, including Louisa May Alcott, Antoinette Brown Blackwell, Caroline Bartlett Crane, William Lloyd Garrison, Florence Kelley, and Julia Ward Howe (editor from 1872 to 1879). In the early 1880s, Lucy

Stone's daughter, Alice Stone Blackwell, became an editor of the *Woman's Journal*. Following her mother's death in 1893 and her father's death in 1909, Alice Stone Blackwell assumed the role of editor in chief of the publication, in which capacity she continued until 1917.

In the late nineteenth century, periodicals by and for women experienced rapid growth in terms of both number and circulation. When it first appeared, the *Woman's Journal* folded together two prior publications, *The Agitator* and the *Woman's Advocate*. It later incorporated *Progress,* the central publication of the National American Woman Suffrage Association (NAWSA). By 1912, the *Woman's Journal* was retitled the *Woman's Journal and Suffrage News*. Advertising for the publication characterized it as a venue "devoted to the interests of women—to their educational, industrial, legal and political Equality, and especially to their right of Suffrage."

In 1917, Carrie Chapman Catt acquired the journal, joining it with the *Woman Voter* and *National Suffrage News* under the name *The Woman Citizen*. With the 1920 ratification of the U.S. Constitution's Nineteenth Amendment, *The Woman Citizen* became a monthly rather than weekly publication. Having realized its original intent in achieving American women's right to vote, the publication had fulfilled the goal its founders held paramount. In 1927, the publication was once again issued as the *Woman's Journal,* appearing with that title until publication was suspended in June 1931.

For 61 years, the *Woman's Journal* championed women's equality and, in particular, fought for women's suffrage. In the process, it empowered female and male readers alike with information, purpose, and a sense of women's capacity as agents of social change.

Linda S. Watts

Further Reading

Carver, Mary M. "Everyday Women Find Their Voice in the Public Sphere." *Journalism History* 34, no. 1 (Spring 2008): 15–22.

Easton-Flake, Amy. "Fiction and Poetry in the Revolution and the *Woman's Journal*: Clarifying History." *American Journalism* 36, no. 1 (2019): 32–50.

Endres, Kathleen L., and Therese L. Lueck, eds. *Women's Periodicals in the United States: Social and Political Issues*. Westport, CT: Greenwood Press, 1996.

Richardson, Todd H. "Transcendentalist Periodicals." In *The Oxford Handbook of Transcendentalism*, edited by Joel Myerson, Sandra Harbert Petrulionis, and Laura Dassow Walls, 361–372. New York: Oxford University Press, 2010.

Women's Political Union

The Women's Political Union (WPU) was an organization that actively promoted the cause of women's suffrage in the first two decades of the twentieth century. Modeled on the British suffrage organization, the Women's Social and Political Union, the American WPU both complemented and competed with the ongoing efforts of the National American Woman Suffrage Association (NAWSA). Once women's suffrage advocates had all achieved their goal of securing the enactment of the Nineteenth Amendment, the WPU merged with other groups to form the National Woman's Party (NWP).

Central to the efforts of the WPU was its founder Harriot Stanton Blatch. Blatch was born in Seneca Falls, New York, in 1856, the sixth of seven children born to feminist icon Elizabeth Cady Stanton. A graduate of Vassar College, she lived in England for over 20 years, where she was active in the suffrage movement. Upon returning to the United States in 1902 following the death of her mother, she found the American suffrage movement in decline. Her experience in England led her to believe that the American effort needed to take a more radical approach and engage a broader number of women. Convinced that the working class needed the vote to advance their interests, she sought to involve working women more directly in the suffrage effort.

Blatch created the Equality League of Self-Supporting Women in 1907, the group that was renamed the Women's Political Union in late 1910, to bridge the chasm between upper-class women reformers and the working class. Blatch and her allies adopted many of the tactics and strategies of the British activists, undertaking for the first-time marches, parades, and demonstrations. Using a combination of publicity, education, and civil action, they quickly established a public presence. They organized mass meetings and, well aware of the politics involved in their efforts, in the election years 1908, 1910, and 1912, the group organized suffrage parades. The 1912 effort in New York City had 20,000 marchers and was witnessed by 80,000 spectators.

In addition, the WPU was active in the 1915 New York suffrage effort and Blatch brought working women to testify before the New York legislature as it considered a women's suffrage amendment for the state. True to form, the group employed theater stars such as Ethel Barrymore in public presentations aimed at developing public support. While the 1915 effort fell short, the WPU played an equally active and important part in the successful follow-up effort of 1917.

The WPU was known for its ability to create media attention for women's suffrage. For example, the organization took advantage of the New York law that allowed anyone to be a poll watcher. Stationing disenfranchised women at all-male polling places, the WPU highlighted the disenfranchisement of women. Blatch also encouraged her friend Emmeline Pankhurst, an immensely well-known British suffragette, to come to the United States to speak on behalf of women's suffrage. The organization also published a biweekly newspaper, *Women's Political World*, and in 1913 collaborated on a film, *What 80 Million Women Want*, a drama in which real and fictional suffragists plotted to expose a corrupt politician. Not only did the WPU directly impact the public debate over suffrage, but it also forced the more established organizations to reassess their efforts, in the end raising the level of activity and energy of the entire suffrage movement.

In 1916, the WPU merged with Alice Paul's Congressional Union, and eventually they evolved into the National Woman's Party. While the WPU was actively involved in the 1917 New York campaign, in joining with Paul, WPU veterans abandoned their previous state-based approach and instead focused on securing passage of the Nineteenth Amendment, an accomplishment that was achieved in 1920 in time for women to cast their vote in the presidential election.

William H. Pruden III

Further Reading

DuBois, Ellen Carol. *Harriot Stanton Blatch and the Winning of Women's Suffrage*. New Haven, CT: Yale University Press, 1999.

Rosen, Andrew. *Rise up, Women! The Militant Campaign of the Women's Social and Political Union, 1903–1914*. New York: Routledge, 2014.

Women's Trade Union League (WTUL)

The Women's Trade Union League (WTUL) was founded in 1903 to push for protections for women in the workforce. The organization advocated for an eight-hour day, membership in trade unions, equal pay for equal work, a living wage, and full citizenship (including voting rights) for all women.

The WTUL was founded by working-, middle-, and upper-class women, which marked a unique development in the history of similar organizations,

The National Women's Trade Union League Convention in St. Louis, Missouri, 1913. (Library of Congress)

which were often segregated by race and class. Prior to the WTUL, women who did not have to work outside the home regarded themselves as reformers with a duty to provide moral leadership and charity to the lower and working classes. But in the WTUL, while middle-class reformers made up the bulk of leadership in the early years, the goal was to grow working-class women into leaders who would determine the direction and goals of the organization. In 1921, Maud Swartz, a typographer, was elected president of the WTUL.

The WTUL was also established in spite of—or perhaps because of—the indifference of the American Federation of Labor (AFL) to wage-earning women, and it was at an AFL convention that organizers began to construct their platform in 1903. The AFL never supported the WTUL fully, mostly ignoring its efforts. The history of integrating women into the labor movement was never easy in the United States, with objections from both men and women as early as 1836, when a Committee of Female Labor argued against the employment of women on moral grounds. Eventually, even AFL president Samuel Gompers, who was once angry at the WTUL for meeting apart from the AFL, realized that women did and would continue to work out of the necessity to support themselves and their families.

Among the most prominent American organizers of the WTUL were Jane Addams, Lillian Wald, and Mary McDowell. Addams was prominent in the development of settlement houses in inner cities, Wald was the founder of community nursing, and McDowell established settlement houses in Chicago and worked for the rights of laborers, immigrants, and minorities. Harriot Stanton Blatch was one of the socioeconomic elites present at the birth of the WTUL who was committed to the working-class leadership of the organization, as well as being the daughter of Elizabeth Cady Stanton, one of the founders of the American suffrage movement and organizer of the Seneca Falls Convention of 1848. Blatch disagreed publicly with her mother on the role of non-educated women in the suffrage movement: Stanton wanted the suffrage movement to include an educational restriction, and Blatch did not. Blatch also understood that women who were doctors, lawyers, educators, and journalists were dependent on domestic help. Thus, professional women were freed to pursue their potential due to the labor of working women. In 1907, Blatch established the Equality League of Self-Supporting Women, which helped bridge the divide between working women and middle-class women by highlighting the concerns as well as the tactics of trade union women.

Issues of workplace safety and the employment of children were priorities of the WTUL. After the infamous Triangle Shirtwaist Factory fire in 1911 that killed 146 people, mostly women and girls, the WTUL was at the forefront of the investigations. The president of the WTUL, Margaret Dreier Robins, participated in the subsequent investigation of the tragedy. Under the leadership of Robins, the WTUL supported striking workers, organized picket lines, and created a Training School, not to teach women a trade, but to train them to be leaders and organizers. This initiative to encourage working-class women to become their own leaders, and to promote grass-roots organization and power, was part of the general trend of suffrage and feminism in the United States as well as Great Britain. Organizer Rose Schneiderman, speaking after the Triangle Shirtwaist Factory fire, exhorted more privileged women to remember that the working classes wanted and deserved quality of life as well.

Leslie Birdwell Shortlidge

Further Reading

Diemand, Kelsey. "Labor and Feminism: Margaret Dreier Robins and the Women's Trade Union League." Library of Congress Blog. https://blogs.loc.gov/inside_adams/2019/04/unions-feminism-and-margaret-dreier-robins/.

DuBois, Ellen Carol. *Harriot Stanton Blatch and the Winning of Woman Suffrage*. New Haven, CT: Yale University Press, 1997.

Orleck, Annelise. *Common Sense and a Little Fire: Women and Working-Class Politics in the United States, 1900–1965*. Chapel Hill: University of North Carolina Press, 1995.

Woodhull, Victoria (1838–1927)

Victoria Claflin Woodhull Blood Martin was the first female candidate for president of the United States. She was a charismatic speaker, publisher, and stockbroker as well as an advocate for women's suffrage, reproductive freedom, women's rights, labor reforms, civil rights, and the abolition of slavery.

Victoria California Claflin was born on September 23, 1838, in the central Ohio rural community of Homer. She was the seventh of 10 children born to the impoverished Roxanna and Buck Claflin. Her mother was an illiterate follower of mysticism, and her father was described as a con man and snake oil salesman. Victoria and Tennessee "Tennie" Celeste Claflin, her youngest sister, became especially close. Victoria only had three years of formal education but felt that she was the medium for spirit voices, and her father put both girls to work as faith healers to support the family. When her father was accused of arson, the township raised funds to send the family elsewhere.

An engraving from *Frank Leslie's Illustrated Newspaper* depicts Victoria Woodhull reading her argument supporting women's suffrage to the Judiciary Committee of the House of Representatives on January 11, 1871. (Library of Congress)

In 1853, Victoria, who had just turned 15, married a man about twice her age, Canning (or Channing) Woodhull, who practiced as a doctor in Ohio. She bore two children, Byron, who had severe brain damage, and Zulu (later Zula Maud), and had to support the family. Victoria divorced Woodhull in 1864, and then met Colonel James H. Blood, who left his wife for Woodhull. They are alleged to have married in 1866, divorced, and remarried on subsequent occasions. The couple took in Tennessee Claflin, who had been indicted for manslaughter in 1864 following the death of a patient in her father's clinic. Woodhull, Blood, and Tennie moved to New York in 1868, taking with them a large extended family including Woodhull's parents.

In New York, the sisters met 73-year-old Cornelius Vanderbilt, one of the richest men in America, who was charmed by Tennie and fascinated by the sisters' apparent gift of clairvoyance. He backed the sisters in a brokerage firm, and in 1870 they became the first women stockbrokers on Wall Street. In 1870, Woodhull and her sister used some of the profits from their brokerage firm to start a newspaper, *Woodhull & Claflin's Weekly*, which printed the first English version of Karl Marx's *Communist Manifesto*.

The newspaper promoted reform issues, women's rights, female suffrage, legalized prostitution, sex education, less restrictive women's clothing, spiritualism, and free love, or the right to marry, divorce, and make one's own reproductive decisions. Woodhull had some allies in the women's suffrage movement despite her controversial beliefs. She was invited to join the National Woman Suffrage Association (NWSA) by Susan B. Anthony, but they soon became rivals for leadership. In 1872, Woodhull was nominated for president of the United States by the Equal Rights Party. Although he never acknowledged the nomination, former slave and abolitionist leader Frederick Douglass was nominated as her vice president. Some questioned the legality of her candidacy since she was younger than 35, the minimum age for the office, though this was a minor issue. In 1872, Woodhull became the center of a national scandal when she published an accusation of adultery against Henry Ward Beecher, one of the country's most renowned clergymen and one of her most severe critics. Woodhull and Claflin were jailed several days before the election for obscenity in publicizing the affair, but later acquitted. However, her arrest interfered with her campaigning and, in the 1872 election, Woodhull received no electoral votes and only a minuscule portion of the popular vote.

In 1876, Woodhull and Blood were officially divorced. Within a year, she left for England and the start of a new life. She married banker John

Biddulph Martin in 1883. In London, Woodhull founded the *Humanitarian*, a magazine she edited with her daughter, Zula. Victoria Woodhull Martin was noted as the author of several works including *Arguments for Woman's Electoral Rights*, *Aristocracy of Blood*, *The Origin, Tendencies and Principles of Government*, *Pharmacy of the Soul*, and *Social Freedom*. After her husband's death, she retired to the country in Worcestershire, England.

Victoria Woodhull died in her sleep on June 9, 1927. Her obituary in the *New York Times* was headed "Victoria Martin, Suffragist, Dies." She was cremated, with her ashes scattered at sea in England. There is a memorial to her at Tewkesbury Abbey in Gloucestershire, England.

Nancy Hendricks

Further Reading

Frisken, Amanda. *Victoria Woodhull's Sexual Revolution: Political Theater and the Popular Press in Nineteenth-Century America*. Philadelphia, PA: University of Pennsylvania Press, 2004.

Gabriel, Mary. *Notorious Victoria: The Life of Victoria Woodhull*. New York: Algonquin Books, 1998.

Goldsmith, Barbara. *Other Powers: The Age of Suffrage, Spiritualism, and the Scandalous Victoria Woodhull*. New York: Harper Perennial, 1998.

Primary Source Documents

Elizabeth Cady Stanton, Declaration of Sentiments (1848)

Elizabeth Cady Stanton drew directly from the Declaration of Independence to draft a women's manifesto at the Women's Rights Convention in Seneca Falls, New York, in July 1848. By comparing the two documents, and replacing the charges of American colonists against England's King George III to women's grievances against men, she opposed a double standard that denied female humanity and reduced women to partial citizenship. The document was also the first time that the vote for women—"the inalienable right to the elective franchise"—was named as a demand by the American women's movement.

When, in the course of human events, it becomes necessary for one portion of the family of man to assume among the people of the earth a position different from that which they have hitherto occupied, but one to which the laws of nature and of nature's God entitle them, a decent respect to the opinions of mankind requires that they should declare the causes that impel them to such a course.

We hold these truths to be self-evident: that all men and women are created equal; that they are endowed by their Creator with certain inalienable rights; that among these are life, liberty, and the pursuit of happiness; that to secure these rights governments are instituted, deriving their just powers from the consent of the governed. Whenever any form of government becomes destructive of these ends, it is the right of those who suffer from it to refuse allegiance to it, and to insist upon the institution of a new government, laying its foundation on such principles, and organizing its powers in such form, as to them shall seem most likely to effect their safety and happiness.

Prudence, indeed, will dictate that governments long established should not be changed for light and transient causes; and, accordingly, all experience has shown that mankind are more disposed to suffer, while evils are sufferable, than to right themselves by abolishing the forms to which they were accustomed. But when a long train of abuses and usurpations, pursuing invariably the same object, evinces a design to reduce them under absolute despotism, it is their duty to throw off such government and to provide new guards for their future security. Such has been the patient sufferance of the women under this government, and such is now the necessity which constrains them to demand the equal station to which they are entitled.

The history of mankind is a history of repeated injuries and usurpations on the part of man toward woman, having in direct object the establishment of an absolute tyranny over her. To prove this, let facts be submitted to a candid world.

He has never permitted her to exercise her inalienable right to the elective franchise. He has compelled her to submit to law in the formation of which she had no voice.

He has withheld from her rights which are given to the most ignorant and degraded men, both natives and foreigners. Having deprived her of this first right as a citizen, the elective franchise, thereby leaving her without representation in the halls of legislation, he has oppressed her on all sides.

He has made her, if married, in the eye of the law, civilly dead.

He has taken from her all right in property, even to the wages she earns.

He has made her morally, an irresponsible being, as she can commit many crimes with impunity, provided they be done in the presence of her husband.

In the covenant of marriage, she is compelled to promise obedience to her husband, he becoming, to all intents and purposes, her master—the law giving him power to deprive her of her liberty and to administer chastisement.

He has so framed the laws of divorce, as to what shall be the proper causes and, in case of separation, to whom the guardianship of the children shall be given, as to be wholly regardless of the happiness of the women—the law, in all cases, going upon a false supposition of the supremacy of man and giving all power into his hands.

After depriving her of all rights as a married woman, if single and the owner of property, he has taxed her to support a government which recognizes her only when her property can be made profitable to it.

He has monopolized nearly all the profitable employments, and from those she is permitted to follow, she receives but a scanty remuneration. He closes against her all the avenues to wealth and distinction which he considers most honorable to himself. As a teacher of theology, medicine, or law, she is not known.

He has denied her the facilities for obtaining a thorough education, all colleges being closed against her.

He allows her in church, as well as state, but a subordinate position, claiming apostolic authority for her exclusion from the ministry, and, with some exceptions, from any public participation in the affairs of the church.

He has created a false public sentiment by giving to the world a different code of morals for men and women, by which moral delinquencies which exclude women from society are not only tolerated but deemed of little account in man.

He has usurped the prerogative of Jehovah himself, claiming it as his right to assign for her a sphere of action, when that belongs to her conscience and to her God.

He has endeavored, in every way that he could, to destroy her confidence in her own powers, to lessen her self-respect, and to make her willing to lead a dependent and abject life. Now, in view of this entire disfranchisement of one-half the people of this country, their social and religious degradation, in view of the unjust laws above mentioned, and because women do feel themselves aggrieved, oppressed, and fraudulently deprived of their most sacred rights, we insist that they have immediate admission to all the rights and privileges which belong to them as citizens of the United States.

In entering upon the great work before us, we anticipate no small amount of misconception, misrepresentation, and ridicule; but we shall use every instrumentality within our power to effect our object. We shall employ agents, circulate tracts, petition the state and national legislatures, and endeavor to enlist the pulpit and the press in our behalf. We hope this Convention will be followed by a series of conventions embracing every part of the country.

Resolutions

Whereas, the great precept of nature is conceded to be that "man shall pursue his own true and substantial happiness." Blackstone in his Commentaries remarks that this law of nature, being coeval with mankind and dictated by God himself, is, of course, superior in obligation to any other. It is binding over all the globe, in all countries and at all times; no human laws are of any validity if contrary to this, and such of them as are valid derive all their force, and all their validity, and all their authority, mediately and immediately, from this original; Therefore,

Resolved, that such laws as conflict, in any way, with the true and substantial happiness of woman, are contrary to the great precept of nature and of no validity, for this is "superior in obligation to any other."

Resolved, that all laws which prevent woman from occupying such a station in society as her conscience shall dictate, or which place her in a position inferior to that of man, are contrary to the great precept of nature and therefore of no force or authority.

Resolved, that woman is man's equal, was intended to be so by the Creator, and the highest good of the race demands that she should be recognized as such.

Resolved, that the women of this country ought to be enlightened in regard to the laws under which they live, that they may no longer publish their degradation by declaring themselves satisfied with their present position, nor their ignorance, by asserting that they have all the rights they want.

Resolved, that inasmuch as man, while claiming for himself intellectual superiority, does accord to woman moral superiority, it is preeminently his duty to encourage her to speak and teach, as she has an opportunity, in all religious assemblies.

Resolved, that the same amount of virtue, delicacy, and refinement of behavior that is required of woman in the social state also be required of man, and the same transgressions should be visited with equal severity on both man and woman.

Resolved, that the objection of indelicacy and impropriety, which is so often brought against woman when she addresses a public audience, comes with a very ill grace from those who encourage, by their attendance, her appearance on the stage, in the concert, or in feats of the circus.

Resolved, that woman has too long rested satisfied in the circumscribed limits which corrupt customs and a perverted application of the Scriptures have marked out for her, and that it is time she should move in the enlarged sphere which her great Creator has assigned her.

Resolved, that it is the duty of the women of this country to secure to themselves their sacred right to the elective franchise.

Resolved, that the equality of human rights results necessarily from the fact of the identity of the race in capabilities and responsibilities.

Resolved, that the speedy success of our cause depends upon the zealous and untiring efforts of both men and women for the overthrow of the monopoly of the pulpit, and for the securing to woman an equal participation with men in the various trades, professions, and commerce.

Resolved, therefore, that, being invested by the Creator with the same capabilities and same consciousness of responsibility for their exercise, it is demonstrably the right and duty of woman, equally with man, to promote every righteous cause by every righteous means; and especially in regard to the great subjects of morals and religion, it is self-evidently her right to participate with her brother in teaching them, both in private and in public, by writing and by speaking, by any instrumentalities proper to be used, and in any assemblies proper to be held; and this being a self-evident truth growing out of the divinely implanted principles of human nature, any custom or authority adverse to it, whether modern or wearing the hoary sanction of antiquity, is to be regarded as a self-evident falsehood, and at war with mankind.

Source: Stanton, Elizabeth Cady, Susan Brownell Anthony, and Matilda Joslyn Gage, eds. *History of Woman Suffrage: 1861–1876.* Vol. II. New York: Fowler & Wells, 1882, 70–73.

Lucretia Coffin Mott, Discourse on Woman (1849)

A self-educated Quaker theologian and revered abolitionist, Lucretia Coffin Mott of Nantucket, Massachusetts, displayed skill at logic in refuting Lyceum lecturer Richard Henry Dana Sr. of Boston. In a speaking tour to major cities, he had delivered "An Address on Woman," which demeaned women as physically, mentally, and morally inferior to men. After hearing his lecture several days earlier, Mott cited the faulty claims by laypersons and the clergy that males were innately superior to women. Her sermon charged men with mocking females and ignoring biblical affirmation of women's ability to prophesy. She anticipated social progress as a result of full citizenship for women, which she claimed that women had deserved from the beginning of creation.

There is nothing of greater importance to the wellbeing of society at large—of man as well as woman—than the true and proper position of woman. Much has been said, from time to time, upon this subject. It has been a theme for ridicule, for satire and sarcasm. We might look for this from the ignorant and vulgar; but from the intelligent and refined we have a right to expect that such weapons shall not be resorted to—that gross comparisons and vulgar epithets shall not be applied, so as to place woman, in a point of view, ridiculous to say the least.

This subject has claimed my earnest interest for many years. I have long wished to see woman occupying a more elevated position than that which custom for ages has allotted to her. It was with great regret, therefore, that I listened a few days ago to a lecture upon this subject, which, though replete with intellectual beauty, and containing much that was true and excellent, was yet fraught with sentiments calculated to retard the progress of woman to the high elevation destined by her Creator. I regretted the more that these sentiments should be presented with such intellectual vigor and beauty, because they would be likely to ensnare the young.

The minds of young people generally, are open to the reception of more exalted views upon this subject. The kind of homage that has been paid to woman, the flattering appeals which have too long satisfied her—appeals to her mere fancy and imagination, are giving place to a more extended recognition of her rights, her important duties and responsibilities in life. Woman is claiming for herself stronger and more profitable food. Various are the indications leading to this conclusion. The increasing attention to female education, the improvement in the literature of the age, especially in what is called the "Ladies' Department," in the periodicals of the day, are among the proofs of a higher estimate of woman in society at large. Therefore we may hope that the intellectual and intelligent are being prepared for the discussion of this question, in a manner which shall tend to ennoble woman and dignify man. . . .

This age is notable for its works of mercy and benevolence—for the efforts that are made to reform the inebriate and the degraded, to relieve the oppressed and the suffering. Women as well as men are interested in these works of justice and mercy. They are efficient co-workers, their talents are called into profitable exercise, their labors are effective in each department of reform. The blessing to the merciful, to the peacemaker is equal to man and to woman. It is greatly to be deplored, now that she is increasingly qualified for usefulness, that any view should be presented, calculated to retard her labors of love.

Why should not woman seek to be a reformer? If she is to shrink from being such an iconoclast as shall "break the image of man's lower worship," as so long held up to view; if she is to fear to exercise her reason, and her noblest powers, lest she should be thought to "attempt to act the man," and not "acknowledge his supremacy;" if she is to be satisfied with the narrow sphere assigned her by man, nor aspire to a higher, lest she should transcend the bounds of female delicacy; truly it is a mournful prospect for woman. We would admit all the difference, that our great and beneficent Creator has made, in the relation of man and woman, nor would we seek to disturb this relation; but we deny that the present position of woman, is her true sphere of usefulness: nor will she attain to this sphere, until the disabilities and disadvantages, religious, civil, and social, which impede her progress, are removed out of her way. These restrictions have enervated her mind and paralyzed her powers. While man assumes that the present is the original state designed for woman, that the existing "differences are not arbitrary nor the result of accident," but grounded in nature, she will not make the necessary effort to obtain her just rights, lest it should subject her to the kind of scorn and contemptuous manner in which she has been spoken of. . . .

Woman has never wakened to her highest destinies and holiest hopes. The time is coming when educated females will not be satisfied with the present objects of their low ambition. When a woman now leaves the immediate business of her own education, how often, how generally do we find her, sinking down into almost useless inactivity. To enjoy the social circle, to accomplish a little sewing, a little reading, a little domestic duty, to while away her hours in self-indulgence, or to enjoy the pleasures of domestic life—these are the highest objects at which many a woman of elevated mind, and accomplished education aims. . . .

A new generation of women is now upon the stage, improving the increased opportunities furnished for the acquirement of knowledge. Public education is coming to be regarded the right of the children of a republic. The hill of science is not so difficult of ascent as formerly represented by poets and painters; but by fact and demonstration smoothed down, so as to be accessible to the assumed weak capacity of woman. She is rising in the scale of being through this, as well as other means, and finding heightened pleasure and profit on the right hand and on the left. The study of physiology, now introduced into our common schools, is engaging her attention, impressing the necessity of the observance of the laws of health. The intellectual Lyceum and instructive lecture room are becoming, to many, more attractive than the theatre and the ballroom. The sickly and sentimental novel and pernicious romance are giving place to works calculated to call forth the benevolent affections and higher nature. . . .

The question is often asked, "What does woman want, more than she enjoys? What is she seeking to obtain? Of what rights is she deprived? What privileges are withheld from her?" I answer, she asks nothing as favor, but as right, she wants to be acknowledged a moral, responsible being. She is seeking not to be governed by laws in the making of which she has no voice. She is deprived of almost every right in civil society and is a cypher in the nation except in the right of presenting a petition. In religious society her disabilities, as already pointed out, have greatly retarded her progress. Her exclusion from the pulpit or ministry—her duties marked out for her by her equal brother man, subject to creeds, rules, and disciplines made for her by him—this is unworthy her true dignity. In marriage, there is assumed superiority, on the part of the husband, and admitted inferiority, with a promise of obedience, on the part of the wife. This subject calls loudly for examination, in order that the wrong may be redressed. . . .

May these statements lead you to reflect upon this subject, that you may know what woman's condition is in society—what her restrictions are, and seek to remove them. In how many cases in our country, the husband and wife begin life together, and by equal industry and united effort accumulate to themselves a comfortable home. In the event of the death of the wife, the household remains undisturbed, his farm or his workshop is not broken up, or in any way molested. But when the husband dies, he either gives his wife a portion of their joint accumulation, or the law apportions to her a share; the homestead is broken up, and she is dispossessed of that which she earned equally with him; for what she lacked in physical strength, she made up in constancy of labor and toil, day and evening. The sons then coming into possession of the property, as has been the custom until of latter time, speak of having to keep their mother, when she in reality is aiding to keep them. Where is the justice of this state of things? . . .

Women's property has been taxed, equally with that of men's, to sustain colleges endowed by the states; but they have not been permitted to enter those high seminaries of learning. Within a few years, however, some colleges have been instituted, where young women are admitted, nearly upon equal terms with young men; and numbers are availing themselves of their long denied rights. This is among the signs of the times, indicative of an advance for women. The book of knowledge is not opened to her in vain. Already is she aiming to occupy important posts of honor and profit in our country. . . .

Let woman then go on—not asking as favor, but claiming as right, the removal of all the hindrances to her elevation in the scale of being—let her receive encouragement for the proper cultivation of all her powers, so that she may enter profitably into the active business of life; employing her own hands, in ministering to her necessities, strengthening her physical being by proper exercise, and observance of the laws of health. Let her not be ambitious to display a fair hand, and to promenade the fashionable streets of our city, but rather, coveting earnestly the best gifts, let her strive to occupy such walks in society, as will befit her true dignity in all the relations of life.

Source: Mott, Lucretia. *Lucretia Mott's Discourse, at the Friend's Quarterly Meeting, in the Hester Street House.* New York: Ross & Tousey, 1850.

Ernestine Rose, *On Woman's Rights* (1851)

One of New York's passionate orators of the mid-1800s, suffragist Ernestine Rose, a Jewish immigrant from Russo-Poland, incorporated in her plea for women's rights memories of the French Revolution and the immediacy of the rhetorical "woman question." By dramatizing the American struggle for equality within the panorama of world history, she interwove the style and purpose of colonial pamphleteer Thomas Paine in demanding independence for women. To explain women's subservience to men, she charged society's ignorance and the traditions that pictured the female as delicate and helpless.

. . . Like man, woman comes involuntarily into existence. Like him she possesses physical and mental and moral powers on the proper cultivation of which depends her happiness. Like him she is subject to all the vicissitudes of life. Like him she has to pay the penalty for disobeying nature's laws, and far greater penalties has she to suffer from ignorance of her far more complicated nature than he. Like him she enjoys or suffers with her country.

Yet she is not recognized as his equal! In the laws of the land she has no rights, in government she has no voice. And in spite of another principle, recognized in this republic, namely, that "taxation without representation is tyranny," yet she is taxed without being represented. Her property may be consumed by taxes to defray the expenses of that unholy, unrighteous custom called war, yet she has no power to give her veto against it. From the cradle to the grave she is subject to the power and control of man. Father, guardian, or husband, one conveys her like some piece of merchandise over to the other.

At marriage she loses her entire identity and her being is said to have become merged in her husband. . . .

It is high time to denounce such gross injustice, to compel man by the might of right to give to woman her political, legal, and social rights. Open to her all the avenues of emolument, distinction, and greatness. Give her an object for which to cultivate her powers, and a fair chance to do so, and there will be no need to speculate as to her proper sphere. She will find her own sphere in accordance with her capacities, powers, and tastes, and yet she will be woman still. Her rights will not change, but strengthen, develop, and elevate her nature. Away, then, with that folly and absurdity, that a possession of her rights would be detrimental to her character; that if she is recognized as the equal to man, she would cease to be woman. . . .

It is from ignorance not malice that man acts towards woman as he does. In ignorance of her nature and the interest and happiness of both sexes, he conceived ideas, laid down rules, and enacted laws concerning her destiny and rights. The same ignorance, strengthened by age, sanctified by superstition, engrafted into his being by habit, makes him carry these convictions out to the detriment of his own as well as her happiness; for is he not the loser by his injustice? Oh! How severely he suffers. Who can fathom the depth of misery and suffering to society from the subjugation and injury inflicted on woman? The race is elevated excellence and power or kept back in progression, in accordance with the scale of woman's position in society. But so firmly has prejudice closed the eyes of man to the light of truth, that though he feels the evils, he knows not their cause. . . .

To achieve this glorious victory of right over might, woman has much to do. Man may remove her legal shackles, and recognize her as his equal, which will greatly aid in her elevation, but the law cannot compel her to cultivate her mind and take an independent stand as a free being. . . . Woman must think for herself, and use for herself that greatest of all prerogatives—judgment of right and wrong. And next she must act according to her best convictions, irrespective of any other voice than that or right and duty. The time, I trust, will come, though slowly, yet surely, when woman will occupy that high and lofty position, for which nature has so eminently fitted her, in the destinies of humanity.

Source: Rose, Ernestine Louise. *An Address on Woman's Rights*. Boston, MA: J. P. Mendum, 1851.

"The Nonsense of It" (1866)

This pamphlet, titled "The Nonsense of It," was entered into the records of the U.S. House of Representatives in 1866. It is an early version of a pamphlet attributed to Thomas Wentworth Higginson, a social reformer who strongly supported abolition and women's suffrage. In this document, he cites arguments commonly used against woman suffrage at the time. The pamphlet rejects each of these arguments, concluding that prohibiting women from the ballot box would be undemocratic.

"It would never do for women to vote, it would lead to such divisions in families." But political divisions do not, after all, make men quarrel half so much as religious divisions; and if you allow wives to do their own thinking in religion, why not in politics? Besides, nothing makes a man so coaxing and persuasive as when he tries to induce his neighbor to vote "our ticket." Husbands who are boors all the rest of the year would become patterns of politeness for a month before election day, —if the wives only had a vote!

"The polls are not decent places for women, at present." Then she is certainly needed there to make them decent. Literature was not decent, nor the dinner table, till she was admitted to them, on equal terms. But already, throughout most parts of the country, the ballot-box is as quiet a place to go to as the Post-office; and where it is not so, the presence of one woman would be worth a dozen policemen.

"Politics are necessarily corrupting." Then why not advise good men, as well as good women, to quit voting?

"I should not wish to hear my wife speak in town meeting." I should think not, unless she spoke more to the point than the average of men. Perhaps she would; no telling till she tries. And you are willing to pay a high price occasionally to hear somebody's else wife sing in public—and if it is proper for a woman to sing nonsense before an audience, why not to speak sense?

"Woman is sufficiently represented already, through her influence on men." How is it then that the whole legislation of Christendom, in regard to her, was "a disgrace to any heathen nation," till the Women's Rights Conventions began to call attention to it, ten years ago?

"Women are entirely distinct from men, altogether unlike, quite a different order of beings." Are they indeed? Then if they are so distinct, how can men represent them, make laws for them, administer their rights, judge them in court, spend their tax-money? If they are the same with men, they have the same rights; if they are distinct, they have a right to distinct representation, distinct, laws, courts, property, and all the rest. Arrange it as you please, it comes to the same thing.

"A woman who takes proper care of her household, has no time to know anything about politics." Why not say, "a man who properly supports his household, has no time to know anything about politics?" Show me the husband who does not assure his wife that his day's work is harder than her's. How absurd, then, to suppose that he has time to read the newspaper every day, and step round to the ballot-box once a year—and she has not?

"Women, after all, are silly creatures." No doubt they are, often enough. As the old lady says in a late English novel, "God Almighty made some of them foolish, to match the men." And the men have done their best to turn the heads of others, who were no fools by nature. But it is the theory of democracy that every man has a right to express his own folly at the ballot-box, if he will—and in time, perhaps, learn more sense by so doing. And why not every woman too?

The amount of it all is, that woman must be enfranchised; it is a mere question of time. All attempts to evade this, end in inconsistency and nonsense. Either she must be a slave or an equal; there is no middle ground. Admit, in the slightest degree, her right to education or to property, and she must have the right of suffrage in order to protect the property and use the education. And there are no objections to this, except such as would equally hold against the whole theory of democratic government.

Source: "The Nonsense of It," A Printed Pamphlet Arguing for Women's Suffrage; 12/26/1865; Petitions and Memorials Referred to the Committee on the Judiciary, 6/3/1813–1998; Records of the U.S. House of Representatives; National Archives Building, Washington, D.C.

Sojourner Truth, Address to the American Equal Rights Association (1867)

Former slave Sojourner Truth became one of the most popular orators of the mid-nineteenth century, speaking out against slavery and for women's rights.

She is best known in the historical record for her "Ar'n't I a Woman?" speech, delivered at the 1851 Women's Rights Convention in Akron, Ohio. In that address, she challenged the hypocrisy of nineteenth-century gender ideologies as applied to black women. On May 9, 1867, Truth delivered the following address at the first annual meeting of the American Equal Rights Association, formed by many prominent reformers to fight for universal suffrage. Truth spoke up for the rights of black women caught in the middle of discussions about rights based on race versus sex.

My friends, I am rejoiced that you are glad, but I don't know how you will feel when I get through. I come from another field the country of the slave. They have got their liberty so much good luck to have slavery partly destroyed; not entirely. I want it root and branch destroyed. Then we will all be free indeed. I feel that if I have to answer for the deeds done in my body just as much as a man, I have a right to have just as much as a man. There is a great stir about colored men getting their rights, but not a word about the colored women; and if colored men get their rights, and not colored women theirs, you see the colored men will be masters over the women, and it will be just as bad as it was before. So I am for keeping the thing going while things are stirring; because if we wait till it is still, it will take a great while to get it going again. White women are a great deal smarter, and know more than colored women, while colored women do not know scarcely anything. They go out washing, which is about as high as a colored woman gets, and their men go about idle, strutting up and down; and when the women come home, they ask for their money and take it all, and then scold because there is no food. I want you to consider on that, chil'n. I call you chil'n; you are somebody's chil'n, and I am old enough to be mother of all that is here. I want women to have their rights. In the courts women have no right, no voice; nobody speaks for them. I wish woman to have her voice there among the pettifoggers. If it is not a place fit for women, it is unfit for men to be there.

I am above eighty years old; it is about time for me to be going. I have been forty years a slave and forty years free, and would be here forty years more to have equal rights for all. I suppose I am kept here because something remains for me to do; I suppose I am yet to help to break the chain. I have done a great deal of work; as much as a man, but did not get so much pay. I used to work in the field and bind grain, keeping up with the cradler; but men doing no more, got twice as much pay; so with the German women. They work in the field and do as much work, but do not get the pay. We do as much, we eat as much, we want as much. I suppose I am about the only colored woman that goes about to speak for the rights of the colored women. I want to keep the thing stirring, now that the ice is cracked. What we want is a little money. You men know that you get as much again as women when you write, or for what you do. When we get our rights we shall not have to come to you for money, for then we shall have money enough in our pockets; and may be you will ask us for money. But help us now until we get it. It is a good consolation to know that when we have got this battle once fought we shall not be coming to you any more. You have been having our rights so long, that you think, like a slave-holder, that you own us. I know that it is hard for one who has held the reins for so long to give up; it cuts like a knife. It will feel all the better when it closes up again. I have been in Washington about three years, seeing about these colored people. Now colored men have the right to vote. There ought to be equal rights now more than ever, since colored people have got their freedom. I am going to talk several times while I am here; so now I will do a little singing. I have not heard any singing since I came here.

Source: "American Equal Rights Association," *New York Tribune*, May 10, 1867, 8.

Fourteenth Amendment (1868)

The Fourteenth Amendment was one of three Reconstruction Era amendments ratified in the years immediately following the American Civil War. The Fourteenth Amendment expanded the definition of U.S. citizenship to include all African Americans, including formerly enslaved people, equal protection under the law at the federal level. These provisions would be used (unsuccessfully) by suffragists to claim women's right to vote as citizens of the United States. The amendment passed Congress in 1866 and was ratified by the required number of states and adopted as part of the U.S. Constitution in 1868.

Section 1. All persons born or naturalized in the United States and subject to the jurisdiction thereof, are citizens of the United States and of the State wherein they reside. No State shall make or enforce any law which shall abridge the privileges or immunities of citizens of the United States; nor shall any State deprive any person of life, liberty, or property, without due process of law; nor deny to any person within its jurisdiction the equal protection of the laws.

Section 2. Representatives shall be apportioned among the several States according to their respective numbers, counting the whole number of persons in each State, excluding Indians not taxed. But when the right to vote at any election for the choice of electors for President and Vice President of the United States, Representatives in Congress, the Executive and Judicial officers of a State, or the members of the Legislature thereof, is denied to any of the male inhabitants of such State, being twenty-one years of age, and citizens of the United States, or in any way abridged, except for participation in rebellion, or other crime, the basis of representation therein shall be reduced in the proportion which the number of such male citizens shall bear to the whole number of male citizens twenty-one years of age in such State.

Section 3. No person shall be a Senator or Representative in Congress, or elector of President and Vice President, or hold any office, civil or military, under the United States, or under any State, who, having previously taken an oath, as a member of Congress, or as an officer of the United States, or as a member of any State legislature, or as an executive or judicial officer of any State, to support the Constitution of the United States, shall have engaged in insurrection or rebellion against the same, or given aid or comfort to the enemies thereof. But Congress may by a vote of two-thirds of each House, remove such disability.

Section 4. The validity of the public debt of the United States, authorized by law, including debts incurred for payment of pensions and bounties for services in suppressing insurrection or rebellion, shall not be questioned. But neither the United States nor any State shall assume or pay any debt or obligation incurred in aid of insurrection or rebellion against the United States, or any claim for the loss or emancipation of any slave; but all such debts, obligations and claims shall be held illegal and void.

Section 5. The Congress shall have power to enforce, by appropriate legislation, the provisions of this article.

Source: The House Joint Resolution proposing the 14th amendment to the Constitution, June 16, 1866; Enrolled Acts and Resolutions of Congress, 1789–1999; General Records of the United States Government; Record Group 11; National Archives.

An Act to Grant to the Women of Wyoming Territory the Right of Suffrage (1869)

Wyoming was the first territory to grant women the right to vote and, upon statehood, in 1890, became the first state with full women's suffrage. Several western states and territories granted women's suffrage before national suffrage rights were gained with ratification of the Nineteenth Amendment in 1920, primarily to attract more women settlers to sparsely populated areas and to the spread of the populist ideas. In Wyoming, however, the early push for white women's suffrage may have also been a maneuver by the local Democratic Party to counter Republican support for the African American vote under the Fifteenth Amendment.

Be it enacted by the Council and House of Representatives of the Territory of Wyoming:

Sec. 1. That every woman of the age of twenty-one years, residing in this territory, may at every election to be holden under the laws thereof, cast her vote. And her rights to the elective franchise and to hold office shall be the same under the election laws of the territory, as those of electors.

Sec. 2. This act shall take effect and be in force from and after its passage.

(Approved, December 10, 1869)

Source: General Laws, Memorials and Resolutions of the Territory of Wyoming, Passed at the First Session of the Legislative Assembly, Convened at Cheyenne, October 12, 1869. Cheyenne, W.T.: S. Allan Bristol, Public Printer, Tribune Office, 1870, 371.

Fifteenth Amendment (1870)

One of three Reconstruction Era amendments enacted in the years immediately following the Civil War, the Fifteenth Amendment protected the voting rights of African American men by prohibiting states from denying the right to vote based on race. Before the adoption of the Fifteenth Amendment, the matter of suffrage had been purely a matter for the states. Debates over the exclusion of "sex" as a protected category, and over the extension of national voting rights to black men before white women, led to a split in the women's movement that lasted more than 20 years. Congress approved the Fifteenth Amendment in 1869, and it was ratified by the states and adopted as part of the U.S. Constitution in 1870.

Section 1. The right of citizens of the United States to vote shall not be denied or abridged by the United States or by any State on account of race, color, or previous condition of servitude.

Section 2. The Congress shall have power to enforce this article by appropriate legislation.

Source: The House Joint Resolution proposing the 15th amendment to the Constitution, December 7, 1868; Enrolled Acts and Resolutions of Congress, 1789–1999; General Records of the United States Government; Record Group 11; National Archives.

Victoria Woodhull, Address before the House of Representatives (1871)

Controversial reformer and suffragist Victoria Claflin Woodhull was the first woman to address a congressional committee when she spoke before the House Judiciary Committee on the subject of women's suffrage on January 11, 1871. She was joined in the House by Susan B. Anthony and Isabella Hooker and the suffragists sought to claim women's right to vote as a condition of citizenship under the recently ratified Fourteenth and Fifteenth Amendments to the U.S. Constitution. Only two representatives present supported the women's suffrage argument and the proposal was tabled. The following year, Woodhull ran for president as the candidate for the Equal Rights Party.

The public law of the world is founded upon the conceded fact that sovereignty can not be forfeited or renounced. The sovereign power of this country is perpetually in the politically organized people of the United States, and can neither be relinquished nor abandoned by any portion of them. The people in this republic who confer sovereignty are its citizens; in a monarchy the people are the subjects of sovereignty. All citizens of a republic by rightful act or implication confer sovereign power. . . .

As sovereignty can not be forfeited, relinquished, or abandoned, those from whom it flows—the citizens—are equal in conferring the power, and should be equal in the enjoyment of its benefits and in the exercise of its rights and privileges. One portion of citizens have no power to deprive another portion of rights and privileges such as are possessed and exercised by themselves. The male citizen has no more right to deprive the female citizen of the free, public, political, expression of opinion than the female citizen has to deprive the male citizen thereof.

The sovereign will of the people is expressed in our written Constitution, which is the supreme law of the land. The Constitution makes no distinction of sex. The Constitution defines a woman born or naturalized in the United States, and subject to the jurisdiction thereof, to be a citizen. It recognizes the right of citizens to vote. It declares that the right of citizens of the United States to vote shall not be denied or abridged by the United States or by any State on account of "race, color, or previous condition of servitude."

Women, white and black, belong to races, although to different races. A race of people comprises all the people, male and female. The right to vote can not be denied on account of race. All people included in the term race have the right to vote, unless otherwise prohibited. Women of all races are white, black, or some intermediate color. Color comprises all people, of all races and both sexes. The right to vote can not be denied on account of color. All people included in the term color have the right to vote unless otherwise prohibited. . . .

The citizen who is taxed should also have a voice in the subject matter of taxation. "No taxation without representation" is a right which was fundamentally established at the very birth of our country's independence; and by what ethics does any free government impose taxes on women without giving them a voice upon the subject or a participation in the public declaration as to how and by whom these taxes shall be applied for common public use? . . .

. . . The American nation, in its march onward and upward, can not publicly choke the intellectual and political activity of half its citizens by narrow statutes. The will of the entire people is the true basis of republican government, and a free expression of that will by the public vote of all citizens, without distinctions of race, color, occupation, or sex, is the only means by which that will can be ascertained. As the world has advanced into civilization and culture; as mind has risen in its dominion over matter; as the principle of justice and moral right has gained sway, and merely physical organized power has yielded thereto; as the might of right has supplanted the right of might, so have the rights of women become more fully recognized, and that recognition is the result of the development of the minds of men, which through the ages she has polished, and thereby heightened the lustre of civilization. . . .

Therefore, Believing firmly in the right of citizens to freely approach those in whose hands their destiny is placed under the Providence of God, your memorialist has frankly, but humbly, appealed to you, and prays that the wisdom of Congress may be moved to action in this matter for the benefit and the increased happiness of our beloved country.

Source: Woodhull, Victoria. "Address to the Judiciary Committee of the House of Representatives." January 11, 1871. In United States Congress, *Congressional Reports on Woman Suffrage*. New York: Woodhull, Glaflin, & Co., 1871, 40c–40f.

United States v. Susan B. Anthony, U.S. District Court, Canandaigua, New York (1873)

On November 5, 1872, Susan B. Anthony cast a ballot in the presidential election and was later arrested for illegally voting in Rochester, New York. The trial allowed her a valuable forum in which to argue for women's right to vote as citizens under the Fourteenth Amendment and to present her argument for women's suffrage to a wider audience. The U.S. District Court that heard her case ruled against that argument, and she was fined.

The Court: The prisoner will stand up. Has the prisoner anything to say why sentence shall not be pronounced?

Miss Anthony: Yes, your honor, I have many things to say; for in your ordered verdict of guilty, you have trampled underfoot every vital principle of our government. My natural rights, my civil rights, my political rights, are all alike ignored. Robbed of the fundamental privilege of citizenship, I am degraded from the status of a citizen to that of a subject; and not only myself individually, but all of my sex, are, by your honor's verdict, doomed to political subjection under this so-called republican government.

Judge Hunt: The Court can not listen to a rehearsal of arguments the prisoner's counsel has already consumed three hours in presenting.

Miss Anthony: May it please your honor, I am not arguing the question, but simply stating the reasons why sentence can not, in justice, be pronounced against me. Your denial of my citizen's right to vote is the denial of my right of consent as one of the governed, the denial of my right of representation as one of the taxed, the denial of my right to a trial by a jury of my peers as an offender against law, therefore, the denial of my sacred rights to life, liberty, property, and—

Judge Hunt: The Court can not allow the prisoner to go on.

Miss Anthony: But your honor will not deny me this one and only poor privilege of protest against this high-handed outrage upon my citizen's rights.

May it please the Court to remember that since the day of my arrest last November, this is the first time that either myself or any person of my disfranchised class has been allowed a word of defense before judge or jury—

Judge Hunt: The prisoner must sit down. The Court can not allow it.

Miss Anthony: All my prosecutors, from the Eighth Ward corner grocery politician, who entered the complaint, to the United States Marshal, Commissioner, District Attorney, District Judge, your honor on the bench, not one is my peer, but each and all are my political sovereigns; and had your honor submitted my case to the jury, as was clearly your duty, even then I should have had just cause of protest, for not one of those men was my peer; but, native or foreign, white or black, rich or poor, educated or ignorant, awake or asleep, sober or drunk, each and every man of them was my political superior; hence, in no sense, my peer. Even, under such circumstances, a commoner of England, tried before a jury of lords, would have far less cause to complain than should I, a woman, tried before a jury of men. Even my counsel, the Hon. Henry R. Selden, who has argued my cause so ably, so earnestly, so unanswerably before your honor, is my political sovereign. Precisely as no disfranchised person is entitled to sit upon a jury, and no woman is entitled to the franchise, so, none but a regularly admitted lawyer is allowed to practice in the courts, and no woman can gain admission to the bar—hence, jury, judge, counsel, must all be of the superior class.

Judge Hunt: The Court must insist—the prisoner has been tried according to the established forms of law.

Miss Anthony: Yes, your honor, but by forms of law all made by men, interpreted by men, administered by men, in favor of men, and against women; and hence, your honor's ordered verdict of guilty, against a United States citizen for the exercise of "that citizen's right to vote," simply because that citizen was a woman and not a man. But, yesterday, the same man-made forms of law declared it a crime punishable with $1,000 fine and six months' imprisonment, for you, or me, or any of us, to give a cup of cold water, a crust of bread, or a night's shelter to a panting fugitive as he was tracking his way to Canada. And every man or woman in whose veins coursed a drop of human sympathy violated that wicked law, reckless of consequences, and was justified in so doing. As then the slaves who got their freedom must take it over, or under, or through the unjust forms of law, precisely so now must women, to get their right to a voice in this Government, take it; and I have taken mine, and mean to take it at every opportunity.

Judge Hunt: The Court orders the prisoner to sit down. It will not allow another word.

Miss Anthony: When I was brought before your honor for trial, I hoped for a broad and liberal interpretation of the Constitution and its recent amendments, that should declare all United States citizens under its protecting aegis—that should declare equality of rights the national guarantee of all persons born or naturalized in the United States. But failing to get this justice—failing, even, to get a trial by a jury *not* of my peers—I ask not leniency at your hands—but rather the full rigors of the law.

Judge Hunt: The Court must insist—(Here the prisoner sat down.)

Judge Hunt: The prisoner will stand up. (Here Miss Anthony rose again.) The sentence of the Court is that you pay a fine of one hundred dollars and the costs of the prosecution.

Miss Anthony: May it please your honor, I shall never pay a dollar of your unjust penalty. All the stock in trade I possess is a $10,000 debt, incurred by publishing my paper—*The Revolution*—four years ago, the sole object of which was to educate all women to do precisely as I have done, rebel against your man-made unjust, unconstitutional forms of law, that tax, fine, imprison, and hang women, while they deny them the right of representation in the Government; and I shall work on with might and main to pay every dollar of that honest debt, but not a penny shall go to this unjust claim. And I shall earnestly and persistently continue to urge all women to the practical recognition of the old revolutionary maxim, that "Resistance to tyranny is obedience to God."

Judge Hunt: Madam, the Court will not order you committed until the fine is paid.

Source: *United States v. Susan B. Anthony*, 24 Fed. Case No. 14.459 (1873).

George W. Julian, "The Slavery Yet to Be Abolished" (1874)

Indiana lawyer and politician George Washington Julian was an outspoken social reformer who advocated for liberal causes ranging from the abolition of slavery to land reform to women's suffrage. Representative Julian had supported women's suffrage since before the Civil War, and in 1868 he introduced Congress's first ever bill calling for a federal suffrage amendment.

Julian's speech, "The Slavery Yet to Be Abolished," was delivered on several occasions during an extended tour through Michigan and Iowa in 1874 calling for extending the right to vote to women.

And here, at length, are we brought directly to the question of woman's right to the ballot. We touch the simple, naked and sole issue to be tried. Having demonstrated that the right of representation rests upon personality, that is to say upon humanity itself, being the inherent right of the people to choose their rulers and manage their own affairs, it only remains to inquire whether woman is a part of humanity. Is she a human being? If so, then my argument is clinched, and nothing more need be said. If she is not, then the case must go against her. On this question of fact, I repeat, the whole controversy must turn, for if the opponents of woman's enfranchisement admit the affirmative, they admit away their whole case. I expect them to face this issue as becomes brave men. Twenty years ago, when the champions of slavery were driven to the wall by the humanitarian arguments and appeals of the abolitionists, their respect for logical consistency finally compelled them to deny that the negro belongs to the human species. They pronounced him a monkey, or an orang-outang, and thus made his humanity the single issue in the angry dispute about slavery. Their perfect courage was only equalled by their perfect contempt for common sense. Their absolute fidelity to the logic of an infernal enterprise was so charmingly intrepid that I think it commanded general admiration, when contrasted with the cowardly pettifogging by which the doughfaces sought to reconcile the crime of slaveholding with the rights of humanity. I commend the example of these heroic men to the enemies of woman's enfranchisement, and I trust their courage may prove equally heroic. I think they will be found ready, at all events, to face the only issue involved in the controversy, and either have the gallantry to surrender at discretion, or the matchless audacity to deny the humanity of the mothers who bore them. Taking the latter for granted, I must meet them on their own ground, and insist that woman is a part of the human family. This is my decided opinion. Indeed, I have always understood that fully one-half the human race is feminine. Woman stands related to us as wife, mother, sister and daughter. She is a citizen by the unmistakable words of the constitution. She is a tax-payer, and as to certain positions, in some of the states, she is already allowed to vote and hold office. We are enlarging her sphere of employment, and increasing her compensation for her work. We are recognizing her equality with man by securing to her the same educational opportunities. We imprison her for crime and hang her for murder. We baptize her as a Christian, and send her abroad as a missionary. I suppose Christ died for her in the same sense in which he died for man. She is endowed with the same faculties and affections, is animated by the same hopes, shares with man his joys and sorrows, and strives with him for the same blessings. Indeed, the case seems to me so plain that until those who deny woman's humanity are more particularly heard from, it can hardly be worth while to argue the question further.

But perhaps, after all, they will admit it, and still insist that she shall not vote because of her sex. But in the name of justice and political decency what has sex to do with the question of moral and political right? If you say to woman, "You shall not vote because you are a woman," and she retorts, "You shall not vote because you are a man," is not the account balanced? You agree with me in disowning the principle of an aristocracy founded on property, or nativity, or race, or color, or religion, and yet you approve an aristocracy founded on sex, which is just as anti-republican and indefensible, and if possible still more hateful.

But you will say, perhaps, that you would not withhold the ballot from woman because of her sex, but her inferiority. I answer, that in mere muscle and general physical power she is unquestionably inferior, as a rule, to man; but I have not yet learned that our American democracy has instituted any test of mere bodily strength as a qualification for voting. Do we require a man to be a Samson before we allow him the ballot? On the contrary, the smallest and feeblest men have equal rights with the largest and stoutest. We sometimes carry to the polls cripples, and men in the last stages of incurable disease. Do you tell me that the inferiority you complain of is not physical, but intellectual? Let me, for the sake of the argument, admit this inferiority. Let me accept the declaration so often made that in the higher departments of science, philosophy, and art, woman is inferior to man, and that history has so made the record. What then? Is it a part of the gospel of democracy that none but great scientists, philosophers, and artists shall vote? I think I have seen a good many men vote who would have been excluded by any such rule. Why raise the question of intellectual inferiority, when we give the ballot to the whole mass of our male population above the level of idiots and lunatics? Besides, do you not see that the argument of inferiority is not an argument against, but in favor of, woman's enfranchisement? If she is really inferior to man in capacity, and consequently less fitted to take care of herself, does she not need the ballot all the more for her protection and help? Is not the law intended for the weak? And is not the ballot in the hands of man the gateway to opportunity and the defense of his rights? If woman is man's inferior, and is obliged all the days of her life to encounter the sharpened faculties of a superior order of beings who have thus far made her a slave or a dependent, it must be quite evident that this is the strongest possible argument for giving her a voice in the management of public affairs.

But, in answer to all this, or in evasion of it, I shall be told that woman is not fit for the ballot. Let me ask, what is fitness to vote? I repeat what I said years ago in arguing the question of negro suffrage, that fitness is a relative term. Nobody is perfectly fit to vote, because perfect fitness would require perfect knowledge and perfect virtue. A man would have to be a god, or an angel. The truth is, we are all more or less unfit for all our duties, whether civil, social, religious, or what not. The fitness to govern which must be our reliance, as I have already argued, is not scientific or literary. It is not the fitness of a select few, but of the many. It is aggregate fitness. During the late civil war, and in all our previous trials, our deliverance came through the inconspicuous, unheralded rank and file, "the common people," whose integrity of character, solid sense, and well-ordered homes have given the republic its place among the nations. In the light of this fact, who shall bar the door against the political rights of woman? Who of us can object to her fitness, after giving the ballot to ignorant and untrained masses of males, north and south, white and black? What possible test of fitness would exclude woman that would not disfranchise millions of our male voters?

The plea of unfitness seems still more preposterous if we keep in mind the ugly facts which our masculine voting has brought to the surface. Women, we are told, are unfit to vote. If enfranchised, they would vote on the wrong side. Undoubtedly they would sometimes do so. They would make mistakes; but could they not profit by them? And if a careful search were made, is it not barely possible that cases could be found in which men have voted on the wrong side? I think I have known such cases myself, and probably you can recall others. How stands the account? Have we, in fact, such a record as makes it decent for us to sit in judgment upon the fitness of woman for politics? Look at our Sanborn contracts, our Moiety system, and our custom-house thieving. Look at our eminent Christian statesmen auctioning their consciences to a great railway corporation. Look at the great salary theft of the last Congress. Look at our civil service to-day, as foul and feculent a system of huckstering and plunder as our thoroughly debauched party politics could make it. Look at our drunken libertines elevated to high places by male voting. Look at the open and wholesale pollution of the ballot, and the spectacle of bribery and perjury we have witnessed in so many states. Look at the frightful decay of political morality in every section of the land, and listen to the prayers of good men for a speedy resurrection of conscience as the only possible salvation of the country!

Or look at the wisdom which male suffrage has made manifest in our parties and politicians. Take the tariff question. It is as unsettled as it was a half century ago. Each of the great parties is divided upon it, and neither can define its position. So of the question of railway transportation. Neither is competent to deal with it, and neither, as a party, has any defined position respecting it. The same is true of the finance question. As national parties they are internally divided, while no man can name any vital point on which they stand opposed. Some of the leaders of both are for hard money and a return to specie payments, while others scout this idea, demand more printed money, and refer to Adam Smith and John Stuart Mill as theorists and dreamers whose doctrines of political economy are not applicable to the United States. Take the slavery question. Male suffrage could not settle it, and we were obliged to try it by battle. The labor question succeeds it, and no party has yet appeared that seems at all able to grapple with it. On the temperance question our parties have tried their hand at legislation for more than a generation, but thus far the result is a muddle. The picture thus imperfectly sketched is the picture of our country under the full blaze of masculine wisdom and virtue; and I respectfully submit that it does not warrant the arraignment of woman as unfit to share in our politics. On the contrary, I think it shows the need of her helping hand and saving grace, unless we decide to jump out of our democratic frying pan into the fire of kingly rule, which we have resolved not to do.

But we are told of the dreadful consequences that will ensue if we give the ballot to woman. It will "upheave the whole social system," "destroy the family," inaugurate "free love," and "make Beecher-Tilton scandals the order of the day." This is the current style of argument, and by far the most effective one I find employed; and yet it is palpably no argument at all against woman's enfranchisement, but simply a prediction that certain consequences would follow the event. I meet it in the words of one of the world's greatest living thinkers, in speaking of "logical consequences." He says: "In the course of my experience I have found that they are the scare-crows of fools, and the beacons of wise men," and that "The only question for any man to ask is this: Is this true, or is it false? No other question can possibly be taken into consideration till this one is settled." I have demonstrated woman's equal right with man to share in the government. I have shown that the question of woman's rights is the question of human rights, and consequently that if her right of representation is conventional merely, to be granted or denied at the pleasure of government, the very principle of popular liberty is superseded by the principle of absolutism. Is my argument valid? That is the question first of all to be disposed of, and I may decline to discuss any other till it is settled. Until the opponents of woman's enfranchisement face this question and show the fallacy of my argument, I must treat their "logical consequences" as the "scare-crows of fools." If, as I insist, woman has exactly the same right to a voice in the government as man, it is the duty of man to recognize that right, and the consequences have no more to do with the performance of this duty than with obedience to the commands of the decalogue. They can no more excuse that duty than they can excuse any other duty, whether enjoined by morals or religion. You might just as reasonably object to the Golden Rule that obedience to it would turn the world up-side down, or refuse to do right because the heavens will surely fall if you do, or decline to speak the truth and deal justly because it would "upheave the whole social system." Such arguments are as shallow as they are atheistical, and a good cause would disown them. They are, however, the staple of conservatism, which stupidly turns its back upon all the lessons of experience. When the repeal of the English corn laws was first proposed, national ruin was predicted as a certain result. When Clarkson began his agitation for the abolition of the slave trade, the same prophesy was made. When it was proposed to arm the negroes in the late Civil War, and employ them on the side of the government, it was said they would certainly fight for their masters. It was always confidently predicted that the abolition of slavery would be followed by a general uprising of the negroes, who would lay waste the South, make a general irruption into the free states, put down the wages of our poor whites, and finally marry them.

None of these prophesies ever came true, and yet the enemies of progress have never found it out, and never will. They still "shiver and shrink at the sight of trial and hazard." They still believe in the omnipotence of evil, and forget that the very heavens are built upon justice. They still reject the faith which even a reputed Pagan proclaims, that "the great soul of the World is just," and that there is "one strong thing here below, the just thing, the true thing." They are still prophesying that ruin and disaster will follow in the footsteps of duty, and their children will doubtless take up the trade when they are ready to lay it down, while all history bears witness that loyalty to principle is safety, and truth the only sure lamp to our feet.

In the light of what I have said, it can scarcely be necessary to notice the hackneyed plea that women generally do not desire the ballot. I only remark, in the first place, that a very respectable minority does desire it, and that if the argument I have made is sound, the question of majorities and minorities can have nothing whatever to do with the issue. It is not a problem of mathematics, but a claim of right, and therefore the disclaimer of it by ninety-nine hundredths of the sex could not affect the right of the remainder.

In the next place, this minority includes many earnest and highly gifted women who have given the subject much thought, and whose declared reasons for their position have only been answered by "the gospel of ridicule." On the other hand, the position of the majority is that of indifference, rather than hostility, and results largely from inattention and lack of thought. The mass of the slaves of the South were so accustomed to their lot that they gave no sign of discontent; but Frederick Douglas[s] and scores of others ran away from their masters, and denounced the whole system of oppression as an outrage upon humanity and a crime against God. The world has accepted their testimony, and rejected the negative evidence of the great majority, whose very contentedness with their condition was itself the strongest condemnation of their enslavement.

In the third place, this minority is rapidly growing. It is already quite as large as minorities usually are in the early stages of a reform. A great cause never musters a majority in its beginning, and does not need it. It has the truth on its side, and that never fails to prove all-sufficient. The cause of woman's enfranchisement is so woven into the logic of progress and the spirit of the age that its failure is impossible. It is coming, in the language of Colonel Higginson, as "a part of the succession of civilizations." It is coming as the final product and ripe fruit of democratic institutions. It is coming in obedience to the law which has made the progress of society and the elevation of woman go hand in hand in the past. It is coming through the principle of social evolution which has made the condition of woman constantly approach that of equality with man in the history of the world. It is coming in response to the spirit of humanity which centuries ago swept away the code which gave woman in marriage without her consent and made her the chattel slave of her husband, who could exercise over her the power of life and death; while that same spirit is now reforming and humanizing our laws respecting her personal and property rights, enlarging the sphere of her occupations, increasing her wages, and promoting her higher education. Its enemies may throw obstacles in its way, and distress themselves by the childish dread of consequences, but they will be as powerless to defeat it as to stay the tides of the sea.

Source: Julian, George W. *Later Speeches on Political Questions with Select Controversial Papers.* Indianapolis, IN: Carlon and Hollenbeck, 1889, 71–78.

Alexander Graham Bell, Letters on Woman Suffrage (1875)

In 1877 the famed Scottish-born inventor Alexander Graham Bell married Mabel Hubbard of Massachusetts, a woman to whom he had been long engaged. The two had corresponded frequently during their engagement, and in the following letter from Bell to "Miss Mabel" in the fall of 1875, he attempts to explain his admittedly "puzzled" thoughts about the subject of women's rights. Bell acknowledges that women generally have been treated unfairly in American society, and he expresses sympathy with some of their goals. But he also expresses profound discomfort with what he views as the radicalism of the women's rights movement, complaining that women should be patient about seeing their roles and rights expanded.

Salem, Mass.
Oct. 18th, 1875

Dear Miss Mabel,
I wonder if you know what it is to have more correspondence upon your hands than you can possibly attend to.

It is with a despairing countenance that I sometimes open letters to find that I am expected to write volumes in reply.

I have been so busy lately writing upon the subjects of Telebraphym Visible Speech, and Orthöepy that I have allowed quite a number of letters to accumulate on my hands unanswered.

This evening feeling some premonitory twinges of conscience I sat down to write—and have just accomplished a feat of which I really feel quite proud. I have written nine letters at one sitting—most of them quite lengthy epistles too!!

And now—having eased my conscience in regard to these letters—I shall rest myself by writing a few lines to you in answer to your kind note. I fear I must have left you last night about as much puzzled as you were at first in regard to my real feelings on the subject of "Woman's Rights". To tell the truth I am somewhat puzzled in the matter myself!

I have a vague sort of feeling that there has been-and-is-injustice somewhere in the position that woman holds in the world—but where to locate that injustice—or how to define its boundaries—I know not.

The fact is that my mind has been so occupied with scientific matters that I have given very little attention to the question at all.

I am quite at sea in the matter—in a fog—and I do not even know the latitude and longitude of the port for which I am bound!

When I heard from Mrs. Hubbard that you were interested in the subject—I felt curious to ascertain what your ideas were. On the spur of the moment I strung a few disjointed thoughts together and forwarded them to you in Bethel hoping to rouse your indignation to a reply!

It was a dangerous experiment and I am glad I did not succeed. You were not angry with me. Indeed I do not know whether you are ever angry with anybody!

All is well that ends well and I am glad that I have escaped this time. One of my latest resolves has been to keep my letters for a day before posting them. Had I done so in that instance the letter would not have been posted at all. As I stated to you yesterday I am a passive advocate of Woman's Rights and not an active one—although you would scarcely believe it could you hear the debates that sometimes arise between Mr. Sanders and myself upon the subject. In Salem I come out strongly for the plaintiff in the action "Woman versus Man"—because Mr. Sanders will take the other side. In Cambridge however I suspect I shall have to plead for the defendant in the suit! if you are such a Woman's Rightist as I take you to be. The true way to look at a subject is to look at it from all sides—to view it in its totality with impartial eye. I confess that I am unable to as yet to do this with Woman's Rights as I have thought too little upon the subject.

I recognize that women have many just grounds of complaint against society—and yet I think that there is much to be thankful for in the position accorded to them in this nineteenth century. The evils of this life obtrude themselves upon our notice—the blessings have to be sought for to be appreciated. It is always much more easy to find fault with established usages than to propose remedies that will be above criticism. An illustration occurs to me at this moment.

I remember in England having my attention called to the case of a very good, honest worthy woman who had married unhappily. Her husband was a great drunkard and at last she was obliged to open a millinery store in order to support herself and her little child. The man left her but returned every now and then for the purpose of carrying off what money she had in the house!

The poor woman lived in continual dread of his visits--but, as she believed the marriage tie to be too sacred a one to be broken by human hands, she could obtain no redress.

It was not "robbery" for a husband to take from his wife—for what belonged to the one belonged to the other! Now here was a manifest injustice! And yet I would not hold that the law should be laid on one side because it may be unjust in certain cases. It is easy to find fault with it—but very difficult to frame a better one.

There is to me something extremely beautiful in the idea of marriage—as the union and complete identity of two beings—so perfect a union that what belongs to the one belongs to the other and that each becomes to the other a second self.

And yet how hard does that law become which recognizes and compels a union that does not exist in heart.

My best wishes go with those who try to reform the world—and I should like to help them out—even though they are women!

When I look out upon the world of real life I see much to deplore—much that needs rightin—but I think there is much also that is good. Indeed the good and evil are pretty evenly balanced. I do not think we should open our eyes to the one and close them to the other. In the rough contacts of life the rocks seem very hard and angular—huge stones encumber the ground—Still—viewed from a lofty point—the details of the landscape melt into a harmonious whole. The blessings of this life stand out all the more brightly that they are contrasted with evils. The brightest picture—we know—would seem tame without its shadows. There are lights and shadows in our own lives. There is a bright and a dark side to the world itself. I do not approve of the plan of looking at one side and ignoring the other—but if I must look at one side more than the other—give me that which is brightest and best.

Were we to spend a winter in the Arctic Regions we might become sceptical of the existence of warmth and sunshine upon earth. We live in the Tropics ice and snow would be matters of faith. The African and the Hindoo laugh at the Englishman who tells them that water becomes solid in his country—and that white rain falls from the sky!

Give me the temperate regions of the earth where Spring and Summer, Autumn and Winter succeed each other in every-pleasing variety.

We do not appreciate those blessings that we possess continually—half as much as those which we are still to come—or which we have lost.

I think that women have a brighter and freer future before them, but I must say that I cannot fully sympathize with or appreciate sudden revolutions. The mightiest physical changes upon the face of the earth have been accomplished by silent and gentle upheavals of the crust continued through long periods of time. Sudden movements are always destructive in their tendencies. I believe in Woman's Rights as a matter sure to be accomplished in the future.

For ages past there have been a steady and continuous improvement in the condition of the sex—but I cannot feel that extremists are right. Were everything granted at once there would be a sudden and disastrous change in the condition of society—and a catastrophe would ensue.

But I must bring this epistle to a close or I fear I should have Mr. Sanders upon me for breaking my promise about sitting up at night.

I hope that you are not going to New York on Friday but if you are—I trust you may have a pleasant visit.

With kindest regards
Believe me
Yours very sincerely
A. Graham Bell

Source: Bell, Alexander Graham. Letter to Mabel Hubbard Bell, October 18, 1875. Alexander Graham Bell Family Papers, 1862–1939. Library of Congress.

Minor v. Happersett (1875)

In Minor v. Happersett, *Virginia Minor argued that the State of Missouri had violated her First, Thirteenth, and Fourteenth Amendment rights when it prohibited her from registering to vote in 1872. The U.S. Supreme Court found that the U.S. Constitution does not grant the right of suffrage as a condition of citizenship and the states' decision to limit voting to men was not unconstitutional.*

Minor contended that the First Amendment provided voting rights as a form of free expression, that under the Thirteenth Amendment being denied the vote was a form of involuntary servitude, and that the Fourteenth Amendment made voting for federal officials a privilege of citizenship. The U.S. Supreme Court refused to consider the first two arguments and focused on the Fourteenth Amendment argument. Although agreeing that women were citizens and that women were persons because they were counted as part of the total population, the Court found that the Fourteenth Amendment did not add to the privileges and immunities of citizens but only added a guaranty of protection for those already in place.

1. The word "citizen" is often used to convey the idea of membership in a nation.

2. In that sense, women, if born of citizen parents within the jurisdiction of the United States, have always been considered citizens of the United States, as much so before the adoption of the Fourteenth Amendment to the Constitution as since.

3. The right of suffrage was not necessarily one of the privileges or immunities of citizenship before the adoption of the Fourteenth Amendment, and that amendment does not add to these privileges and immunities. It simply furnishes additional guaranty for the protection of such as the citizen already had.

4. At the time of the adoption of that amendment, suffrage was not coextensive with the citizenship of the states; nor was it at the time of the adoption of the Constitution.

5. Neither the Constitution nor the Fourteenth Amendment made all citizens voters.

6. A provision in a state constitution which confines the right of voting to "male citizens of the United States" is no violation of the federal Constitution. In such a state women have no right to vote.

[. . .]

In this state of things, on the 15th of October, 1872. . . . Mrs. Virginia Minor, a native-born free white citizen of the United States and of the State of Missouri over the age of twenty-one years wishing to vote for electors for President and Vice-President of the United States and for a representative in Congress and for other officers at the general election held in November, 1872, applied to one Happersett, the registrar of voters, to register her as a lawful voter, which he refused to do, assigning for cause that she was not a "male citizen of the United States," but a woman. She thereupon sued him in one of the inferior state courts of Missouri for willfully refusing to place her name upon the list of registered voters, by which refusal she was deprived of her right to vote.

The registrar demurred, and the court in which the suit was brought sustained the demurrer and gave judgment in his favor, a judgment which the [state] supreme court affirmed. Mrs. Minor now brought the case here [to the U.S. Supreme Court] on error.

THE CHIEF JUSTICE delivered the opinion of the [U.S. Supreme] Court.

[. . .]

It is contended that the provisions of the constitution and laws of the State of Missouri which confine the right of suffrage and registration therefor to men are in violation of the Constitution of the United States, and therefore void. The argument is that as a woman, born or naturalized in the United States and subject to the jurisdiction thereof, is a citizen of the United States and of the state in which she resides, she has the right of suffrage as one of the privileges and immunities of her citizenship which the state cannot by its laws or constitution abridge.

There is no doubt that women may be citizens. They are persons, and by the Fourteenth Amendment "all persons born or naturalized in the United States and subject to the jurisdiction thereof" are expressly declared to be "citizens of the United States and of the state wherein they reside." But in our opinion it did not need this amendment to give them that position. Before its adoption, the Constitution of the United States did not in terms prescribe who should be citizens of the United States or of the several states, yet there were necessarily such citizens without such provision. There cannot be a nation without a people.

[. . .]

When used in this sense, ["citizen"] is understood as conveying the idea of membership of a nation, and nothing more.

[. . .]

. . . certainly more cannot be necessary to establish the fact that sex has never been made one of the elements of citizenship in the United States. In this respect, men have never had an advantage over women. The same laws precisely apply to both. The Fourteenth Amendment did not affect the citizenship of women any more than it did of men. In this particular, therefore, the rights of Mrs. Minor do not depend upon the amendment. She has always been a citizen from her birth and entitled to all the privileges and immunities of citizenship. The amendment prohibited the state, of which she is a citizen, from abridging any of her privileges and immunities as a citizen of the United States, but it did not confer citizenship on her. That she had before its adoption.

If the right of suffrage is one of the necessary privileges of a citizen of the United States, then the Constitution and laws of Missouri confining it to men are in violation of the Constitution of the United States, as amended, and consequently void. The direct question is therefore presented whether all citizens are necessarily voters.

The Constitution does not define the privileges and immunities of citizens. For that definition we must look elsewhere. In this case, we need not determine what they are, but only whether suffrage is necessarily one of them.

It certainly is nowhere made so in express terms . . . The power of the state in this particular is certainly supreme until Congress acts.

The [Fourteenth] amendment did not add to the privileges and immunities of a citizen... No new voters were necessarily made by it.

[. . .]

In this condition of the law in respect to suffrage in the several states, it cannot for a moment be doubted that if it had been intended to make all citizens of the United States voters, the framers of the Constitution would not have left it to implication. So important a change in the condition of citizenship as it actually existed, if intended, would have been expressly declared.

[. . .]

Women were excluded from suffrage in nearly all the states by the express provision of their constitutions and laws . . . The right of suffrage, when granted, will be protected. He who has it can only be deprived of it by due process of law, but in order to claim protection, he must first show that he has the right.

[. . .]

No new state has ever been admitted to the Union which has conferred the right of suffrage upon women, and this has never been considered a valid objection to her admission. On the contrary, as is claimed in the argument, the right of suffrage was withdrawn from women as early as 1807 in the State of New Jersey without any attempt to obtain the interference of the United States to prevent it. Since then, the governments of the insurgent states have been reorganized under a requirement that before their representatives could be admitted to seats in Congress, they must have adopted new constitutions, republican in form. In no one of these constitutions was suffrage conferred upon women, and yet the states have all been restored to their original position as states in the Union.

Besides this, citizenship has not in all cases been made a condition precedent to the enjoyment of the right of suffrage.

[. . .]

Certainly if the courts can consider any question settled, this is one. For nearly ninety years, the people have acted upon the idea that the Constitution, when it conferred citizenship, did not necessarily confer the right of suffrage. If uniform practice long continued can settle the construction of so important an instrument as the Constitution of the United States confessedly is, most certainly it has been done here. Our province is to decide what the law is, not to declare what it should be.

[. . .]

No argument as to woman's need of suffrage can be considered. We can only act upon her rights as they exist.

[. . .]

Being unanimously of the opinion that the Constitution of the United States does not confer the right of suffrage upon anyone, and that the constitutions and laws of the several states which commit that important trust to men alone are not necessarily void, we *Affirm the judgment.*

Source: *Minor v. Happersett*, 88 U.S. 21 Wall. 162 (1875).

The Declaration of Rights of the Women of the United States (1876)

In 1876, the centennial of the United States was celebrated in Philadelphia. The National Woman Suffrage Association, led by Susan B. Anthony and Elizabeth Cady Stanton, used this event to bring women together and to publicize the unequal status of women. It prepared a Declaration of Rights of the Women of the United States, *stating that women, as citizens, were entitled to the same privileges as male citizens and demanding civil and political rights for women in keeping with the spirit of 1776. The group requested permission to read the document during the Fourth of July celebration at Independence Hall but was turned down. At a bandstand outside Independence Hall, Anthony read the declaration to a large crowd.*

While the nation is buoyant with patriotism, and all hearts are attuned to praise, it is with sorrow we come to strike the one discordant note, on this one-hundredth anniversary of our country's birth. When subjects of kings, emperors, and czars, from the old world join in our national jubilee, shall the women of the republic refuse to lay their hands with benedictions on the nation's head? Surveying America's exposition, surpassing in magnificence those of London, Paris, and Vienna, shall we not rejoice at the success of the youngest rival among the nations of the earth? May not our hearts, in unison with all, swell with pride at our great achievements as a people; our free speech, free press, free schools, free church, and the rapid progress we have made in material wealth, trade, commerce and the inventive arts? And we do rejoice in the success, thus far, of our experiment of self-government. Our faith is firm and unwavering in the broad principles of human rights proclaimed in 1776, not only as abstract truths, but as the corner stones of a republic. Yet we cannot forget, even in this glad hour, that while all men of every race, and clime, and condition, have been invested with the full rights of citizenship under our hospitable flag, all women still suffer the degradation of disfranchisement.

The history of our country the past hundred years has been a series of assumptions and usurpations of power over woman, in direct opposition to the principles of just government, acknowledged by the United States as its foundation, which are:

First—The natural rights of each individual.

Second—The equality of these rights.

Third—That rights not delegated are retained by the individual.

Fourth—That no person can exercise the rights of others without delegated authority.

Fifth—That the non-use of rights does not destroy them.

And for the violation of these fundamental principles of our government, we arraign our rulers on this Fourth day of July, 1876,—and these are our articles of impeachment:

Bills of attainder have been passed by the introduction of the word "male" into all the State constitutions, denying to women the right of suffrage, and thereby making sex a crime—an exercise of power clearly forbidden in Article I, sections 9, 10, of the United States constitution.

The writ of habeas corpus, the only protection against lettres de cachet and all forms of unjust imprisonment, which the constitution declares "shall not be suspended, except when in cases of rebellion or invasion the public safety demands it," is held inoperative in every State of the Union, in case of a married woman against her husband—the marital rights of the husband being in all cases primary, and the rights of the wife secondary.

The right of trial by a jury of one's peers was so jealously guarded that States refused to ratify the original constitution until it was guaranteed by the sixth amendment. And yet the women of this nation have never been allowed a jury of their peers—being tried in all cases by men, native and foreign, educated and ignorant, virtuous and vicious. Young girls have been arraigned in our courts for the crime of infanticide; tried, hanged, convicted—victims, perchance, of judge, jurors, advocates—while no woman's voice could be heard in their defense. And not only are women denied a jury of their peers, but in some cases jury trial altogether. . . . During the last presidential campaign a woman, arrested for voting, was denied the protection of a jury, tried, convicted, and sentenced . . . , by the absolute power of a judge of the Supreme Court. . . .

Taxation without representation, the immediate cause of the rebellion of the colonies against Great Britain, is one of the grievous wrongs the women of this country have suffered during this century. Deploring war, . . . we have been taxed to support standing armies, with their waste of life and wealth. Believing in temperance, we have been taxed to support the vice, crime and pauperism of the liquor traffic. While we suffer its wrongs and abuses infinitely more than man, we have no power to protect our sons. . . . During the temperance crusade, mothers were arrested, fined, imprisoned, for even praying and singing in the streets, while men blockade the sidewalks with impunity, even on Sunday, with their military parades and political processions. Believing in honesty, we are taxed to support a dangerous army of civilians, buying and selling the offices of government and sacrificing the best interests of the people. . . . [W]e are taxed to support the very legislators and judges who make laws, and render decisions adverse to woman. And for refusing to pay such unjust taxation, the houses, lands, bonds, and stock of women have been seized and sold . . . , thus proving Lord Coke's assertion, that "The very act of taxing a man's property without his consent is, in effect, disfranchising him of every civil right."

Unequal codes for men and women. Held by law a perpetual minor, deemed incapable of self protection, even in the industries of the world, woman is denied equality of rights. The fact of sex, not the quantity or quality of work, in most cases, decides the pay and position; and because of this injustice thousands of fatherless girls are compelled to choose between a life of shame and starvation. Laws catering to man's vices have created two codes of morals in which penalties are graded according to the political status of the offender. Under such laws, women are fined and imprisoned if found alone in the streets, or in public places of resort, at certain hours. Under the pretense of regulating public morals, police officers seizing the occupants of disreputable houses, march the women in platoons to prison, while the men, partners in their guilt, go free. . . .

Special legislation for woman has placed us in a most anomalous position. Women invested with the rights of citizens in one section—voters, jurors, office-holders—crossing an imaginary line, are subjects in the next. In some States, a married woman may hold property and transact business in her own name; in others, her earnings belong to her husband. In some States, a woman may testify against her husband, sue and be sued in the courts; in others, she has no redress in case of damage to person, property, or character. In case of divorce on account of adultery in the husband, the innocent wife is held to possess no right to children or property, unless by special decree. . . . But in no State of the Union has the wife the right to her own person, or to any part of the joint earnings of the co-partnership during the life of her husband. In some States, women may enter the law schools and practice in the courts; in others they are forbidden. In some universities girls enjoy equal educational advantages with boys, while many of the proudest institutions in the land deny them admittance, though the sons of China, Japan and Africa are welcomed there. But the privileges already gained in the several States are by no means secure. The right of suffrage once exercised by women in certain States and territories has been denied by subsequent legislation. A bill is now pending in congress to disfranchise the women of Utah, thus interfering to deprive United States citizens of the same rights which the Supreme Court has declared the national government powerless to protect anywhere. Laws passed after years of untiring effort, guaranteeing married women certain rights of property, and mothers the custody of their children, have been repealed in States where we supposed all was safe. Thus have our most sacred rights been made the football of legislative caprice, proving that a power which grants as a privilege what by nature is a right, may withhold the same as a penalty when deeming it necessary for its own perpetuation.

Representation of woman has had no place in the nation's thought. Since the incorporation of the thirteen original States, twenty-four have been admitted to the Union, not one of which has recognized woman's right of self-government. On this birthday of our national liberties, July Fourth, 1876, Colorado, like all her elder sisters, comes into the Union with the invidious word "male" in her constitution.

Universal manhood suffrage, by establishing an aristocracy of sex, imposes upon the women of this nation a more absolute and cruel despotism than monarchy; in that, woman finds a political master in her father, husband, brother, son. The aristocracies of the old world are based upon birth, wealth, refinement, education, nobility, brave deeds of chivalry; in this nation, on sex alone; exalting brute force over moral power, vice above virtue, ignorance above education, and the son above the mother who bore him.

The judiciary above the nation has proved itself but the echo of the party in power, by upholding and enforcing laws that are opposed to the spirit and letter of the constitution. When the slave power was dominant, the Supreme Court decided that a black man was not a citizen, because he had not the right to vote; and when the constitution was so amended as to make all persons citizens, the same high tribunal decided that a woman, though a citizen, had not the right to vote. Such vacillating interpretations of constitutional law unsettle our faith in judicial authority, and undermine the liberties of the whole people.

These articles of impeachment against our rulers we now submit to the impartial judgment of the people. To all these wrongs and oppressions woman has not submitted in silence and resignation. From the beginning of this century . . . until now, woman's discontent has been steadily increasing, culminating nearly thirty years ago in a simultaneous movement among the women of the nation, demanding the right of suffrage. In making our just demands, a higher motive than the pride of sex inspires us; we feel that national safety and stability depend on the complete recognition of the broad principles of our government. Woman's degraded, helpless position is the weak point in our institutions to-day [and] a disturbing force everywhere. . . . It was the boast of the founders of the republic, that the rights for which they contended were the rights of human nature. If these rights are ignored in the case of one-half the people, the nation is surely preparing for its downfall. Governments try themselves. The recognition of a governing and a governed class is incompatible with the first principles of freedom. Woman has not been a heedless spectator of the events of this century, nor a dull listener to the grand arguments for the equal rights of humanity. From the earliest history of our country woman has shown equal devotion with man to the cause of freedom, and has stood firmly by his side in its defense. Together, they have made this country what it is. Woman's wealth, thought and labor have cemented the stones of every monument man has reared to liberty.

And now, at the close of a hundred years . . . , we declare our faith in the principles of self government; our full equality with man in natural rights; that woman was made first for her own happiness, with the absolute right to herself—to all the opportunities and advantages life affords for her complete development; and we deny that dogma of the centuries, incorporated in the codes of all nations—that woman was made for man—her best interests, in all cases, to be sacrificed to his will. We ask of our rulers, at this hour, no special favors, no special privileges, no special legislation. We ask justice, we ask equality, we ask that all the civil and political rights that belong to citizens of the United States, be guaranteed to us and our daughters forever.

[Signed by Lucretia Mott, Elizabeth Cady Stanton, Pauline Wright Davis, Ernestine Rose, Clarina Nichols, Mary Ann McClintock, Mathilde Franceske Anneke, Sarah Pugh, Amy Post, Catharine Stebbins, Susan B. Anthony, Matilda Joslyn Gage, Clemence Lozier, Olympia Brown, Mathilde Wendt, Adeline Thomson, Ellen Clark Sargent, Virginia Minor, Catherine Waite, Elizabeth Schenk, Phoebe Couzins, Elizabeth Boynton Harbert, Laura DeForce Gordon, Sara Andres Spencer, Lillie Devereux Blake, Jane Graham Jones, Abigail Scott Duniway, Belva Lockwood, Isabella Beecher Hooker, Sara Williams, and Abby Ela.]

Source: Stanton, Elizabeth Cady, Susan B. Anthony, and Matilda Joslyn Gage, eds. *History of Woman Suffrage*. Vol. 3. 1886, Rochester, NY: National American Woman Suffrage Association, 1886, 31.

Isabella Beecher Hooker, *The Constitutional Rights of the Women of the United States* (1888)

A pivotal organizer of the drive for women's rights, Isabella Beecher Hooker directed the suffrage campaign from a state concern to a national crusade. By examining the Declaration of Independence and the Constitution, she pointed out precepts affecting women's lives and choices. Her lecture described suffrage as a rational argument based on law, the foundation of democracy.

In the month of August 1774, that eminent statesman and true patriot, Thomas Jefferson in a little tract entitled "A Summary View of the Rights of British America" used certain words which I will take for my text while addressing you to-day on the "Constitutional Rights of the Women Citizens of the United States." They are these: "The whole art of government consists in the art of being honest." And again: "The God who gave us life gave us liberty at the same time; the hand of force may destroy, but cannot disjoin them."

May I ask your patient attention while I attempt to show: First, that under a proper interpretation of the constitution of the United States, which he had so large a part in preparing, women have a right to vote today, on precisely the same terms with men; and secondly, that they ought, for various reasons, to exercise this right without subjection to molestation or delay, and men ought to help them to do so by every means in their power.

First let me speak of the Constitution of the United States, and assert that there is not a line in it, nor a word, forbidding women to vote; but, properly interpreted, that is, interpreted by the Declaration of Independence, and by the assertions of the Fathers, it actually guarantees to women the right to vote in all elections, both state and national. Listen to the preamble to the constitution, and the preamble you know, is the key to what follows; it is the concrete, general statement of the great principles which subsequent articles express in detail. The preamble says:

> We, the People of the United States, in order to form a more perfect union, establish justice, insure domestic tranquility, provide for the common defense, promote the general welfare, and secure the blessings of liberty to ourselves and our posterity, do ordain and establish this Constitution for the United States of American.

Commit this to memory, friends; learn it by heart as well as by head, and I should have no need to argue to question before you of my right to vote. For women are "people" surely, and desire, as much as men, to say the least, to establish justice and to insure domestic tranquility; and, brothers, you will never insure domestic tranquility in the days to come unless you allow women to vote, who pay taxes and bear equally with yourselves all the burdens of society; for they do not mean any longer to submit patiently and quietly to such injustice, and the sooner men understand this and graciously submit to become the political equals of their mothers, wives, and daughters—aye, of their grandmothers, for that is my category, instead of their political masters, as they now are, the sooner will this precious domestic tranquility be insured. Women are surely "people," I said, and were when these words were written, and were as anxious as men to establish justice and promote the general welfare, and no one will have the hardihood to deny that our foremothers (have we not talked about our forefathers alone long enough?) did their full share in the work of establishing justice, providing for the common defense, and promoting the general welfare in all those early days.

The truth is, friends, that when liberties had to be gained by the sword and protected by the sword, men necessarily came to the front and seemed to be the only creators and defenders of these liberties; hence all the way down women have been content to do their patriotic work silently and through men, who are the fighters by nature rather than themselves, until the present day;

but now at last, when it is established that ballots instead of bullets are to rule the world, and we in this country are making and upholding our just laws by ballots alone, keeping our bullets for the few wretched Indians on the frontiers, whom we are wicked enough to wish to exterminate rather than to civilize and educate, now, it is high time that women ceased to attempt to establish justice and promote the general welfare, and secure the blessings of liberty to themselves and their posterity, through the votes of men, because they cannot control these votes and turn them to high moral uses in government; on the contrary, our brothers, the best of them, are at their wit's end to-day, and so appalled at the moral corruptions of the body politic that they are ready, some of them, to throw away their own power to vote and go back upon the whole theory of our government of the many, of the people (our government nominally of the people, by the people, and for the people), and to ask for the government of the few once more—the few rich, the few wise, the few educated.

But I shall deal with this point hereafter. I only wish to fasten upon your minds now this thought, that women are included in this word "people" of the preamble, and were intended to be included as much as men, and that their non-use of the ballot in all the past, because they chose to exercise their people's powers in other ways, has not cut them off from their right to use the ballot at any time they may see fit; and you will perceive by a careful examination of the whole constitution which follows the preamble, and which became the law of the land so early as 1789, that women were embraced in its provisions precisely as men were, and that the word "people," so frequently used, always included them.

This is true of the four articles which I will consider, and of every other article in the constitution where the word "people" is used. Article I of the amendments is: "The right of the people to peaceably assemble and petition for a redress of grievances," etc. No one doubts that women have that right equally with men; in fact, this is about the only political right that is cheerfully accorded to us to-day, because it is so easy to get rid of us and silence us in that way.

For years and years women have been petitioning Congress and the state legislatures to take down the political bars which men have put up, contrary to the national constitution and the whole spirit of our government, and allow them to become active co-workers in promoting the general welfare; but the reply has been "leave to withdraw," or its equivalent; and this simply because these women petitioners had no power to cut off the heads of these congressmen and assemblymen; (their political heads, I mean, because we do not believe much in bloodshed of any sort). So long ago as 1871 I got an order from a Senator to the clerk of the Senate for a search for petitions then on file his office, and here is the clerk's report. He found the names of 20,000 women slumbering in the dusty pigeon holes of his office, and the honorable gentleman who asked me with a smile of contempt "How many women really want to vote?" was surprised at the record, which was not a tenth part of the number who had been wearily petitioning our legislative bodies year after year since 1848.

And then there is Article II, with its provision for "the right of the People to keep and to bear arms," etc., which right women assuredly have equally with men, and which, unless some new protective element is brought into society, women will be compelled to use in self-defense as never before, for the crimes against woman in her very womanhood are becoming unendurably frequent all over our land. The new protective element I hardly need say is the ballot in her own hands, since it is already in the hands of these ruffians who make night hideous and who virtually close the thoroughfares of our cities and villages even to all honest women the moment the sun has gone down. Have you ever thought of it, gentlemen, you who are opposed to woman's use of the ballot, that among her so-called protectors who are to use her ballot for her, are these very men for whom we build most of our jails and penitentiaries, taxing the women to do it, and that every election day sees paupers and vagrants taken from the workhouse to elect the men who are to make and administer the laws for all women no less than all men?

Article IV provides for "the right of the people to be secure against unreasonable searches and seizures," etc. Women surely need to be and are thus secured. And Article IX provides that the "enumeration in the constitution of certain rights shall not be construed to deny others retained by the People."

Is it not perfectly clear that all these are the rights of women equally with men, and that the term "people" as here used was intended to embrace both?

Thus, then, the preamble and the constitution under which our government was formed and began its work of protective legislation, plainly embraced women in all its provisions; and when the preamble declares that the object of all was to secure the blessings of liberty to ourselves and our posterity, it surely did not mean to secure to men alone and their posterity these blessings of liberty, to the half of ourselves and the half of our posterity, but to the whole people, women as well as men . . .

Source: Hooker, Isabella Beecher. *The Constitutional Rights of the Women of the United States*. Hartford, CT: Hartford Press, 1900.

Frances E. W. Harper, "Woman's Political Future" (1893)

African American abolitionist, poet, novelist, and suffragist Frances Ellen Watkins Harper was active in the women's rights, civil rights, and temperance movements. She regularly addressed suffrage organizations and was involved with the international women's movement as well. Harper presented this address on May 20, 1893, before the World Congress of Representative Women, a gathering of international women's rights activists as part of the World's Columbian Exposition in Chicago, Illinois, marking the 400th-year anniversary of Christopher Columbus's arrival in the New World.

If before sin had cast its deepest shadows or sorrow had distilled its bitterest tears, it was true that it was not good for man to be alone, it is no less true, since the shadows have deepened and life's sorrows have increased, that the world has need of all the spiritual aid that woman can give for the social advancement and moral development of the human race. The tendency of the present age, with its restlessness, religious upheavals, failures, blunders, and crimes, is toward broader freedom, an increase of knowledge, the emancipation of thought, and a recognition of the brotherhood of man; in this movement woman, as the companion of man, must be a sharer. So close is the bond between man and woman that you can not raise one without lifting the other. The world can not move without woman's sharing in the movement, and to help give a right impetus to that movement is woman's highest privilege.

If the fifteenth century discovered America to the Old World, the nineteenth is discovering woman to herself. Little did Columbus imagine, when the New World broke upon his vision like a lovely gem in the coronet of the universe, the glorious possibilities of a land where the sun should be our engraver, the winged lightning our messenger, and steam our beast of burden. But as mind is more than matter, and the highest ideal always the true real, so to woman comes the opportunity to strive for richer and grander discoveries than ever gladdened the eye of the Genoese mariner.

Not the opportunity of discovering new worlds, but that of filling this old world with fairer and higher aims than the greed of gold and the lust of power, is hers. Through weary, wasting years men have destroyed, dashed in pieces, and overthrown, but today we stand on the threshold of woman's era, and woman's work is grandly constructive. In her hand are possibilities whose use or abuse must tell upon the political life of the nation, and send their influence for good or evil across the track of unborn ages.

As the saffron tints and crimson flushes of morn herald the coming day, so the social and political advancement which woman has already gained bears the promise of the rising of the full-orbed sun of emancipation. The result will be not to make home less happy, but society more holy; yet I do not think the mere extension of the ballot a panacea for all the ills of our national life. What we need today is not simply more voters, but better voters. Today there are red-handed men in our republic, who walk unwhipped of justice, who richly deserve to exchange the ballot of the freeman for the wristlets of the felon; brutal and cowardly men, who torture, burn, and lynch their fellow-men, men whose defenselessness should be their best defense and their weakness an ensign of protection. More than the changing of institutions we need the development of a national conscience, and the upbuilding of national character.

. . .

Today women hold in their hands influence and opportunity, and with these they have already opened doors which have been closed to others. By opening doors of labor woman has become a rival claimant for at least some of the wealth monopolized by her stronger brother. In the home she is the priestess, in society the queen, in literature she is a power, in legislative halls law-makers have responded to her appeals, and for her sake have humanized and liberalized their laws. The press has felt the impress of her hand. In the pews of the church she constitutes the majority; the pulpit has welcomed her, and in the school she has the blessed privilege of teaching children and youth. To her is apparently coming the added responsibility of political power; and what she now possesses should only be the means of preparing her to use the coming power for the glory of God and the good of mankind; for power without righteousness is one of the most dangerous forces in the world.

Political life in our country has plowed in muddy channels, and needs the infusion of clearer and cleaner waters. I am not sure that women are naturally so much better than men that they will clear the stream by the virtue of their womanhood; it is not through sex but through character that the best influence of women upon the life of the nation must be exerted.

I do not believe in unrestricted and universal suffrage for either men or women. I believe in moral and educational tests. I do not believe that the most ignorant and brutal man is better prepared to add value to the strength and durability of the government than the most cultured, upright, and intelligent woman. I do not think that willful ignorance should swamp earnest intelligence at the ballot-box, nor that educated wickedness, violence, and fraud should cancel the votes of honest men. The unsteady hands of a drunkard can not cast the ballot of a freeman. The hands of lynchers are too red with blood to determine the political character of the government for even four short years. The ballot in the hands of woman means power added to influence. How well she will use that power I can not foretell. Great evils stare us in the face that need to be throttled by the combined power of an upright manhood and an enlightened womanhood; and I know that no nation can gain its full measure of enlightenment and happiness if one-half of it is free and the other half is fettered. China compressed the feet of her women and thereby retarded the steps of her men. The elements of a nation's weakness must ever be found at the hearthstone.

More than the increase of wealth, the power of armies, and the strength of fleets is the need of good homes, of good fathers, and good mothers.

. . .

O women of America! into your hands God has pressed one of the sublimest opportunities that ever came into the hands of the women of any race or people. It is yours to create a healthy public sentiment; to demand justice, simple justice, as the right of every race; to brand with everlasting infamy the lawless and brutal cowardice that lynches, burns, and tortures your own countrymen.

To grapple with the evils which threaten to undermine the strength of the nation and to lay magazines of powder under the cribs of future generations is no child's play.

Let the hearts of the women of the world respond to the song of the herald angels of peace on earth and good will to men. Let them throb as one heart unified by the grand and holy purpose of uplifting the human race, and humanity will breathe freer, and the world grow brighter. With such a purpose Eden would spring up in our path, and Paradise be around our way.

Source: Frances E. W. Harper. "Woman's Political Future." In *World's Congress of Representative Women*, edited by Mary Wright Sewall. Chicago, IL: Rand McNally, 1894, 433–437.

Alice Stone Blackwell, *Why Women Should Vote* (1896)

Largely remembered for impromptu oratory and radical journalism as editor of the Woman's Journal, *Alice Stone Blackwell, daughter of prominent reformers and suffragists Lucy Stone and Henry Browne Blackwell, addressed the House Judiciary Committee in 1896 and outlined 16 reasons why women deserved full citizenship. Her list appealed to justice, fairness, and universal humanity as well as to public welfare.*

1. Because it is fair and right that those who must obey the laws should have a voice in making them, and that those who must pay taxes should have a vote as to the size of the tax and the way it shall be spent.

2. Because the moral, educational, and humane legislation desired by women would be got more easily if women had votes. New York women have worked in vain for years to secure a legislative appropriation to found a state industrial School for Girls. Colorado women worked in vain for one till they got the ballot; then the Legislature promptly granted it.

3. Because laws unjust to women would be amended more quickly. It cost Massachusetts women 55 years of effort to secure the law making mothers equal guardians of their children with the fathers. In Colorado, after women were enfranchised, the very next Legislature granted it. After more than half a century of agitation by women for this reform only 13 out of 46 States now give equal guardianship to mothers.

4. Because disfranchisement helps to keep wages down. The Honorable Carroll D. Wright, National Commissioner of Labor said in an address delivered at Smith College on February 22, 1902: "The lack of direct political influence constitutes a powerful reason why women's wages have been kept at a minimum."

5. Because equal suffrage would increase the proportion of educated voters. The high schools of every state in the Union are graduating more girls than boys—often twice or three times as many.

6. Because it would increase the proportion of native-born voters. In three years from June 30, 1900, to June 30, 1903, there landed in the United States 1,344,622 foreign men, and only 576,746 foreign women.

7. Because it would increase the moral and law-abiding vote very much, while increasing the vicious and criminal vote very little. The U.S. Census of 1890 gives the statistics of men and women in the state prisons of the different States. Omitting fractions, they are as follows: In the District of Columbia, women constitute 17 percent of the prisoners; in Massachusetts and Rhode

Island, 14 percent; in New York, 13; in Louisiana, 12; in Virginia, 11; in New Jersey, 10; in Pennsylvania and Maryland, 9; in Connecticut, 8; in Alabama, New Hampshire, Ohio and South Carolina, 7; in Florida, Maine, Mississippi, New Mexico and Tennessee, 6; in Georgia, Illinois, Indiana, Kentucky, Michigan, Missouri, North Carolina and West Virginia, 5; in Arkansas and Delaware, 4; in California, Minnesota, North Dakota, Texas and Vermont, 3; in Colorado, Iowa, Montana, Nebraska and Utah, 2; in Arizona, Kansas, Nevada and South Dakota, 1; in Washington, four-fifths of 1 percent; in Oregon and Wisconsin, two-fifths of 1 percent; in Wyoming and Idaho, none.

8. Because it leads to fair treatment of women in the public service. In Massachusetts the average pay of a female teacher is about one-third that of a male teacher, and in almost all the States it is unequal. In Wyoming and Utah, the law provides that they shall receive equal pay for usual work.

9. Because legislation for the protection of children would be secured more easily. Judge Lindsey of the Denver Juvenile Court writes in *Progress* for July, 1904: "We have in Colorado the most advanced laws of any state in the Union for the care and protection of the home and the children. These laws in my opinion, would not exist at this time if it were not for the powerful influence of woman suffrage."

10. Because it is the quietest, easiest, most dignified and least conspicuous way of influencing public affairs. It takes much less expenditure of time, labor and personal presence to go up to the ballot box, drop in a slip of paper, and then come away, than to persuade a multitude of miscellaneous voters to vote right.

11. Because it would make women more broadminded. Professor Edward H. Griggs says: "The ballot is an educator, and women will become more practical and more wise in using it."

12. Because woman's ballot will make it hard for the notoriously bad candidates to be nominated or elected. In the equal suffrage states, both parties have to put men of respectable character or lose the women's vote.

13. Because it would increase women's influence. Mrs. Mary C. C. Bradford, president of the Colorado State Federation of Women's clubs, said at the National Suffrage Convention in Washington in February: "Instead of woman's influence being lessened by the ballot, it is greatly increased. Last year there were so many members of the legislature with bills which they wanted

the club women to indorse that the Social Science department of the State Federation had to sit one day each week to confer with these legislators who were seeking our endorsement. Clubwomen outside the suffrage states do not have this experience.

14. Because it would help those women who need help the most. Theodore Roosevelt recommended woman suffrage in his message to the New York Legislature. On being asked why, he reported to have answered that many women have a very hard time, working women especially, and if the ballot would help them, even a little, he was a willing to see it tried. Mrs. Maud Nathan, President of the National Consumers' League, said in an address at the National Suffrage Convention in Washington, in February, 1904: "My experience in investigating the condition of women wage-earners warrants the assertion that some of the evils from which they suffer would not exist if women had the ballot. In the States where women vote, there is far better enforcement of the laws which protect working girls."

15. Because it is a maxim in war: "Always do the thing to which your adversary particularly objects." Every vicious interest in the country would rather continue to contend with woman's indirect influence than try to cope with woman's vote.

16. Because experience has proved it to be good. Women have for years been voting literally by hundreds of thousands, in England, Scotland, Ireland, Australia, New Zealand, Canada, Wyoming, Colorado, Kansas, Utah, and Idaho, in all these places put together, the opponents have not yet found a dozen respectable men who assert over their own names and addresses that the results have been bad, while scores of prominent men and women testify that it has done good. An ounce of fret is worth a ton of theory.

Source: Blackwell, Alice Stone. *Why Women Should Vote.* Philadelphia: Pennsylvania Woman Suffrage Association, 1915.

Harriot Stanton Blatch, "Woman as an Economic Factor" (1898)

An economist and advocate for working women, suffragist Harriot Eaton Stanton Blatch, daughter of Elizabeth Cady Stanton, grew up in a radical environment committed to gender equality. In "Woman as an Economic Factor" she argued for women's right to vote based on their economic contribution to society, arguing against those who argued that women had no "worth" relevant to or interest in political life.

It is often urged that women stand greatly in need of training in citizenship before being finally received into the body politic. This argument is usually put forward in a tone of weighty wisdom by the opponent who thinks his demand is only prompted by a question of national welfare, but which in truth results from never taking cognizance of the fact that women are the first class who have asked for the right of citizenship after their ability for political life had been proved.

I have seen in my time two enormous extensions of the suffrage to men—one in America and one in England. But neither the negro in the South nor the agricultural laborer in Great Britain had showed before they got the ballot any capacity for government; for they had never had the opportunity to take the first baby steps in political action.

Very different has been the history of the march of women toward a recognized position in the state. We have had to prove our ability at each stage of progress, and have gained nothing without having satisfied a test of capacity. The history of the conferring upon women of the right to vote for and be elected members of school boards in England illustrates this point, and is typical of our political achievements in other lines. Before the education acts of 1870, women were appointed here and there as school managers, because some local circumstance made the need of them felt. When the new departure in education was made and election boards established, it was but a natural development, a conservative recognition of their usefulness, for women to become elected representatives on the new educational bodies. By proved worth in the first position, women gained popular assent to the exercise of a further privilege of citizenship. And so in America, after having been appointed or elected to small township offices, they have passed on to wider spheres in county or state, and finally have been elected to legislatures. In England there are to-day over 2,000 women sitting as popularly elected representatives on school boards, boards of guardians, on parish and district councils. These women are elected to perform these important duties of citizenship time after time, and are almost invariably returned at the head of the poll. All this surely is a quiet, steady, reasonable verdict upon how women carry out their work as administrative officers.

The right to vote has always been considered more sacred than the right to be elected to office, and has consequently been more safe-guarded and more cautiously conferred. Therefore, to urge that women have proved useful to the community as officials does not convince a political student that they are fitted to be electors. Nor do I wish to claim their fitness on such grounds. I rest our demand here, as in the other case, upon the safe foundation of proved ability. We were given a small local vote here, or the school suffrage there, and wider and wider duties were conferred only after capacity for government was shown in the narrow sphere. Nowhere has complete enfranchisement been conferred on women, as it was on negroes, with the stroke of the pen. Slowly, step by step, women have gained every vote in England except the parliamentary suffrage.

Just as slowly, in America, they have made their way, until, in a few states, they are now full citizens. The last franchise in England will be conferred when public opinion is fully convinced of the conscientious manner in which women are exercising the rights they have, and the older and more conservative states of the union will give vote after vote to us as we prove the value of our work in political life. The contention of our opponents, then, that we must get political training before claiming citizenship, is but a display of ignorance regarding the history of our emancipation; for our political evolution has not come through abstract reasoning about man's natural rights, but as the result, if I may be permitted the phrase, of a civil-service examination of a searching nature into our capacity for citizenship.

Now, as "proved worth" has been the cause of our progress so far, it is evident that along that line future efforts must be made. The value of a voter depends largely upon the conscientious manner in which he endeavors to inform himself upon public questions; and therefore such associations as the league directed by Dr. Jacobi and Mrs. Sanders in New York, in so far as they are forming a scholarly habit in the study of political questions among women, are building up a class which will prove in time of the highest value to the State, and which will have on that account an irresistible claim to citizenship. When the various clubs of women the country over have developed more thoroughly their study of political and economic problems, they will have educated all their members into seeing that a republic must have from each and all of its citizens self-denial and devotion—that there is no room for the shirk except under a Russian despotism.

The public demand for "proved worth" suggests, too, another, and what appears to me the chief and most convincing argument upon which our future claims must rest. I refer to the growing recognition of the economic value of the work of women. I intentionally do not say an increase in their work, for it is a popular mistake to suppose that women are rushing in large numbers into gainful pursuits. This false impression has come about by women of the well-to-do class taking it for granted that the doings of their tiny body are of great importance and typical of all classes. For instance, because women architects increased from 1 to 22 in the years between 1870 and 1890, chemists, assayers, and metallurgists from nothing to 46, and women in the ministry from 67 to 1,237, it has been hastily concluded that these enormous percentages (though, mark you, absurdly small absolute numbers) were characteristic of industrial employments; but no less an authority than Carroll D. Wright truly says: "The proportion of women laborers is increasing a little less than 3 per cent."

However, although it is a mistake to say that women are adopting gainful pursuits in largely increased proportion, and although we cannot claim for them any great advance in efficiency, there has been a marked change in the estimate of our position as wealth producers. We have never been supported by men; for if all men labored hard every hour of the twenty-four, they could not do all the work of the world. A few worthless women there are, but even they are not so much supported by the men of their family as by the overwork of the "sweated" women at the other end of the social ladder. From creation's dawn our sex has done its full share of the world's work; sometimes we have been paid for it, but oftener not.

Unpaid work never commands respect. It is the paid worker that has brought to the public mind conviction of our worth. The spinning and weaving done by our great-grandmothers in their own homes was not reckoned as national wealth, until the work was carried to the factory and organized there; and the women, who followed their work, were paid according to its commercial value. It is the women of the industrial class, the wage-earners, reckoned by the hundreds of thousands, and not by units, the women whose work has been submitted to a money test, who have been the means of bringing about the altered attitude of public opinion toward woman's work in every sphere of life.

If we recognize the democratic side of our cause and make an organized appeal to industrial women on the ground of their need of citizenship and to the nation on the ground of its need that all wealth producers should form part of its body politic, the close of the century might witness the building up of a true republic in the United States.

Source: Blatch, Harriot Stanton. "Woman as an Economic Factor." In *History of Woman Suffrage*. Vol. 4. Indianapolis, IN: Hollenbeck Press, 1902.

Florence Kelley, "Child Labor and Women's Suffrage" (1905)

Social reformer and secretary of the National Consumers League, Florence Kelley worked as an investigator for the Illinois Bureau of Labor Statistics in 1892 and reported on the conditions of sweatshops in the garment industry. She spoke out against child labor and was influential in the passage of wage and hour laws as well as in the creation of the Children's Bureau of the U.S. Department of Labor. In this speech, delivered in Philadelphia, Pennsylvania, in July 1905, Kelley argues that if women could vote they would vote with their consciences against abusive labor practices.

We have, in this country, two million children under the age of sixteen years who are earning their bread. They vary in age from six and seven years (in the cotton mills of Georgia) and eight, nine and ten years (in the coal-breakers of Pennsylvania), to fourteen, fifteen and sixteen years in more enlightened States.

No other portion of the wage earning class increased so rapidly from decade to decade as the young girls from fourteen to twenty years. Men increase, women increase, youth increase, boys increase in the ranks of the breadwinners; but no contingent so doubles from census period to census period (both by percent and by count of heads), as does the contingent of girls between twelve and twenty years of age. They are in commerce, in offices, in manufacture.

To-night while we sleep, several thousand little girls will be working in textile mills, all the night through, in the deafening noise of the spindles and the looms spinning and weaving cotton and woolen, silks and ribbons for us to buy.

In Alabama the law provides that a child under sixteen years of age shall not work in a cotton mill at night longer than eight hours, and Alabama does better in this respect than any other Southern State. North and South Carolina and Georgia place no restriction upon the work of children at night; and while we sleep little white girls will be working to-night in the mills in those States, working eleven hours at night.

In Georgia there is no restriction whatever! A girl of six or seven years, just tall enough to reach the bobbins, may work eleven hours by day or by night. And they will do so to-night, while we sleep.

Nor is it only in the South that these things occur. Alabama does better than New Jersey. For Alabama limits the children's work at night to eight hours, while New Jersey permits it all night long. Last year New Jersey took a long backward step. A good law was repealed which had required women and [children] to stop work at six in the evening and at noon on Friday. Now, therefore, in New Jersey, boys and girls, after the 14th birthday, enjoy the pitiful privilege of working all night long.

In Pennsylvania, until last May it was lawful for children, 13 years of age, to work twelve hours at night. A little girl, on her thirteenth birthday, could start away from her home at half past five in the afternoon, carrying her pail of midnight luncheon as happier people carry their midday luncheon, and could work in the mill from six at night until six in the morning, without violating any law of the Commonwealth.

If the mothers and the teachers in Georgia could vote, would the Georgia Legislature have refused at every session for the last three years to stop the work in the mills of children under twelve years of age?

Would the New Jersey Legislature have passed that shameful repeal bill enabling girls of fourteen years to work all night, if the mothers in New Jersey were enfranchised? Until the mothers in the great industrial States are enfranchised, we shall none of us be able to free our consciences from participation in this great evil. No one in this room to-night can feel free from such participation. The children make our shoes in the shoe factories; they knit our stockings, our knitted underwear in the knitting factories. They spin and weave our cotton underwear in the cotton mills. Children braid straw for our hats, they spin and weave the silk and velvet wherewith we trim our hats. They stamp buckles and metal ornaments of all kinds, as well as pins and hat-pins. Under the sweating system, tiny children make artificial flowers and neckwear for us to buy. They carry bundles of garments from the factories to the tenements, little beasts of burden, robbed of school life that they may work for us.

We do not wish this. We prefer to have our work done by men and women. But we are almost powerless. Not wholly powerless, however, are citizens who enjoy the right of petition. For myself, I shall use this power in every possible way until the right to the ballot is granted, and then I shall continue to use both.

What can we do to free our consciences? There is one line of action by which we can do much. We can enlist the workingmen on behalf of our enfranchisement just in proportion as we strive with them to free the children. No labor organization in this country ever fails to respond to an appeal for help in the freeing of the children.

For the sake of the children, for the Republic in which these children will vote after we are dead, and for the sake of our cause, we should enlist the workingmen voters, with us, in this task of freeing the children from toil.

Source: Kelley, Florence. Speech read at the National Suffrage Convention, Philadelphia, PA, July 22, 1905. Reprinted in *Everyday Housekeeping*, Vol. 23:1, August 1906.

Women Opponents of Suffrage, "Why the Home Makers Do Not Want to Vote" (1909)

The Illinois Association Opposed to the Extension of Suffrage to Women was founded and led by Caroline Fairchild Corbin, a Chicago socialite who was convinced that the drive for women's suffrage was a socialist plot to undermine the stability of American homes. Corbin was the primary author of most of the Illinois Association's tracts and pamphlets decrying women's suffrage. One such essay from the organization was this 1909 work, titled "Why the Home Makers Do Not Want to Vote," which asserts that once women are exposed to the world of business, they will be forever spoiled for carrying out the traditional duties of wife and mother.

The independent position of American women in the home and society is the wonder of Europe. Scarcely an intelligent foreigner, man or woman, who comes to us, but expresses this astonishment. The burdens which nature puts upon women everywhere, they bear in common with their sex, but under circumstances of such freedom, homage and chivalrous respect as obtain nowhere else in the world. Their rights, privileges and immunities as faithful wives and mothers, although they may not attain to the perfect ideal, are nevertheless beyond what any other body of women enjoy.

The history of American legislation proves that for fifty years or more men have been busy, often quite of their own unsolicited goodwill, in improving the legal status of women in matters of property rights, inheritance rights and the custody of their children. And these prerogatives extend far beyond woman's immediate social and domestic sphere. It is the testimony of many excellent women workers in philanthropic enterprises, both public and private, that when legal aid is necessary in carrying out their plans for the wellbeing of the poor and unfortunate, if they go to the legislatures as women, not as politicians working in connection with any political party, they have no difficulty in gaining their ends; while as members of opposing parties their bills would be held up session after session. Thoughtful women who are engaged in the highest enterprises of womanhood, home making and soul building, the work of social amelioration, and the care of the poor and unfortunate, cannot see how they would be the gainers by possessing the ballot.

...

A temporary disarrangement of the equal division of labor between the sexes has been caused by the absorption of much that was formerly considered woman's household work into great manufacturing and commercial enterprises, thus drawing the women after their work into shops and factories, and indeed into almost all the occupations which have been considered as belonging to men and boys as wage earners. It requires little observation and study to see that this process has many evil results. It lowers the wages of men and obliges them to forego or to postpone marriage, thus tempting them to immorality; and it draws off from household service the very class upon which householders have hitherto depended for help. The great dearth of household service has become a serious trial to families, and together with the raising of wages in the home to a degree approximately corresponding to the lowering of men's wages—a very noticeable gain to women let us observe with which the ballot has nothing to do—contributes another impediment to marriage....

But the evil, dark and discouraging as it is, is already turning a brighter side, a remedy very different from that proposed by women suffragists, who view with great complacency a state of things which under their management would soon show, is indeed now showing, signs of the disintegration of all marriage relations. In almost every state of the Union, women of experience, intelligence and character, have taken up with great zeal and earnestness, the education of young girls who would naturally fall into the ranks of wage earners, in the housewifely arts and sciences. The work is followed by the opening of doors to them into womanly pursuits which are auxiliary to the home, without being dependent upon it. A needed relief is thus afforded to the housekeeper, which does not destroy the independent character of the worker.

. . .

Many voices are being raised in both church and state, calling attention to the decay of family life, and in more than one instance the evil is emphatically traced to the false doctrines concerning the emancipation of women, which are being disseminated.

. . .

It is for reasons like these that the great body of American women do not wish to vote. They love their own sphere in life, they feel their own adaptation to it, and fifty years of relentless agitation has not convinced them that participation in the duties which belong to men, would make them more honored, more useful, or happier.

Source: "Why the Home Makers Do Not Want to Vote." Illinois Association Opposed to the Extension of Suffrage to Women, Chicago, 1909. Collection Development Department. Widener Library, Harvard University.

Theodore Roosevelt, "Women's Rights; and the Duties of Both Men and Women" (1912)

As the Progressive Party presidential candidate in 1912, Theodore Roosevelt tentatively campaigned in favor of woman suffrage, although he felt that it was up to the states to decide whether or not it should be granted. He also explained that men and women had different roles in society and would therefore have a different relationship to political participation.

I believe in women's rights. I believe even more earnestly in the performance of duty by both men and women; for unless the average man and the average woman live lives of duty, not only our democracy but civilization itself will perish. I heartily believe in equality of rights as between man and woman, but also in full and emphatic recognition of the fact that normally there cannot be identity of function. Indeed, there must normally be complete dissimilarity of function between them, and the effort to ignore this patent fact is silly. I believe in woman's suffrage where the women want it. Where they do not want it, the suffrage should not be forced upon them. I think that it would be well to let the women themselves, and only the women, vote at some special election as to whether they do or do not wish the vote as a permanent possession.

In other words, this is peculiarly a case for the referendum to those most directly affected—that is, the women themselves. I believe such a referendum was held in Massachusetts, in which a majority of the women who voted, voted in favor of the ballot. But they included only about five percent of the women who were entitled to vote, and where the vote is so light, those not voting should be held to have voted no. This was in 1895. It would be well to try to the experiment again in the more doubtful States like Massachusetts or New York. I should be entirely content to abide the decision, either way; for, though I do not think that the damage prophesied from women's voting would come, or has come where it has been tried, I also think that very much less effect would be produced, one way or the other, than the enthusiasts believe. In other words,

I do not regard the movement as anything like as important as either its extreme friends or extreme opponents think. It is so much less important than many other reforms that I have never been able to take a very heated interest in it.

Perhaps one reason why so many men who believe as emphatically as I do in woman's full equality with man take little interest in the suffrage movement is to be found in the very unfortunate actions of certain leaders in that movement, who seem desirous of associating it with disorderly conduct in public and with thoroughly degrading and vicious assaults upon the morality and the duty of women within and without marriage.

. . .

If the woman suffrage movement were to be judged only by those advocates of it who discredit themselves and their sex by disorderly antics in public, and who assail the foundations of private and public morality in their endeavor, not to raise the sense of moral duty in man, but to lower the sense of moral duty in women, I should certainly oppose the movement. But I do not believe these undesirable apostles are in any way to be accepted as exponents of the cause, and I call attention to the fact that they are prominent, not in the region where woman suffrage does exist, but in regions where it does not exist.

I pin my faith to woman suffragists of the type of the late Julia Ward Howe. Julia Ward Howe was one of the foremost citizens of this Republic; she rendered service to the people such as few men in any generation render; and yet she did, first of all, her full duty in the intimate home relations that must ever take precedence of all other relations. . . . We are fortunate in being able to point to such a woman as exemplifying all that we mean when we insist that the good woman's primary duties must be those to the home and the family, those of wife and mother; but that the full performance of those duties may be helped and not hindered if she also possess a sense of duty to the public, and the power and desire to perform this duty.

In our Western States where the suffrage has been given to women I am unable to see that any great difference has been caused, as compared with neighboring States of similar social and industrial conditions where women have not the suffrage. There has been no very marked change in general political conditions, nor in the social and industrial position of woman. . . . In those Western States it is a real pleasure to meet women, thoroughly womanly women, who do every duty that any woman can do, and who also are not only in fact but in theory on a level of full equality with men. I fail to see that these women are any less efficient in their households, or show any falling off in the sense of duty; I think the contrary is the case; and so far as their influence has affected political life at all it has affected it for good. . . .

. . .

Most of the women whom I know best are against woman suffrage precisely because they approach life from the standpoint of duty. They are not interested in their "rights" so much as in their obligations. They tell me that they feel that already they have as much to do as they can well attend to; that their duties are numerous and absorbing—although they are happy in doing them; and that, for the very reason that they take their duties seriously, and would accept suffrage seriously as a duty, they do not think that such a heavy additional burden should be put on their shoulders, It is, however, with me a question whether these women, with busy, happy, duty-filled lives, are really typical of those other women who are more or less defense-less. These other women, wage-earning girls for instance, and wives whose husbands are brutal or inconsiderate, would, I believe, be helped by the suffrage, if they used it wisely and honorably. I hope that if women voted we should be able to wage a more rapidly successful war against the "white salve" traffic and kindred iniquities.

. . .

I most earnestly desire to emphasize my feeling that the question of woman suffrage is unimportant compared to the great fundamental questions that go to the root of right conduct as regards both men and women. There should be equality of rights and duties, but not identity of function; and with the man, as with the woman, the prime duties are those related to the home and the family. . . . The first duty of the average citizen is to be a good father or mother, husband or wife. . . . Other fools, advising women to forsake their primary duties and "go into industry" prattle about the "economic dependence" of the wife. Economic dependence, forsooth! Any husband who regards his wife as "economically dependent," or who fails to recognize her as a full partner, needs severe handling by society or the State. The service of the good mother to society is the most valuable economic asset that the entire commonwealth can show, and is of infinitely more worth to society than any possible service the woman could render by any other, and necessarily inferior, form of industry.

Motherhood must be protected; and the State should make the security of the mothers its first concern. . . . Mothers (and children) should not be allowed to work in any way that interferes with the home duties; and widowed mothers with children and deserted mothers with children must be cared for. *But the care must not be given in such way as to encourage the man to shirk his duty.* His prime duty is to provide for his wife and his children; if he fails to do so, the law should instantly seize him and force him to do so. It should be even more severe in thus forcing him to care for his children if he has not married their mother. In such case the man has not merely grievously sinned against another human being, but has grievously sinned against society, against the commonwealth. . . . Our aim must be the healthy economic interdependence of the sexes, based on equality of rights and of obligations, including the obligations of sexual and domestic morality; any attempt to bring about the kind of "economic independence" which means a false identity of economic function spells mere ruin. The home, based on the love of one man for one woman and the performance in common of their duty to their children, is the finest product of Christianity and civilization. Our consistent effort must be to strengthen it, and any movement to destroy it marks the nadir of folly and wickedness. . . .

Source: Roosevelt, Theodore. "Women's Rights: And the Duties of Both Men and Women." *Outlook* (February 3, 1912): 262–266.

Helen Keller, "Why Men Need Woman Suffrage" (1913)

Left deaf and blind by an illness as a toddler, Helen Keller overcame these challenges to become a politically astute and outspoken writer, reformer, and suffragist. In this article published in the New York Call *on October 17, 1913, Keller emphasized the plight and conditions of working women and children and the need for women to have a say in laws affecting the home and the workplace. As a socialist, she also hoped that women with the vote would bring about the end of a capitalist system built on exploitation. In addition to her work for women's suffrage and labor rights, Keller advocated for the blind and was a member of the Socialist Party of America, the Industrial Workers of the World, and cofounded the American Civil Liberties Union.*

Many declare that the woman peril is at our door. I have no doubt that it is. Indeed, I suspect that it has already entered most households. Certainly a great number of men are facing it across the breakfast table. And no matter how deaf they pretend to be, they cannot help hearing it talk.

Women insist on their "divine rights," "immutable rights," "inalienable rights." These phrases are not so sensible as one might wish. When one comes to think of it, there are no such things as divine, immutable or inalienable rights. Rights are things we get when we are strong enough to make good our claim to them. Men spent hundreds of years and did much hard fighting to get the rights they now call divine, immutable and inalienable. Today women are demanding rights that tomorrow nobody will be foolhardy enough to question.

Anyone that reads intelligently knows that some of our old ideas are up a tree, and that traditions are scurrying away before the advance of their everlasting enemy, the questioning mind of a new age. It is time to take a good look at human affairs in the light of new conditions and new ideas, and the tradition that man is the natural master of the destiny of the race is one of the first to suffer investigation.

The dullest can see that a good many things are wrong with the world. It is old-fashioned, running into ruts. We lack intelligent direction and control. We are not getting the most out of our opportunities and advantages. We must make over the scheme of life, and new tools are needed for the work. Perhaps one of the chief reasons for the present chaotic condition of things is that the world has been trying to get along with only half of itself. Everywhere we see running to waste woman-force that should be utilized in making the world a more decent home for humanity. Let us see how the votes of women will help solve the problem of living wisely and well.

When women vote men will no longer be compelled to guess at their desires—and guess wrong. Women will be able to protect themselves from man-made laws that are antagonistic to their interests. Some persons like to imagine that man's chivalrous nature will constrain him to act humanely toward woman and protect her rights. Some men do protect some women. We demand that all women have the right to protect themselves and relieve man of this feudal responsibility.

Political power shapes the affairs of state and determines many of the everyday relations of human beings with one another. The citizen with a vote is master of his own destiny. Women without this power, and who do not happen to have "natural protectors," are at the mercy of man-made laws. And experience shows that these laws are often unjust to them. Legislation made to protect women who have fathers and husbands to care for them does not protect working women whose only defenders are the state's policemen.

The wages of women in some states belong to their fathers or their husbands. They cannot hold property. In parts of this enlightened democracy of men the father is the sole owner of the child. I believe he can even will away the unborn babies. Legislation concerning the age of consent is another proof that the voice of woman is mute in the halls of the lawmakers. The regulations affecting laboring women are a proof that men are too busy to protect their "natural wards."

Economic urgencies have driven women to demand the vote. To a large number of women is entrusted the vitally important public function of training all childhood. Yet it is frequently impossible for teachers to support themselves decently on their wages. What redress have these overworked, underpaid women without the vote? They count for nothing politically.

An organization of women recently wanted to obtain a welfare measure from a Legislature in New York. A petition signed by 5,000 women was placed before the chairman of a committee that was to report on the bill. He said it was a good bill and ought to pass. After the women had waited a reasonable time, they sent up a request to know what had become of the bill. The chairman said he did not know anything about it. He was reminded of the petition that had been brought to him signed by 5,000 women. "Oh," replied the chairman, "a petition signed by 5,000 women is not worth the paper it is written on. Get five men to sign and we'll do something about it." That is one reason we demand the vote—we want 5,000 women to count for more than five men.

A majority of women that need the vote are wage-earners. A tremendous change has taken place in the industrial world since power machines took the place of hand tools. Men and women have been compelled to adjust themselves to a new system of production and distribution. The machine has been used to exploit the labor of both men and women as it was never exploited before. In the terrific struggle for existence that has resulted from this change women and children suffer even more than men. Indeed, economic pressure drives many women to market their sex.

Yet women have nothing to say about conditions under which they live and toil. Helpless, unheeded, they must endure hardships that lead to misery and degradation. They may not lift a hand to defend themselves against cruel, crippling processes that stunt the body and brain and bring on early death or premature old age.

Working men suffer from the helplessness of working women. They must compete in the same offices and factories with women who are unable to protect themselves with proper laws. They must compete with women who work in unsanitary rooms called homes, work by dim lamps in the night, rocking a cradle with one foot. It is to the interest of all workers to end this stupid, one-sided, one-power arrangement and have suffrage for all.

. . .

Women are even now more active in working for social legislation and laws affecting the schools, the milk supply and the quality of food than are the men who have the votes. Fundamentally, woman is a more social being than man. She is concerned with the whole family, while man is more individualistic. Social consciousness is not so strong in him. Many questions can be solved only with the help of woman's social experience—questions of the safety of women in their work, the rights of little children.

. . .

We shall not see the end of capitalism and the triumph of democracy until men and women work together in the solving of their political, social and economic problems. I realize that the vote is only one of many weapons in our fight for the freedom of all. But every means is precious and, equipped with the vote, men and women together will hasten the day when the age-long dream of liberty, equality and brotherhood shall be realized upon earth.

Source: Keller, Helen. "Why Men Need Woman Suffrage." *New York Call*, October 17, 1913.

Jane Addams, "If Men Were Seeking the Franchise" (1913)

In this article, published in Ladies Home Journal *in June 1913, Jane Addams turns the tables on her opponents in this satire that imagines a world run by women in which men must seek the vote. The piece is an attack on anti-women's suffrage arguments and exposes the reality and hypocrisy of female oppression.*

LET US IMAGINE THROUGHOUT this article, if we can sustain an absurd hypothesis so long, the result upon society if the matriarchal period had held its own; if the development of the State had closely followed that of the Family until the chief care of the former, as that of the latter, had come to be the nurture and education of children and the protection of the weak, sick and aged. In short let us imagine a hypothetical society organized upon the belief that "there is no wealth but life." With this Ruskinian foundation let us assume that the political machinery of such a society, the franchise and the rest of it, were in the hands of women because they had always best exercised those functions. Let us further imagine a given movement when these women, who in this hypothetical society had possessed political power from the very beginnings of the State, were being appealed to by the voteless men that men might be associated with women in the responsibilities of citizenship.

Plagiarizing somewhat upon recent suffrage speeches let us consider various replies which these citizen women might reasonably make to the men who were seeking the franchise; the men insisting that only through the use of the ballot could they share the duties of the State.

First, could not the women say: "Our most valid objection to extending the franchise to you is that you are so fond of fighting—you always have been since you were little boys. You'd very likely forget that the real object of the State is to nurture and protect life, and out of sheer vainglory you would be voting away huge sums of money for battleships, not one of which could last more than a few years, and yet each would cost ten million dollars; more money than all the buildings of Harvard University represent, although it is the richest educational institution in America. Every time a gun is fired in a battleship it expends, or rather explodes, seventeen hundred dollars, as much as a college education costs many a country boy, and yet you would be firing off these guns as mere salutes, with no enemy within three thousand miles, simply because you so enjoy the sound of shooting.

"Our educational needs are too great and serious to run any such risk. Democratic government itself is perilous unless the electorate is educated; our industries are suffering for lack of skilled workmen; more than half a million immigrants a year must be taught the underlying principles of republican government. Can we, the responsible voters, take the risk of wasting our taxes by extending the vote to those who have always been so ready to lose their heads over mere military display?"

Second, would not the hypothetical women, who would have been responsible for the advance of industry during these later centuries, as women actually were during the earlier centuries when they dragged home the game and transformed the pelts into shelter and clothing, say further to these disenfranchised men:

"We have carefully built up a code of factory legislation for the protection of the workers in modern industry; we know that you men have always been careless about the house, perfectly indifferent to the necessity for sweeping and cleaning; if you were made responsible for factory legislation it is quite probable that you would let the workers in the textile mills contract tuberculosis through needlessly breathing the fluff, or the workers in machine shops through inhaling metal filings, both of which are now carried off by an excellent suction system which we women have insisted upon, but which it [would be] almost impossible to have installed in a man-made State because the men think so little of dust and its evil effects. In many Nations in which political power is confined to men, and this is notably true in the United States of America, there is no protection even for the workers in white lead, although hundreds of them are yearly incapacitated from lead poisoning, and others actually die.

"We have also heard that in certain States, in order to save the paltry price of a guard which would protect a dangerous machine, men legislators allow careless boys and girls to lose their fingers and sometimes their hands, thereby crippling their entire futures. These male legislators do not make guarded machinery obligatory, although they know that when the heads of families are injured at these unprotected machines the State must care for them in hospitals, and when they are killed, that if necessary the State must provide for their widows and children in poorhouses."

These wise women, governing the State with the same care they had always put into the management of their families, would further place against these men seeking the franchise the charge that men do not really know how tender and delicate children are, and might therefore put them to work in factories, as indeed they have done in man-made States during the entire period of factory production. We can imagine these women saying: "We have been told that in certain States children are taken from their beds in the early morning before it is light and carried into cotton mills, where they are made to run back and forth tending the spinning frames until their immature little bodies are so bent and strained that they never regain their normal shapes; that little children are allowed to work in canneries for fifteen and seventeen hours until, utterly exhausted, they fall asleep among the debris of shells and husks."

Would not these responsible women voters gravely shake their heads and say that as long as men exalt business profit above human life it would be sheer folly to give them the franchise; that, of course, they would be slow to make such matters the subject of legislation? Would not the enfranchised women furthermore say to these voteless men:

"You have always been so eager to make money; what assurance have we that in your desire to get the largest amount of coal out of the ground in the shortest possible time you would not permit the mine supports to decay and mine damp to accumulate, until the percentage of accidents among miners would be simply heartbreaking? Then you are so reckless. Business seems to you a mere game with big prizes, and we have heard that in America, where the women have no vote, the loss of life in the huge steel mills is appalling; and that the number of young brakemen, fine young fellows, every one of them the pride of some mother, killed every year is beyond belief; that the average loss of life among the structural iron workers who erect the huge office buildings and bridges is as disastrous in percentages as was the loss of life in the Battle of Bull Run. When the returns of this battle were reported to President Lincoln he burst into tears of sorrow and chagrin; but we have never heard of any President, Governor or Mayor weeping over the reports of this daily loss of life, although such reports have been presented to them by Governmental investigators; and this loss of life might easily be reduced by protective legislation."

Having thus worked themselves into a fine state of irritation, analogous to that ever-recurrent uneasiness of men in the presence of insurgent women who would interfere in the management of the State, would not these voting women add: "The trouble is that men have no imagination, or rather what they have is so prone to run in the historic direction of the glory of the battle-field, that you cannot trust them with industrial affairs. Because a crew in a battle-ship was once lost under circumstances which suggested perfidy the male representatives of two great Nations voted to go to war; yet in any day of the year in one of these Nations alone—the United States of America—as many men are killed through industrial accidents as this crew contained. These accidents occur under circumstances which, if not perfidious, are at least so criminally indifferent to human life as to merit Kipling's characterization that the situation is impious."

Certainly these irritated women would designate such indifference to human life as unpatriotic and unjustifiable, only to be accounted for because men have not yet learned to connect patriotism with industrial affairs.

These conscientious women responsible for the State in which life was considered of more value than wealth would furthermore say: "Then, too, you men exhibit such curious survivals of the mere savage instinct of punishment and revenge. The United States alone spends every year five hundred million dollars more on its policemen, courts and prisons than all its works of religion, charity and education. The price of one trial expended on a criminal early in life might save the State thousands of dollars and the man untold horrors. And yet with all this vast expenditure little is done to reduce crime. Men are kept in jails and penitentiaries where there is not even the semblance of education or reformatory measure; young men are returned over and over again to the same institution until they have grown old and gray, and in all of that time they have not once been taught a trade, nor have they been in any wise prepared to withstand the temptations of life.

"A homeless young girl looking for a lodging may be arrested for soliciting on the streets, and sent to prison for six months, although there is no proof against her save the impression of the policeman. A young girl under such suspicion may be obliged to answer the most harassing questions put to her by the city attorney, with no woman near to protect her from insult; she may be subjected to the most trying examination conducted by a physician in the presence of a policeman, and no matron to whom to appeal. At least these things happen constantly in the United States—in Chicago, for instance—but possibly not in the Scandinavian countries where juries of women sit upon such cases, women whose patience has been many times tested by wayward girls and who know the untold moral harm which may result from such a physical and psychic shock."

Then these same women would go further, and, because they had lived in a real world and had administered large affairs and were therefore not prudish and affected, would say: "Worse than anything which we have mentioned is the fact that in every man-ruled city the world over a great army of women are so set aside as outcasts that it is considered a shame to speak the mere name which designates them. Because their very existence is illegal they may be arrested whenever any police captain chooses; they may be brought before a magistrate, fined and imprisoned. The men whose money sustains their houses, supplies their tawdry clothing and provides them with intoxicating drinks and drugs, are never arrested, nor indeed are they even considered lawbreakers."

Would not these fearless women, whose concern for the morals of the family had always been able to express itself through State laws, have meted out equal punishment to men as well as to women, when they had equally transgressed the statute law?

Did the enfranchised women evoked by our imagination speak thus to the disenfranchised men, the latter would at least respect their scruples and their hesitation in regard to an extension of the obligation of citizenship. But what would be the temper of the masculine mind if the voting women representing the existing State should present to them only the following half-dozen objections, which are unhappily so familiar to many of us: If the women should say, first, that men would find politics corrupting; second, that they would doubtless vote as their wives and mothers did; third, that men's suffrage would only double the vote without changing results; fourth, that men's suffrage would diminish the respect for men; fifth, that most men do not want to vote; sixth, that the best men would not vote?

I do not believe that women broadened by life and its manifold experiences would actually present these six objections to men as real reasons for withholding the franchise from them, unless indeed they had long formed the habit of regarding men not as comrades and fellow citizens, but as a class by themselves, in essential matters really inferior although always held sentimentally very much above them.

Certainly no such talk would be indulged in between men and women who had together embodied in political institutions the old affairs of life which had normally and historically belonged to both of them. If woman had adjusted herself to the changing demands of the State as she did to the historic mutations of her own house-hold she might naturally and without challenge have held the place in the State which she now holds in the family.

When Plato once related his dream of an ideal Republic he begged his fellow-citizens not to ridicule him because he considered the cooperation of women necessary for its fulfillment. He contended that so far as the guardianship of the State is concerned there is no distinction between the powers of men and women save those which custom has made.

Source: Addams, Jane. "If Men Were Seeking the Franchise." *Ladies' Home Journal* 30:6, June 1913, 20–21.

Emmeline Pankhurst, "Freedom or Death" (1913)

Emmeline Pankhurst was a leading British women's rights activist and founder of the Women's Franchise League, an organization devoted to securing voting rights for married women. In 1903 she helped establish the Women's Social and Political Union (WSPU), which became notorious for its large, "militant" marches and the hunger strikes of jailed suffragettes. She embarked on several speaking tours in the United States and on November 13, 1913, Pankhurst delivered the following speech to a crowd of American suffragists in Hartford, Connecticut.

I do not come here as an advocate, because whatever position the suffrage movement may occupy in the United States of America, in England it has passed beyond the realm of advocacy and it has entered into the sphere of practical politics. It has become the subject of revolution and civil war, and so tonight I am not here to advocate woman suffrage. American suffragists can do that very well for themselves.

I am here as a soldier who has temporarily left the field of battle in order to explain—it seems strange it should have to be explained—what civil war is like when civil war is waged by women. I am not only here as a soldier temporarily absent from the field at battle; I am here—and that, I think, is the strangest part of my coming—I am here as a person who, according to the law courts of my country, it has been decided, is of no value to the community at all; and I am adjudged because of my life to be a dangerous person, under sentence of penal servitude in a convict prison.

It is not at all difficult if revolutionaries come to you from Russia, if they come to you from China, or from any other part of the world, if they are men. But since I am a woman it is necessary to explain why women have adopted revolutionary methods in order to win the rights of citizenship. We women, in trying to make our case clear, always have to make as part of our argument, and urge upon men in our audience the fact—a very simple fact—that women are human beings.

Suppose the men of Hartford had a grievance, and they laid that grievance before their legislature, and the legislature obstinately refused to listen to them, or to remove their grievance, what would be the proper and the constitutional and the practical way of getting their grievance removed? Well, it is perfectly obvious at the next general election the men of Hartford would turn out that legislature and elect a new one.

But let the men of Hartford imagine that they were not in the position of being voters at all, that they were governed without their consent being obtained, that the legislature turned an absolutely deaf ear to their demands, what would the men of Hartford do then? They couldn't vote the legislature out. They would have to choose; they would have to make a choice of two evils: they would either have to submit indefinitely to an unjust state of affairs, or they would have to rise up and adopt some of the antiquated means by which men in the past got their grievances remedied.

Your forefathers decided that they must have representation for taxation, many, many years ago. When they felt they couldn't wait any longer, when they laid all the arguments before an obstinate British government that they could think of, and when their arguments were absolutely disregarded, when every other means had failed, they began by the tea party at Boston, and they went on until they had won the independence of the United States of America.

It is about eight years since the word militant was first used to describe what we were doing. It was not militant at all, except that it provoked militancy on the part of those who were opposed to it. When women asked questions in political meetings and failed to get answers, they were not doing anything militant. In Great Britain it is a custom, a time-honoured one, to ask questions of candidates for parliament and ask questions of members of the government. No man was ever put out of a public meeting for asking a question. The first people who were put out of a political meeting for asking questions, were women; they were brutally ill-used; they found themselves in jail before 24 hours had expired.

We were called militant, and we were quite willing to accept the name. We were determined to press this question of the enfranchisement of women to the point where we were no longer to be ignored by the politicians.

You have two babies very hungry and wanting to be fed. One baby is a patient baby, and waits indefinitely until its mother is ready to feed it. The other baby is an impatient baby and cries lustily, screams and kicks and makes everybody unpleasant until it is fed. Well, we know perfectly well which baby is attended to first. That is the whole history of politics. You have to make more noise than anybody else, you have to make yourself more obtrusive than anybody else, you have to fill all the papers more than anybody else, in fact you have to be there all the time and see that they do not snow you under.

When you have warfare things happen; people suffer; the noncombatants suffer as well as the combatants. And so it happens in civil war. When your forefathers threw the tea into Boston Harbour, a good many women had to go without their tea. It has always seemed to me an extraordinary thing that you did not follow it up by throwing the whiskey overboard; you sacrificed the women; and there is a good deal of warfare for which men take a great deal of glorification which has involved more practical sacrifice on women than it has on any man. It always has been so. The grievances of those who have got power, the influence of those who have got power commands a great deal of attention; but the wrongs and the grievances of those people who have no power at all are apt to be absolutely ignored. That is the history of humanity right from the beginning.

Well, in our civil war people have suffered, but you cannot make omelettes without breaking eggs; you cannot have civil war without damage to something. The great thing is to see that no more damage is done than is absolutely necessary, that you do just as much as will arouse enough feeling to bring about peace, to bring about an honourable peace for the combatants; and that is what we have been doing.

We entirely prevented stockbrokers in London from telegraphing to stockbrokers in Glasgow and vice versa: for one whole day telegraphic communication was entirely stopped. I am not going to tell you how it was done. I am not going to tell you how the women got to the mains and cut the wires; but it was done. It was done, and it was proved to the authorities that weak women, suffrage women, as we are supposed to be, had enough ingenuity to create a situation of that kind. Now, I ask you, if women can do that, is there any limit to what we can do except the limit we put upon ourselves?

If you are dealing with an industrial revolution, if you get the men and women of one class rising up against the men and women of another class, you can locate the difficulty; if there is a great industrial strike, you know exactly where the violence is and how the warfare is going to be waged; but in our war against the government you can't locate it. We wear no mark; we belong to every class; we permeate every class of the community from the highest to the lowest; and so you see in the woman's civil war the dear men of my country are discovering it is absolutely impossible to deal with it: you cannot locate it, and you cannot stop it.

"Put them in prison," they said, "that will stop it." But it didn't stop it at all: instead of the women giving it up, more women did it, and more and more and more women did it until there were 300 women at a time, who had not broken a single law, only "made a nuisance of themselves" as the politicians say.

Then they began to legislate. The British government has passed more stringent laws to deal with this agitation than it ever found necessary during all the history of political agitation in my country. They were able to deal with the revolutionaries of the Chartists' time; they were able to deal with the trades union agitation; they were able to deal with the revolutionaries later on when the Reform Acts were passed: but the ordinary law has not sufficed to curb insurgent women. They had to dip back into the middle ages to find a means of repressing the women in revolt.

They have said to us, government rests upon force, the women haven't force, so they must submit. Well, we are showing them that government does not rest upon force at all: it rests upon consent. As long as women consent to be unjustly governed, they can be, but directly women say: "We withhold our consent, we will not be governed any longer so long as that government is unjust." Not by the forces of civil war can you govern the very weakest woman. You can kill that woman, but she escapes you then; you cannot govern her. No power on earth can govern a human being, however feeble, who withholds his or her consent.

When they put us in prison at first, simply for taking petitions, we submitted; we allowed them to dress us in prison clothes; we allowed them to put us in solitary confinement; we allowed them to put us amongst the most degraded of criminals; we learned of some of the appalling evils of our so-called civilisation that we could not have learned in any other way. It was valuable experience, and we were glad to get it.

I have seen men smile when they heard the words "hunger strike", and yet I think there are very few men today who would be prepared to adopt a "hunger strike" for any cause. It is only people who feel an intolerable sense of oppression who would adopt a means of that kind. It means you refuse food until you are at death's door, and then the authorities have to choose between letting you die, and letting you go; and then they let the women go.

Now, that went on so long that the government felt that they were unable to cope. It was [then] that, to the shame of the British government, they set the example to authorities all over the world of feeding sane, resisting human beings by force. There may be doctors in this meeting: if so, they know it is one thing to feed by force an insane person; but it is quite another thing to feed a sane, resisting human being who resists with every nerve and with every fibre of her body the indignity and the outrage of forcible feeding.

Now, that was done in England, and the government thought they had crushed us. But they found that it did not quell the agitation, that more and more women came in and even passed that terrible ordeal, and they were obliged to let them go.

Then came the legislation—the "Cat and Mouse Act". The home secretary said: "Give me the power to let these women go when they are at death's door, and leave them at liberty under license until they have recovered their health again and then bring them back." It was passed to repress the agitation, to make the women yield—because that is what it has really come to, ladies and gentlemen. It has come to a battle between the women and the government as to who shall yield first, whether they will yield and give us the vote, or whether we will give up our agitation.

Well, they little know what women are. Women are very slow to rouse, but once they are aroused, once they are determined, nothing on earth and nothing in heaven will make women give way; it is impossible. And so this "Cat and Mouse Act" which is being used against women today has failed. There are women lying at death's door, recovering enough strength to undergo operations who have not given in and won't give in, and who will be prepared, as soon as they get up from their sick beds, to go on as before. There are women who are being carried from their sick beds on stretchers into meetings. They are too weak to speak, but they go amongst their fellow workers just to show that their spirits are unquenched, and that their spirit is alive, and they mean to go on as long as life lasts.

Now, I want to say to you who think women cannot succeed, we have brought the government of England to this position, that it has to face this alternative: either women are to be killed or women are to have the vote. I ask American men in this meeting, what would you say if in your state you were faced with that alternative, that you must either kill them or give them their citizenship? Well, there is only one answer to that alternative, there is only one way out—you must give those women the vote.

You won your freedom in America when you had the revolution, by bloodshed, by sacrificing human life. You won the civil war by the sacrifice of human life when you decided to emancipate the negro. You have left it to women in your land, the men of all civilised countries have left it to women, to work out their own salvation. That is the way in which we women of England are doing. Human life for us is sacred, but we say if any life is to be sacrificed it shall be ours; we won't do it ourselves, but we will put the enemy in the position where they will have to choose between giving us freedom or giving us death.

So here am I. I come in the intervals of prison appearance. I come after having been four times imprisoned under the "Cat and Mouse Act", probably going back to be rearrested as soon as I set my foot on British soil. I come to ask you to help to win this fight. If we win it, this hardest of all fights, then, to be sure, in the future it is going to be made easier for women all over the world to win their fight when their time comes.

Source: Parkhurst, Emmeline. "Freedom or Death." Verbatim Report of Mrs. Pankurst's Speech, Connecticut Woman Suffrage Association, November 13, 1913. Available at https://awpc.cattcenter.iastate.edu/2017/03/09/freedom-or-death-part-1-nov-13-1913/

Margaret Hinchey, Address on Working Women (1913)

Margaret Hinchey was an Irish-American immigrant, laundry worker, and labor activist who served as a voice for working women during the fight for women's suffrage. In 1914, Hinchey famously marched at the White House alongside 500 other woman workers, imploring President Woodrow Wilson to grant women the right to vote. In the excerpt below, taken from Hinchey's 1913 speech to the National American Suffrage Convention of 1913, Hinchey detailed the unjust conditions faced by women laborers, suggesting that suffrage would lead to equal representation and a greater balance of power for working women.

When we went to Albany to ask for votes one member of the Legislature told us that a woman's place was at home. Another said he had too much respect and admiration for women to see them at the polls. Another went back to Ancient Rome and told a story about Cornelia and her jewels her children. Yet in the laundries women were working seventeen and eighteen hours a day, standing over heavy machines for $3 and $3.50 a week. Six dollars a week is the average wage of working women in the United States. How can a woman live an honorable life on such a sum? Is it any wonder that so many of our little sisters are in the gutter? When we strike for more pay we are clubbed by the police and by thugs hired by our employers, and in the courts our word is not taken and we are sent to prison. This is the respect and admiration shown to working girls in practice. I want to tell you about Cornelia as we find her case today. The agent of the Child Labor Society made an investigation in the tenements and found mothers with their small children sitting and standing around them standing when they were too small to see the top of the table otherwise. They were working by a kerosene lamp and breathing its odor and they were all making artificial forget-me-nots. It takes 1,620 pieces of material to make a gross of forget-me-nots and the profit is only a few cents.

Four years ago 30,000 shirtwaist girls went on strike and when we went to Mayor McClellan to ask permission for them to have a parade he said: "Thirty thousand women are of no account to me." If they had been 30,000 women with votes would he have said that? We have in New York 14,000 women over sixty-five years old who must work or starve. What is done with them when their bones give out and they cannot work any more? The police gather them and you may then see in jail, scrubbing hard, rough concrete floors that make their knees bleed women who have committed no crime but being old and poor. Don't take my word for it but send a committee to Blackwell's Island or the Tombs and see for yourselves. We have a few Old Ladies' Homes but with most of them it would take a piece of red tape as long as from here to New York to get in. Give us a square deal so that we may take care of ourselves.

Source: Stanton, Elizabeth Cady, Susan B. Anthony, Matilda Joslyn Gage, and Ida Husted Harper. *History of Woman Suffrage.* Vol. 5. New York: National American Woman Suffrage Association, 1922, 365.

Mary Ritter Beard, "The State Rights Shibboleth" (1914)

Mary Ritter Beard was an author, historian, and archivist of women's history. As a Progressive Era reformer, she supported women's suffrage and joined Alice Paul's group, the Congressional Union for Women's Suffrage (later the National Woman's Party). In April 1914, Beard testified before a U.S. Senate committee against suffrage as a state issue and in support of a national amendment.

Women who are asking for a federal amendment abolishing sex discrimination in the suffrage provisions of the Constitution are informed that the determination of the qualifications for voting is purely a state matter. They are dismissed with an air of finality not unlike that which follows a mathematic demonstration. The suffrage is a matter of state, not national, interest, and that is the end of the discussion.

There are some simple-minded persons who accept this dictum as the final word on the subject, but those women who have studied even a little American history and politics know very well that the border line between national and State matters can not be settled by a mathematical process or by an ipse dixit of some interested politician. They know that neither the Republican Party, the champion of nationalism, nor the Democratic Party, the champion of state rights, has been consistent in its attitude toward national and state rights. They know that each of them has leaned toward national or state governments exactly whenever it has suited the party and economic interests.

Did not Thomas Jefferson and James Madison, founders of the Democratic Party, rend the air with cries of State rights against Federal usurpation when the Federalists chartered the first United States bank in 1791, and when the Federalist Court, under the leadership of John Marshall, rendered one ringing nationalist decision after another upholding the rights of the nation against the claims of the states? Yet Jefferson, as president, acquired the Louisiana Territory in what was admitted by him to be open violation of the Constitution; and the same James Madison who opposed the Federalist bank in 1790 as a violation of the Constitution and state rights cheerfully signed the bill rechartering that bank when it became useful to the fiscal interests of the Democratic Party. Jefferson was ready to nullify the alien and sedition laws and the Constitution of the United States in the Kentucky resolutions of 1798: the very Federalists who fought him in that day and denounced him as a traitor and nullifier lived to proclaim and practice doctrines of nullification in behalf of state rights during the War of 1812.

In the administration of Jefferson the National Government began the construction of the great national road without any express authority from the Constitution, and notwithstanding the fact that the construction of highways was admittedly a state matter. Eighteen years later a Democratic president, James Monroe, vetoed an act for the preservation and repair of the Cumberland Road and labored to prove that the whole venture was a violation of the Constitution and an invasion of rights reserved to the states, then controlled by the Democratic Party, voted $500,000 for the construction of experimental and rural-delivery routes and to aid the states in highway construction. From high in the councils of that party we now have the advocacy of national ownership of railways, telegraph, and telephone lines.

In the early days of the republic the Democratic Party protested even in armed insurrection in Pennsylvania against the inquisitorial excise tax, which, to use the language of that day, "penetrated a sphere of taxation reserved to the state." Today this party has placed upon the statute books the most inquisitorial tax ever laid in the history of our country by the act of April 9, 1912—a tax on white phosphorus matches, not for the purpose of raising revenues, for which the taxing power is conferred, but admittedly for the purpose of destroying an industry which it could not touch otherwise. The match industry was found to be injurious to a few hundred workingmen, women and children. The Democratic Party wisely and justly cast to the four winds all talk about the right of states, made the match business a national affair and destroyed the dangerous features of the business. Men and women all over the country rose up and pronounced it a noble achievement. Republicans joined with the Democrats in claiming the honor of that great humane service. Shades of departed Democrats! A taxing power which, according to Calhoun, could not be used for the purpose of protecting industries, may be used to destroy them. Consistency, where is thy virtue, and state rights, where is thy victory?

The state had the right to nullify federal law in 1798—so Jefferson taught and Kentucky practiced. Half a century elapses. The state of Wisconsin, rock-ribbed Republican, nullified the fugitive slave law and in its pronunciamento of nullification quoted the very words which Jefferson used in 1798. A Democratic Supreme Court at Washington, presided over by Chief Justice Taney, the arch apostle of state rights, answered Wisconsin in the very language of the Federalists of 1798, whom Jefferson despised and condemned: "The Constitution and laws of the United States are supreme, and the Supreme Court is the only and final arbiter of disputes between the state and national governments." A few more years elapse. South Carolina declares the right of the state to nullify and Wisconsin answered on the field of battle: "The Constitution and laws of the national government are supreme, so help us God!"

At the close of that ever-to-be-regretted war the nation wrote into the Constitution the fourteenth and fifteenth Amendments the fundamental principle that the suffrage is a national matter. Those amendments were intended to establish forever adult male suffrage throughout the American empire. It is true that those amendments are in many respects nullified by ingenious provisions. But there they stand. You are confronted by this dilemma: Either you must openly flaunt and scorn them, and thus virtually say to the nation, We will obey just as much of the Constitution as we please, which is the doctrine of the anarchist; or you must say suffrage is by the Constitution a national matter and we abide by the Constitution.

All reasonably sophisticated persons know that anything is a state matter which we think is a state matter, and anything is a national matter that we think is a national matter. The women of this country—the women of the enfranchised states and the women of the state not yet enfranchised—think suffrage a national matter. Men may turn aside those women who expect to simper their way to the suffrage by saying, "Just one moment, please," or "Kindly step the other way, please"; but they can not thus dismiss those who had read the long and inconsistent history of all parties.

From history women appeal to political science, and here they cite the example of the only great independent federation that deserves to be compared with the United States—the German Empire. The constitution of that confederation does not leave the determination of the qualifications for voters for the Reichstag to the mercies of the states; but solemnly and emphatically prescribes that every adult male German citizen shall vote for members of the Imperial Congress, whatever may be the qualifications for voters in the several States. The German constitution was made in the full light of modern political science and suffrage was there treated as a national matter.

If we turn to the other great federations of the world—Switzerland, Canada, and Australia—we find that their constitutions treat the suffrage for federal offices as a national matter by empowering the federal parliaments to make uniform the regulations with regard to qualifications for voters. The constitution of the Australian Commonwealth provides that the qualifications imposed on voters by the states shall remain until the (federal) parliament otherwise provides; and in 1902 the Federal Parliament established uniform qualifications throughout the Commonwealth as far as federal elections were concerned, and enfranchised women in spite of the opposition in some of the States.

A study of the constitutional law shows, therefore, that in no federation is the suffrage regarded as a purely state matter. The Constitution of the United States does not allow the states to provide any qualifications they please for voters for members of the House of Representatives or Senators, as is the rule in the case of the choice of presidential electors, where the state legislatures may make any qualifications they see fit. The constitution of Germany established universal manhood suffrage for Reichstag elections; the constitution of the Australian Commonwealth authorizes the Federal Parliament to make uniform qualifications, and the Federal Parliament almost immediately after the adoption of the constitution swept away sex discriminations in federal elections.

Source: Beard, Mary Ritter. "The State Rights Shibboleth." *Congressional Record: Proceedings and Debates of the Congress* 51:5. Washington, D.C.: U.S. Government Printing Office, 1914, 4957–4958.

Anna Howard Shaw, Recollections of NAWSA Conventions (1915)

Minister, physician, and suffragist Anna Howard Shaw was president of the National American Woman Suffrage Association (NAWSA) from 1904 to 1915. In this excerpt from her later autobiography, she describes how the organization was accused by white southern critics of promoting racial equality and even intermarriage, and she specifically recalls how NAWSA addressed the question of race—what she termed "the negro question"—at a 1903 convention held in New Orleans.

From 1887 to 1914 we had a suffrage convention every year, and I attended each of them. In preceding chapters I have mentioned various convention episodes of more or less importance. Now, looking back over them all as I near the end of these reminiscences, I recall a few additional incidents which had a bearing on later events. There was, for example, the much-discussed attack on suffrage during the Atlanta convention of 1895, by a prominent clergyman of that city whose name I mercifully withhold. On the Sunday preceding our arrival this gentleman preached a sermon warning every one to keep away from our meetings, as our effort was not to secure the franchise for women, but to encourage the intermarriage of the black and white races. Incidentally he declared that the suffragists were trying to break up the homes of America and degrade the morals of women, and that we were all infidels and blasphemers. He ended with a personal attack on me, saying that on the previous Sunday I had preached in the Epworth Memorial Methodist Church of Cleveland, Ohio, a sermon which was of so blasphemous a nature that nothing could purify the church after it except to burn it down.

As usual at our conventions, I had been announced to preach the sermon at our Sunday conference, and I need hardly point out that the reverend gentleman's charge created a deep public interest in this effort. I had already selected a text, but I immediately changed my plans and announced that I would repeat the sermon I had delivered in Cleveland and which the Atlanta minister considered so blasphemous. The announcement brought out an audience which filled the Opera House and called for a squad of police officers to keep in order the street crowd that could not secure entrance. The assemblage had naturally expected that I would make some reply to the clergyman's attack, but I made no reference whatever to him. I merely repeated, with emphasis, the sermon I had delivered in Cleveland.

At the conclusion of the service one of the trustees of my reverend critic's church came and apologized for his pastor. He had a high regard for him, the trustee said, but in this instance there could be no doubt in the mind of any one who had heard both sermons that of the two mine was the tolerant, the reverent, and the Christian one. The attack made many friends for us, first because of its injustice, and next because of the good-humored tolerance with which the suffragists accepted it.

The Atlanta convention, by the way, was arranged and largely financed by the Misses Howard—three sisters living in Columbus, Georgia, and each an officer of the Georgia Woman Suffrage Association. It is a remarkable fact that in many of our Southern states the suffrage movement has been led by three sisters. In Kentucky the three Clay sisters were for many years leaders in the work. In Texas the three Finnegan sisters did splendid work; in Louisiana the Gordon sisters were our stanchest allies, while in Virginia we had the invaluable aid of Mary Johnston, the novelist, and her two sisters. We used to say, laughingly, if there was a failure to organize any state in the South, that it must be due to the fact that no family there had three sisters to start the movement.

From the Atlanta convention we went directly to Washington to attend the convention of the National Council of Women, and on the first day of this council Frederick Douglass came to the meeting. Mr. Douglass had a special place in the hearts of suffragists, for the reason that at the first convention ever held for woman suffrage in the United States (at Seneca Falls, New York) he was the only person present who stood by Elizabeth Cady Stanton when she presented her resolution in favor of votes for women. Even Lucretia Mott was startled by this radical step, and privately breathed into the ear of her friend, "Elizabeth, thee is making us ridiculous!" Frederick Douglass, however, took the floor in defense of Mrs. Stanton's motion, a service we suffragists never forgot.

Therefore, when the presiding officer of the council, Mrs. May Wright Sewall, saw Mr. Douglass enter the convention hall in Washington on this particular morning, she appointed Susan B. Anthony and me a committee to escort him to a seat on the platform, which we gladly did. Mr. Douglass made a short speech and then left the building, going directly to his home. There, on entering his hall, he had an attack of heart failure and dropped dead as he was removing his overcoat. His death cast a gloom over the convention, and his funeral, which took place three days later, was attended by many prominent men and women who were among the delegates. Miss Anthony and I were invited to take part in the funeral services, and she made a short address, while I offered a prayer.

The event had an aftermath in Atlanta, for it led our clerical enemy to repeat his charges against us, and to offer the funeral of Frederick Douglass as proof that we were hand in glove with the negro race.

Under the gracious direction of Miss Kate Gordon and the Louisiana Woman Suffrage Association, we held an especially inspiring convention in New Orleans in 1903. In no previous convention were arrangements more perfect, and certainly nowhere else did the men of a community co-operate more generously with the women in entertaining us. A club of men paid the rent of our hall, chartered a steamboat and gave us a ride on the Mississippi, and in many other ways helped to make the occasion a success. Miss Gordon, who was chairman of the programme committee, introduced the innovation of putting me before the audience for twenty minutes every evening, at the close of the regular session, as a target for questions. Those present were privileged to ask any questions they pleased, and I answered them—if I could.

We were all conscious of the dangers attending a discussion of the negro question, and it was understood among the Northern women that we must take every precaution to avoid being led into such discussion. It had not been easy to persuade Miss Anthony of the wisdom of this course; her way was to face issues squarely and out in the open. But she agreed that we must respect the convictions of the Southern men and women who were entertaining us so hospitably.

On the opening night, as I took my place to answer questions, almost the first slip passed up bore these words:

What is your purpose in bringing your convention to the South? Is it the desire of suffragists to force upon us the social equality of black and white women? Political equality lays the foundation for social equality. If you give the ballot to women, won't you make the black and white woman equal politically and therefore lay the foundation for a future claim of social equality?

I laid the paper on one side and did not answer the question. The second night it came to me again, put in the same words, and again I ignored it. The third night it came with this addition:

Evidently you do not dare to answer this question. Therefore our conclusion is that this is your purpose.

When I had read this I went to the front of the platform.

"Here," I said, "is a question which has been asked me on three successive nights. I have not answered it because we Northern women had decided not to enter into any discussion of the race question. But now I am told by the writer of this note that we dare not answer it. I wish to say that we dare to answer it if you dare to have it answered—and I leave it to you to decide whether I shall answer it or not."

I read the question aloud. Then the audience called for the answer, and I gave it in these words, quoted as accurately as I can remember them:

"If political equality is the basis of social equality, and if by granting political equality you lay the foundation for a claim of social equality, I can only answer that you have already laid that claim. You did not wait for woman suffrage, but disfranchised both your black and your white women, thus making them politically equal. But you have done more than that. You have put the ballot into the hands of your black men, thus making them the political superiors of your white women. Never before in the history of the world have men made former slaves the political masters of their former mistresses!"

The point went home and it went deep. I drove it in a little further.

"The women of the South are not alone," I said, "in their humiliation. All the women of America share it with them. There is no other nation in the world in which women hold the position of political degradation our American women hold to-day. German women are governed by German men; French women are governed by French men. But in these United States American women are governed by every race of men under the light of the sun. There is not a color from white to black, from red to yellow, there is not a nation from pole to pole, that does not send its contingent to govern American women. If American men are willing to leave their women in a position as degrading as this they need not be surprised when American women resolve to lift themselves out of it."

For a full moment after I had finished there was absolute silence in the audience. We did not know what would happen. Then, suddenly, as the truth of the statement struck them, the men began to applaud—and the danger of that situation was over.

Another episode had its part in driving the suffrage lesson home to Southern women. The Legislature had passed a bill permitting tax-paying women to vote at any election where special taxes were to be imposed for improvements, and the first election following the passage of this bill was one in New Orleans, in which the question of better drainage for the city was before the public. Miss Gordon and the suffrage association known as the Era Club entered enthusiastically into the fight for good drainage. According to the law women could vote by proxy if they preferred, instead of in person, so Miss Gordon drove to the homes of the old conservative Creole families and other families whose women were unwilling to vote in public, and she collected their proxies while incidentally she showed them what position they held under the law.

With each proxy it was necessary to have the signature of a witness, but according to the Louisiana law no woman could witness a legal document. Miss Gordon was driven from place to place by her colored coachman, and after she had secured the proxy of her temporary hostess it was usually discovered that there was no man around the place to act as a witness. This was Miss Gordon's opportunity. With a smile of great sweetness she would say, "I will have Sam come in and help us out"; and the colored coachman would get down from his box, and by scrawling his signature on the proxy of the aristocratic lady he would give it the legal value it lacked. In this way Miss Gordon secured three hundred proxies, and three hundred very conservative women had an opportunity to compare their legal standing with Sam's. The drainage bill was carried and interest in woman suffrage developed steadily.

The special incident of the Buffalo convention of 1908 was the receipt of a note which was passed up to me as I sat on the platform. When I opened it a check dropped out—a check so large that I was sure it had been sent by mistake. However, after asking one or two friends on the platform if I had read it correctly, I announced to the audience that if a certain amount were subscribed immediately I would reveal a secret—a very interesting secret. Audiences are as curious as individuals. The amount was at once subscribed. Then I held up a check for $10,000, given for our campaign work by Mrs. George Howard Lewis, in memory of Susan B. Anthony, and I read to the audience the charming letter that accompanied it. The money was used during the campaigns of the following year—part of it in Washington, where an amendment was already submitted.

In a previous chapter I have described the establishment of our New York headquarters as a result of the generous offer of Mrs. O. H. P. Belmont at the Seattle convention in 1909. During our first year in these beautiful Fifth

Avenue rooms Mrs. Pankhurst made her first visit to America, and we gave her a reception there. This, however, was before the adoption of the destructive methods which have since marked the activities of the band of militant suffragists of which Mrs. Pankhurst is president. There has never been any sympathy among American suffragists for the militant suffrage movement in England, and personally I am wholly opposed to it. I do not believe in war in any form; and if violence on the part of men is undesirable in achieving their ends, it is much more so on the part of women; for women never appear to less advantage than in physical combats with men. As for militancy in America, no generation that attempted it could win. No victory could come to us in any state where militant methods were tried. They are undignified, unworthy—in other words, un-American.

The Washington convention of 1910 was graced by the presence of President Taft, who, at the invitation of Mrs. Rachel Foster Avery, made an address. It was understood, of course, that he was to come out strongly for woman suffrage; but, to our great disappointment, the President, a most charming and likable gentleman, seemed unable to grasp the significance of the occasion. He began his address with fulsome praise of women, which was accepted in respectful silence. Then he got round to woman suffrage, floundered helplessly, became confused, and ended with the most unfortunately chosen words he could have uttered: "I am opposed," he said, "to the extension of suffrage to women not fitted to vote. You would hardly expect to put the ballot into the hands of barbarians or savages in the jungle!"

The dropping of these remarkable words into a suffrage convention was naturally followed by an oppressive silence, which Mr. Taft, now wholly bereft of his self-possession, broke by saying that the best women would not vote and the worst women would.

In his audience were many women from suffrage states—high-minded women, wives and mothers, who had voted for Mr. Taft. The remarks to which they had just listened must have seemed to them a poor return. Some one hissed—some man, some woman—no one knows which except the culprit—and a demonstration started which I immediately silenced. Then the President finished his address. He was very gracious to us when he left, shaking hands with many of us, and being especially cordial to Senator Owens's aged mother, who had come to the convention to hear him make his maiden speech on woman suffrage. I have often wondered what he thought of that speech as he drove back to the White House. Probably he regretted as earnestly as we did that he had made it.

In 1912, at an official board meeting at Bryn Mawr, Mrs. Stanley McCormack was appointed to fill a vacancy on the National Board. Subsequently she contributed $6,000 toward the payment of debts incident to our temporary connection with the Woman's Journal of Boston, and did much efficient work for us. To me, personally, the entrance of Mrs. Stanley McCormack into our work has been a source of the deepest gratification and comfort. I can truly say of her what Susan B. Anthony said of me, "She is my right bower." At Nashville, in 1914, she was elected first vice-president, and to a remarkable degree she has since relieved me of the burden of the technical work of the presidency, including the oversight of the work at headquarters. To this she gives all her time, aided by an executive secretary who takes charge of the routine work of the association. She has thus made it possible for me to give the greater part of my time to the field in which such inspiring opportunities still confront us—campaign work in the various states.

To Mrs. Medill McCormack also we are indebted for most admirable work and enthusiastic support. At the Washington (D.C.) convention in 1913 she was made the chairman of the Congressional Committee, with Mrs. Antoinette Funk, Mrs. Helen Gardner of Washington, and Mrs. Booth of Chicago as her assistants. The results they achieved were so brilliant that they were unanimously re-elected to the same positions this year, with the addition of Miss Jeannette Rankin, whose energy and service had helped to win for us the state of Montana.

It was largely due to the work of this Congressional Committee, supported by the large number of states which had been won for suffrage, that we secured such an excellent vote in the Lower House of Congress on the bill to amend the national Constitution granting suffrage to the women of the United States. This measure, known as the Susan B. Anthony bill, had been introduced into every Congress for forty-three years by the National Woman Suffrage Association. In 1914, for the first time, it was brought out of committee, debated, and voted upon in the Lower House. We received 174 votes in favor of it to 204 against it. The previous spring, in the same Congress, the same bill passed the Senate by 35 votes for it to 33 votes against it.

The most interesting features of the Washington convention of 1913 were the labor mass-meetings led by Jane Addams and the hearing before the Rules Committee of the Lower House of Congress—the latter the first hearing ever held before this Committee for the purpose of securing a Committee on Suffrage in the Lower House to correspond with a similar committee in the Senate. For many years we had had hearings before the Judiciary

Committee of the Lower House, which was such a busy committee that it had neither time nor interest to give to our measure. We therefore considered it necessary to have a special committee of our own. The hearing began on the morning of Wednesday, the third of December, and lasted for two hours. Then the anti-suffragists were given time, and their hearing began the following day, continued throughout that day and during the morning of the next day, when our National Association was given an opportunity for rebuttal argument in the afternoon. It was the longest hearing in the history of the suffrage movement, and one of the most important.

During the session of Congress in 1914 another strenuous effort was made to secure the appointment of a special suffrage committee in the Lower House. But when success began to loom large before us the Democrats were called in caucus by the minority leader, Mr. Underwood, of Alabama, and they downed our measure by a vote of 127 against it to 58 for it. This was evidently done by the Democrats because of the fear that the united votes of Republican and Progressive members, with those of certain Democratic members, would carry the measure; whereas if this caucus were called, and an unfavorable vote taken, "the gentlemen's agreement" which controls Democratic party action in Congress would force Democrats in favor of suffrage to vote against the appointment of the committee, which of course would insure its defeat.

The caucus blocked the appointment of the committee, but it gave great encouragement to the suffragists of the country, for they knew it to be a tacit admission that the measure would receive a favorable vote if it came before Congress unhampered.

Another feature of the 1913 convention was the new method of electing officers, by which a primary vote was taken on nominations, and afterward a regular ballot was cast; one officer was added to the members of the official board, making nine instead of eight, the former number. The new officers elected were Mrs. Breckenridge of Kentucky, the great-granddaughter of Henry Clay, and Mrs. Catherine Ruutz-Rees of Greenwich, Connecticut. The old officers were re-elected—Miss Jane Addams as first vice-president, Mrs. Breckenridge and Mrs. Ruutz-Rees as second and third vice-presidents, Mrs. Mary Ware Dennett as corresponding secretary, Mrs. Susan Fitzgerald as recording secretary, Mrs. Stanley McCormack as treasurer, Mrs. Joseph Bowen of Chicago and Mrs. James Lees Laidlaw of New York City as auditors.

It would be difficult to secure a group of women of more marked ability, or better-known workers in various lines of philanthropic and educational work, than the members composing this admirable board. At the convention of

1914, held in Nashville, several of them resigned, and at present (in 1914) the "National's" affairs are in the hands of this inspiring group, again headed by the much-criticized and chastened writer of these reminiscences:

Mrs. Stanley McCormack, first vice-president.
Mrs. Desha Breckenridge, second vice-president.
Dr. Katharine B. Davis, third vice-president.
Mrs. Henry Wade Rogers, treasurer.
Mrs. John Clark, corresponding secretary.
Mrs. Susan Walker Fitzgerald, recording secretary.
Mrs. Medill McCormack, Mrs. Walter McNabb Miller, of Missouri, Auditors

In a book of this size, and covering the details of my own life as well as the development of the great Cause, it is, of course, impossible to mention by name each woman who has worked for us—though, indeed, I would like to make a roll of honor and give them all their due. In looking back I am surprised to see how little I have said about many women with whom I have worked most closely—Rachel Foster Avery, for example, with whom I lived happily for several years; Ida Husted Harper, the historian of the suffrage movement and the biographer of Miss Anthony, with whom I made many delightful voyages to Europe; Alice Stone Blackwell, Rev. Mary Saffard, Jane Addams, Katharine Waugh McCullough, Ella Stewart, Mrs. Mary Wood Swift, Mrs. Mary S. Sperry, Mary Cogshall, Florence Kelly, Mrs. Ogden Mills Reid and Mrs. Norman Whitehouse (to mention only two of the younger "live wires" in our New York work), Sophonisba Breckenridge, Mrs. Clara B. Arthur, Rev. Caroline Bartlett Crane, Mrs. James Lees Laidlaw, Mrs. Raymond Brown, the splendidly executive president of our New York State Suffrage Association, and my benefactress, Mrs. George Howard Lewis of Buffalo. To all of them, and to thousands of others, I make my grateful acknowledgment of indebtedness for friendship and for help.

Source: Shaw, Anna Howard. *Anna Howard Shaw, the Story of a Pioneer.* New York: Harper & Brothers Publishers, 1915, 307–322.

Massachusetts Anti-Suffrage Committee (1915)

Massachusetts had long been at the forefront of reform and was home to many prominent women's rights activists. By 1915, the Massachusetts Woman

Suffrage Association boasted nearly 60,000 members. That year, Massachusetts' male voters were asked to vote on an amendment to the state constitution that would have extended the vote to women. The Massachusetts Anti-Suffrage Committee published and disseminated the pamphlet that follows. On November 2, the proposed amendment was soundly defeated.

To The Men of Massachusetts

The question of amending the Constitution to permit women to vote at all elections will be decided by the voters of Massachusetts at the state election November 2.

No more important question has ever appeared upon the Massachusetts ballot.

It profoundly concerns the future of the State and of every man, woman and child within the State.

In this little book we present some of the many reasons for our belief that WOMAN SUFFRAGE IS WRONG IN THEORY AND BAD IN PRACTICE.

We ask you to read it carefully and then to go to the polls on the second day in November and vote as your conscience dictates.

Do not forget that Woman Suffrage has never carried in any state where a majority of the men were sufficiently alive to its importance to vote upon it.

In the states which have adopted it only 44 men out of every 100 were recorded on the issue, for and against.

LET US NOT ALLOW SUCH INDIFFERENCE TO DECIDE THE QUESTION HERE.

Let us take warning by those in suffrage states who are now saying: "I wish I had done something to oppose Woman Suffrage when I had a chance."

THE ISSUE IS TOO BIG, TOO VITAL TO THE INTERESTS OF ALL THE PEOPLE, TO BE DETERMINED BY A MINORITY.

The Case Against Woman Suffrage

1. The vote is not a question of individual "right," or what is best for the individual or for any class, but SOLELY A QUESTION OF WHAT IS BEST FOR THE STATE.

2. The net result of Woman Suffrage wherever tried has been A LOSS TO THE STATE AND A LOSS TO WOMEN.
3. The vote is demanded by only a small minority of women.
4. To force the vote upon the great majority of women to satisfy a small minority would be UNDEMOCRATIC AND UNJUST.
5. Men and women were created different and designed to work in different spheres for the common good—to co-operate with and supplement each other and not to compete.
6. The vote would deprive woman of her non-partisan power which enables her to do for the State what man is unable to do because he is bound by political party obligations.
7. The basis of government is PHYSICAL FORCE, and the physical power to enforce the law, without which the vote is useless, is NEITHER POSSIBLE NOR DESIRABLE FOR WOMEN.
8. Woman Suffrage is demanded by Socialists and Feminists as "a means to an end"—the end being "a complete social revolution."

Such, in briefest outline, is our indictment of the Woman Suffrage movement. In the following pages we shall endeavor to prove our case.

. . .

The Vote Not A Natural Right

Is there any such thing as a natural right to vote? All the legal authorities say NO. The Supreme Court of the United States says NO. Common sense says NO.

"The granting of the franchise," said Chief Justice Marshall, "has always been regarded in the practice of nations as a matter of expediency and not as an inherent right."

"Suffrage," said Judge Cooley, in his work on the Principles of Constitutional Law, "cannot be the right of the individual, because it does not exist for the benefit of the individual, but for the benefit of the State itself."

The Cyclopedia of American Government says: "That the suffrage cannot be a natural right is obvious from the fact that no community can ever enfranchise all its citizens."

The framers of the Federal Constitution, a body of the wisest men this country has ever produced, did not recognize and provide for woman suffrage, and they did recognize, specifically mention, and provide for every right inherent in man or woman.

And as we shall show in a later chapter of this book, THE SUFFRAGE LEADERS THEMSELVES ONCE ABANDONED THE CLAIM THAT THE VOTE WAS A RIGHT AND DEMANDED IT ONLY ON THE GROUND OF EXPEDIENCY.

A Privilege With a Heavy Obligation

The franchise is a privilege of government carrying with it a heavy responsibility, and it is granted only to those to whom the government, for what it conceives to be ITS OWN HIGHEST INTEREST, sees fit to grant it.

If the franchise were a right, like the right, which everyone possesses, to have his person and his property protected, the government would not be justified in withholding it from any individual.

That it is not such a right common sense alone teaches.

The minor, the alien, the Indian, the soldier or sailor in the service of Uncle Sam, the citizen of the District of Columbia, each has a right to have his person and his property protected.

But he has no vote.

From each of these classes the ballot has been withheld on the ground that "their participation in government would be for the disadvantage of the State," the reasons for taking that ground being, of course, different in each case.

. . .

The Woman's Vote in Massachusetts

Evidence to substantiate the foregoing statements is found in abundance in all States where women have either full or partial suffrage.

In Massachusetts women have had the vote for school committee since 1879.

"Give us the school vote," the suffragists then said, "and we will show you what we will do."

Here is what they have done:

For the last seventeen years we have had in Massachusetts an average registration of 4.8 per cent, of the women entitled to vote, and an actual vote of 2.1 per cent, or less than 50 per cent of the registration.

In other words, over 97 per cent of the women entitled to register and vote for school committee in Massachusetts have failed to do their duty.

In many Massachusetts towns years have passed without a single female vote being cast. The town of Dedham is a conspicuous example. The female vote of Dedham in 1889, the first year a record was kept, was 154. In 1903 this vote had dwindled to one, and for eleven years thereafter not one female vote was cast in that town.

. . .

One last word:

DON'T FORGET TO GO TO THE POLLS ON THE SECOND DAY OF NEXT NOVEMBER AND VOTE ON THIS QUESTION.

WHAT WE WANT IS NOT MERELY A DEFEAT FOR WOMAN SUFFRAGE, BUT A DEFEAT SO OVERWHELMING THAT THE QUESTION WILL NOT RISE AGAIN AT LEAST IN THIS GENERATION.

Source: Massachusetts Anti-Suffrage Committee. *The Case Against Woman Suffrage.* Boston, MA: Anchor Linotype Printing, Co., 1915.

NAACP Testimonials on Women's Suffrage (1915)

In 1915, the editors of The Crisis, *the magazine of the National Association for the Advancement of Colored People (NAACP), devoted a significant portion of the August issue to the topic of women's suffrage. The magazine published contributions from 26 distinguished and influential African American men and women supportive of women's rights. Following are three of those testimonials written by Charles W. Chesnutt, a noted novelist, lawyer, and political activist; Mrs. Carrie W. Clifford, honorary chairwoman of the Federation of Colored Women's Clubs of Ohio; and Miss M. E. Jackson, president of the Rhode Island Association of Colored Women's Club.*

Charles W. Chesnutt, "Women's Rights."

I believe that all persons of full age and sound mind should have a voice in the making of the laws by which they are governed, or in the selection of those who make those laws. As long as the family was the social unit, it was perhaps well enough for the householder, representing the family, to monopolize the vote. But with the broadening of woman's sphere the situation has changed, and many women have interests which are not concerned with the family.

Experience has shown that the rights and interests of no class are safe so long as they are entirely in the hands of another class—the rights and interests of the poor in the hands of the rich, of the rich in the hands of the poor, of one race in the hands of another. And while there is no such line of cleavage between the sexes as exists between other social classes, yet so far as women constitute a class as differentiated from men, neither can their rights be left with entire safety solely in the hands of men. In the gradual extension of statutory rights, women are in many countries, the equals of men before the law. They have always been subject to the burdens of citizenship. The burden of taxation, generally speaking, falls more heavily upon them, perhaps because they are more honest in returning their personal property for taxation, or less cunning in concealing it. They are subject, equally with men, to the criminal laws, though there, I suspect, for sentimental reasons, the burden has not fallen so heavily upon them. Their rights need protection, and they should be guarded against oppression, and the ballot is the most effective weapon by which these things can be accomplished.

I am not in favor of woman suffrage because I expect any great improvement in legislation to result from it. The contrary, from woman's lack of experience in government, might not unreasonably be expected. Women are certainly no wiser or more logical than men. But they enjoy equal opportunities for education, and large numbers of them are successfully engaged in business and in the professions and have the requisite experience and knowledge to judge intelligently of proposed legislation. Even should their judgment be at fault—as men's judgment too often is—they have fine intuitions, which are many times a safe guide to action; and their sympathies are apt to be in support of those things which are clean and honest and just and therefore desirable—all of which ought to make them a valuable factor in government.

Mrs. Carrie W. Clifford, "Votes for Children."

It is the ballot that opens the schoolhouse and closes the saloon; that keeps the food pure and the cost of living low; that causes a park to grow where a dump-pile grew before. It is the ballot that regulates capital and protects labor; that up-roots disease and plants health. In short, it is by the ballot we hope to develop the wonderful ideal state for which we are all so zealously working.

When the fact is considered that woman is the chosen channel through which the race is to be perpetuated; that she sustains the most sacred and intimate communion with the unborn babe; that later, she understands in a manner truly marvelous (and explain only by that vague term "instinct") its wants and its needs, the wonder grows that her voice is not the *first* heard in planning for the ideal State in which her child, as future citizen, is to play his part.

The family is the miniature State, and here the influence of the mother is felt in teaching, directing and executing, to a degree far greater than that of the father. At his mother's knee the child gets his first impressions of love, justice and mercy; and by obedience to the laws of the home he gets his earliest training in civics.

More and more is it beginning to be understood that the mother's zeal for the ballot is prompted by her solicitude for her family-circle.

That the child's food may be pure, that his environment shall be wholesome and his surrounding sanitary—these are the things which engage her thought. That his mind shall be properly developed and his education wisely directed; that his occupation shall be clean and his ideals high—all these are things of supreme importance to her, who began to plan for the little life before it was even dreamed of by the father.

Kindergartens, vacation-schools, playgrounds; the movement for the City Beautiful; societies for temperance and for the prevention of cruelty to children and animals—these and many other practical reforms she has brought to pass, *in spite of not having the ballot*. But as she wisely argues, why should she be forced to use indirect methods to accomplish a thing that could be done so much more quickly and satisfactorily by the direct method—by casting her own ballot?

The ballot! the sign of power, the means by which things are brought to pass, the talisman that makes our dreams come true! Her dream is of a State where war shall cease, where peace and unity be established and where love shall reign.

Yes, it is the great mother-heart reaching out to save her children from war, famine and pestilence; from death degradation and destruction, that induces her to demand "Votes for Women," knowing well that fundamentally it is really a campaign for "Votes for Children."

M. E. Jackson, "The Self-Supporting Women and the Ballot."

Looked at from a sane point of view, all objections to the ballot for women are but protests against progress, civilization and good sense.

"Woman's place is in the home." Would that the poorly paid toilers in field, work-shop, mill and kitchen, might enjoy the blessed refreshment of their own homes with accompanying assurance that those dependent upon them might be fed, clothed, properly reared and educated.

Each morning's sun beholds a mighty army of 8,000,000 souls marching forth to do battle for daily bread. You inquire who they are? Why, the mothers, wives, sisters and daughters of the men of America. "The weaker vessels," the majority of whom are constrained from necessity.

There is no field of activity in the country where women are not successfully competing with men. In the agricultural pursuits alone, there are over 900,000. In the ministry 7,000 dare preach the gospel with "Heads uncovered." And 1,010 possess the courage to invade the field of the Solons, bravely interpreting the laws, although their brothers in all but twelve of the forty-five States (so far as the ballot is concerned), class them with criminals, insane and feeble-minded.

The self-supporting woman out of her earnings, pays taxes, into the public treasury and through church, club and civic organization gives her moral backing unstintingly to her Country.

Imagine if you can the withdrawal of this marvelous economic force,—the working women of America! It is a fundamental necessity of modern civilization.

The laboring man has discovered beyond peradventure that his most effective weapon of defence is the *ballot in his own hand*. The self-supporting woman asks for and will accept nothing less.

Source: "Votes for Women: A Symposium by Leading Thinkers of Colored America." *The Crisis* 10, no. 4 (August 1915), 187–188.

Mary Church Terrell, "Woman Suffrage and the 15th Amendment" (1915)

Mary Church Terrell was an African American civil rights activist and vocal supporter of women's suffrage. One of the first black women to earn a college degree in the United States, Terrell went on to become one of the founders of the National Association for the Advancement of Colored People (NAACP). In her pointed essay in The Crisis, *excerpted here, Terrell criticizes African American men who oppose women's suffrage, noting that arguments against a woman's right to vote bear a striking resemblance to arguments used to oppose the African American vote under the Fifteenth Amendment.*

Even if I believed that women should be denied the right of suffrage, wild horses could not drag such an admission from my pen or my lips, for this reason : precisely the same arguments used to prove that the ballot be withheld from women are advanced to prove that colored men should not be allowed to vote. The reasons for repealing the Fifteenth Amendment differ but little from the arguments advanced by those who oppose the enfranchisement of women. Consequently, nothing could be more inconsistent than that colored people should use their influence against granting the ballot to women, if they believe that colored men should enjoy this right which citizenship confers.

What could be more absurd and ridiculous than that one group of individuals who are trying to throw off the yoke of oppression themselves, so as to get relief from conditions which handicap and injure them, should favor laws and customs which impede the progress of another unfortunate group and hinder them in every conceivable way. For the sake of consistency, therefore, if my sense of justice were not developed at all, and I could not reason intelligently, as a colored woman I should not tell my dearest friend that I opposed woman suffrage.

But how can any one who is able to use reason, and who believes in dealing out justice to all God's creatures, think it is right to withhold from one-half the human race rights and privileges freely accorded to the other half, which is neither more deserving nor more capable of exercising them ?

For two thousand years mankind has been breaking down the various barriers which interposed themselves between human beings and their perfect freedom to exercise all the faculties with which they were divinely endowed. Even in monarchies old fetters which formerly restricted freedom, dwarfed the intellect and doomed certain individuals to narrow circumscribed spheres, because of the mere accident of birth, are being loosed and broken one by one. In view of such wisdom and experience the political subjection of women in the United States can be likened only to a relic of barbarism, or to a spot upon the sun, or to an octopus holding this republic in its hideous grasp, so that further progress to the best form of government is impossible and that precious ideal its founders promised it would be it seems nothing more tangible than a mirage.

Source: Terrell, Mary Church. "Woman Suffrage and the 15th Amendment." *The Crisis*, August 1915.

Alice Paul, Letter on Imprisonment (1917)

Co-founder of the National Woman's Party, Lucy Burns, was arrested in 1917 for her part in a silent protest at the White House on the behalf of the women's suffrage movement. Charged with "obstructing traffic," Burns and other protest leaders, including Alice Paul, were sent to the Occoquan Workhouse, where the women undertook a hunger strike based on the principle that suffragettes were political prisoners. Burns, Paul, and others were force-fed with techniques best described as torture. Following is Alice Paul's description of the forced feedings, published in a December 1917 newspaper account.

"I practiced a hunger strike until November 11th. After that date they fed me twice a day by force, except on one day when I was too ill to be touched. . . . I was wrapped in blankets and taken to another cell to be fed, the food being injected through my nostrils.

"During this operation the largest Warden in Holloway sat astride my knees, holding my shoulders down to keep me from bending forward. Two other wardresses sat on either side and held my arms. Then a towel was placed around my throat, and one doctor from behind forced my head back, while another doctor put a tube in my nostril. When it reached my throat my head was pushed forward.

"Twice the tube came through my mouth and I got it between my teeth. My mouth was then pried open with an instrument. Sometimes they tied me to a chair with sheets. Once I managed to get my hands loose and snatched the tube, tearing it with my teeth. I also broke a jug, but I didn't give in."

Source: Winning the Vote for Women: The National American Woman Suffrage Association Collection; American Memory, Library of Congress.

Imprisoned Suffragists' Letter to the Prisoner Commissioners (1917)

In 1917, Mary Winsor, Lucy Branham, and several other women were being held in the Occoquan Workhouse, a District of Columbia prison, for demonstrating on behalf of voting rights for women. During their imprisonment, they wrote the following letter to the prison commission, characterizing themselves as political prisoners unjustly imprisoned for their beliefs.

To the Commissioners of the District of Columbia:

As political prisoners, we, the undersigned, refuse to work while in prison. We have taken this stand as a matter of principle after careful consideration, and from it we shall not recede.

This action is a necessary protest against an unjust sentence. In reminding President Wilson of his pre-election promises toward woman suffrage we were exercising the right of peaceful petition, guaranteed by the Constitution of the United States, which declares peaceful picketing is legal in the District of Columbia. That we are unjustly sentenced has been well recognized when President Wilson pardoned the first group of suffragists who had been given sixty days in the workhouse, and again when judge Mullowny suspended sentence for the last group of picketers. We wish to point out the inconsistency and injustice of our sentences—some of us have been given sixty days, a later group thirty days, and another group given a suspended sentence for exactly the same action.

Conscious, therefore, of having acted in accordance with the highest standards of citizenship, we ask the Commissioners of the District to grant us the rights due political prisoners. We ask that we no longer be segregated and confined under locks and bars in small groups, but permitted to see each other, and that Miss Lucy Burns, who is in full sympathy with this letter, be released from solitary confinement in another building and given back to us.

We ask exemption from prison work, that our legal right to consult counsel be recognized, to have food sent to us from outside, to supply ourselves with writing material for as much correspondence as we may need, to receive books, letters, newspapers, our relatives and friends. Our united demand for political treatment has been delayed, because on entering the workhouse we found conditions so very bad that before we could ask that the suffragists be treated as political prisoners, it was necessary to make a stand for the ordinary rights of human beings for all the inmates. Although this has not been accomplished we now wish to bring the important question of the status of political prisoners to the attention of the commissioners, who, we are informed, have full authority to make what regulations they please for the District prison and workhouse.

The Commissioners are requested to send us a written reply so that we may be sure this protest has reached them.

Signed by, MARY WINSOR, Lucy BRANHAM, ERNESTINE HARA, HILDA BLUMBERG, MAUD MALONE, PAULINE F. ADAMS,

ELEANOR A. CALNAN, EDITH AINGE, ANNIE ARNEIL, DOROTHY J. BARTLETT, MARGARET FOTHERINGHAM.

Source: Stevens, Doris. *Jailed for Freedom*. New York: Boni and Liveright, 1920.

A. Philip Randolph, "Woman Suffrage and the Negro" (1917)

African American civil rights leader A. Philip Randolph was an early champion of working-class blacks and their interests from the Progressive Era through the civil rights movement of the 1960s. In the 1910s, he added his voice in support of woman's suffrage, using many of the same arguments for equality that African Americans were using in their long struggle against racial segregation. The following is an essay that Randolph wrote for the civil rights magazine he cofounded, The Messenger, *in 1917, the magazine's first year of publication.*

Woman suffrage is coming.

Some women want it, and some women don't want it.

Women are taxpayers, producers and consumers just the same as men are, and they are justly entitled to vote.

The sentimental and puritanical objections advanced by the squeamish moralists won't stand. Sex is no bar to woman's participating in the industrial world and it should be none to her participating in the political world.

Negro men should realize their responsibility and duty in the coming election on the question of woman suffrage. Remember that if the right to vote benefits the Negro man, the right to vote will also benefit the Negro woman.

If white women ought to have the right to vote, then colored women ought to have the right to vote. If it will be beneficial to one, it will be beneficial to the other. Colored women are taxpayers, producers and consumers and they have a right to express their sentiment as regards the school systems, sanitation, the high cost of living, war, and everything which affects the general public. Of course, there are some colored women who will speak against woman suffrage, just as there are some white women who will speak for it. There were some Negro slaves who were opposed to freedom. Such kinks in the mind of the common people are not unusual.

Of course, when they are seen among the aristocracy, the reason is not difficult to see. Throughout history the few have attempted to keep the many in economic and political slavery.

But the great sweep of democracy moves on. The artificial standards of sex or race should not stand against it.

All peoples, regardless of race, creed or sex will be drawn into the vortex of world democracy.

Just as there could not be any union while some men were slaves and some men were free, so there can be no democracy while white men vote and white women, colored women, and colored men in the South don't vote.

Mr. Negro Voter, do your "bit."

Source: Randolph, A. Philip. "Woman Suffrage and the Negro." *The Messenger*, November 1917.

Carrie Chapman Catt, Address to Congress on Women's Suffrage (1917)

In an open letter directed to the U.S. Congress, Carrie Chapman Catt followed up on a major address made as president of the National American Woman Suffrage Association (NAWSA) in 1917. She encouraged the legislators to adopt a constitutional amendment guaranteeing women's suffrage, and she demanded that they move beyond the idea of leaving the issue of women's voting rights to individual states. Through Catt's efforts, NAWSA lobbied Congress during the next two years until the amendment was passed in 1919.

Woman suffrage is inevitable. Suffragists knew it before November 4, 1917; opponents afterward. Three distinct causes made it inevitable.

First, the history of our country. Ours is a nation born of revolution, of rebellion against a system of government so securely entrenched in the customs and traditions of human society that in 1776 it seemed impregnable. From the beginning of things, nations had been ruled by kings and for kings, while the people served and paid the cost. The American Revolutionists boldly proclaimed the heresies: "Taxation without representation is tyranny." "Governments derive their just powers from the consent of the governed." The colonists won, and the nation which was established as a result of their victory has held unfailingly that these two fundamental principles of democratic government are not only the spiritual source of our national existence but have been our chief historic pride and at all times the sheet anchor of our liberties.

Eighty years after the Revolution, Abraham Lincoln welded those two maxims into a new one: "Ours is a government of the people, by the people, and for the people." Fifty years more passed and the president of the United States, Woodrow Wilson, in a mighty crisis of the nation, proclaimed to the world: "We are fighting for the things which we have always carried nearest to our hearts: for democracy, for the right of those who submit to authority to have a voice in their own government."

All the way between these immortal aphorisms political leaders have declared unabated faith in their truth. Not one American has arisen to question their logic in the 141 years of our national existence. However stupidly our country may have evaded the logical application at times, it has never swerved from its devotion to the theory of democracy as expressed by those two axioms . . .

With such a history behind it, how can our nation escape the logic it has never failed to follow, when its last un-enfranchised class calls for the vote? Behold our Uncle Sam floating the banner with one hand, "Taxation without representation is tyranny," and with the other seizing the billions of dollars paid in taxes by women to whom he refuses "representation." Behold him again, welcoming the boys of twenty-one and the newly made immigrant citizen to "a voice in their own government" while he denies that fundamental right of democracy to thousands of women public school teachers from whom many of these men learn all they know of citizenship and patriotism, to women college presidents, to women who preach in our pulpits, interpret law in our courts, preside over our hospitals, write books and magazines, and serve in every uplifting moral and social enterprise. Is there a single man who can justify such inequality of treatment, such outrageous discrimination? Not one . . .

Second, the suffrage for women already established in the United States makes women suffrage for the nation inevitable. When Elihu Root, as president of the American Society of International Law, at the eleventh annual meeting in Washington, April 26, 1917, said, "The world cannot be half democratic and half autocratic. It must be all democratic or all Prussian. There can be no compromise," he voiced a general truth. Precisely the same intuition has already taught the blindest and most hostile foe of woman suffrage that our nation cannot long continue a condition under which government in half its territory rests upon the consent of half of the people and in the other half upon the consent of all the people; a condition which grants representation to the taxed in half of its territory and denies it in the other half a condition which permits women in some states to share in the election of the president, senators, and representatives and denies them that privilege in others. It is too obvious to require demonstration that woman suffrage, now covering half our territory, will eventually be ordained in all the nation. No one will deny it. The only question left is when and how will it be completely established.

Third, the leadership of the United States in world democracy compels the enfranchisement of its own women. The maxims of the Declaration were once called "fundamental principles of government." They are now called "American principles" or even "Americanisms." They have become the slogans of every movement toward political liberty the world around, of every effort to widen the suffrage for men or women in any land. Not a people, race, or class striving for freedom is there anywhere in the world that has not made our axioms the chief weapon of the struggle. More, all men and women the world around, with farsighted vision into the verities of things, know that the world tragedy of our day is not now being waged over the assassination of an archduke, nor commercial competition, nor national ambitions, nor the freedom of the seas. It is a death grapple between the forces which deny and those which uphold the truths of the Declaration of Independence . . .

Do you realize that in no other country in the world with democratic tendencies is suffrage so completely denied as in a considerable number of our own states? There are thirteen black states where no suffrage for women exists, and fourteen others where suffrage for women is more limited than in many foreign countries.

Do you realize that when you ask women to take their cause to state referendum you compel them to do this: that you drive women of education, refinement, achievement, to beg men who cannot read for their political freedom?

Do you realize that such anomalies as a college president asking her janitor to give her a vote are overstraining the patience and driving women to desperation?

Do you realize that women in increasing numbers indignantly resent the long delay in their enfranchisement?

Your party platforms have pledged women suffrage. Then why not be honest, frank friends of our cause, adopt it in reality as your own, make it a party program, and "fight with us"? As a party measure—a measure of all parties—why not put the amendment through Congress and the legislatures? We shall all be better friends, we shall have a happier nation, we women will be free to support loyally the party of our choice, and we shall be far prouder of our history.

"There is one thing mightier than kings and armies"—aye, than Congresses and political parties—"the power of an idea when its time has come to move." The time for woman suffrage has come. The woman's hour has struck. If parties prefer to postpone action longer and thus do battle with this idea, they challenge the inevitable. The idea will not perish; the party which opposes it may. Every delay, every trick, every political dishonesty from now on will antagonize the women of the land more and more, and when the party or parties which have so delayed woman suffrage finally let it come, their sincerity will be doubted and their appeal to the new voters will be met with suspicion. This is the psychology of the situation. Can you afford the risk? Think it over.

We know you will meet opposition. There are a few "women haters" left, a few "old males of the tribe," as Vance Thompson calls them, whose duty they believe it to be to keep women in the places they have carefully picked out for them. Treitschke, made world famous by war literature, said some years ago, "Germany, which knows all about Germany and France, knows far better what is good for Alsace-Lorraine than that miserable people can possibly know." A few American Treitschkes we have who know better than women what is good for them. There are women, too, with "slave souls" and "clinging vines" for backbones. There are female dolls and male dandies. But the world does not wait for such as these, nor does liberty pause to heed the plaint of men and women with a grouch. She does not wait for those who have a special interest to serve, nor a selfish reason for depriving other people of freedom. Holding her torch aloft, liberty is pointing the way onward and upward and saying to America, "Come."

To you and the supporters of our cause in Senate and House, and the number is large, the suffragists of the nation express their grateful thanks. This address is not meant for you. We are more truly appreciative of all you have done than any words can express. We ask you to make a last, hard fight for the amendment during the present session. Since last we asked a vote on this amendment, your position has been fortified by the addition to suffrage territory of Great Britain, Canada, and New York.

Some of you have been too indifferent to give more than casual attention to this question. It is worthy of your immediate consideration. A question big enough to engage the attention of our allies in wartime is too big a question for you to neglect.

Some of you have grown old in party service. Are you willing that those who take your places by and by shall blame you for having failed to keep pace with the world and thus having lost for them a party advantage? Is there any real gain for you, for your party, for your nation by delay? Do you want to drive the progressive men and women out of your party?

Some of you hold to the doctrine of states' rights as applying to woman suffrage. Adherence to that theory will keep the United States far behind all other democratic nations upon this question. A theory which prevents a nation from keeping up with the trend of world progress cannot be justified.

Gentlemen, we hereby petition you, our only designated representatives, to redress our grievances by the immediate passage of the Federal Suffrage Amendment and to use your influence to secure its ratification in your own state, in order that the women of our nation may be endowed with political freedom before the next presidential election, and that our nation may resume its world leadership in democracy.

Woman suffrage is coming—you know it. Will you, Honorable Senators and Members of the House of Representatives, help or hinder it?

Source: Catt, Carrie Chapman. *An Address to the Congress of the United States.* New York: National Woman Suffrage Publishing Company, 1917.

Nineteenth Amendment (1920)

The result of decades of political turmoil, the Nineteenth Amendment marked the culmination of the woman suffrage movement of the late nineteenth and early twentieth centuries. On June 4, 1919, the U.S. Congress approved the Nineteenth Amendment, thus recognizing women's right to vote on the national level, as well as asserting their right to vote in all state and local elections that had not already expanded the suffrage to them. The requisite number of states ratified the amendment by August 18, 1920, thus officially putting the amendment into effect.

The right of citizens of the United States to vote shall not be denied or abridged by the United States or by any State on account of sex.

Congress shall have power to enforce this article by appropriate legislation.

Source: Joint Resolution of Congress proposing a constitutional amendment extending the right of suffrage to women, approved June 4, 1919; Ratified Amendments, 1795–1992; General Records of the United States Government; Record Group 11; National Archives.

Crystal Eastman, "Now We Can Begin" (1920)

Crystal Eastman was a prominent American lawyer and women's rights activist who fought tirelessly during the suffrage movement. In 1918, Eastman and her brother founded and edited The Liberator, *a socialist magazine focusing on national and international politics. Eastman often contributed to this monthly publication, calling for American society to support women's independence, equality, and overall empowerment by redefining a woman's role in the home. In the following excerpt, Eastman considers where women might focus their efforts in the wake of the ratification of the Nineteenth Amendment, which had just granted them the right to vote.*

What, then, is "the matter with women"? What is the problem of women's freedom? It seems to me to be this: how to arrange the world so that women can be human beings, with a chance to exercise their infinitely varied gifts in infinitely varied ways, instead of being destined by the accident of their sex to one field of activity—housework and child-raising. And second, if and when they choose housework and child-raising, to have that occupation recognized by the world as work, requiring a definite economic reward and not merely entitling the performer to be dependent on some man. . . .

Freedom of choice in occupation and individual economic independence for women: How shall we approach this next feminist objective? First, by breaking down all remaining barriers, actual as well as legal, which make it difficult for women to enter or succeed in the various professions, to go into and get on in business, to learn trades and practice them, to join trades unions. . . .

Second, we must institute a revolution in the early training and education of both boys and girls. It must be womanly as well as manly to earn your own living, to stand on your own feet. And it must be manly as well as womanly to know how to cook and sew and clean and take care of yourself in the ordinary exigencies of life. . . .

Sons? Daughters? They are born of women—how can women be free to choose their occupation, at all times cherishing their economic independence, unless they stop having children? This is a further question for feminism. If the feminist program goes to pieces on the arrival of the first baby, it is false and useless. For ninety-nine out of every hundred women want children, and seventy-five out of every hundred want to take care of their own children, or at any rate so closely superintend their care as to make any other full-time occupation impossible for at least ten or fifteen years. Is there any such thing then as freedom of choice in occupation for women? And is not the family the inevitable economic unit and woman's individual economic independence, at least during that period, out of the question?

The feminist must have an answer to these questions, and she has. The immediate feminist program must include voluntary motherhood. Freedom of any kind for women is hardly worth considering unless it is assumed that they will know how to control the size of their families. "Birth control" is just as elementary an essential in our propaganda as "equal pay." Women are to have children when they want them, that's the first thing. That ensures some freedom of occupational choice; those who do not wish to be mothers will not have an undesired occupation thrust upon them by accident, and those who do wish to be mothers may choose in a general way how many years of their lives they will devote to the occupation of childraising.

But is there any way of insuring a woman's economic independence while child-raising is her chosen occupation? Or must she sink into that dependent state from which, as we all know, it is so hard to rise again? That brings us to the fourth feature of our program—motherhood endowment. It seems that the only way we can keep mothers free, at least in a capitalist society, is by the establishment of a principle that the occupation of raising children is peculiarly and directly a service to society, and that the mother upon whom the necessity and privilege of performing this service naturally falls is entitled to an adequate economic reward from the political government. It is idle to talk of real economic independence for women unless this principle is accepted. But with a generous endowment of motherhood provided by legislation, with all laws against voluntary motherhood and education in its methods repealed, with the feminist ideal of education accepted in home and school, and with all special barriers removed in every field of human activity, there is no reason why woman should not become almost a human thing.

Source: Eastman, Crystal. "Now We Can Begin." *The Liberator* 3 (December 1920): 23–24.

Documents from the League of Women Voters (1921)

The League of Women Voters was founded by suffrage leaders Carrie Chapman Catt and Emma Smith DeVoe in 1920 to support women's participation in the political process after gaining the right to vote with the Nineteenth Amendment. This 1921 brochure states some reasons to join the League of Women Voters and provides evidence of the commitment and purpose guiding the new organization.

Why Join the League of Women Voters?

BECAUSE it is the only organization in existence for the political education of women.

BECAUSE it develops the intelligence of the individual voter through forums, discussions and the spread of information on public affairs.

BECAUSE it gives disinterested unpartisan information on parties, candidates and measures.

BECAUSE it offers programs for practical civic work in your state, your city, your town.

BECAUSE it works for better law enforcement.

BECAUSE it works for better legislation on matters for which women should be primarily responsible.

BECAUSE it provides a meeting ground for women of all parties and all groups, where they may exchange ideas, make plans and work together for things in which they have a common interest.

BECAUSE it urges women to enroll in the political parties and work through them to improve the machinery of government.

BECAUSE it is organized in every state and you can accomplish more through a great National organization than by working alone.

BECAUSE it unites the country's woman power into a new force for the humanizing of government.

"If ever the world sees a time when women shall come together purely and simply for the benefit and good of mankind, it will be a power such as the world has never known." —Matthew Arnold.

Source: "Why Join the League of Women Voters?" 1921 brochure, League of Women Voters Papers, Library of Congress.

National Woman's Party Platform (1922)

The National Woman's Party (formerly the Congressional Union for Woman Suffrage) was founded in 1916 by Alice Paul and Lucy Burns to seek a national women's suffrage amendment. The group broke away from the National American Woman Suffrage Association (NAWSA) in order to focus on a national amendment rather than individual state victories. Following the passage of the Nineteenth Amendment in 1920 granting women's suffrage, the organization fought for the Equal Rights Amendment (ERA), an issue highlighted in their national platform in 1922.

Declaration of Principles

WHEREAS, Women today, although enfranchised, are still in every way subordinate to men before the law, in government, in educational opportunities, in professions, in the church, in industry, and in the home:

BE IT RESOLVED, That as a part of our campaign to remove all form of the subjection of women, we shall work for the following immediate objects:

That women shall no longer be regarded and shall no longer regard themselves as inferior to men, but the equality of the sexes shall be recognized.

That women shall no longer be the governed half of society, but shall participate equally with men in the direction of life.

That women shall no longer be denied equal educational opportunities with men, but the same opportunities shall be given to both sexes in all schools, colleges, and universities which are supported in any way by public funds.

That women shall no longer be barred from any occupation, but every occupation to men shall be open to women and restrictions upon the hours, conditions and remuneration of labor shall apply alike to both sexes.

That women shall no longer be discriminated against in the legal, the medical, the teaching, or any other profession, but the same opportunities shall be given to women as to men in training for professions and in the practice of these professions.

That women shall no longer be discriminated against in civil and government service, but shall have the same right as men to pay in the executive, the legislative, and the judicial branches of the government service.

That women shall no longer be discriminated against in the foreign trade, consular and diplomatic service, but women as well as men shall represent our country in foreign lands.

That women shall no longer receive less pay than men for the same work, but shall receive equal compensation for equal work in public and private employment.

That women shall no longer be barred from the priesthood or ministry, or any position of authority in the church, but equally with men shall participate in ecclesiastical offices and dignities.

That a double moral standard shall no longer exist, but one code shall obtain for both men and women.

That exploitation of the sex of women shall no longer exist, but women shall have the same right to control of their persons as have men.

That women shall no longer be discriminated against in treatment of sex diseases and in punishment of sex offenses, but men and women shall be treated in the same was for sex diseases and sex offenses.

That women shall no longer be deprived of the right of trial by a jury of their peers, but jury service shall be open to women as to men.

That women shall no longer be discriminated against in inheritance laws, but men and women shall have the same right to inherit property.

That the identity of the wife shall no longer be merged in that of her husband, but the wife shall retain her separate identify after marriage and be able to contract with her husband concerning the marriage relationship.

That a woman shall no longer be REQUIRED by law or custom to assume the name of her husband upon marriage but shall have the same right as a man to retain her own name after marriage.

That the wife shall no longer be considered as supported by the husband, but their mutual contribution to the family maintenance shall be recognized.

That the headship of the family shall no longer be in the husband alone, but shall be equally in the husband and the wife.

That the husband shall no longer own his wife's services, but these shall belong to her alone as in the case of any free person.

That the husband shall no longer own his wife's earnings, but these shall belong to her alone.

That the husband shall no longer own or control his wife's property, but it shall belong to her and be controlled by her alone.

That the husband shall no longer control the joint property of his wife, but the wife shall have the right to obtain divorce on the same grounds as the husband.

That the husband shall no longer have a greater right to make contracts than the wife, but a wife shall have equal right with her husband to make contracts.

That married women shall no longer be denied the right to choose their own citizenship, but shall have the same independent choice of citizenship as is possessed by their husbands.

That women shall no longer be discriminated against in the economic world because of marriage, but shall have the same treatment in the economic world after marriage as have men.

That the father shall no longer have the paramount right to the care, custody, and control of the child, to determine its education and religion, to the guardianship of its estate and to the control of its services and earnings, but these rights shall be shared equally by the father and mother in the case of all children, whether born within or without the marriage ceremony.

That no form of the Common Law or Civil Law disabilities of women shall any longer exist, but women shall be equal with men before the law.

In short—That women shall no longer be in any form of subjection to man in law to custom, but shall in every way be on an equal plane in rights, as she has always been and will continue to be, in responsibilities and obligations.

THE OUTLINE OF THE Women's Party PLAN OF CAMPAIGN is as follows:

I. National Work—Make certain that your United States Senators and your Congressmen give their whole-hearted support and their vote to all Equal Rights legislation before Congress.

II. State Work—Make certain that your Senators and your Representatives in the State Legislature give their whole-hearted support and their vote to All Equal Rights legislation.

III. Local Work—Make certain that your own locality is at least one spot in the United States where every girl that is born has an equal chance in life with every boy and where, throughout life, there are not handicaps of any kind placed upon women because of their sex.

To this end make certain:

(1) That women are nominated for all elective offices in your local community, your county and your state, and are supported in the elections and are placed equally with men in the offices which control the life of your community.

(2) That women are appointed equally with men to all appointive positions under your local, your county, and your state government.

(3) That the same opportunities are given to girls as to boys in all schools, colleges, and universities in your community which are supported in whole or in part by public funds; that in these educational institutions girls have the same opportunities as boys to study in all department; that entrance requirements are equal; the opportunity for trade and vocational training is equal; that opportunity for physical training and for entrance into the athletic life of the institutions is equal; the opportunity for physical training and for entrance into the athletic life of the institution is equal; that opportunity for obtaining academic honors, scholarships, fellowships, and all other honors is equal.

(4) That in your community, all occupations and professions, whether public or private, are open to women on the same terms as to men; that women equally with men are appointed to the administrative and other positions involving power and high salaries; that women have the same opportunities to advancement in these occupations and professions; that they are paid equally for the same work; that they have equal opportunity to enter the Unions of their trade and to participate in the government of the Unions; that women engaged in business or working at any paid occupations are

encouraged and supported; that whenever public money is spent, women receive the appointments, contracts, or commissions equally with men.

(5) That in the churches in your community women have an equal share with men in the governing of the church, and in participation in the ministry and all ecclesiastical offices and dignities.

(6) That in your community, the public sentiment supports a single moral and ethical code for men and women, and that all acts which are considered dishonorable or wrong in one sex, are considered the same in the other sex.

(7) That in your community one sex in no way preys upon the other by the white slave trade; by forcing it into prostitution or in any other way; that men and women receive the same examination, quarantine and treatment for sex diseases; that when men and women are punished for sex offenses they are punished in the same way for the same offense.

(8) That in your community married women are not dismissed from government service, the schools, or from private employment because of their marriage.

Source: "National Woman's Party Platform." *New York Times*, December 10, 1922, 90.

About the Editor and Contributors

EDITOR

Tiffany K. Wayne, PhD, is an independent scholar in Northern California who specializes in U.S. women's history and is the author or editor of several books, including *Women's Roles in Nineteenth-Century America*, *American Women of Science since 1900*, and *Women's Rights in the United States: A Comprehensive Encyclopedia of Issues, Events, and People*.

CONTRIBUTORS

Rolando Avila, Department of History, University of Texas, Rio Grande Valley

Elizabeth Bass, Oklahoma Historical Society

Nancy Beach, Technical Analyst, University of North Carolina at Chapel Hill

Roshunda L. Belton, Department of History, Grambling State University

Amy Bizzarri, Freelance Travel Writer, Chicago

Barbara Burrell, Department of Classics, Brock University

Dianne G. Bystrom, Center for Women and Politics, Iowa State University

Keri Dearborn, Independent Scholar, United States

Tessa Ditonto, Department of Political Science, Iowa State University

About the Editor and Contributors

Kathleen L. Endres, School of Communication, University of Akron

Amy H. Forss, Department of History, Metropolitan Community College

Elizabeth Frost-Knappman, Agent Emeritus, New England Publishing Associates

M. Carmen Gómez-Galisteo, Associate Professor, Universidad Isabel I in Burgos, Spain

Nancy Snell Griffith, Independent Scholar, United States

Nancy Hendricks, Independent Scholar, United States

Julie Holcomb, Associate Professor in Museum Studies, Baylor University

Marilyn K. Howard, Department of the Humanities, Columbus State Community College

Joan Marie Johnson, Lecturer, Northeastern Illinois University

Jenna L. Kubly, Independent Scholar, United States

William McGuire, Department of Psychology, Yale University

Patit Paban Mishra, Independent Scholar, India

Sean Morton, Independent Scholar, Canada

Sarah Nation, Independent Scholar, United States

Jason Newman, Independent Scholar, United States

Jennifer Oliver O'Connell, Independent Scholar, United States

Deirdre Benia Cooper Owens, Director of the Humanities in Medicine Program, University of Nebraska–Lincoln

William H. Pruden III, College Counselor/Director of Civic Engagement, Ravenscroft School

Larissa Brown Shapiro, Head of Global Diversity and Inclusion, Mozilla

Leslie Birdwell Shortlidge, Editor, Ohioana Library

Kathleen R. Simonton, Department of Social Sciences, Edmonds Community College

Robert L. Thornton, Urban Education Program, Westfield State University

Christopher Allen Varlack, Lecturer, University of Maryland, Baltimore County

John R. Vile, Department of Political Science, Middle Tennessee State University

Katherine Warming, Independent Scholar, United States

Linda S. Watts, School of Interdisciplinary Arts and Sciences, University of Washington, Bothell

Leslie Wheeler, Independent Scholar, United States

Geoff Wickersham, History Teacher, Wylie E. Groves High School

Cynthia M. Zavala, Independent Scholar, United States

Index

Note: Page numbers in **bold** indicate the location of main entries; page numbers in *italics* indicate photos.

Abolitionism
  and African American women in suffrage movement, 4–5
  American Anti-Slavery Society, 9, 10, 15, 95
  and Anthony, Susan B., 14, 15
  and Mott, Lucretia Coffin, 95–96
  Philadelphia Female Anti-Slavery Society, 95
  and Rose, Ernestine, 127–128
  and Stanton, Elizabeth Cady, 141–142
  and Stone, Lucy, 144–145
  World Anti-Slavery Convention, xxii, 95, 133
Aboriginal women, xxxv, xxxvi
Abzug, Bella, xxxix, xl
Adams, Abigail, xxi
Addams, Jane, **1–3**
  American Civil Liberties Union cofounder, 3
  and American settlement house movement, 1–3, 124, 187
  criticism and controversy, 3
  death, 3
  Democracy and Social Ethics, 2
  family and early years, 1–3, 124
  Hull House (Chicago) cofounder, 1–3, 124
  Hull House Maps and Papers, 2
  Immigrants' Protective League founder, 2
  and National American Woman Suffrage Association, 3, 279, 280, 281
  Newer Ideals of Peace, 2
  Nobel Peace Prize recipient, 3, 49
  pacifism of, 1, 2–3
  and Second International Congress of Women for Permanent Peace, 124
  The Second Twenty Years at Hull-House, 2
  Shaw, Anna Howard, on, 279, 280, 281
  social research, 2
  The Spirit of Youth and the City Streets, 2

Addams, Jane (*Continued*)
   Twenty Years at Hull-House, 2
   and Weil, Gertrude, 168
   "The Woman and the State," 3
   Woman's Peace Party cofounder, 3, 39
   and Women's International League for Peace and Freedom, 49
   and Women's Trade Union League, 2, 131, 187
   and World War I, 2–3
Addams, Jane, "If Men Were Seeking the Franchise" (1913) (primary document), 257–262
   on children, 259
   on criminal justice system, 260–261
   on education, 258
   on factory work, 258–259
   on fighting and war, 258
   on industrial accidents, 260
   on money and profit, 259–260
   on Plato, 262
Adkins v. Children's Hospital (1923), 113
Afghanistan, 77
African American women and suffrage, **4–6**
   and abolitionism, 4–5
   Alpha Suffrage Club (Chicago), 5, 6–8, 170–171
   and intersectionality, 6
   and National American Woman Suffrage Association, 5–6
   racism and discrimination, 6
   and Seneca Falls Convention, 4
   Stewart, Maria, 4
   See also Bethune, Mary McLeod; Ruffin, Josephine St. Pierre; Terrell, Mary Church; Truth, Sojourner; Wells-Barnett, Ida Bell
Albright, Madeline, xlii
Alcott, Louisa May, 142, 183
Alpha Suffrage Club, **6–8**
   Alpha Suffrage Record, 7
   and Brooks, Virginia, 7
   founding, 6, 170–171
   purpose and goal, 6–7, 170–171
   and Squire, Belle, 7
   and Wells-Barnett, Ida Bell, 5, 6–8, 170–171
American Anti-Slavery Society, 9, 10, 15, 95
American Association of University Women (AAUW), **8–9**
   founding, 8
   headquarters and membership, 9
   Health Statistics of Women College Graduates, 8
   notable activities, 8–9
   purpose and goals, 8
   and Richards, Ellen Swallow, 8
   support for women's suffrage, 9
   and Talbot, Marion, 8
American Civil Liberties Union
   Addams, Jane, cofounder, 3
   formerly National Civil Liberties Bureau, 48–50
   Keller, Helen, cofounder, 254
American Equal Rights Association, **9–11**
   and American Woman Suffrage Association (AWSA), 9, 11
   and Brown, Olympia, 32

dissolution of, 9, 10, 71
founding, xxiv, 9, 57, 96
history, 9–10
and National Woman Suffrage Association (NWSA), 9, 11, 103
purpose and goal, xxiv, 9, 57, 96
and Stanton, Elizabeth Cady, 142
state-level political campaigns, 10
and Stone, Lucy, 145
and Truth, Sojourner, 160, 204–206
See also Truth, Sojourner, address to the American Equal Rights Association
American Federation of Labor (AFL), xl, 187
American settlement house movement, 1–3, 124
and Addams, Jane, 1–3, 124, 187
Hull House (Chicago), 1–3, 124
and McDowell, Mary, 187
and Phyllis Wheatley Club, 151
Telegraph Hill Neighborhood Association (San Francisco), 123
American Temperance Society, 153
American Woman Suffrage Association (AWSA), **11–13**
Blackwell, Henry, cofounder, 11, 15, 25, 145, 149
and Blackwell, Lucy Stone, 15, 25
founding, 9, 10, 11–12, 15, 57, 110–111, 125, 145
and Hooker, Isabella, 72
and Howe, Julia Ward, 11
merger with NWSA to form National American Woman Suffrage Association, xxvii, 5, 11, 13, 15, 58, 62, 70, 72, 97, 103, 104, 112, 142, 145
and Mott, Lucretia Coffin, 96
purpose and goals, 10, 11–13, 57, 103, 104, 108, 110–111, 145
schism with National Woman Suffrage Association, xxiv–xxv, 5, 12–13, 57–58, 59, 70, 96, 108, 110–111, 142
Stone, Lucy, cofounder, 15, 25, 57–58, 70, 125, 144, 149
support of Fifteenth Amendment, xxiv–xxv, 5, 11–12, 96, 104, 108
and Truth, Sojourner, 160
and Woman's Christian Temperance Union, 13
Woman's Journal, xxv, 25, 125, 144, 145, 149, 183–184
Anthony, Daniel R., 50
Anthony, Susan B., **14–16**
and abolitionism, 14, 15
and American Anti-Slavery Society, 15
and American Civil War, 15
American Equal Rights Association cofounder, xxiv, 57
Anthony Amendment, xxvii, 16, 100, 112, 122, 135, 136 (*see also* Nineteenth Amendment)
arrest, xxv, 61, 93, 108
and Blake, Lillie Devereux, 27
and Brown, Olympia, 32
and Daughters of Temperance, 15
death, 16, 39, 176
and Dorr, Rheta Childe, 45, 46
education, 14
family and early years, 14–15

Anthony, Susan B. (*Continued*)
  and Fifteenth Amendment, 14, 15, 37, 44, 47, 57, 104, 110, 145
  and Fourteenth Amendment, xxv, 15, 37, 59, 104, 108
  and Harper, Ida Husted, 67, 68–69, 281
  and *History of Woman Suffrage* (coeditor), xxvi, 15, 28, 29, 61, 67, 69–71
  International Woman Suffrage Alliance cofounder, 74
  The Life and Work of Susan B. Anthony (with Harper), 15, 67, 68–69
  and Lockwood, Belva, 87
  and National American Woman Suffrage Association, xxvii, 15–16, 39, 97, 98, 104, 156, 275, 279
  National Woman Suffrage Association cofounder, xxiv, 10, 14, 15, 37, 44, 57, 104, 145
  and National Women's Rights Conventions, xxiii, xxv, 10, 108
  and New Departure strategy, 107, 108, 109, 161
  New York Temperance Society cofounder, 15
  Petition for Universal Suffrage, xxiv
  Portrait Monument (U.S. Capitol), 56
  reading of Declaration of Rights of the Women of the United States, 228–233
  and *The Revolution*, xxiv, 15, 125–126, 183
  and Rose, Ernestine, 128
  Senate Committee on Women's Suffrage testimony (1892), 72
  and Shaw, Anna Howard, 138, 275, 279
  and Stanton, Elizabeth Cady, *14*, 142
  and Stone, Lucy, 145
  support for Horace Greeley, 53
  Susan B. Anthony: The Woman Who Changed the Mind of a Nation (Dorr), 46–47
  and temperance movement, 15, 153, 156
  Woman's National Loyal League founder, 15
  Woman's State Temperance Society cofounder, 142
  and Woodhull, Victoria, 190
  writer for *The Lily*, 30
  See also United States v. Susan B. Anthony
Anti-lynching movement
  Association of Southern Women for the Prevention of Lynching, 169
  and Bethune, Mary McLeod, 24
  and Commission on Interracial Cooperation, 101
  and Harper, Frances E. W., 238, 239
  and National Association of Colored Women's Clubs, 167
  and Talbert, Mary Burnett, 151
  and Weil, Gertrude, 169
  and Wells-Barnett, Ida B., xxvii, 6, 129, 156, 169–170
  and *The Woman Citizen*, 179

and *The Woman's Era,* 182
Anti-Semitism, 79, 80
Antisuffrage movement, **16–18**
  Anti-Suffrage Review, 18
  The Anti-Suffragist, 18
  Congressional testimonies, xxx–xxxi, 280
  and *Fairchild v. Hughes* (1922), xxxii
  and feminism, 18
  and *Leser v. Garnett* (1922), xxxii, 113
  membership, 16
  National Association Opposed to Woman Suffrage headquarters, *17*
  petition to U.S. Congress, 17
  purpose and goals, 16–17
  and temperance movement, 18
  The Women's Protest, 18
  See also Massachusetts Anti-Suffrage Committee (1915) (primary document); National Association Opposed to Woman Suffrage
Argentina, 77
Armenia, 26
Association of Southern Women for the Prevention of Lynching, 169
Australia, 242, 272

Bass, Mrs. George, *12*
Beard, Charles Austin, 19, 20
Beard, Mary Ritter, **19–21**
  contributions to women's history archives, 20
  death, 20
  education and early career, 19
  family and early years, 19
  and National Woman's Party, 19
  and *The Suffragist* (editor), 19
  textbooks by, 20
  and Women's Trade Union League, 19
  World Center for Women's Archives founder, 20
Beard, Mary Ritter, "The State Rights Shibboleth" (1914) (primary document), 269–273
  on Founding Fathers, 270
  on Fourteenth and Fifteenth Amendments, 271–272
  on protest of inquisitorial excise tax, 271
  on states' nullification of federal law, 271
  on suffrage as state matter, 269–273
  on world federations and constitutions, 272–272
Beecher, Catharine, 30, 71
Beecher, Henry Ward, 72, 190
Beecher-Tilton Scandal, 72, 190, 217
Bell, Alexander Graham, letters on woman suffrage (1875) (primary document), 220–223
  on good and evil, 222–223
  on marriage, 222–223
  on sudden versus slow change, 223
  on "woman's rights," 221
Belmont, Alva Vanderbilt, **21–23**
  as benefactor, 22
  death, 22
  and Field, Sara Bard, 56

Belmont, Alva Vanderbilt (*Continued*)
influences on, 21
and International Women's Suffrage Association, 22
and National American Woman Suffrage Association, 21, 22
and National Woman's Party, 21, 22
Political Equality League founder, 21–22
and Women's Trade Union League, 21
Bethune, Mary McLeod, 5, **23–25**
death, 25
and Federal Committee on Fair Employment Practices, 24
National Council of Negro Women founder, xxxiii, 101
and Roosevelt, Eleanor, 24
and Roosevelt, Franklin, administration, 24
Women's Army Corps assistant director, 24
Bethune-Cookman College, 25
Birth control. *See* Contraception
Blackwell, Alice Stone, **25–26**
and American Woman Suffrage Association, 25
Armenian Poems, 26
blindness and death, 26
education, 25
family and early years, 25
Friends of Armenia cofounder, 26
Lucy Stone: Pioneer of Woman's Rights, 26, 146
Massachusetts League of Women Voters honorary president, 25–26
Massachusetts Woman Suffrage Association president, 26
and National American Woman Suffrage Association, 25
New England Woman Suffrage Association, president, 26
parents of, 25, 145
sale of *Woman's Journal* to Carrie Chapman Catt, 177–178, 184
and social reform groups, 26
The Woman Citizen contributing editor, 178
Woman's Journal editor in chief, 25, 26, 183
Blackwell, Alice Stone, *Why Women Should Vote* (1896) (primary document), 239–242
on broadmindedness, 241
on criminal versus law-abiding vote, 240–241
on educated voters, 240
on efficiency in influencing public affairs, 241
on fairness, 239–242
on help for women, 241–242
on legislation, 240
on low wages, 240
on native-born voters, 240
on protection of children, 241
on unjust laws, 240
on women's influence, 241–242
Blackwell, Antoinette Brown, 15, 32, 145, 183
Blackwell, Elizabeth, 25
Blackwell, Henry, 11, 15, 25, 145, 149
Blackwell, Lucy Stone. *See* Stone, Lucy

Blake, Lillie Devereux, **26–28**
    and Anthony, Susan B., 27
    death, 28
    early years and education, 27
    Fettered for Life; or, Lord and Master, 27
    journalism career, 26–27
    and National American Woman Suffrage Association, 27
    New York City Woman Suffrage League president, 27
    New York State Woman Suffrage Association president, 27
    Southwold, 27
Blatch, Harriot Stanton, **28–30**, 46, 70
    Challenging Years: The Memoirs of Harriot Stanton Blatch (with Lutz), 30
    death, 30
    early years and education, 28
    Elizabeth Cady Stanton: As Revealed in Her Letters, Diary, and Reminiscences (coeditor), 29–30
    Equality League of Self-Supporting Women founder, xxviii, 29, 132
    and *History of Woman Suffrage,* 28–29
    marriage and loss of U.S. citizenship, 29
    Mobilizing Woman-Power, 29
    and National American Woman Suffrage Association, 29, 98
    National Woman's Party cofounder, 176
    parents of, 28, 142
    and reform societies, 29
    and Silent Sentinels, 139
    Socialist Party membership, 29
    student protest rally, 90
    Women's Political Union founder, 185–186
    and Women's Trade Union League, 187–188
    and World War I, 29
Blatch, Harriot Stanton, "Woman as an Economic Factor" (1898) (primary document), 242–246
    on citizenship training, 243
    on "proved worth," 244–245
    on right to hold office, 244
    on school board elections, 243
    on unpaid work, 245
Bloomer, Amelia Jenks, **30–32**
    and Anthony, Susan B., 15
    death, 31
    dress reform and bloomers, 30–31
    Iowa Women's Suffrage Association president, 31
    journalism career, 30
    and *The Lily,* xxii, 30
    at Seneca Falls Convention, 30
    teaching career, 30
    and temperance movement, 30
Bradwell v. Illinois, 59
Brazil, 77, 100
Brown, John, 65
Brown, Olympia, **32–33**
    and Anthony, Susan B., 32
    and Congressional Union for Woman Suffrage, 33
    death, 33
    early years and education, 32
    Federal Suffrage Association cofounder, xxvii, xxvii, 32–33

Brown, Olympia (*Continued*)
   first woman ordained by full denominational authority, 32
   influences on, 32, 41
   National Woman Suffrage Association vice president, 32
   and National Woman's Party White House picket protest, 33
   Old and New, among Reformers, 33
   Racine Times manager, 33
   Wisconsin Woman Suffrage Association president, 32
   and Women's International League for Peace and Freedom, 33
Brown v. Board of Education, 60, 157
Burns, Lucy, **33–35**
   arrests, 34–35, 42, 140, 143, 290, 291
   and Catholicism, 35
   Congressional Committee for the National American Woman Suffrage Association chair, 34
   Congressional Union for Woman Suffrage cofounder, xxix, 41, 98, 143
   death, 35
   early years and education, 33
   and Eastman, Crystal, 49
   and imprisoned suffragists' letter to prisoner commissioners, 291
   and letter on imprisonment (Paul), 290
   and National American Woman Suffrage Association, 22, 34, 98, 146
   National Woman's Party cofounder, 33, 34, 91, 105, 106, 176, 301
   and Night of Terror (Occoquan Workhouse), 34
   and Pankhursts (Emmeline and Christabel), 33
   and Paul, Alice, 33–34, 41, 105, 106
   and "The Prison Special" train tour, 34–35
   role in passage of Nineteenth Amendment, 33, 35
   and Silent Sentinels White House picket protest, xxx, 22, 34, 122, 140, 156
   split with National American Woman Suffrage Association, 97–98, 106
   and suffrage procession of 1913, 143, 146
   The Suffragist coeditor, 150
Bush, George W., xlii

Canada, 36–38, 65, 76, 212, 242, 272, 297
Caraway, Hattie Wyatt, xxxiii
Carter, Jimmy, xl, xli
Cary, Mary Ann Shadd, **36–38**
   and abolitionism, 36
   and American Civil War, 37
   death, 38
   early years and education, 36
   father of, 36
   House Judiciary Committee on women's suffrage testimony, 37
   journalism career, 36–37
   law school education, 37

missionary career, 36
and National Woman Suffrage
  Association, 37
*A Plea for Emigration; or Notes
  of Canada West,* 37
Provincial Freeman publisher, 37
Catt, Carrie Chapman, **38–40**
  address to U.S. Congress
    advocating passage of suffrage
    amendment, 39
  American Hebrew Medal
    recipient, 39
  campaign for vice president
    (Georgist Commonwealth Land
    Party), 39
  Carrie Chapman Catt Center for
    Women and Politics (Iowa State
    University), 40
  and Congressional Union, 41
  death, 40
  early years and education, 38
  first woman superintendent of
    schools, 38
  and International Woman
    Suffrage Alliance, 39, 74
  League of Women Voters founder,
    xxxii, 38, 39, 84, 300
  National American Woman
    Suffrage Association delegate,
    12
  National American Woman
    Suffrage Association president,
    xxviii, xxx, 38, 39, 41, 84, 97,
    98, 99, 118, 122, 138, 176–177
  Winning Plan strategy, xxx, 39,
    99, 176–177
  and *The Woman Citizen,* 177–178,
    184
  *Woman Suffrage and Politics:
    The Inner Story of the Suffrage
    Movement* (with Shuler), 39
  and Woman's Centennial
    Conference (1940), 39–40
  Woman's Peace Party cofounder,
    38, 39
Catt, Carrie Chapman, address to
  Congress on women's suffrage
  (1917) (primary document),
  293–297
  on American Revolution, 293–294
  on inevitability of woman
    suffrage, 293
  on nation-wide suffrage for
    women, 294–295
  on opposition to woman suffrage,
    296
  on party platforms, 296
  on states' rights, 297
  on taxation with representation,
    293–294
  on U.S. world leadership, 295
Child labor reform and issues
  and Addams, Jane, 1, 2
  and Gordon, Kate, 64
  and Progressive Movement, 120,
    121
  and *The Woman Citizen,* 179
  See also Kelley, Florence, "Child
    Labor and Women's Suffrage"
China, 86, 239
Chinese Exclusion Act (1882),
  xxxiv, 86, 87
Chisholm, Shirley, xxxviii, xxxix
Civil Rights Act (1964), xxxvii
Clinton, Bill, xlii
Clinton, Hillary, xlii, xliv

College Equal Suffrage League, **40–41**
  founding, 40, 115
  and Irwin, Inez Haynes, 40, 115
  legacy, 41
  and National College Equal Suffrage League, 40–41
  and Park, Maud Wood, 40, 115
  purpose and activities, 40
Comstock Law, 54, 72
Congressional Union, **41–42**
  background and history, 41–42
  and Beard, Mary Ritter, 269
  and Belmont, Alva Vanderbilt, 21
  and Brown, Olympia, 33, 41
  and Burns, Lucy, xxix, 41–42, 49, 98–99, 143, 146
  and Eastman, Crystal, 49
  founding, xxix, 41, 98–99, 112, 143, 146
  membership, 42
  merger with Political Equality League, 22
  merger with Women's Political Union to form National Woman's Party, 42, 98–99, 105, 186
  and Panama-Pacific International Exposition, 55
  and Paul, Alice, xxix, 41–42, 49, 98–99, 112, 143, 146
  purpose and goals, 41
  role in passage of Nineteenth Amendment, 42, 46
  and Shafroth-Palmer Amendment, 135–136
  and Silent Sentinel White House picket protest, 156
  and Stevens, Doris, 143
  strategies of, 41–42
  The Suffragist, 42, 45, 149–150
  and Vernon, Mabel, 41, 163, 164
  and World War I, 42
Constitution, U.S.
  Eighteenth Amendment, 112, 153, 154
  Equal Protection Clause, xxiv, 12, 52, 58–60, 85, 108, 206
  First Amendment, 85, 224
  on minimum age to serve as president, 53
  ratification of, xxi
  Thirteenth Amendment, xxiv, 57, 58, 107, 224
  Twenty-First Amendment, 154
  Twenty-Fourth Amendment, xxxvi
  Twenty-Sixth Amendment, xxxix
  Twenty-Third Amendment, xxxvi
  See also Equal Rights Amendment; Fifteenth Amendment; Fourteenth Amendment; Nineteenth Amendment
Constitutional Rights of the Women of the United States, The (Hooker). *See* Hooker, Isabella, *The Constitutional Rights of the Women of the United States*
Contraception
  and the "woman question," 76
  American Birth Control League (later Planned Parenthood Federation of America), xxxii
  first birth control clinic, xxx
  Food and Drug Administration approval of oral contraceptives, xxxvi

and *Griswold v. Connecticut,*
xxxvii
and Milholland, Inez, 90
Curtis, Charles, 50

Davis, Paulina Kellogg Wright,
43–45
and abolitionism, 43
death, 44
family and early years, 43
*A History of the National
Woman's Rights Movement,*
xxv, 44
and National Woman Suffrage
Association, 44
and National Women's Rights
Conventions, xxii, 44, 95, 145
New England Woman Suffrage
Association cofounder, 44
and *The Revolution,* 44, 126
Rhode Island Suffrage
Association president, 44
and *The Una,* 44
*Davis v. Monroe County Board of
Education* (1999), xlii
Declaration of Rights of the Women
of the United States (1876)
(primary document), 228–233
on assumptions and usurpations
of power over women, 229
on habeas corpus, 229
on ignorance of representation of
women, 231
on judiciary, 232
on special legislation for women,
230–231
on taxation without
representation, 230

on trial by jury, 229–230
on unequal codes for men and
women, 230
on universal manhood suffrage,
231
on use of "male" in state
constitutions, 229
Declaration of Sentiments (1848)
(primary document). *See*
Stanton, Elizabeth Cady,
Declaration of Sentiments
Denmark, 76
Dorr, Rheta Childe, **45–47**
death, 47
early years and education, 45
and General Federation of
Women's Clubs, 46
journalism career, 45–46
The Suffragist editor, 45, 46, 150
*Susan B. Anthony: The Woman
Who Changed the Mind of a
Nation* (Dorr), 46–47
What Eight Million Women Want,
46
A Woman of Fifty, 45
and Women's Trade Union
League, 46
Douglass, Frederick
American Equal Rights
Association cofounder, xxiv, 57
and "Declaration of Sentiments,"
134
Douglass Day, 155
home purchased by National
Association of Colored Women,
100, 152
and Howe, Julia Ward, 110
and Mott, Lucretia Mott, 95

Douglass, Frederick (*Continued*)
   and National American Woman Suffrage Association, 274–275
   nominated as Equal Rights Party vice presidential candidate, xxv, 53, 190
   North Star newspaper, 36
   and Stanton, Elizabeth Cady, 142
   and Truth, Sojourner, 159
   and Wells-Barnett, Ida Bell, 171
Douglass, Sarah, 95
Dred Scott v. Sandford (1857), xxiii
Du Bois, W. E. B., 171

Eastman, Crystal Catherine, **48–50**
   American Union Against Militarism executive director, 49
   blacklisting of, 50
   and Congressional Union, 49
   death, 50
   education, 48
   Equal Rights Amendment coauthor, 49
   family and early years, 48
   journalism career, 48, 50
   National Civil Liberties Bureau (later American Civil Liberties Union) cofounder, 48, 49–50
   and National Woman's Party, 49
   pacifism of, 49
   Work Accidents and the Law, 48
Eastman, Crystal Catherine, "Now We Can Begin" (1920) (primary document), 298–300
   on economic independence, 299–300
   on education of boys and girls, 299
   on feminism, 299
   on freedom of choice, 298
   on voluntary motherhood, 299
Edmunds-Tucker Act (1887), xxvii
El Salvador, 77
Emerson, Ralph Waldo, 142
Enforcement Acts (1871), xxv
Equal Pay Act (1963), xxxvii, 106
Equal Rights Amendment (ERA), **50–53**
   AFL-CIO endorsement of, xl
   anti-ERA movement, 52
   and Carter, Jimmy, xli
   core provision, 52
   Equal Rights envoys of the National Woman's Party in Rapid City, *51*
   ERA Club, 63
   introduced in Congress, xxxiii, 50
   March for Equality, xl
   as Mott Amendment, 51
   and National Woman's Party, 106, 301
   passage in House (1971) and Senate (1972), xxxix, 50–51, 52
   and Paul, Alice, xxxiii, 50, 51, 117, 118
   and Stevens, Doris, 144
   and Vernon, Mabel, 165
Equal Rights Party, **53–54**
   Douglass, Frederick, vice presidential nominee, xxv, 53, 190
   election of 1872, 53–54
   election of 1884, 54
   election of 1888, 54
   Lockwood, Belva Ann, presidential candidate, 53, 54, 87, 89

Woodhull, Victoria, presidential candidate, xxv, 53–54, 190, 209
Equality League of Self-Supporting Women, xxviii, xxix, 29, 132, 185, 188

Fairchild v. Hughes (1922), xxxii
Federal Suffrage Association, xxvii, 32
Female Labor Reform Association, xxii
Ferraro, Geraldine, xli
Field, Sara Bard, **55–56**
  death, 56
  delivery of suffrage petition to Woodrow Wilson, 55–56
  early years, 55
  and National American Woman Suffrage, 55
  and National Woman's Party, 55
  poetry volumes, 56
Fifteenth Amendment, **56–58**
  and African American women, 4–5
  and American Equal Rights Association, 9, 11
  debates, xxiv–xxv
  model for women's suffrage amendment, 112
  and New Departure strategy, 107–108
  ratification, xxv, 11, 56
  Terrell, Mary Church, on, 288–289
  text of, 56–57, 208
  and *United States v. Susan B. Anthony*, 161
  and Voting Rights Act, xxxvii
  and women's movement schism, xxiv, 5, 11–12, 14, 15, 37, 44, 47, 57–58, 59, 96, 103–104, 110, 111–112, 125, 145, 160
Fifteenth Amendment (1870) (primary document), 208–209
  on enforcement, 208
  on right to vote, 208
Finland, 76, 147
Fourteenth Amendment, **58–60**
  and *Bradwell v. Illinois,* 59
  and *Brown v. Board of Education,* 60
  due process clause, 12, 58, 60, 206
  equal protection clause, xxiv, 12, 52, 58, 59, 60, 108, 206
  and *Minor v. Happersett,* xxvi, 92–94, 104, 108, 112, 162, 224–228
  and New Departure strategy, 107–108, 161
  and Nineteenth Amendment, 111–113
  and *Obergefell v. Hodges,* 60
  provisions, 58–59
  ratification, xxiv, 58
  and *Reed v. Reed,* 60
  and *Roe v. Wade,* 60
  text of, 206–207
  and *United States v. Susan B. Anthony,* xxv, 211
  and women's movement schism, 10, 11–12, 15, 59–60, 103–104
Fourteenth Amendment (1868) (primary document), 206–207
  citizenship clause, 206
  due process clause, 206
  equal protection clause, 206

France, 76, 77
"Freedom or Death" (Pankhurst). See Pankhurst, Emmeline, "Freedom or Death"
Friedan, Betty
 The Feminine Mystique, xxxvii
 National Organization for Women cofounder, xxxvii

Gage, Matilda Joslyn, **61–63**
 and abolitionism, 61
 and "Ar'n't I a Woman" (Truth), 159–160
 and American Civil War, 61
 death, 62
 Declaration of the Rights of the Women of the United States coauthor, 62
 early years, 61
 and *History of Woman Suffrage,* xxvi, 15, 62, 69–70, 109
 Liberal Thinker editor, 62
 The National Citizen and Ballot Box editor, 70
 and National Woman Suffrage Association, 61–62
 National Women's Rights Convention speaker and president, xxiii, 61
 and Native American rights, 61, 62
 The Woman's Bible coauthor, 62
 Woman's National Liberal Union founder, 62
Gardener, Helen H., 12
Garvey, Marcus, 101, 171
Gender gap (voting), xli
General Federation of Women's Clubs, xxx, 46, 129–130, 175

Germany, 76, 272
Gerrymandering, 85
Gilman, Charlotte Perkins, 72, 90, 168, 173
Ginsburg, Ruth Bader, xlii
Gordon, Kate, **63–64**
 death, 64
 ERA Club cofounder, 63
 family and early years, 63
 healthcare activism, 63
 justice system reform, 63, 64
 Louisiana Anti-Tuberculosis League founder, 63
 and Louisiana State Suffrage Association, 63–64
 and National American Woman Suffrage Association, 275, 277
 and Portia Club, 63
 and Southern States Woman Suffrage Conference founder, xxix, 64
Griffiths, Martha, xxxviii
Grimké, Angela, xxii, 109, 145
Grimké, Sarah, xxi–xxii, 109, 145
Griswold v. Connecticut (1965), xxxvii
Guinn v. United States (1915), xxx

Haiti, 36, 100
Harlem Renaissance, 101
Harper, Frances Ellen Watkins, **65–67**
 The Life and Work of Susan B. Anthony (with Anthony), 15, 67, 68–69
 and National Women's Rights Convention, xxiv

Harper, Frances E. W., "Woman's
   Political Future" (1893)
   (primary document),
   237–239
  on demand for justice, 239
  on discovery of new worlds, 237
  on moral and education tests for
   suffrage, 238–239
  on social and political
   advancement, 238
Harper, Ida Husted, **67–69**
  and Belmont, Alva Vanderbilt, 21
  and *History of Woman
   Suffrage,* xxviii, xxxii, 67,
   69, 70, 136
  journalism career, 67–68
  and Leslie Bureau of Suffrage
   Education, 69
  *The Life and Work of Susan B.
   Anthony* (with Anthony), 15,
   68–69
  National American Woman
   Suffrage Association press
   secretary, 68
*Harper v. Virginia Board of
   Elections* (1966), xxxviii
Help America Vote Act, xlii
Hinchey, Margaret, address on
   working women (1913)
   (primary document), 268–269
  on child labor, 269
  on labor strikes, 268
  on shirtwaist workers strike, 269
  on woman's place, 268
*History of the National Woman's
   Rights Movement, A* (Davis),
   xxv, 44
History of Woman Suffrage, **69–71**
  and Anthony, Susan B., xxvi, 15,
   28, 29, 61, 67, 69–71
  and Blatch, Harriot Stanton, 28,
   29
  and Gage, Matilda Joslyn, xxvi,
   15, 62, 69–70, 109
  and Harper, Ida Husted, xxviii,
   xxxii, 67, 69, 70, 136
  history and origins, 69–70
  and Stanton, Elizabeth Cady, xxvi,
   15, 28, 29, 61, 69, 70, 135, 141
  Volume 1 (1881), xxvi, 62, 70–71,
   135, 141
  Volume 2 (1882), xxvi, 29, 62, 70,
   109, 141
  Volume 3 (1886), xxvi, 62, 70, 141
  Volume 4 (1902), xxviii, 69, 70
  Volume 5 (1922), xxxii, 69, 70,
   136
  Volume 6 (1922), xxxii, 69, 70
Holtzman, Elizabeth, xl
Hooker, Isabella, **71–73**
  and abolitionism, 71
  and Beecher-Tilton Scandal Case,
   72
  Connecticut Woman Suffrage
   Association founder and
   president, 71–72
  death, 73
  education, 71
  family and early years, 71
  and House Judiciary Committee
   (1871), 209
  and International Convention of
   Women, 72
  and Senate Committee on
   Women's Suffrage (1892), 209
  and Spiritualism, 72

Hooker, Isabella Beecher, *The Constitutional Rights of the Women of the United States* (1888) (primary document), 233–236
  on Article I, 235–236
  on Article II, 236
  on Article IV, 236
  on the Constitution, 234
  on Jefferson, Thomas, 233
  on patriotic work, 234–235
  on use of the word "people," 235
Hull House (Chicago), 1–3, 124. *See also* Addams, Jane; American settlement house movement
Hungary, 80

Iceland, 76
"If Men Were Seeking the Franchise" (Addams). *See* Addams, Jane, "If Men Were Seeking the Franchise"
Illinois Suffrage Act, xxix
Immigrants' Protective League, 2
Immigration and immigrants
  and Addams, Jane, 1, 3, 258
  and anti-Semitism, 79, 80
  and Cary, Mary Ann Shadd, 36
  Catt, Carrie Chapman, on, 294
  and Chinese Exclusion Act (1882), xxxiv
  and Hull House (Chicago), 1, 3
  and international women's movement, 75
  and Jewish women and suffrage, 79–80
  and Ku Klux Klan, 154
  and Lee, Mabel Ping-Hua, 87
  and Magnuson Act (1943), xxxiv
  and McCarran-Walter Act (Immigration and Nationality Act) (1952), xxxv
  and Pollitzer, Anita Lily, 119
  and Progressive Movement, 120
  and Shaw, Anna Howard, 138
  and Triangle Factory Fire (1911), 132
  and Women's Trade Union League, 187
Immigration and Nationality Act (1952), xxxv
Imprisoned suffragists' letter to the prisoner commissioners (1917) (primary document) (primary document), 290–292
  on exemption from prison work, 291
  on rights of political prisoners, 291
  on unjust sentencing, 291
India, 77
Indian Citizenship Act (Snyder Act) (1924), xxxiii, 173
International Ladies' Garment Workers' Union (ILGWU), xxviii, xxviii, 132
International Woman Suffrage Alliance (IWSA), **74–75**
  Addams, Jane, 1908 address, 3
  Anthony, Susan B., cofounder, 74
  Catt, Carrie Chapman, cofounder and first president, 39, 74
  founding, 74
  history and origins, 74
  and International Council of Women, 74
  Jus Suffragi (The Right of Suffrage) (later *International Women's News*), 74

and League of Nations, 75
meetings and activities, 74–75, 76
and Pollitzer, Anita Lily, 120
purpose, 74–75, 76
renamed International Women's Alliance, 74, 76
Stanton, Elizabeth Cady, cofounder, 74
International women's movement, **75–78**
eras, 75–76
and International Suffrage Alliance, 74–75, 76
legal and economic rights, 76–77
and "woman question," 76–77
See also individual nations
Ireland, 242
Italy, 77

Japan, 77
Jewish women and suffrage, **79–81**
and anti-Semitism, 79, 80
and immigration, 79–80
and Jacobs, Aletta, 80
Jewish League for Woman Suffrage, 79
and Katzenstein, Caroline, 81
and Meyer, Annie Nathan, 80
and Nathan, Frederick, 80
and Nathan, Maud, 80, 242
National Council of Jewish Women, 79
in New York, 80
and Schwimmer, Rosika, 20, 80
and temperance movement, 79
and Wise, Steven, 80
and women's club movement, 79
See also Schneiderman, Rose; Weil, Gertrude

Johnson, Lyndon B.
Civil Rights Act (1964), xxxvii
Executive Order 11375 (banning gender discrimination in federal employment), xxxviii
Voting Rights Act (1965), xxxvii
Julian, George W., "The Slavery Yet to Be Abolished" (1874) (primary document), 213–220
on consequences of women's suffrage, 217–219
on fitness to vote, 216–217
on inferiority as reason for disenfranchisement, 215–216
on male suffrage, 217
on sex as reason for disenfranchisement, 215
on women as human beings, 214–215
on women's desire to vote, 219–220

Katzenstein, Caroline, 81
Keller, Helen, "Why Men Need Woman Suffrage" (1913) (primary document), 254–257
on consequences of woman suffrage, 255
on impact on men of helplessness of working women, 256
on rights, 254
on wages and economic urgencies, 255–256
on "woman peril," 254
on women as social beings, 256–257
on world wrongs, 255

Kelley, Florence, 22, 120, 183
Kelley, Florence, "Child Labor and Women's Suffrage" (1905) (primary document), 246–248
   on child labor statistics, 246
   on increase of young girls in wage earning class, 246
   on state child labor laws, 246–248
Kennedy, John F., xxxvii
Ku Klux Klan
   anti-immigration views, 154
   and Enforcement Acts, xxv

La Follette, Belle Case, **82–83**
   death, 83
   early years and education, 82
   La Follette's Weekly Magazine (later *The Progressive*), 82
   and National American Woman Suffrage Association, 82–83
   and Progressive reform, 82–83
   U.S. Senate on Women's Suffrage testimony (1913), xxix, 82–83
   and Wilson, Woodrow, 82
   and Wisconsin suffrage referendum, 83
   Woman's Peace Party cofounder, 83
La Follette, Robert, xxix, 82–83
labor
   and Dorr, Rheta Childe, 45–46
   farm labor, 33
   Female Labor Reform Association, xxii
   International Ladies' Garment Workers' Union, xxviii, 132
   and Jewish women in suffrage movement, 79, 80
   and Lemlich, Clara, 80
   and Milholland, Inez, *91*
   and *Mueller v. Oregon* (1908), 121
   and National American Woman Suffrage Association, 279
   and National Woman's Party, 106
   and Progressive Movement, 120–121
   and Schneiderman, Rose, 131–132
   shirtwaist factory strike, 21, 131, 269
   Triangle Shirtwaist Factory fire (1911), 80, 132, 188
   and Weil, Gertrude, 169
   and Woman's Christian Temperance Union, 174
   women's integration into labor movement, 187
   See also Blatch, Harriot Stanton, "Woman as an Economic Factor"; Child labor reform and issues; Hinchley, Margaret, address on working women; Keller, Helen, "Why Men Need Woman Suffrage"; Women's Trade Union League
League of Women Voters, **83–85**
   and Blackwell, Alice Stone, 25–26
   campaigns and activities, 84–85
   Catt, Carrie Chapman, founder, 38, 39, 84, 177
   Equal Rights Amendment endorsed by, xxxix, 85
   founding, xxxii, 38, 39, 83–84, 97, 99, 177
   Gill v. Whitford amicus brief, 85
   headquarters, *84*
   League of Women Voters Education Fund, 85

and National American Woman
    Suffrage Association, 84, 97,
    99
The National Voter, 85
and Park, Maud Wood, 84, 115,
    116
Power the Vote campaign, 85
purpose and goals, 83–85
and United Nations, 85
and *The Woman Citizen,* 178
Lee, Mabel Ping-Hua, **86–87**
    death, 86
    director of First Chinese Baptist
        Church, 86–87
    early years and education, 86
    first Asian women to graduate
        from Columbia University, 86
    migration to United States, 86
    and New York City suffragists
        parade (1912), 86
    "The Submerged Half" (1915
        speech to Women's Political
        Union), 86
Leser v. Garnett (1922), xxxii, 113
Lily Ledbetter Fair Pay Restoration
    Act, xliii
Literacy tests, xxx, 4, 5, 24, 58, 167
Lockwood, Belva, **87–89**
    and Anthony, Susan B., 87–88
    and antiwar movement, 89
    death, 89
    early years and education, 87
    Equal Rights Party presidential
        candidate, 53, 54, 87, 89
    first woman to present in front of
        U.S. Supreme Court, 87, 89
    and labor reform, 88
    law career, 88–89

and National Woman Suffrage
    Association, 88
teaching career, 87–88
Universal Franchise Association
    cofounder, 88
Lynching. *See* Anti-lynching
    movement

Magnuson Act (1943), xxxiv
Married Women's Property Law
    (New York), xxii
Massachusetts Anti-Suffrage
    Committee (1915) (primary
    document), 281–285
    case against woman suffrage,
        282–283
    to the men of Massachusetts, 282
    a privilege with a heavy
        obligation, 284
    vote is not a natural right,
        283–284
    woman's vote in Massachusetts,
        284–285
McCain, John, xliii
McCarran-Walter Act (Immigration
    and Nationality Act) (1952),
    xxxv
McKinney, Cynthia, xliii
Mexico, 178
Meyer, Annie Nathan, 80
Milholland, Inez, **90–92**
    death, 91–92
    early political activism, 90
    early years and education, 90
    and National American Woman
        Suffrage Association, 90, 91
    and National Woman's Party, 90,
        91–92

Milholland, Inez (*Continued*)
  and Silent Sentinel campaign, 92
  suffrage procession of 1913 organizer, 90, 91, 147
Minor, Francis, 92–94, 108, 109
Minor, Virginia, 92–94, 104, 107, 108, 162, 224, 225
Minor v. Happersett, xxvi, **92–94**
  background, 92–93
  and Fourteenth Amendment, 92–93, 104, 112
  impact and legacy, 93–94
  and New Departure strategy, 108–109
  and *United States v. Susan B. Anthony,* 162
Minor v. Happersett, 88 U.S. 162 (1875) (primary document), 224–228
  on "citizen" and citizenship, 224, 225
  on Fourteenth Amendment, 224–226
  on "male citizens," 224
  on right of suffrage, 224
  on suffrage rights in Constitution, 227–228
  on women as citizens, 225
Miss America Pageant, protests, xxxviii
Mitchell, Charlene, xxxviii
Mondale, Walter, xli
Mott, James, 134
Mott, Lucretia Coffin, **94–96**
  and abolitionism, 95–96
  American Anti-Slavery Society cofounder, 95
  American Equal Rights Association cofounder, 9, 96
  and Anthony, Susan B., 15
  death, 70, 96
  Discourse on Woman, 95, 197–201
  and Douglass, Frederick, 95, 96
  early years and education, 94
  and *History of Woman Suffrage,* 70
  Mott Amendment, 70 (*see also* Equal Rights Amendment)
  and National Woman Suffrage Association, 96
  and National Women's Rights Conventions, xxiii, xxv, 44, 95
  Pennsylvania Peace Society president, 96
  Philadelphia Female Anti-Slavery Society founder, 95, 96
  Portrait Monument (U.S. Capitol), 56
  and Quakerism, 94–95
  Seneca Falls Convention co-organizer, xxii, 95, 133–134, 142
  and Stanton, Elizabeth Cady, 274
  Universal Peace Union vice president, 96
  Women's National Loyal League cofounder, xxiv
  and World Anti-Slavery Convention, xxii
Mott, Lucretia Coffin, Discourse on Woman (1849) (primary document), 197–201
  on importance of position of woman for society, 197–198
  on new generation of women, 199
  on what women want, 199–200
  on women as reformers, 198–199

on women's education, 198
on women's property, 200
Mount Holyoke College, xxi, 32, 145

NAACP testimonials on women's suffrage (1915) (primary document), 285–288
  Chesnutt, Charles W. ("Women's Rights"), 285–286
  Clifford, Carrie W. ("Votes for Children"), 286–287
  Jackson, M. E. ("The Self-Supporting Women and the Ballot"), 287–288
Nathan, Frederick, 80
Nathan, Maud, 80, 242
National Advisory Committee on Women, xl
National American Woman Suffrage Association (NAWSA), **97–99**
  and Anthony, Susan B., xxvii, xxvii, 15–16, 39, 97, 98, 104, 156, 275, 279
  and Blatch, Harriot Stanton, 29, 98
  and Burns, Lucy, 22, 34, 98, 146
  and Catt, Carrie Chapman, xxviii, xxx, 38, 39, 41, 84, 97, 98, 99, 118, 122, 138, 176–177
  delegation of officers, *12*
  founding, xxvii
  National Suffrage Bulletin, xxviii
  purpose and goals, 97
  role in passage of Nineteenth Amendment, 97–99
  and Shafroth-Palmer Amendment, 135–136
  split with Paul and Burns, 97–98
  See also Congressional Union; League of Women Voters; Suffrage procession of 1913; Winning Plan
National Association for the Advancement of Colored People (NAACP)
  founding, xxviii
  and Milholland, Inez, 90
  and Ovington, Mary White, 90
  and Ruffin, Josephine St. Pierre, 130
  and Talbert, Mary Burnett, 151, 152
  and Terrell, Mary Church, 90, 157, 288
  and Wells-Barnett, Ida Bell, 171
  See also NAACP testimonials on women's suffrage (1915) (primary document)
National Association of Colored Women (NACW), **99–101**
  Better Homes drive, 101
  founding, xxvii
  history and origins, 99–100
  membership, 99, 100
  purchase of home of Frederick Douglass, 100, 152
  purpose and goals, 100
  renamed National Association of Colored Women's Clubs, 101
  Ruffin, Josephine St. Pierre, cofounder, 100, 129
  support of Susan B. Anthony Amendment, 100
  Terrell, Mary Church, cofounder, xxvii, 99–100, 129, 155, 157
National Association Opposed to Woman Suffrage, **102–103**

National Association Opposed to
   Woman Suffrage (*Continued*)
 disbandment, 103
 and Dodge, Josephine, 18, 102
 founding, 17–18, 102
 headquarters and organization,
   17, 102
 history, 102–103
 membership, 103
 purpose and goals, 102–103
 and Wadsworth, Alice Hay,
   xxx–xxxi, 102
 See also Antisuffrage movement
National Council of Jewish Women,
   79
National Council of Negro Women,
   xxxiii, 24, 101
National Organization for Women
   (NOW)
 and Equal Rights Amendment, 52
 founding, xxxvii
 March for Equality (1978), xl
National Suffrage Bulletin, xxviii
National Voter Registration Act
   (1993), xlii
National Woman Suffrage
   Association (NWSA), **103–105**
 Anthony, Susan B., cofounder,
   xxiv, xxiv, 10, 14, 15, 37, 44, 57,
   104, 145
 headquarters and conventions, 104
 history and founding, 103–104
 merger with AWSA to form
   National American Woman
   Suffrage Association, xxvii, 5,
   11, 13, 15, 58, 62, 70, 72, 97,
   103, 104, 112, 142, 145
 purpose and goals, 103
 schism with American Woman
   Suffrage Association, xxiv–
   xxv, 5, 12–13, 57–58, 59, 70, 96,
   108, 110–111, 142
 See also Revolution, The
National Woman's Party (NWP),
   105–107
 Burns, Lucy, cofounder, 33, 34,
   91, 105, 106, 176, 301
 campaigns and activities, 106–107
 and Equal Pay Act (1963), 106
 Equal Rights, 106
 and Equal Rights Amendment,
   106
 history and founding, xxx,
   105–106
 Paul, Alice, cofounder, 105,
   106–107, 117, 118
 purpose and goals, 105
 See also Silent Sentinels
National Woman's Party Platform
   (1922) (primary document),
   301–305
 declaration of principles, 301–303
 local work, 304
 national work, 304
 plan of campaign, 304–305
 state work, 304
National Women's Political Caucus,
   xxxix, 52
National Women's Rights
   Conventions
 1855 (Cincinnati, Ohio), xxiii
 1853 (Cleveland, Ohio), xxiii
 1856 (New York City), xxiii, 10
 1858 (New York City), xxiii
 1859 (New York City), xxiii
 1860 (New York City), xxiii

1866 (New York City), xxiv
1854 (Philadelphia, Pennsylvania), xxiii, 128
1852 (Syracuse, New York), xxiii, 61
1869 (Washington, D.C.), xxv
1850 (Worcester, Massachusetts), xxii, 4, 110, 127
1851 (Worcester, Massachusetts), xxii
and Anthony, Susan B., xxiii, xxiii, xxv, xxv, 10, 108
and Davis, Paulina Wright Kellogg, xxii
and Gage, Matilda Joslyn, xxiii, 61
and Harper, Frances Ellen Watkins, xxiv
and Mott, Lucretia, xxiii, xxv
and Rose, Ernestine, xxiii, 127, 128
and Stanton, Elizabeth Cady, xxiv, xxv
and Stone, Lucy, 10, 110
and Truth, Sojourner, 4
and Wright, Martha Coffin, xxiii
Netherlands, 80
New Deal, 131, 132
New Departure, **107–109**
and Anthony, Susan B., 107, 108, 109, 161
history and origins, 107–108
and *History of Woman Suffrage,* 109
and *Minor v. Happersett,* 108–109
and *United States v. Susan B. Anthony,* 108–109
New England Woman Suffrage Association, **109–111**

and American Woman Suffrage Association, 110–111
and Blackwell, Alice Stone, 26
and Brown, Olympia, 32
Davis, Paulina Kellogg Wright, cofounder, 43, 44
and Fifteenth Amendment, 110
history and founding, 44, 109–110
and Hooker, Isabella, 71
and Howe, Julia Ward, 109, 110
state-by-state strategy, 110
and Stone, Lucy, 109–110, 145
New Jersey state constitution, xxi, 227
New York Radical Women, xxxviii
New Zealand (first independent nation to grant women right to vote), xxvii, 242
Niagara Movement, 151, 171
Night of Terror, xxx, 34, 140. *See also* Imprisoned suffragists' letter to the prisoner commissioners
Nineteenth Amendment, **111–114**
and *Adkins v. Children's Hospital* (1923), 113
as Anthony Amendment, xxvii, 16, 100, 112, 122, 135, 136
and Burns, Lucy, 33
and *Fairchild v. Hughes* (1922), xxxii
formally adopted as part of Constitution, xxxii
and Harper, Ida Husted, 69
history, 111–112
impact and legacy, 113
and *Leser v. Garnett* (1922), xxxii, 113

Nineteenth Amendment (*Continued*)
  and National American Woman Suffrage Association, 97, 99
  and National Woman's Party, 42
  opposition to, 64, 112, 113
  passage in houses of Congress, xxxii, 112
  and Paul, Alice, 33, 112, 117, 118, 149
  and Pollitzer, Anita Lily, 120
  provisions, 112–113
  ratification, 111–113
  role of western states in ratification of, 171–173
  and Shafroth-Palmer Amendment, 112, 135–136
  and Silent Sentinels, 139–141
  and Stanton, Elizabeth Cady, 141
  and states' voting rights, xxxi, 112
  text of (1920) (primary document), 297–298
  thirty-sixth state to ratify (Tennessee), xxxii, 122
  and Winning Plan strategy, 176–177
Nixon, Richard, xxxix
"Nonsense of It, The" (1866) (primary document), 203–204
  on corruption of politics, 203
  on men's and women's sameness, 204
  on need for enfranchisement of women, 204
  on political divisions, 203
  on political knowledge, 204
  on polls as proper places for women, 203
  on public speech by women, 203
  on women as "silly creatures," 204
  on women's influence, 203

Obama, Barack, xliii
Obergefell v. Hodges, xliii, 60
Oberlin College, xxi, 25, 143, 145, 151, 155
O'Connor, Sandra Day, xli
On Woman's Rights (1851) (primary document), 201–202
Overseas Citizens Absentee Voting Act, xli
Ovington, Mary White, 90

Pacifism
  and Addams, Jane, 1, 2–3
  and American Union Against Militarism (AUAM), 49
  and antisuffrage activism, 18
  and Blatch, Harriot Stanton, 29
  and Catt, Carrie Chapman, 39
  and Eastman, Crystal Catherine, 48
  and La Follette, Belle, 83
  and Mott, Lucretia Coffin, 94
  and Rankin, Jeannette, xxx, 49, 123–124
  and Vernon, Mabel, 163
Palin, Sarah, xliii
Pankhurst, Christabel, 19, 33, 46, 117
Pankhurst, Emmeline, 19, 22, 33, 46, 117, 118, 186, 278
Pankhurst, Emmeline, "Freedom or Death" (1913) (primary document), 262–268

on determination of women, 267
on hunger strikes, 266–267
on imprisonment, 265–266
on industrial action, 265
on legislation, 266–267
on militancy, 264
on representation for taxation, 264
on warfare, 264–265
on women as human beings, 263
Park, Maud Wood, **115–117**
  and Boston Equal Suffrage Association for Good Government, 115
  and Cable Act (1922), 116
  College Equal Suffrage League, cofounder, 40–41, 115
  first president of League of Woman Voters, 84, 115, 116
  Front Door Lobbying, 116
  and League of Nations, 116
  and Massachusetts Woman Suffrage Association, 115
  maternal-based Progressive Era activism, 116
  and National American Woman Suffrage Association, *12,* 115, 178
  and National College Equal Suffrage League, 115
  and Schlesinger Library on the History of Women in America, 116–117
  and Sheppard-Towner Maternity and Infancy Protection Act (1921), 116
Paul, Alice, **117–119**
  and Burns, Lucy, 33–34, 41, 105, 106
  and Congressional Union, xxix, 41–42, 49, 98–99, 112, 143, 146
  death, xl, 119
  education, 117
  and Equal Rights Amendment, xxxiii, 50, 51, 117, 118–119
  family and early years, 117
  influence of Pankhursts on, 117–118
  law education, 118
  and National American Woman Suffrage Association, 118
  National Woman's Party cofounder, 105, 106–107, 117, 118
  and Quakerism, 94–95
  role in ratification of Nineteenth Amendment, 33, 112, 117, 118, 149
  and Silent Sentinels, 118
  split with National American Woman Suffrage Association, 97–98, 106, 118
  and suffrage procession of 1913, 146, 148
Paul, Alice, letter on imprisonment (1917) (primary document), 290
  on force feeding, 290
  on hunger strike, 290
  on physical restraint, 290
Pelosi, Nancy, xliii
Perkins, Frances, 20, 120
Pillsbury, Parker, 125–126
Poland, 80, 127, 131, 201
Poll taxes, xxxvii, xxxviii, 4, 5, 24, 58, 167

Pollitzer, Anita Lily, **119–120**
   death, 120
   early years and education, 119
   and International Woman Suffrage Alliance, 120
   and National Woman's Party, 119–120
   and O'Keefe, Georgia, 119
   and Paul, Alice, 119, 120
   and Silent Sentinel White House picket protests, 119–120
Pomeroy, Samuel C., xxiv
Portrait Monument (U.S. Capitol), 56
Pregnancy Discrimination Act, xli
Presidential politics and suffrage, **120–122**
   and Kelley, Florence, 120
   and labor legislation, 121
   and Perkins, Frances, 120
   Progressive Movement, 120–122
   Roosevelt (Theodore) era, 121
   Taft era, 121
   Wilson era, 121–122
   See also Roosevelt, Franklin; Roosevelt, Theodore; Silent Sentinels; Taft, William Howard; Wilson, Woodrow
President's Commission on the Status of Women, xxxvi
Progressive Era and presidential politics. *See* Presidential politics and suffrage
Progressive Party, xxix, 3, 250
property rights
   and antisuffrage movement, 249
   and coverture, 134
   and Declaration of Rights of the Women of the United States, 230–231
   and "Declaration of Sentiments," 194
   Julian, George W., on, 220
   Keller, Helen, on, 255
   for married women, xxii, 44, 72, 127, 134, 220
   Married Women's Property Act (1848), xxii, 44, 127
   Mott, Lucretia Coffin, on, 200
   and National Woman's Party Platform, 302, 303
   and "The Nonsense of It" (pamphlet), 204
   Rose, Ernestine, on, 201
   and Stone, Lucy, 144, 145
   and suffrage, xxi, xxiii, 31, 63, 76, 284, 286
   and taxation, 31, 200, 201, 230
   and women's rights, 15, 31, 200

Quakerism
   and African American women in suffrage movement, 4
   and Anthony, Susan B., 14
   Hicksites, 94–95, 133
   and Mott, Lucretia Coffin, 94–95, 197
   and Paul, Alice, 94–95
   and Seneca Falls Convention, 133
   and Vernon, Mabel, 163
   and Washington, Margaret Murray, 166

Randolph, A. Philip, 24
Randolph, A. Philip, "Woman Suffrage and the Negro" (1917) (primary document), 292–293
   on inevitability of woman suffrage, 292

on suffrage for colored women, 292
on women as taxpayers, 292
Rankin, Jeannette, **123–125**
  death, 124
  education, 123
  family and early years, 123
  first woman elected to U.S. Congress, xxx, 123, 124
  Georgia Peace Society founder, 124
  Jeannette Rankin Brigade, 124
  legacy, 124
  and National American Woman Suffrage Association, 124, 279
  pacifism of, xxx, 49, 123–124
  and Women's International League for Peace and Freedom, 124
Reagan, Ronald, xli
Reconstruction Era, xxiv, 57, 58. *See also* Fifteenth Amendment; Fourteenth Amendment; Thirteenth Amendment
Revolution, The, **125–126**
  and Anthony, Susan B., xxiv, 15, 125–126, 183, 213
  controversy, 125
  and Davis, Paulina Kellogg Wright, 44, 126
  founding, xxiv, 125
  and Gage, Matilda Joslyn, 61
  and Stanton, Elizabeth Cady, 125–126, 142
  subscribers, 126
Ridley, Florida Ruffin, 129, 182
Roe v. Wade, xxxix, 60
Roosevelt, Eleanor
  and Bethune, Mary McLeod, 24
  head of President's Commission on the Status of Women, xxxvi
  and Universal Declaration of Human Rights, xxxv, 24
  and World Center for Women's Archives, 20
Roosevelt, Franklin
  and Bethune, Mary McLeod, 24
  Executive Order prohibiting racial or ethnic discrimination in defense industries, xxxiv
  New Deal, 131, 132
  and World War II, 124
Roosevelt, Theodore
  election of 1912, xxix, 3
  introduction to *Mobilizing Woman-Power* (Blatch), 29
  New Freedom platform, 121
  and Progressive Era, 121
  and woman's suffrage, xxix, 121, 242, 250–254
Roosevelt, Theodore, "Women's Rights; and the Duties of Both Men and Women" (1912) (primary document), 250–254
  on duty, 252–253
  on equality of rights, 250–251
  on equality of rights but not identity of function, 253
  on Howe, Julia Ward, 252
  on protection of motherhood, 253–254
  on state suffrage referendums, 251
  on suffrage advocates who discredit themselves, 251–252
  on western states, 252
Rose, Ernestine, **126–128**
  and abolitionism, 127–128

Rose, Ernestine (*Continued*)
  and American Civil War, 128
  early years and education, 127
  influence of Robert Owen on, 127
  and National Women's Rights Conventions, xxiii, 127, 128
  political and religious views, 126–127
Rose, Ernestine, *On Woman's Rights* (1851) (primary document), 201–202
  on inequality of women, 201–202
  on men's ignorance, 202
  on women's education and efficacy, 202
Ruffin, Josephine St. Pierre, 5, **128–130**
  and American Civil War, 129
  death, 130
  education, 128–129
  family and early years, 128
  and National Association for the Advancement of Colored People, 130
  National Association of Colored Women founder, 100, 129
  National Federation of Afro-American Women founder, 100
  and racism, 128–129
  Woman's Era editor and publisher, 100, 128, 129, 182
  Women's Era Club cofounder, 129, 182
Russia and Soviet Union, xxxi, 34, 76–77, 178
  Bolshevik Revolution, 46, 76–77

Sanger, Margaret
  American Birth Control League founder (later Planned Parenthood Federation of America), xxxii
  opens first birth control clinic, xxx
Sargent, Aaron, xxvi, 89
Saudi Arabia, 77
Schlafly, Phyllis, xxxix, 52
Schneiderman, Rose, **131–133**
  death, 132
  and Equality League of Self-Supporting Women, 132
  family and early years, 131
  and labor reform, 131–132
  and National American Woman Suffrage Association, 132
  representative at Paris Peace Conference, 132
  and Roosevelt (Franklin) administration, 132
  and shirtwaist workers strike, 131–132
  on Triangle Shirtwaist Factory fire, 80, 188
  and Women's Trade Union League, 131–132
Schwimmer, Rosika, 20, 80
Select Committee on Woman Suffrage, xxvi
Seneca Falls Convention, xxii, 4, **133–135**
  and Bloomer, Amelia Jenks, 30
  "Declaration of Sentiments," xxii, 95, 133–135, 141, 142
  and Douglass, Frederick, 133, 134, 142, 274

history and origins, 133–134
impact and legacy, 134
location, 133
and Mott, Lucretia, xxii, 44, 95, 96, 133, 134, 142
participants and attendees, 133, 134
and Pierce, Charlotte Woodward, 135
and Stanton, Elizabeth Cady, xxii, 44, 95, 97, 111, 126, 133–135
thirtieth anniversary, 96
See also Declaration of Sentiments (1848) (primary document); Stanton, Elizabeth Cady, Declaration of Sentiments
Settlement house movement
in London, 117
in United States, 1–3, 123, 124, 151, 187
See also Addams, Jane
Shafroth-Palmer Amendment, **135–136**
and Addams, Jane, 3
and Congressional Union of NAWSA, 135–136
history and origins, 135–136
provisions, 135
Southern support for, 112
Shaw, Anna Howard, **136–138**
and Anthony, Susan B., 138, 275, 279
death, 138
Distinguished Service Medal recipient, 138
early years and education, 137, *137*

International Women's Suffrage Association delegate, 22
and Massachusetts Women's Suffrage Association, 137
National American Woman Suffrage Association delegate, *12*
and National American Women's Suffrage Association, xxviii, 97, 98, 136, 138
The Story of a Pioneer, 138
and Woman's Christian Temperance Union, 138
and World War I, 138
Shaw, Anna Howard, recollections of NAWSA conventions (1915) (primary document), 273–281
on Atlanta convention (1895), 273–274
on board meeting at Bryn Mawr (1912), 279
on Buffalo convention (1908), 277
on Nashville convention (1914), 280–281
on New Orleans convention (1903), 275–276
on Seattle convention (1909), 277–278
on Washington convention (1910), 278
on Washington convention (1913), 279–280
on Washington convention (1914), 279–280
on Washington convention of National Council of Women, 274–275
Shelby v. Holder, xliii

Silent Sentinels, **139–141**
  arrests and jail times, 140
  controversy, 140
  and Night of Terror, xxx, 34, 140
  origins of name, 139–140
  picket at White House (1917), *139*
  purpose and goal, 139
  See also Imprisoned suffragists' letter to the prisoner commissioners
"The Slavery Yet to Be Abolished" (Julian). *See* Julian, George W., "The Slavery Yet to Be Abolished"
Smith, Adam, 217
Smith, Gerrit, 141
Smith, Margaret Chase, xxxvii
Smith College, xxi, 168–169
Smith v. Allwright (1944), xxxiv
Society of Friends. *See* Quakerism
South Africa, xlii, 77, 100
Stanton, Elizabeth Cady, **141–143**
  and abolitionism, 141–142
  American Equal Rights Association cofounder, 57
  and Anthony, Susan B., *14,* 142
  death, 142
  early years and education, 141
  Eighty Years and More: Reminiscences 1815-1897, 142
  and *History of Woman Suffrage,* xxvi, 15, 28, 29, 61, 69, 70, 135, 141
  International Woman Suffrage Alliance cofounder, 74
  Portrait Monument (U.S. Capitol), 56
  and *The Revolution,* 125–126, 142
  and Seneca Falls Convention, xxii, 44, 95, 97, 111, 126, 133–135
  support for Horace Greeley, 53
  The Woman's Bible, xxvii, xxvii, 62, 80, 141, 142
  Woman's State Temperance Society cofounder, 142
  and World Anti-Slavery Convention (1840), xxii, 133
Stanton, Elizabeth Cady, Declaration of Sentiments (1848) (primary document), 193–197
  on education, 195
  on equality of sexes, 193
  on marriage, 194
  on patient suffering of women, 194
  resolutions, 195–197
  on tyranny of men over women, 194–195
  on women's employments, 194–195
Starr, Ellen Gates, 1
"State Rights Shibboleth" (Beard). *See* Beard, Mary Ritter, "The State Rights Shibboleth"
Stein, Jill, xliii, xliv
Steinem, Gloria, xxxix
Stevens, Doris, **143–144**
  and Congressional Union, 143
  death, 144
  early years, 143
  and Equal Rights Amendment, 144
  first chair of Inter-American Commission of Women, 143
  Jailed for Freedom, 143
  and National Woman's Party, 143

and Silent Sentinels, 143
and Sixth International
   Conference of American States
   (Havana), 144
Stone, Lucy, **144–146**
   and abolitionism, 144–145
   American Equal Rights
      Association cofounder, 57
   American Woman Suffrage
      Association cofounder, 15, 25,
      57–58, 70, 125, 144, 149
   death, 15, 25, 57–58, 70, 125, 144,
      149
   early years and education, 144–145
   legacy, 146
   *Lucy Stone: Pioneer of Woman's
      Rights* (Blackwell), 26, 146
   and National American Woman
      Suffrage Association, 145–146
   and National Women's Rights
      Conventions, 10, 110
   and New England Woman
      Suffrage Association, 109–110,
      145
   and property rights, 144, 145
   Woman's Journal founder, 13,
      144, 145, 183
STOP ERA campaign, xxxix, 52
Stowe, Harriet Beecher, 71, 72, 160
Suffrage procession of 1913,
   146–149
   background and history, 146
   and Burns, Lucy, 143, 146
   events and participants, 147–148
   and Milholland, Inez, 90, 91, 147
   official program, *147*
   and Paul, Alice, 146, 148
   spectators, 148

and Wells-Barnett, Ida Bell, 148
and Wilson, Woodrow, xxix, 7,
   90, 91, 98, 105–106, 143,
   146–148, 171
Suffragist, The, **149–150**
   contents, 150
   Dorr, Rheta Childe, editor, 150
   history and purpose, 149
   Paul, Alice, founder, 149
Sweden, 76, 147

Taft, William Howard, 121, 138, 278
Talbert, Mary Burnett, **151–152**
   activism and journalism career,
      151–152
   death, 152
   early years and education, 151
   and National Association for the
      Advancement of Colored
      People, 151
   and National Association for the
      Advancement of Colored
      Women, 151
   and Niagara Movement, 151
   Phyllis Wheatley Club founding
      member, 151
Temperance movement, **152–155**
   American Temperance Society,
      153
   and Anthony, Susan B., 15, 153,
      156
   Anti-Saloon League, 153–154
   and Daughters of Temperance, 15
   and Eighteenth Amendment, 112,
      153, 154
   New York Temperance Society
      cofounder, 15
   purpose and goals, 152–153

Temperance movement (*Continued*)
    and Twenty-First Amendment, 154
    and Volstead Act, 154
    Woman's State Temperance Society, 142
    "Women's Holy War" (Currier and Ives lithograph), *153*
    See also Woman's Christian Temperance Union
Terrell, Mary Church, 5, **155–158**
    and Anthony, Susan B., 156
    and anti-lynching movement, 156
    A Colored Woman in a White World, 157
    and Coordinating Committee for the Enforcement of the Washington, D.C., Anti-Discrimination Laws, 157
    death, 157
    deaths of children, 156
    and Douglass, Frederick, 155
    early years and education, 155
    first black woman appointed to Washington, D.C., Board of Education, 155
    and International Congress of Women (Berlin), 124, 156
    and National American Woman Suffrage Association, 156
    and National Association for the Advancement of Colored People, 90, 155, 157
    National Association of Colored Women founder and first president, xxvii, 99–100, 129, 155, 157
Terrell, Mary Church, "Woman Suffrage and the 15th Amendment" (1915), 288–289
    on barriers between human beings, 289
    on Fifteenth Amendment, 289
Thirteenth Amendment
    and *Minor v. Happersett,* 224
    provisions, 57, 58, 107
    ratification, xxiv, 107
Title IX (Education Amendments of 1972), xxxix, xlii
Truth, Sojourner, 4, **158–160**
    "Ar'n't I a Woman" (1851), xxii, 159–160, 205
    death, 160
    and Douglass, Frederick, 159
    early years and slavery, 158
    freedom from slavery, 158–159
    name of, 159
    Narrative of Sojourner Truth: A Northern Slave, 158, 159
    and Second Great Awakening, 159
    speeches and activism, 110, 159–160
    turned away from voting, xxv
Truth, Sojourner, address to the American Equal Rights Association (1867) (primary document), 204–206
    on money, 206
    on rights of colored women, 205–206
    on slavery, 205–206
    on women's rights, 205

Union movement. *See* labor
United Arab Emirates, 77
United Kingdom, 76, 79, 128
United Nations
    and Catt, Carrie Chapman, 39

charter, 106
Commission on the Status of Women, xxxiv
Declaration on the Elimination of Discrimination against Women, xxxviii
Fourth World Conference on Women, xlii
and League of Women Voters, 85
and Paul, Alice, 106
Universal Declaration of Human Rights, xxxv
Year of the Woman (1975), xl
United States v. Susan B. Anthony, **161–162**
background and history, 161–162
decision, xxv, 162
and New Departure strategy, 108–109
United States v. Susan B. Anthony, U.S. District Court, Canandaigua, New York (1873) (primary document), 211–213
on denial of rights, 211
on lack of due process, 212
plea for full rigors of the law, 213
on refusal to pay penalty, 213
Universal Franchise Association, 88
Universal Negro Improvement Association (UNIA), 101

Vassar College, xxi, 8, 28, 29, 33, 48, 90, 102, 185
Venezuela, 77
Vernon, Mabel, **163–165**
arrests, 140
and Congressional Union, 41
death, 165
education, 163, 164

family and early years, 163, 164
and National American Woman Suffrage Association, 163
and National Woman's Party, 164, *164*
and Silent Sentinels, 140, 164
and World War I, 164
Vietnam War, 124
Violence against Women Act (1994), xlii
Voting Rights Act (1965), xxxvii, 58
and *Shelby v. Holder,* xliii

Wadsworth, Alice Hay, xxx–xxxi, 102
Waite, Morrison, 93–94
Washington, Booker T., 166, 171, 182
Washington, Margaret Murray, **166–168**
death, 168
education, 166
family and early years, 166
and International Council of Women of the Darker Races, 168
and *National Association News,* 167, 182
and National Association of Colored Women, 166
National Association of Colored Women's Clubs founder, 167
and Tuskegee Institute, 166–168
and Wells-Barnett, Ida Bell, 167
Weil, Gertrude, **168–169**
death, 169
education, 168–169
family and early years, 168
Goldsboro Equal Suffrage Association cofounder, 169

Weil, Gertrude (*Continued*)
   and National American Woman Suffrage Association, 81, 169
   North Carolina League of Women Voters founder, 169
   and Women's Club Movement, 169
Wellesley College, xxi
Wells-Barnett, Ida Bell, **169–171**
   Alpha Suffrage Club founder, 5, 6–8, 171
   anti-lynching campaign, xxvii, 129, 156, 170
   death, 171
   early years and slavery, 169–170
   Equal Rights Party vice-presidential candidate, 54
   journalism career, 170
   and National American Woman Suffrage Association, 5, 171
   and National Association for the Advancement of Colored People, 171
   and Niagara Movement, 171
   and suffrage procession of 1913, 5–6, 148
   and Washington, Margaret Murray, 167
Wesleyan College, xxi
Western states and suffrage, **171–173**
   journals and newspapers, 172
   Native American women, 173
   notable suffragists, 172, 173
   and socioeconomic class, 172
   states' and territories' voting rights, 172
   and temperance movement, 173
White, Ruth, *12*
"Why Men Need Woman Suffrage" (Keller). *See* Keller, Helen, "Why Men Need Woman Suffrage"
"Why the Home Makers Do Not Want to Vote" (1909) (primary document), 248–250
   on education of girls in home making, 249–250
   on independence of American home makers, 248–249
   on unequal division of labor, 249
Why Women Should Vote (Blackwell), 239–242. *See* Blackwell, Alice Stone, *Why Women Should Vote*
Willard, Frances, **174–175**
   and Association for the Advancement of Women, 174
   death, 174
   early years and education, 174
   Woman's Christian Temperance Union cofounder and president, xxvi, 153, 154, 174–175, 176, 179, 180–181
   and World WCTU, 175
Wilson, Woodrow
   election of 1912, 121
   and imprisoned suffragists' letter to prisoner commissioners, 291
   meetings with suffragists, 82
   and Silent Sentinels White House picket protests, xxx, 33, 34, 92, 106, 118, 119–120, 122, 139–141, 164
   suffrage petition delivered to, 55–56

and suffrage procession of 1913, xxix, 7, 90, 91, 98, 105–106, 143, 146–148, 171
and "The Prison Special" train tour, 34–35
and women's suffrage, xxxi, 42, 113, 122, 177
Winning Plan, **176–177**
background and history, 176
and Catt, Carrie Chapman, xxx, 39, 99, 176–177
four-pronged strategy, 176
Wittenmyer, Annie, xxvi, xxvi, 154, 179–181
"Woman as an Economic Factor" (Blatch). See Blatch, Harriot Stanton, "Woman as an Economic Factor"
Woman Citizen, The, **177–179**
and Catt, Carrie Chapman, 177–178, 184
contents, 178–179
final issue, 179
financial backing, 177
history and creation, 177–178
and League of Women Voters, 178
renamed *The Woman's Journal,* 179
"Woman Suffrage and the Negro" (Randolph). See Randolph, A. Philip, "Woman Suffrage and the Negro"
The Woman's Bible (Stanton), xxvii, 62, 80, 141, 142
Woman's Christian Temperance Union (WCTU), **179–181**
and American Woman Suffrage Association, 13

founding, xxvi, 179–180
and labor, 174
reasons women were drawn to temperance movement, 180
and Shaw, Anna Howard, 138
and temperance movement, 153–154
The Union Signal, 181
Willard, Frances, cofounder and president, xxvi, 153, 154, 174–175, 176, 179, 180–181
Wittenmyer, Annie, cofounder and president, xxvi, 154, 179–181
and women's suffrage, 180–181
Woman's Era, The, **182–183**
contents and purpose, 182
and Ruffin, Josephine St. Pierre, 100, 128, 129, 182
Woman's Journal, **183–184**
Blackwell, Alice Stone, editor in chief, 25, 26, 183
founding, xxv
history and creation, 25, 26, 183
purchased by Carrie Chapman Catt, 177–178, 184
purpose and contents, 183
renamed *Woman's Journal and Suffrage News,* 184
Stone, Lucy, founder, 13, 144, 145, 183
Women's History Month, xli
Women's International League for Peace and Freedom (WILPF)
and Addams, Jane, 49
and Brown, Olympia, 33
founding, 75
and Rankin, Jeannette, 124

Women's International League for Peace and Freedom (WILPF) (*Continued*)
   and Vernon, Mabel, 164
   and Woman's Peace Party, 83
Women's National Loyal League, xxiv
Women's Political Union, **185–186**
   background and origins, 185
   and Blatch, Harriot Stanton, 185–186
   first major suffrage parade (1910), xxix
   and media attention, 186
   merger with Congressional Union to form National Woman's Party, 42, 98–99, 105, 186
   and New York suffrage effort, 185
   What 80 Million Women Want, 186
   Women's Political World, 186
Women's rights conventions
   first statewide convention (1850) (Ohio), xxii
   Truth, Sojourner, "Ar'n't I a Woman" (1851) (Ohio), xxii, 159, 160, 205
   See also National Women's Rights Conventions; Seneca Falls Convention
Women's Trade Union League (WTUL), **186–188**
   and Addams, Jane, 2, 187
   and American Federation of Labor (AFL), 187
   and Beard, Mary Ritter, 19
   and Belmont, Ava Vanderbilt, 21
   and Blatch, Harriot, 29, 188
   and Dorr, Rheta Childe, 46
   founding, xxviii, 2, 80, 186–187
   and McDowell, Mary, 187
   and Milholland, Inez, 90
   national convention (1913), *187*
   purpose and priorities, xxviii, 186–188
   and Robins, Margaret Dreier, 188
   and Schneiderman, Rose, 80, 131, 188
   and Triangle Shirtwaist Factory fire, 188
   and Wald, Lillian, 187
Woodhull, Victoria, **189–191**
   and Anthony, Susan B., 190
   and Beecher-Tilton Scandal, 72, 190, 217
   death, 191
   Equal Rights Party presidential candidate, xxv, 53–54, 190, 209
   family and early years, 189–190
   first woman to run for U.S. president, xxv, 189, 190–191
   House Judiciary Committee testimony (1871), 209
   Humanitarian, 191
   published works, 191
   Woodhull & Claflin's Weekly, 190
Woodhull, Victoria, address before House of Representatives (1871) (primary document), 209–211
   on civilization, 210
   on race, 210
   on sovereignty, 209–210
   on taxation, 210
World Anti-Slavery Convention (1840) (London), xxii

and Mott, Lucretia Coffin, xxii, 95, 133
and Stanton, Elizabeth Cady, xxii, 133
World Center for Women's Archives, 20

Wyoming Territory, An Act to Grant to Women the Right of Suffrage (1869) (primary document), 207–208

Young, Rose, *12,* 178

www.ingramcontent.com/pod-product-compliance
Lightning Source LLC
Chambersburg PA
CBHW072131220426
43664CB00013B/2204